Inter-Plays Works and Words of Writers and Critics

Inter-Plays: Works and Words of Writers and Critics

A Festschrift Published in honour of Albert-Reiner Glaap

Editors: Rolf Althof
Rurik von Antropoff
Klaus Peter Müller

BREAKWATER

BREAKWATER
100 Water St.
P.O. Box 2188
St. John's, NF
Canada
A1C 6E6

Canadian Cataloguing in Publication Data
Main entry under title:

Inter-plays

Includes bibliographical references.
ISBN 1-55081-078-2

1. Glaap, Albert-Reiner. 2. Canadian drama
(English) — 20th Century. * 3. English drama —
20th century. 4. New Zealand drama — 20th century.
5. English drama — 20th century — History and
criticism. I. Glaap, Albert-Reiner. II. Althof,
Rolf. III. Antropoff, Rurik von. IV. Müller, Klaus
Peter, 1950-

| PN6112.I67 1994 | 822 | C94-950246-4 |

CONTENTS

PREFACE

This book is about a large number of interplays on many levels. First, there are the authors of plays, short stories, poetry and prose who have kindly given us their creative writings. Most of these texts are published here for the first time, and they widen our understanding of the works of these authors. Then there are critics, who have commented upon these fictional texts so that the reader can find out which reactions these texts may provoke.

The authors who are represented in this volume have dealt with a great variety of topics. **Marion Andre**, who now lives in Canada, has written a play, *Captive of Yesteryear*, that is greatly influenced by the European past and in particular the Holocaust. **Alan Ayckbourn**, the well-known playwright and theatre director in Scarborough, England, satirizes the rather loose morals at a dreadful office party in a tv-play. **Henry Beissel**, German-born Canadian dramatist and poet, expresses his concern about the future of our planet in view of the atrocities of mankind. **Michael Cook**, Newfoundland's best-known playwright, has made use of a historic event of Canada's past to question traditional myths. **David French**, who is also from Newfoundland, recalls significant moments of a father-son relationship in his *Memoir*. **Linda Griffiths** reflects her position in Canada's alternate theatre movement in *The Red Spray Can*, a provocative extract from her as yet unpublished monoplay *Spiral Woman and The Dirty Theatre*. **Kristjana Gunnars**, a Canadian of Icelandic descent, plays with concepts of fiction and language in her *'Forged Letters.'* **Roger Hall**, who emigrated from England to New Zealand, has his protagonist forge dreams into reality and makes fun of both the Hollywood film industry and psychoanalysis. **Ronald Harwood** recollects the feelings and imaginings of a South African boy who is frustrated in his eager wish to meet the famous actor Laurence Olivier. Canadian playwright **James Reaney** has puppets replay the harassment of the Donnelly family by the local community and provides also an intertextual commentary on his own well-known trilogy. **Banuta Rubess**, a Latvian Canadian, has created visions of the loneliness and separateness of human beings leading to violence and destruction. In his tv-play *Terraces*, **Willy Russell** contrasts attitudes of the individual with demands of the community.

All these writers have either offered these texts or written them for publication in honour of Albert-Reiner Glaap, a well-known scholar in the field of English, Canadian and New Zealand literature, the translation of literary texts and the methodology of language teaching, especially the teaching of literature. His eminent role in mediating between the British and German theatre was officially acknowledged when he was made an Officer of the British Empire in 1992. The contributors to this volume have known Albert-Reiner Glaap for many years and have had a close and friendly relationship with him. On the occasion of his 65th birthday they all thank him for his outstanding work and great generosity and wish him all the very best for many years to come.

Rolf Althof, Rurik von Antropoff, Klaus Peter Müller

Marion Andre

CAPTIVE OF YESTERYEAR

The action of the play takes place in Toronto and Anna Maria Island, Florida, in March of 1990. It develops on a fairly large stage and is supported by scenery that is scant, striking and very mobile; changes should be brief and "mysteriously" evolved. The images from the past that are basically of surrealistic quality, come from the days of the Warsaw Uprising (Poland), September 1944, and from the ghetto in a Polish city in 1943. They should appear upstage, and should be located on a level much higher than the rest of the scenery. When they materialize they must strongly draw attention to themselves, "dissolving" for a moment the focus on the rest of the stage.

Cast

EDGAR BROUT, a Jew, born in Poland in 1923, now 67 years old, an immigrant to Canada. He arrived in the spring of 1946 after being released by the allied forces from a prisoner-of-war camp in Germany where he was imprisoned when the Warsaw Uprising in 1944— in which he took an active part —was crushed by the German army. A member of his family, a dentist and a Canadian citizen lived in Toronto. With his assistance Edgar, now a professor of political science at York University, was granted immigrant status, immersed himself in cultural studies, the mastery of the English language included, and eventually became a respected Canadian academician. He is married to Miriam.

MIRIAM, nee MARTIN, a Canadian born woman, 55 years old—a C.B.C. radio producer.

MARITA SOLUBEK, a slim, attractive, 44-year-old Polish woman (but looks much younger), a journalist and a writer who is on a visit to North America preparing a book about Americans and Canadians of Polish origin who have achieved important status in the U.S. and Canada.

ROLF MILBAUER, a German in his late forties, a professor of contemporary history at the University of Düsseldorf and a recent friend of Marita.

"WHALE MAN," a university colleague of Edgar's and most briefly Miriam's lover.

JOHNNY, a young, black driver of Edgar Brout during his stay in Florida.

WAITER, in the "Sand Bar."

And several characters appearing in the various brief images relating to Edgar Brout's *distant past*. The main characters of those are:

EDGAR BROUT, as a 21-year-old member of the Polish underground during the Nazi occupation.

JADWIGA, an 18-year-old very attractive girl, a 'warrior' during the Warsaw Uprising and for a short time Edgar's loving companion during his last few months in Poland, prior to and during the Warsaw uprising.

Other characters from the *distant past* appear only briefly and are played by actors who are seen on stage within the *framework of the present* but have the 'space' to appear as other people.

Prologue

A wintry, late afternoon in Toronto. A living room in an unpretentious but good looking house in the annex that belongs to Professor Edgar Brout and his wife, Miriam. It is already quite dark outside, the light from the lamp-post nearby pierces through the window and reveals the couch occupied by a man—his friends call him "Whale Man"—and a woman who is only partly dishevelled. They are in the process of making love. The man is huge, paunchy. The woman underneath him, Miriam Brout, practically disappears. For a moment or two we see her face, quite lovely, but "cool," perhaps even sad, showing no enjoyment caused by the action that involves her body. The man keeps "pumping," then the ejaculation takes place. When it's finished he slips off her body, and holding his pants, covered with sweat, breathing hard and sighing with pleasure, rolls down on the carpet beside a low table. There are a few bottles of liquor on it and two half empty glasses. The woman remains on the sofa, and as before seems distant, untouched by what took place.

WHALE MAN (*Mutters*): Oh, I surely had an explosion! Haven't experienced anything like that for quite a while. (*He laughs*) Are you flattered?

MIRIAM (*Almost sarcastically*): Yes, Whale Man, I am. And how …

Then we hear the clank of the front door and a man's voice, that of EDGAR, the woman's husband:

EDGAR: My lecture was a triumph! McGill wants me to come again next year! Miriam, are you in? Are you in?

And in the doorway of the living room the silhouette of a slim, medium height, man—a small suitcase in his hand— appears. He absorbs the scene before him, then he exclaims in horror:

EDGAR (*Dropping the suitcase*): Whale Man! Ah!

The "WHALE MAN" jumps up from the floor, pulling up his pants, grabbing hold of his jacket from the sofa and screaming:

WHALE MAN: Ah! Ah! (*And he runs out almost bumping EDGAR of his feet and yelling*) Don't blame me! Blame her! The Madame bitch! The tippling whore!

MIRIAM (*Sobbing*): You weren't to arrive today! You were to be back home tomorrow!

The "WHALE MAN" is gone. EDGAR moves closer to his wife. He grabs her by the arms, lifts her off the sofa and vehemently throws her against the wall. We see him better now, intelligent face, grey bearded but well trimmed. His eyes, now distorted by anger shoot arrows of contempt. His lips spill words of barely contained fury.

EDGAR: Sorry for the surprise! Madame bitch! It's your lover who gave you that nickname, not me! Should I challenge him for it? God, how you stink with your panties at your knees! I should whack you but the smell you exude ...

MIRIAM (*Sobbing*): My smell is no different than yours when you played the ... cloying game with your secretaries! You climbed on them on the same sofa I did my ... reclining! And one of them told me, you invited her to our bedroom!

They stare at each other with pain and fury.

Then black out.

ACT I, SCENE 1

Morning hours of a wintry day in Toronto one week later. The bedroom in the house of EDGAR and MIRIAM BROUT. The room is in a messy state. On the king sized bed centered under a window there are two opened suitcases partly packed with male clothing—shirts, socks, underwear, stacks of books and papers. On the carpeted floor there are shoes and an electric typewriter in a case—a constant obstacle for PROFES-SOR BROUT who is now involved in packing. He is clearly very tense, his face shows it. So do his actions. He walks to and from the two opened closets filled with men and women's clothing. He tears his pants and jackets off the hangers, examines them with a furious stare. Those he doesn't approve of he dumps on the floor, others he rumples together and squeezes them into the suitcases. The door leading to the bedroom is half closed. Suddenly it is pushed open and MIRIAM BROUT appears. For a moment or two she remains silent watching her husband flying back and forth from the closet. Then she addresses him.

MIRIAM: Are you packing?

EDGAR (*Sharply*): Don't you see?

MIRIAM (*Softly*): So you're leaving ...

EDGAR (*Sarcastically*): Would I be putting my clothes into the suitcases if I were not leaving?

MIRIAM: I thought ...

EDGAR: Please don't tell me what you think! I told you that we must part! I explained, I thought, the reason for it! And, I assumed that my argument was potent enough for you to accept it! But if you want me to make a show of it once more, I am willing to do it, but briefly. The cab that's to drive me to the airport (*He looks at his watch*) will be here in an hour!

MIRIAM (*Straightforwardly*): Your time is as precious as mine. I have work to do. I'm expected at the studio in an hour.

EDGAR (*Errupting*): Fuck your work! Fuck your studio!

MIRIAM (*Ironically*): Who should do the fucking, you or me? I think you're the expert at it.

EDGAR (*With 'ready to kill' intensity*): Are you sure?!

He moves towards her with his fist raised and almost falls down, stumbling over the typewriter. MIRIAM reacts to it exclaiming:

MIRIAM: Ah!

EDGAR straightens up, they both giggle a little. Then MIRIAM continues:

MIRIAM: God's wisdom, don't you think? Now seriously—why won't you consider some delay?

EDGAR: A delay? Why?

MIRIAM: (*Softly*) Because ...

EDGAR (*Sharply*): No! (*After a pause*) Miriam, delaying my departure will change nothing. It would make matters worse. (*In response to her sadly ironic smile*) Yes, worse! At least we talk to one another. But another few days of this ... mutually recognized collapse of our marriage—we would not only keep on fighting! We would ... spit venom at each other! Raise fists ... with hatred!

MIRIAM: Hatred?

EDGAR: Yes, hatred! I can barely suppress that feeling now! I look at you and I think ...

MIRIAM (*Cuts in, holding her forehead, and repeating with dramatic intensity*): Why did she do it?! Why did she do it?! (*Then directly*) You know why! Because I was alone, troubled. In need of affection!

EDGAR (*With brutal sarcasm*): In need of affection! From whom?! That balding jerk who screwed you behind my back professing at the same time his esteem for me?! He couldn't offer affection even if he wanted to because his heart is made of cement! No! It's like a rubber balloon, full of hot air and devoid of feeling! He screwed you, because ...

MIRIAM (*Softly, but again imitating EDGAR*): He wanted to examine the motivation of your coolness towards me. Investigate the inadequacy of your prick!

EDGAR (*With fury and kicking the bed*): Miriam!

MIRIAM (*Shocked*): Edgar!

EDGAR (*With unabated intensity*): Don't "Edgar" me, because you succumbed to it! You swallowed his philosophical garbage, oblivious to the slime oozing from him, blind to the consequences of this action!

MIRIAM (*Softly*): And how blind were you when you did it? Your last one, Lolita! Was her chapter built on thoughtful consideration?

EDGAR: Miriam!

MIRIAM (*With growing intensity*): Yes, I know I made a solemn promise not to ever mention that name again in your presence. But I thought of her nevertheless during many sleepless nights, trying to figure out what you saw in that brainless nymph!

EDGAR (*Kicking the bed again*): Miriam!

MIRIAM (*In the same manner as before*): Her slimness, her blue eyes and pale complexion after she washed off that paint, were quite enticing I grant you that, but ...

EDGAR (*Interrupting with fury*): Now you know why I'm leaving! 'Cause of the pleasure you derive from sending me on this ... guilt trip! What I did was foolish, I admit it, I purged myself, **voluntarily**, without being prodded to do so, but ...

MIRIAM (*Cutting in, angrily*): Twelve times in the last three years ... Come on, Edgar, your breast beating exercises were too frequent to be taken seriously! And they didn't diminish the distance that spread between us! To talk to me you had to be in real trouble! To embrace me you had to be sloshed? And so ...

EDGAR: You jumped on the bandwagon! With an associate of mine, this loathsome galoot who voluptuously spread the news around! Who ...

MIRIAM (*Cutting in again, imitating EDGAR'S way of speaking*): Thusly undermined, your standing in the scholastic community, making you the butt of sickly jokes among your students! (*In her normal tone*) You have used that line so many times that it got pinned on the membrane of my brain! Forever! (*Calmer now*) Well, enough's enough. You'd better finish your packing and be gone or you will miss the plane. As usual ... (*After a pause*) Incidentally, where are you going?

EDGAR: I told you! To Florida.

MIRIAM: To Florida? The "rich trash land" you used to call it! You must be kidding.

EDGAR: No, I am not! I rented a condo on an Island which is ... quite unusual. Serene and beautiful.

MIRIAM: Who owns it?

EDGAR: Dr. Merner's brother. He went to Europe. That's why his condo is free this winter.

MIRIAM: Dr. Merner's brother? Don't tell me that your psychiatrist had something to do with it?! If he did ...

EDGAR: You'd give him hell, right?! You'd make his peers look into it!

MIRIAM: But ...

EDGAR (*Not letting her finish the sentence*): No highrises! No fancy stores! I've seen the photographs! I rented it on the spot! And a car too!

MIRIAM: Good for you. For the first time in our twenty five years of marriage you have done something on your own. Without asking me to look after the "boring technicalities that are a part of human existence." You must have been really pressed to make a go of it. Really pressed. (*Pausing briefly*) So what will you do there? Keep on walking on the beach?

EDGAR: Yes, at the same time pulling my thoughts together. That's what I need. Refresh my mind. Put my thoughts together!

MIRIAM (*Pointing at the typewriter*): You really believe you will write? Without access to a research centre—you will write?

EDGAR: What business is it of yours whether I write or not? For your information I finished the rough draft of my memoirs. "THE REFUGEE OF THE HOLOCAUST" is done. I need to go through it, make corrections, changes. I'll be doing it in Florida. But the main body of the work is done!

MIRIAM (*Taken aback*): I am glad you told me. Finally a nice reward for the hours I spent encouraging you to work on it. Collecting data, rifling through your notes, documents. Well, well, well ... As I said before you must have been really pressed to keep quiet about it. And to make arrangements for your trip. (*After a brief pause*) You'll be gone for how long?

EDGAR: Six to eight weeks.

MIRIAM: That long?! What about your classes? Did you quit teaching?

EDGAR: Have you forgotten how old I am? And that I'm not a full time teacher? My contract permits me to be absent from the University for two months in winter and four months during the summer! I'm the first Senior Citizen within the Ontario teaching profession ...

MIRIAM (*Takes over and as if quoting*): Who in recognition of his outstanding merits was allowed to pursue his career on a freelance basis at the University where he was enrolled as a student and then joined his mentors as a knowledgeable colleague and a teaching magician! (*Now in her normal tone*) I know that you know by heart the crescendo of the speech delivered in your honour by the President of the University when your plea not to be 'done away with' because of your age was accepted. So spare me this jeremiad! Don't burden me with that quotation! (*After a moment of silence*) What about your depression? Your ... visits to your past? "The paralysis of your mind" as you used to call it. If those attacks occur, who will take care of that? Do you believe that ...

EDGAR: "The paralysis of my mind" is gone! Yes, it is! I'm on the mend, you know that! And I discussed my trip with Dr. Merner. He gave me the name of his colleague in Sarasota, and took it upon himself to inform him about my ... existence. I'm to call the man if necessary. (*After a pause*) But he also told me that my separation from the tension at home might do me a lot of good. It may help me to ... come to grips ...

MIRIAM (*Interrupting*): Did you have a bath this morning?

EDGAR: What? Yes, I did. Why ...

MIRIAM: I have a question to ask. Only don't blow up. Did you ... masturbate?

EDGAR: What?! Surely that's not your bloody business!

MIRIAM (*Softly*): I am asking because I know how troubled you are by your condition. It is you who kept telling me that when you take a bath ...

EDGAR: No! You're asking because you want to know if I'll be able to fuck a woman if I meet one who'd appeal to my senses! Yes, I will be able to do it! I'm alright! In perfect condition! And don't tell me you haven't experienced it! Don't you ...

MIRIAM (*Softly*): Don't worry, I won't. I'm glad you feel so secure. I sincerely hope you will not call me to come to your rescue, in Florida.

EDGAR puts three framed photographs in one of the suitcases

MIRIAM: You're taking the pictures of your parents! And your sister! What for?

EDGAR: I like their company. At least they're silent. They don't berate me for whatever I do.

MIRIAM: But they stare at you nevertheless. As you told me, you're under their scrutiny all the time. They're your entry into your past.

EDGAR: So?

MIRIAM: But you want to get out of it! You want to stop cursing yourself for being alive while they're dead! Why can't you be like me?! I also lost my parents! Not the way you lost yours, nonetheless ... abnormally! How often does it happen that one's father dies during surgery after a train crash and one's mother, soon afterwards, out of despair suffers a stroke! Which turns her into a zombie! And stays that way for several years, sitting in her rocker, muttering to herself but addressing nobody, seeing nobody including her teenaged daughter! Who had to take care of her until she died, at the same time taking care of herself, going to school, studying, learning to make some sense of life on her own until she met her man! And fell in love with him! And he with her! And then faced the mystery of existence together with him! My past, harsh as it was did not interfere with our daily life! I did not sulk about it! I blocked it out! My only link with the joys of life or the pain of it was you! I have told you this many times, you're shortening your life by clinging to the past! Quit it! And find something that will fill you with joy! The choice is simple! A happy life or a ... (*She glances at her wrist watch*) Oh, my God! It's late! I'm expected at work in the next twenty minutes. I'm sorry for not being able to hold your hand until you depart, but that's life, you know it. To be tranquil my mind requires that I work a lot.

EDGAR (*Ironically*): One of the few reasons for my search for ... enjoyment outside our bedroom. As long as I have known you—you craved for a busy life more than I did. "No children! I'm too busy!" Putting together the fast forgotten radio programs at your studio!

MIRIAM (*Sarcastically*): "Children? Who needs them? In the mad world of today!" Wasn't that your sacred conviction? We saw eye to eye on it. (*Softly*) Not speaking about my inadequacy to bear them ... (*Then a touch more sharply*) And about "fast forgotten"! Weren't you the one who used to tell me how "wonderful" those programs were: How "timely, enlightening and wonderful"? To remind you, one of them dealing with 'Orphans of the Holocaust' made you phone me. And meet me for dinner. And spill out to me your life story.

(With a smile) The early days in this 'colonial land' included. How battered you were by your 'teeth drilling' uncle who brought you here and then wanted you to quit dreaming about a teaching career but sell lamps or socks door to door to make a living! Your mind was so clear in those days. And for many years afterwards. Marked yet not trammelled, trampled by the viciousness of your past. I so much wish you could … Enough. *(She walks to him and kisses him on the cheek)* Well goodbye, my husband. But not my "ex." Not yet. It'll be up to you to come up with that decision. Have a good time wherever you go. Whatever you do.

EDGAR: You too.

MIRIAM: Do a lot of thinking.

EDGAR: You too.

MIRIAM: And if you need something …

(The telephone rings EDGAR picks it up)

EDGAR: Hallo … *(He listens, hangs up, then addresses his wife)* It was for you. Some crisis. You're badly needed at the studio.

MIRIAM *(Running out)*: Some crisis! Oh, my God! *(She disappears from the room. EDGAR walks to the window, sees her running across the street.)*

Suddenly, an image of a woman appears to him. The setting is a grungy basement of a house in Warsaw (1944) that's in ruin caused by artillery fire. There's a huge hole in the side wall, the moonlight shines through it, creating an eerie feeling to the scene. The woman is young, lovely, dressed in worn out, old fashioned clothes. She is holding a rifle in her hands, her face exudes the feeling of a person who's angry, hurt. She whispers:

JADWIGA: So you are leaving me! Deserter! Deserter!

The image disappears as fast as it appeared. EDGAR is shaken by it. He interlaces his fingers, there are tears in his eyes. He whispers:

EDGAR: You again! Why? Why?

The sound of a car stopping in front of the house. The driver honks a few times, making EDGAR aware that the taxi has arrived. He dries his eyes with his fists, opens the window and shouts:

EDGAR: I'm ready to go. Will you come up to pick up my luggage?

(The voice of the DRIVER calls back) DRIVER: Yes. Yes, sir.

EDGAR closes the window, walks back to the bed, picks up his raincoat, puts it on, zips up his suitcases, then collapses on the bed, his fists clenched, his face showing inner torment. And he whispers:

EDGAR: I'm a haunted man! And bruised! Not a deserter! Not a deserter!

Then he forces himself to get up. He picks up his luggage, the typewriter included and leaves the room. A moment later he is on his way. We hear the heavy noise of the traffic, honking cars, some kind of explosions, the roar of a plane taking off, then:

Black out.

ACT I, SCENE 2

A lovely, unspoiled and uncrowded beach on Anna Maria Island basking in the golden radiance of the sun, takes over the stage. The sand on the beach is powdery and white. Two large palm trees enclose it, stage right and left.

Somewhat off centre is a boulder beside which spreads a reclining chair that belongs to EDGAR BROUT who is just coming out of the water upstage. He dries himself with a towel he left on the ground. We see him now without his clothes. He is well built, quite muscular, his body is a bit red from the scorching sun, and his face tells us how much he enjoyed his swimming experience. He is on his way to one of the boulders where he lingered before. There is a noisy sound of squealing gulls and then his eyes are caught by an unusual event. A young, blond, blue-eyed, attractive woman—her name is MARITA, she wears a rather provocative swimsuit—runs onstage waving her hands, hiding her face under her arms and screaming:

MARITA: Zgnile ptaki! Get lost! Get lost! (*Then, overcome with fear, she slides down on the sand. EDGAR runs to her rescue, waving his beach towel and screaming like a madman.*)

EDGAR: Get lost, you feathered monkeys! Get lost, you dumb, hungry birds!

Then he kneels down beside the woman and asks with real concern:

EDGAR: Are you alright? Are you alright? What happened? What happened?

MARITA (*With a slight Eastern European accent coloured by a British one*): Gulls … Gulls …

EDGAR: What?

MARITA (*Slowly recovering*): Gulls! They attacked me! I was feeding them with the crumbs that I bought especially for them! I was throwing them in the air. (*Showing him*) Like this! And they came down on me! Like a black cloud! Pinched my arms! Pinched my face!

EDGAR: Are you hurt? Are you bleeding?

MARITA: Yes! No! I'm only shocked by what happened! I only wanted to be nice to them. I love gulls. I love birds.

EDGAR (*Trying to address her in Polish*): Eh … Pani jest … (*Then in English*) Are you Polish?

MARITA: Yes. How did you guess?

EDGAR (*In a joking fashion*): Simple. You are so alive. So … volcanic. The Polish temperament was oozing out of you.

MARITA: What?

EDGAR (*With a smile*): Zgnile Ptaki. That's Polish. Also your accent. When you screamed, outside of being worried for you, I thought … I know where she comes from. Poland! I have a very good ear for vocal sounds. I'm an expert on accents.

MARITA (*Posing as a British lady*): And you didn't think I was British?

EDGAR: Well ... (*They both burst ot laughing, then he continues*) You're not in pain, are you?

MARITA (*Slowly rising*): No, I'm not. I'm fine. Fine. (*Smiling softly*) Thank you for your help.

EDGAR: My help? I have done nothing! I only yelled at the top of my lungs ... (*Then absolutely astounded*) I can't believe it! I can't believe it!

MARITA: What can't you believe? That I'm o.k.?

EDGAR: No, no! I mean ... I'm astounded that I met a woman here, my second day on the beach who's Polish! And who can speak English so fluently!

MARITA (*Somewhat offended*): What's so unusual about that? Aren't you Polish? I heard you say a few words ... And don't you speak English?

EDGAR (*Somewhat embarassed*): Eh ... I can't converse in Polish. I used to be quite fluent, but ... Who are you anyway?

MARITA: A Polish woman. And who are you?

EDGAR: A monk. On vacation.

MARITA (*Shocked*): Who?

EDGAR (*Laughing*): No! No! Don't take it seriously. When I am overwhelmed by something, I crack those silly jokes. My wife ... Let me introduce myself. (*Stretching out his hand*) I am Edgar Brout. I'm a Canadian, vacationing in Florida.

MARITA (*Shaking his hand*): And I am Marita Solubek, a Polish journalist, exploring Florida.

EDGAR: A journalist?! I didn't know that Polish journalists have the means to travel! I thought ...

MARITA: Yes, we travel a lot, nowadays. Cheaply, but we travel! Particularly those who work on interesting projects. Like me. A lot has changed since you left Poland. When was that?

EDGAR: Years and years ago. The way I see you, you were still ... unborn. Did not inhabit the Polish Earth. (*After a brief pause, he continues*) So who are you? What's your project? (*Raising his hands*) No! First let's sit down. If you'd like to, that is. We've met, in a fashion, that's ...

MARITA (*Giggling*): Unusual, to say the least. Yes, I'd like to sit down. I'd like us to explore one another. Where should we go?

EDGAR (*Pointing to the boulder where his chair is*): See that rock? With the chair beside it? And the bag ... (*With a wink*) There's a bottle of wine in it. (*He takes her by the hand*) Let's go and let's sit down. Then we'll talk.

MARITA (*Smiling*): Sit down I will. Providing ...

EDGAR (*As if reading her thoughts*): I will not invite the birds ...

MARITA: Nor will you invite me to drink wine. Not on the beach and not so early in the morning.

EDGAR (*Pretending to be shocked*): So early in the morning?! It's about midday! The sun's right above our heads!

MARITA: Yes, but ...

EDGAR (*Not allowing her to speak*): And you came from Poland?! When I lived there ... we drank day and night! Not wine but vodka! Twenty four hours "labour" it was called. To drink vodka non-stop, that's Polish.

MARITA: When you were there, there must have been a lot of vodka around and about. But today ...

EDGAR (*Nodding wisely and sadly*): There's a serious shortage of essential products. Those that are needed to keep sturdy. Caviar, shish-kabob. (*They both burst out laughing*)

MARITA: You're a comedian, you know that?

EDGAR (*In the same manner*): What else can I be? When you meet a woman who tugs at your heart ...

MARITA (*Sarcastically*): You mean a lady! In our country those who clean floors are called women. All others ...

EDGAR (*Cuts in*): Prostitutes included ...

MARITA (*Finishing the sentence*): Are ladies. What did you say? That calling ceased to matter in our country. We may lack some freedoms but sexual give and take is free for all, and is sharply etched (*She knocks at her body*) in our constitution. The services apply equally to both our genders. Our gentlemen and ladies follow passionately the challenge and the enjoyment of having **free** access to sex!

EDGAR: I'm astounded. Astounded.

MARITA (*Straightens up*): By what this time?

EDGAR: By your bathing suit. It's so ... progressive. Allows the sun to reach your whole body.

MARITA: I love it. Makes me feel so unleashed. So comfortable. Let's go.

They start walking toward the boulder where EDGAR'S reclining chair and a small leather bag are situated.

MARITA: Now seriously, who are you? What do you do to earn a living?

EDGAR: I teach political science at a University in Toronto. Toronto, you know, the unofficial capital of the Canucks, of Canada.

MARITA: I know Toronto, I stayed there a few weeks ago.

EDGAR: Did you? I thought ...

MARITA: What you thought is immaterial, my dear professor of political science. Why is it that teachers are so often one track minded? My mother told me that my father ...

EDGAR (*Teasing her*): You had a father?

MARITA (*Replying in kind*): I wish I didn't. I would have been free of bad memories. (*After a pause*) Have you ever heard of the Warsaw Uprising? I was born soon afterwards. The following year, to be exact. But how did you ...

EDGAR (*Cutting in*): Jump over the hurdle? It's funny that you mentioned the Uprising. I took part in it. Shot some Nazis. Then I was sent to a camp.

MARITA: Concentration camp?

EDGAR: No, no. A prisoner of war camp. Stalag XIII it was called. (*After a pause*) It took a lot of me to survive that camp. Some memories still haunt me. (*With an ironic smile*) They appear without warning. And yet stick on the sky. What a strange place for mind rotting memories. To see them glued to the sky.

MARITA (*Lightly*): Can't you be more specific? There's an intriguing twist to your words. And it ...

EDGAR (*Without looking at her, his eyes on the sky, very softly*): In that camp I was once abused by a priest.

MARITA: Abused?

EDGAR (*Nodding gently*): Yes, abused. The mildest word I can use to describe the experience.

An image in slow motion unfolds before EDGAR'S eyes. He is 21 years old, in a prisoner of war camp, in a barrack with several bunk beds in it. He stands beside one of them, in front of three men in grubby, civilian clothes. Their features are unclear, they look like puppets. They are members of the Home Army (ak) now Germans captives, like him. One of them is a CAPTAIN, another is a PRIEST, one can recognize that by a silver cross that is hanging on his neck. The third one, a thin young man, who stands behind the CAPTAIN is his ADJUTANT. The CAPTAIN addresses EDGAR:

CAPTAIN: Do you know who I am?

EDGAR: My commander, yes.

CAPTAIN: Your code name is Emil, yes?

EDGAR: Yes.

CAPTAIN: Sounds strange for a code name. Why did you adopt it?

EDGAR: It was my father's name. He's dead. And I wanted ...

CAPTAIN (*Interrupting*): You understand German, yes?

EDGAR: Yes, I do. Yes.

CAPTAIN: I'm to supply the German commander of the camp with a few men who speak German. They're to put in order the stack of papers that relate to us, the members of the Home Army who took part in the Uprising. You're appointed to do that job. (*He hands him a piece of paper*) When you come across the documents carrying those names ... no, (*He stresses it*) **connecting their code names** with their real ones, slip them under your shirt, **discreetly**, and bring them to me. These men were on the list of the Gestapo, for many years. Now they're here. If the S.S. men get hint of it, they will be dead. We need to save their lives. Are you ready to risk yours to save theirs?

EDGAR: Yes, I am.

Then the PRIEST interferes.

PRIEST: You look like a Jew. Are you a Jew?

EDGAR (*After a slight hesitation*): Yes, I am.

PRIEST (*Holding the cross that hangs on his neck, and speaking harshly*): Then you're no good for the job! (*Turning to the CAPTAIN*) Captain, let him go! If something goes wrong, he'll squeal. To save his life. That's what Jews do. Squeal!

The image disappears. A new one takes its place.

EDGAR is outside the barrack, in an empty yard. At some distance but visible there is a barbed wire fence and high towers with armed guards overlooking the field. EDGAR, his face contorted by pain, runs through it towards the fence. He is clearly suicidal, ready to be shot by the guards. Then from behind a barrack another prisoner appears. He is the same YOUNG MAN who silently stood beside the CAPTAIN, watching the "scene." He sees EDGAR, races to him, grabs hold of him and pushes him down to the ground and whispers:

YOUNG MAN: Go back, you fool! Don't give up! What the priest said to you is not worth dying for! You must live to take vengeance for it! You must not die! You must live!

The image fades away.

We are back on the beach watching EDGAR and MARITA.

MARITA (*Tensely*): What happened to you? You were somewhere else! Staring at the sky! You didn't tell me anything about your story. Got stuck on your memories? Something to do with the camp?

EDGAR (*Softly*): Yes. But don't ask me to … talk about it. Not now. It is still so painful. (*After a pause*) In a book I'm writing, my yesteryear memoir … there's mention of it. If you would like to glance at it … in its unfinished form …

MARITA (*Quickly*): You bet I would. The Warsaw Uprising, for many reasons means so much to me. And after the camp, what did you do? How did you come to Canada?

EDGAR (*Again in his joking manner*): By plane. Like many others. I had an uncle. My mother's brother. A dentist. He left Poland in the thirties. Migrated to Canada. I contacted him, he stretched his helping hand to me … I was twenty-three when I crossed the Atlantic. And from then on I sweated blood to make a go of it. In the free world. In Canada.

MARITA: It's free alright. As a friend of mine would say: "Free to do good and bad at the same time."

EDGAR: Meaning?

MARITA: Not now! Not now! So, political science is your speciality. How exciting and rewarding it must be. It pays for your meals. You eat well, don't you?

EDGAR: You bet I do!

MARITA: But does it cover your other expenses? Your wife, your movies and your vodka? You mentioned that you have a wife …

EDGAR: Did I? I must have. Otherwise how would you know? It's a tricky subject. We'll talk about it at a later date. Are you married?

MARITA: That's a tricky subject. But we'll talk about it. When our minds collate.

They laugh, then MARITA continues her questioning.

MARITA: What do you focus on in your work? What countries? What periods?

EDGAR: Right now I'm focussing on … you. (*Pointing to the chair they have just arrived at*) You are welcome to spread out on it. And if by some chance a glass of wine would … loosen you …

MARITA (*Explodes with laughter*): Loosen me? I'm the loosest person you have met, I bet! If I were not, would I have accepted the … bed of a stranger? This chair is like a bed. One could comfortably …

EDGAR: Make love on it?

MARITA (*Pretending to be on the alert*): Oh?! Is that what you have in mind? If the answer is "yes" or "maybe"— just forget it! I'm loose but not in that field. I'm curious about you. I would want to hear about the shape of your life, but that's all. Would you accept me under those conditions?

EDGAR: I accept! I accept! My hospitality will never climb onto the sexual level. But let me tell you this …

MARITA: My ears are closed. So is the chapter. But if you would want to offer me a glass of wine …

EDGAR: I'm tickled pink by your surrender. (*Taking out the half filled bottle, a plastic glass, pouring into it, and handing it to her with a graceful gesture.*) Madame … I hope you will not find it … gross if I have my sip directly from the bottle. Cheers!

MARITA (*Giggling*): To which she replied in Polish: Na zdrowie! My friend! Na zdrowie!

They drink, smiling happily while looking at each other. Then EDGAR sits on the sand beside the chair and says:

EDGAR: I want to tell you, I'm mystified by our meeting. Two total strangers. And such a joy filled connection! So much laughter. So much fun.

MARITA: The same thought crossed my mind. But I suspect I'm more cynical than you are. So my brain wave had another part to it. That fun … where will it lead? What bitter bite will it carry?

EDGAR: Only time will tell. But now, let's have fun. You can drill into me as much as you want. And I'll be upright with my answers. But first, would you mind telling me who you really are? No, I don't propose that you're a spy! But what's the purpose of your visit to North America?

MARITA (*Straightening up and delivering her response*): As you wish, Sir. I mean—Professor. My name is Marita Solubek. That you know. I'm fourty-four years old, a journalist. It was my mother who invoked in me the dream to become a journalist. So upon learning the basics at the University, (*With a smile*) and studying a dictionary, and sharpening my conversational skills with my tutor, I became a journalistic linguist, of sorts. (*With a giggle*) I also learned a lot from the songs of Elvis Presley. From his lyrics, I mean. I liked his slang. His words were so punchy. So full of bang, bang!

EDGAR (*Interrupting*): My father used to think that if you spoke English you had a chance to make a go of it in the world. Was that your mother's vision?

MARITA: You bet it was. She regretted that in that language she was … speechless. But she worked hard to feed me the right mental nutrient. And it paid off well! (*In her previous, somewhat 'distant' way of speaking.*) I was married for a while, now I'm divorced. It took me some time to get used to being parted from my husband, but c'est la vie was what I said to myself one day, and that was it! And I started to live again. Now the aim of my tantalising visit to North America has to do with my desire to connect with Americans (*With emphasis*) and with Canadians of Polish origin who made an impact on their new Mother/Fatherland. You know what I mean. I intend to write their life stories and make them famous in the country they left—the Polish Republic we call it. For that reason I spent some time in Toronto. I interviewed a number of people who were suggested to me by the Polish Congress. People of importance of both genders, who at some point migrated to Canada and who made a go of it on a big scale. You weren't one of them, but as you're an ex-Pole, and I suspect a person of … stature, I think I would want you to be included in my book. None of those that I talked to was a scholar, though they were writers, doctors, radio people and politicians …

EDGAR (*Cutting in*): No cattlemen? No musicians?

MARITA (*Disregarding his teasing comments*): So, I want you in my book! And a refusal of my offer is not accepted unless … (*She stops, catching her breath, giggles and says to EDGAR*) Have I done it well? The recitation, I mean. I was once told that frankness is the very virtue in America. So I'm trying to be frank. (*Responding to the amused but also admiring stare of EDGAR*) I have impressed you, didn't I? (*With a serious face now*) But you were born in Poland, weren't you?

EDGAR: I was. I'm also a Jew. Doesn't that revelation bring your interest to a … crashing halt?

MARITA: On the contrary, my sweet, Polish Jew. It would ignite my passion to write your story. You see, I am pro … no, Philosemite. The man I loved and who left me was a Jew.

EDGAR (*In his usual comedic manner*): Oh, smells fishy. Were you married, or only …

MARITA: We were married. And lived together for ten years.

EDGAR: For ten years? No children?

MARITA: No children, yes. You see, my ex was a devoted condomite. He wouldn't touch me without enclosing his … you know what … in a condom.

EDGAR (*Giggling*): Well, well, well. A prudent man one might say. But too prudent for my liking. And he left you? Why?

MARITA (*After a moment of hesitation*): He hated the country of his birth. He lost his parents when he was four years old. He was brought up by his nanny. Her name was Solubek. She took him at the request of his parents, once they understood what was in store for him if he remained with them in the ghetto. She adopted him. She was a kind, good hearted, simple woman who saved his life.

EDGAR: And he hated her for it?

MARITA: Yes. Once he learned about the fate of his parents. They were gassed in a concentration camp. He would often say: "Why did she save only me? Why didn't she save my parents?" And he spat venom at other people of this land. For their cruel compliance as he called it. "For their muted giggle at the sight of armbands and the rise of the ghetto walls! For their silent approval of beatings, jailing, and the whistle of trains on their way to concentration camps."

An image "fills up" EDGAR'S brain. He sees it as usual on the sky. It is a cloudy, fall day. EDGAR is 19 years old and standing on a street in the ghetto during the selection of those who are to be "re-settled" into a concentration camp. His parents are torn away from him by a huge surrealistic figure of an S.S. MAN, who's screaming:

S.S. MAN: Raus! Raus!

EDGAR left alone catches his parents' eyes— unlike the surrealistic figure of the S.S. MAN they look real. They are in their forties. His father wears glasses, is clean shaven. His mother is dark haired, looks very young and not semitic. And he hears them whisper softly, he really reads their lips.

EDGAR'S PARENTS: Run away! To the other side! And when this is all over, run away, to America!

Then, the image is gone. EDGAR looks at MARITA and says after a moment of silence:

EDGAR: But you were too young to be one of those people. Yet he left you. Why?

MARITA (*With an ironic smile*): Mystery of the Universe—as the saying goes. I was too crazy. Too progressive. He wanted to live in an old fashioned way. That is why he went to South Africa.

EDGAR (*Utterly bewildered*): To South Africa?!

MARITA: That's where he lives. He and his family. He learned that his cousins survived the Holocaust and built their new homestead in South Africa. He wrote to them, they urged him to come. He wanted me to go with him, but I couldn't. I couldn't become rich exploiting Blacks. Suppressing them and exploiting. That's what his family does. They own a factory. They believe in white supremacy. And they are Polish Jews who in their earlier life tasted the Nazis but who sought refuge and a better life in ... South Africa!

EDGAR is deeply moved by her words. He lowers his head and is silent for a moment.

MARITA notices his shaken state and gently continues: Have I done you harm by my confession? I hope not. I don't know why but I feel so strongly that you and I share this common ground. That we do not wish to do any harm to people whoever they are. Even if they would hurt us, we couldn't pay them back in kind. We just couldn't do it! Am I right to believe that you and I share this conviction? Am I right?

EDGAR (*Whispers*): Yes, yes.

At that moment an image of the past rises before his eyes. He sees JADWIGA. She stands on the same ground as in the previous apparition. She is dressed in the same way, with a rifle in her hand and she whispers:

JADWIGA: Deserter ... deserter.

Quickly this image is superceded by another image. We are in the home of the BROUTS. MIRIAM stands against the wall and she whispers:

MIRIAM: And how blind were you when you did it? Your last one, Lolita! Was her ... chapter built on thoughtful consideration?

The image vanishes. We're back at the beach. MARITA notices a briefly vacuous expression on EDGAR'S face and bending over and touching him she asks:

MARITA: Are you alright? Are you alright? (*Then she notices the time on his wrist watch. She exclaims:*) Holy Jesus! It's almost one o'clock! I was to meet my boyfriend at 12:30! At the Sand Bar! He's a professor, like you. We met in Toronto! Oh, I need to get dressed! I'm late! Late!

She's ready to run away. Then she stops, looking at the "crumbled" figure of EDGAR. Full of concern, she moves to him and says:

MARITA: Are you o.k? I must go, but I can't unless you tell me you're alright! Tell me! Tell me!

EDGAR (*Now in control of himself*): I'm alright. Thanks.

MARITA: Good. So I'm off. But I want to see you again. I want to know all the details of your life. You'll be in my book! I will phone you ... Do you know your phone number?

EDGAR: Yes, I do. It's 778-3736.

MARITA (*Repeats*): 778-3736. An easy number. I won't forget.

Totally unexpectedly she bends over, kisses EDGAR'S cheek and is gone, running across the beach towards the sand bar restaurant. EDGAR watches her go and he whispers:

EDGAR: Marita ... Marita ...

Black out.

ACT II, SCENE 1

We are in the condo that EDGAR rented at Westbay Point & Moorings, the housing development on Anna Maria Island. It's midnight, the only light that brightens the room comes from the full moon and hundreds of stars that are glimmering in the sky. EDGAR, in his pyjamas, lies on a sofa bed. He's asleep but obviously "possessed by a demon" his body is in constant shivering motion, he whines, his face is marked by the pangs of fear. Suddenly he wakes up, jumps up, turns on the light, grabs hold of the telephone receiver—the telephone is on a small desk by the window, just beside the lamp. Mumbling the numbers, he is calling long distance, to his psychiatrist, in Toronto. His name is Dr. Merner. The telephone rings, then we hear a voice:

VOICE: Hallo …

EDGAR: Dr. Merner? This is Edgar speaking. Edgar Brout. Your patient. I know it's late but I needed to call you. I had this horrible dream! I was again in Warsaw. During the Uprising.

VOICE: Hallo … Hallo …

EDGAR: Can you hear me? Can I talk to you? I didn't wake you up, did I? Did I make you leave your bed?

VOICE: No, you didn't.

EDGAR: Oh, good. So I can talk. I was with Jadwiga. We were running away from the Old City through the canal to Zoliborz. Remember? The outskirts of Warsaw. The suburb of the City. I told you all about it! O.k. I'll continue. The water was up to our knees, no, up to our ankles, but it was dark, very chilly. Jadwiga was frightened, she was crying. Then I was making love to her, on the beach of the Vistula River. We were in a hole. A hole that looked like a burial ground. Deep enough for a coffin. (*After a pause*) Yes, a coffin! That's what I said. I felt that she was dragging me to the grave. Though I made love to her I was in a grave. I was on top of her but … felt like a corpse! Making love to a corpse! In a grave!

When he delivers the last words there's a humming sound, as if the connection was out of order. EDGAR is shaking the receiver and shouting

EDGAR: Hallo … Hallo …

He dials the number again but to no avail. He cannot establish the connection. He calls the operator.

EDGAR: Operator, I called Toronto. I talked to my … to the person I wanted. Then, there was some noise and the line went dead. Could you … (*After a pause*) The number was 489-8889. In Toronto, Canada.

There is a moment of silence. EDGAR listens, his tension is palpable then he says:

EDGAR: There's no reply? Why? You mean the phone is out of order! Ok. I'll try it tomorrow! (*Exploding*) Shit! Shit! Shit!

He smashes down the receiver, angrily walks out on the small deck outside. The star filled night is splendid. The silence is overwhelming. The moon a gigantic circle—seems nearby. EDGAR stares at the moon, and he says softly:

EDGAR: I want a house on the moon.

Again an image from the past fills his mind. It's the time of the Warsaw Uprising —September 1944. EDGAR is in the cellar of a house where the members of the underground (ak—Polish Home Army) who are off duty, sleep at night. The place is dark, some moonlight is seeping through the low windows. There are three other men in the cellar, each on a mattress, their bodies and heads covered with blankets. Their snoring indicates how far "gone" they are. Then, on the steps leading to the cellar, a figure appears. It's JADWIGA, barefooted. She is wearing a short slip and holds a small hurricane lamp in her hand. The candle inside of it gives a touch of flickering light. JADWIGA'S other hand is around the lamp. She is trying to diminish the glare as much as possible, and her eyes are searching for EDGAR. When she finds him, she quietly tiptoes towards him, extinguishes the candle with her thumb and she whispers, barely audibly:

JADWIGA: I couldn't sleep. I was watching the moon. I wanted to live there. But not alone. With you ... (*She kneels beside him, caressing his body, and she whispers again:*) Love me. I think I'm pregnant. Love me. Yes, here. And then, let's live on the moon. Dance a tango on the moon.

She slips under him. They are ready to make love. Then suddenly the other men who are in the cellar jump out from their mattresses. One of them is holding a lit flashlight. They move towards EDGAR and JADWIGA, we see their large, grotesque bodies and they scream, kicking them:

VOICES: He's fucking her! In our bedroom! This Jewish shithead! He's fucking this whore! This Jewish shithead! This Polish whore!

The image is gone. EDGAR is on the deck staring at the moon. His face expresses an indescribable despair. He covers his face with the palm of his hand and almost screams:

EDGAR: Ah ...

Then realizing that he's outside of his apartment and that the noise he made could wake up the neighbours, he rapidly re-enters the room and collapses on the sofa bed. He curls up on it and whispers:

EDGAR: Dr. Merner ... Dr. Merner ... I didn't tell you what they said ... He fucks her! In our bedroom! This Jewish shithead! And this Polish whore! Dr. Merner, I'm losing my mind! What am I to do? What am I to do?

Then out of nowhere the image of MARITA appears to him. She is on the beach, moving backwards and waving to him. The image disappears as fast as it appeared. And EDGAR whispers:

EDGAR: Marita ... Marita ...

Blackout.

ACT II, SCENE 2

The same location, the next day about 11 o'clock in the morning. The sun is up, and light pours into the room which is sparsely but elegantly furnished. EDGAR is asleep on the sofa bed. The telephone rings. He jumps up, but not fully awake, and not certain where the sound is coming from, runs in the opposite direction. The phone rings again. He turns around and picks up the receiver.

EDGAR (*Exclaiming*): Dr. Merner?! (*Then his tone changes completely*) Ah, it's you ... How are you, Miriam? (*Then in his usual infuriated fashion*) He asked you to call me?! Why didn't he make the call himself? Why did he have to burden you with my problem?! (*Sarcastically now*) He had some problem with his phone. Sure, sure. And he was busy with patients. That's why he called you! (*Erupting angrily*) I had a bad dream, that's all! Yes! That's why I called him in the middle of the night! Because I needed to talk to him! And I knew he wouldn't be asleep! I knew he'd be watching ... (*Responding to her words*) What? Enough of this ... shit?! Right?! That's what you were going to say, right?! I supplied you with a phrase you so often use in your studio! DON'T GIVE ME THIS SHIT! You may talk like this to your handyman, not to me! And that's why I left! Because ... (*After a pause*) No! I'm not coming home, no matter how concerned you are! And stop calling me! Don't load that guilt trip on me! O.k. O.k. Sorry for losing my temper. It's because I find it odious that Dr. Merner ... Yes, tell him you talked to me. And that I'm well. My anxiety is gone. I'm well. Bye.

He hangs up, goes to the table where there is a bottle of vodka and a pitcher of orange juice. He is ready to mix a drink, but is stopped by a soft and singing male voice.

VOICE: Mr. Brot ... Mr. Brot ... Mr. Brot ...

EDGAR (*Stepping out on the deck*): Brout. Who are you?

He addresses a skinny, young, black man—his name is JOHNNY. He stands on the grounds below the deck and is somewhat startled by the sudden apparition of the man he was looking for.

JOHNNY (*Ingratiating himself*): Oh! Nice meeting you Mr. Brot. I'm Johnny, your driver who'll take you wherever you ... plan to go. It's all arranged. The office told me to tell you that. But for my work you'll have to pay. You see ...

EDGAR: Slow down, will you? To start with, my name is Brout. Not Brot! I dislike the grotesque sound that flows from your mouth and stands for my name!

JOHNNY: Oh, sorry Mr. Bb ...

EDGAR: Brout. Then who told you to knock at my door? So early in the morning? I don't need a driver. You must be looking for someone else. Hey, right! You're searching for someone who's called Brot!

JOHNNY: That's not so, Mr. Brrout. Did I pronounce it correctly?

EDGAR: Yes, you did.

JOHNNY (*He smiles graciously and continues*): You see, I'm not only a driver but I work in the office. I'm the Boss's handyman. He's the manager of this estate. I've seen you before, on the day you arrived here. Hey ... didn't you come to the office?

EDGAR: I did. But I still don't understand why you're here. As I said, I don't need a driver. So go back to your desk. In your office.

JOHNNY: But you're wrong, Mr. Brout. You need a driver. Mr. Merner called us. Mr. Merner who owns the place you live in. His brother is a doctor in the city you come from. And he knows you. And he called his brother who called our office to tell us that you're out of order—healthwise—that you need to be watched and that you cannot drive. Under no condition can you use the driving wheel. And as we know Mr. Merner very well, he's owned this property for many years, and as he is a very rich man and has a very ... booming voice ... ha ... ha ... ha ...

EDGAR: I don't need you now. I will call the office when I require a driver.

JOHNNY: One more thing, you'll have to pay for it. For my service. You'll have to pay for it. I was told you will—but I thought I should mention it to you. I can't drive you without ...

EDGAR: How much will it cost?

JOHNNY: Not too much. Eight dollars an hour. When I'm behind the wheel. And when I wait for you ...

EDGAR: O.k. I'll pay.

JOHNNY (*With a smile*): Good, good. I drive fast. I will drive you around the Island. And off it if you wish. But nothing compares to our village. (*Pointing out*) Out there! There are high rise winter resorts! Scandal loaded garbage dumps! Whores! Drugs! *He notices a grimace of discomfort on EDGAR'S face and reacts to it.*

JOHNNY: Hey, have I hurt your feelings? You're not on drugs, are you?

EDGAR: Yes, I am. But not on those you have in mind. I buy mine at the drugstore.

JOHNNY (*With enthusiasm*): Oh! How lucky can you be!

EDGAR (*Impatiently*): Anything else? As I've told you ... *The telephone rings again.*

EDGAR: I have to go.

He leaves the deck in a hurry and picks up the receiver of the phone in the living room.

EDGAR: Hallo ... (*Then with happy surprise*) Oh, Marita? Oh ... oh ... I'm pleased to hear your voice, yes. So, how are you? Having a nice time with your friend? (*After a pause*) I'm speaking of the man you ran to while you and I ... Oh, I see. He's your lover, not your friend. I'm glad you told me. I shall remember the distinction. (*After a pause*) You want me to be one of the heroes of your book! I'll be damned! O.k, yes, I'll be a victim of your drilling, if that's what you want. Mind you I'm not convinced that I'm too keen to undergo ... yes, your pushy entry—my words not yours—into my personality, but ... I'll meet you any time, anywhere. In an hour on the deck of the Sand Bar? Sure! Sure! We'll have a spicy lunch together, cooled by champagne. (*Responding to her comment*) Not cooled but sparkled! Right again. Will you ever be wrong, allowing me to be right? Once in a lifetime? (*Listening to her words and laughing*) Right again! You are not my spouse so "lifetime" is beyond my claim! You are a bright dame! That's for sure! A stunning, bright dame! I almost wish ... Enough! My mouth's zipped ... until we see each other ... (*Looking at the sky which is much more cloudy now*) Whether it rains or not, right?

He hangs up and returns to the deck.

JOHNNY (*Who was sitting on the ground gets up to leave*): Sorry for being on your turf for so long. I love it here. Particularly early in the morning when the sun rises. Or in the evening, when it sets ...

For a moment an image from the past flashes through EDGAR'S mind. The sun is setting over the old city of Warsaw. We see the silhouettes of buildings basking in the red glare. And the same young woman that we saw in the previous 'return' to the past, JADWIGA, is seen, wearing her grubby outfit and holding a rifle in her hand. EDGAR stands beside her. He too is dressed shabbily, his face is covered with dirt. Yet he looks strong and attractive. A rifle hangs on his shoulder. He's holding JADWIGA'S hand, they're both facing the huge, red glow of the sun. And she whispers:

JADWIGA: The sun's setting. Will we see it rising?

EDGAR (*With painful conviction*): We will, my love. We will. We will. (*He embraces her.*)

Then there is an outburst of gun and machine gun fire and the image dissolves, abruptly. We are again in Tampa Bay. JOHNNY is watching EDGAR and he says:

JOHNNY: Are you sick or something? Shouldn't you take your pill?

EDGAR (*Roughly*): No, thank you. You'd better go ... No! Wait for me. I'll get dressed. Then you'll take me to the other side. I'm to meet ... a bird, and feed her at the Sand Bar.

JOHNNY (*Giggling*): Sir ...

EDGAR (*Pretending to be angry*): Don't "sir" me, or I'll "sir" you!

He runs down the small staircase and lightly punches the drivers's belly.

EDGAR: See!

JOHNNY: Oh, I like that! I want more! Sir! Sir! Sir!

They both stare at each other then burst out laughing.

EDGAR: You're a ... funny guy, let me tell you. I like your gentleness. And your humour.

JOHNNY: I'm glad. D'you think that I could survive here—a nigger like me—if I didn't play the kidder?

EDGAR (*Shocked*): A nigger like you?! What does that mean?! For me, you're like me! A man! A human being!

JOHNNY: Oh sir ... you rubbed my heart. Oh, sir ... sir ... sir ...

They both burst out laughing, then EDGAR invites JOHNNY to sit on a chair that's on the deck.

EDGAR: Relax on that chair and wait for me. I'll be with you in a few minutes.

JOHNNY: Your kindness makes me sick. Sir ... sir ... sir ...

They laugh again then JOHNNY collapses on the chair and EDGAR is about to re-enter the room, but he stops at the door and addresses JOHNNY.

EDGAR: Tell me, are you married?

JOHNNY: You bet I am. (*Imitating the sexual act with his arm in a pumping motion*) A good pusher like me, why wouldn't I be married?

EDGAR: I just … left my wife. I caught her under the belly of a friend of mine. And so …

JOHNNY (*His eyes blazing with fury*): Is she still alive?

EDGAR: Sure she is. Why …

JOHNNY: Good for her! I would have left mine too, but dead. I would have broken her neck! Clobbered her skull!

EDGAR: And if she caught you in the same position? On the body …

JOHNNY: It couldn't happen! I would never let her see it! She's a good cook. A good mother (*With a wink*) to me and our children. Why would I be so dumb to let her catch me on top of another broad? Even if I were filled with liquor, pissed, I would never … so your woman caught you. How? What's the story?

EDGAR: She saw through me many times. And the last time … It was a black woman.

JOHNNY: A black woman? You're kidding me! Why would you fish in a pond that you didn't know? I don't believe you. She wasn't black. (*With a giggle*) Though for sure she was a woman.

EDGAR: Listen to this. I once invited some students to a party at my house. One of them was a young person who I slept with. She seduced me. No, I seduced her. She knew that she would meet my wife, she wanted to be anonymous, unrecognizable, so she painted herself dark brown. Almost black. Her face, her neck, her arms and legs … I screamed seeing her. My wife said: "Who are you, little phoney?" And she replied, pointing at me. "Ask him. He always has less respect for whites than for blacks!"

JOHNNY: So, what happened? What happened?

EDGAR: All who were present burst out laughing, then my wife invited her to wash herself in our bathroom. To remove the paint.

JOHNNY: And?

EDGAR: She told my wife the reason for her … disguise.

JOHNNY: She told your wife that she slept with you?!

EDGAR: She did, overcome with remorse. Then she ran away spoiling the party, disappointing all the other guests who wanted to chat with her.

JOHNNY: And then?

EDGAR: My wife dismissed the party and took me to task. She called me a "disloyal prick!"(*After a pause*) It was not the first time I betrayed her. I needed to do it, to prove to myself that I was alive.

JOHNNY: And then?

EDGAR: She spread her legs for a friend of mine. I walked into it. I saw it. (*After a pause clenching his fist*) And then I knew that our life together was over. (*After a pause*) I left her in the house we shared for twenty years. I packed my bags and ran to Florida.

JOHNNY (*With real compassion*): So you're a cuckold?

EDGAR: You've chosen the right word. I'm a cuck! And old ...

JOHNNY (*Laughing*): You're a cuck! Never heard that before ... (*Again with compassion*) And old ...

EDGAR (*Bitterly*): Yes, man. Old. Well, I'd better get ready. If you want a drink, pour yourself one. But not two! Vodka ...

JOHNNY (*Reading his train of thought*): It's good for your soul! So-so for your brain. I'll take you up on your offer. Sir ... sir ... sir ...

They laugh again, EDGAR unexpectedly, hugs him, then they both enter into the room. JOHNNY looks around. He notices three photographs of EDGAR'S parents and his sister sitting on the desk. He bends over to see them better then asks suddenly:

JOHNNY: Who are they?

EDGAR: My parents. And my sister.

JOHNNY: Are they ... Are you a Jew?

EDGAR: Yes, I am. What brought this about?

JOHNNY: You ... hugging me. Only a Jew would embrace a black man ... And those photographs ... they're dead, aren't they?

EDGAR: Yes.

JOHNNY: Murdered!

EDGAR: Yes.

JOHNNY: Once I saw them, I knew. Yes, my good man, yes. Your race and mine know what pain is. Our bodies are covered with wounds. We both know the ... taste, the smell of suffering.

They look at each other, warmly, then, an image rises before EDGAR'S eyes.

He is 18 years old in a street of a small town ghetto in Poland, walking home and holding hands with his lovely looking, 15 year old sister, ANNA. They both are grungilly dressed, on their right arm there is an arm band with the star of David on it. Suddenly a huge and grotesque looking S.S. MAN pulls ANNA away from EDGAR and kicks him down to the ground. Then holding ANNA by her arm and her hair, and laughing uproariously he drags her away. A few seconds later, he is gone, leaving EDGAR on his knees, crying.

EDGAR: Anna! Anna!

The image disappears.

We are back in the room with EDGAR and JOHNNY who saw and understood EDGAR'S "withdrawal" to the past. He says with pain:

JOHNNY (*Very gently*): Right now, did you taste it? Did you smell it?

EDGAR (*Softly*): Yes, I did. The loss of my sister.

JOHNNY embraces him, and he says:

JOHNNY: Get hold of yourself, Mr. Brout, or you won't survive! You're sinking! Live now, not in the past! Drink, make love, shift your gears to NOW, or you won't survive! (*Then, after a pause*) That ... bird you're going to meet ... couldn't she help you?

EDGAR (*Smiling gently*): A good thought. (*He calls*) Marita, will you help me? Will you help me, Marita …

Blackout.

ACT II, SCENE 3

The same day a short while later. We are on the deck of the sand bar. The place is rather empty. The sky is somewhat cloudy. EDGAR is sitting on the deck at a table close to the railing. He is alone, watching the beach and the swimmers, but he is also checking his watch with growing impatience. He is obviously perturbed that MARITA hasn't appeared as yet. He also, occasionally glances at the bottle of champagne which is stuck in an ice filled bucket, on the table. He would like to open it and have a drink but resists the temptation. Then MARITA appears. EDGAR jumps up, the pleasure of seeing her is strongly etched on his face. But the expression of joy evaporates at the sight of a man, who follows MARITA. He is middle aged, sturdy, good looking. His name is ROLF MILBAUER. He wears a light cotton suit and a tie, a manner of dress that is quite foreign to the place. There is evident coolness about MARITA'S companion. The impression that he makes is that of a person who's puzzled, perhaps even disdained by the forthcoming encounter with EDGAR. MARITA notices EDGAR standing by his table. She runs towards him and calls:

MARITA: Professor Brout! Forgive me for being late: My day got all screwed up because … (*In response to a "warning" sound coming from the throat of her friend she changes her tune and says:*) I misplaced my watch! (*Pointing at ROLF*) Only when he found it, I knew what time it was, and … Ah! (*She turns to her companion*) Rolf, this is Dr. Edgar Brout, Professor of political science, University of Toronto, (*Then pointing at her friend*) and this is Rolf Milbauer, professor of modern history at a German University. In Duesseldorf.

ROLF (*Correcting her with a benign smile*): West German University. So far. But with the Berlin Wall down there's a good chance that one of these days … (*Then extending his hand to EDGAR*) I'm pleased to meet you Dr. Brout.

EDGAR (*Shaking ROLF'S hand*): Nice meeting you too, Dr. Milbauer. You're a doctor, aren't you. Most German professors I have met …

ROLF (*Interrupting, with an ironic smile*): Yes, I am. In my country to carry some scholastic weight that title must be seen before the name. The same as in Canada.

There are only two chairs at the table that EDGAR occupies. ROLF walks away to find a chair for himself. While he is absent MARITA says softly:

MARITA: I'm sorry for the surprise. I'll explain later … (*Then at the sight of ROLF who is only a few steps away holding a chair, to EDGAR, quite loudly*) You're a doctor, aren't you?

EDGAR: You bet I am. At my age to carry some scholastic weight … Please sit down. Sit down.

A WAITER passes by. EDGAR addresses him.

EDGAR: Waiter!

WAITER (*Clearly British*): Sir?

EDGAR: Don't "Sir" me! As if I were your master and you were my slave! I hate it!

WAITER (*Totally confused*): Sir?

EDGAR: Never mind! (*Pointing at the bottle*) Would you open it please? (*Pointing at ROLF*) And bring us one more glass. And menus. My guests are hungry. So am I. And another bottle! This one will be empty before you return. (*To ROLF*) Am I right? You will not object if I fill you up with champagne?

ROLF: Not at all. Providing that I pay for it. (*He addresses the WAITER*) Waiter, bring us another bottle and give me the bill.

EDGAR: Dr. Milbauer ...

ROLF: As I said, I'm paying for it. And for whatever I eat. I'm an uninvited guest. The least I can do ...

EDGAR: Is to stop making such a big deal of it! (*Pointing at MARITA*) This lady brought you here. And I'm the host!

While they were chatting the WAITER brought a glass for ROLF, opened the bottle, poured the champagne and was gone, leaving the menus on the table. EDGAR comments on it.

EDGAR: I like that man. Deft and silent. What more can one ask? Cheers!

MARITA & ROLF (*Together*): Cheers!

They all enjoy the taste of the bubbly, decide what to order, then ROLF, looking at the sky that is getting darker, says:

ROLF: Shouldn't we go inside? It's going to rain.

EDGAR: Who cares. (*To ROLF, with a wink*) So, let's straighten this matter. You're here to ... discover who I am, right?

ROLF: Sort of. But first, how old are you, may I ask?

EDGAR: You may not! (*Pointing his finger at MARITA*) If she'd asked the question, I might answer it, who knows ...

MARITA: Well, how old are you, my dear Dr. B.?

EDGAR: Old enough to be your father. Whether wise enough, that's another story! (*Then to ROLF*) Why do you want to know how old I am? To assess the virility ... I mean, fertility of my mind?

ROLF: Something like that. Marita spoke about you with such fervour, described you as a man "so full of vigour, really a young man," and that ...

MARITA: A man young for his age, that's what I said.

ROLF: "A spunky, middle aged man"—that's what I heard. "Captivatingly youthful." So I decided ...

EDGAR (*Cutting him off*): Did you say "useful?" You can bet I am! Long winded at times, yes, but sharp minded! Vice free! That is why my students sing my praises! They say, he's vigorous! Zestful!

MARITA (*Cuts in with a giggle*): Lustful!

EDGAR: Buoyant! Gleeful!

MARITA: Crustacean! Trustful!

EDGAR (*Astounded, then laughing*): I drink to that! Cheers! (*He gulps his drink then addresses ROLF*) Dr. M. I interrupted you. Sorry. You were saying …

ROLF: That I decided to be prudent and face that … lustful guy. I'm always ready to stand up to a challenge.

EDGAR (*Responding in kind*): To dismantle the competition? Sounds good! Very good! How do we do it? The fight I mean? And who'll be the judge? Can you imagine a contest without a judge? And what are the rules of the competition?

ROLF: There's only one rule. The winner takes all. (*Putting his hand on the table for arm wrestling*) Are you ready Dr. Brout?

EDGAR: You bet I am! But if you win …

MARITA (*Pretending to be insulted*): Wait a minute! Don't I have a word on the subject? You're teasing one another, but underneath you're deadly serious! And the prize of the contest is me! Don't I have a say in the matter?! (*At the sight of the WAITER carrying a large tray with meals on it*) Food! Hey, we didn't order!

EDGAR: You're damn right! We didn't! (*To the WAITER*): What's that all about?! What have you got there, sir?!

WAITER (*Very shaky*): O..o..nion soup! Sh..shrimps! C..c.. crab legs! But you're right! I made a mistake! You didn't order!

EDGAR: Never mind. We call that God sent! Spread it around. And we will eat.

ROLF: And drink. Don't forget! The other bottle!

The WAITER places the plates filled with food in front of the occupants of the table and quickly vanishes. EDGAR, ROLF and MARITA start eating, find their food delicious, the noises they make clearly indicate that.

EDGAR: Uhm!

MARITA: Uhm!

ROLF: Uhm!

EDGAR: God sent! I've told you … So where did you meet, the two of you: Oh, I know. In Toronto. Verdict of Fate, I call it. And from then on you're exploring Florida. So who are you, Rolf? What brought you here? I am eager to hear a few words about your career. You don't mind if I call you by your first name? I was once told that when you share a drink with somebody—no family names! Mind you it was not champagne that we drank. It was pure … vodka!

ROLF (*Laughing*): I like that Edgar! No surnames! I like it! And I drink to that! Cheers! (*He swallows all the champagne he had in his glass*)

MARITA & EDGAR (*Together*): In one gulp?! (*Then raising their glasses*) Cheers!

ROLF (*Teasingly*): So how old are you, Edgar? As you can see I'm in love with the subject. Confined to it! But, let me first answer your question. I was born in Germany. My mother was a nurse. My father was an officer of the Wehrmacht. The German army.

EDGAR (*Sarcastically*): Oh, one of those …

ROLF: Yes, indeed. He became an officer when the war broke out. And he served according to his conscience.

EDGAR (*Ironically*): Meaning?

ROLF (*Calmly*): After the entry into Poland and when he saw the atrocities that were committed …

EDGAR (*Seriously this time*): Are you referring to the treatment of the Jews?

ROLF: Yes, and no. The onslaught on the rights of human beings went beyond the Jewish question. Poles were murdered too. Gypsies. Incarcerated and slaughtered in concentration camps.

EDGAR: So what did your father do? How did he appease his conscience?

ROLF: Once he learned what Hitler was up to, he deserted. To the Soviet Union. Where he died. Eventually. In a labour camp.

MARITA: Oh, my God! Oh, my God! You never told me!

ROLF (*Affectionately*): There was no time for that. We were busy … talking about so many other things. I'm saying it not to hurt your feelings but to … enlighten this gentleman. (*Then to EDGAR*) As Marita probably told you she and I met in Canada only recently. In Toronto to be exact. I was attending a conference where I delivered a lecture. On the state of the world, today. (*With a light smile*) And on its state—tomorrow. If there is such a thing. The world of tomorrow.

EDGAR: Any doubts about it?

ROLF: Yes, I question its future. I ask, will it survive the vitriolic disease that is … freely flowing through its veins or …

EDGAR: What disease? What are you talking about?

ROLF: It's a long story.

EDGAR: Well, time's on our side. Isn't that so, Marita?

MARITA: I wouldn't be so certain if I were you. When Rolf gets the podium … (*Pretending to make an aside of it*) Hopefully not in his preaching manner …

ROLF (*Cutting in*): I sometimes talk a lot and Marita objects to it. She calls it "preaching." Nevertheless I believe that the topic I'm dealing with is the most crucial of our times! And that I'm voicing the truth!

EDGAR: Whatever that is. The truth, I mean. Continue, please …

ROLF: We may not see eye to eye on the subject. On the other hand you might become a convert …

EDGAR: Get to the point! Get to the point!

ROLF: We're in a mess, don't you think? World-wide. Bloodshed, despotism, starvation—these are the features of our global existence. And so little is done about it. We seem to accept this … sickly state of affairs with as little murmur as possible. We lower our heads as an expression of sympathy for the victims or whisper our … antipathetic slogans. That's about all we're doing.

EDGAR: What do you propose?

ROLF: That we spend more time, more effort to expose the philosophy that brought the world to such a condition! Initiated, instigated by the ruthless manipulations of the two evil empires that form the modus vivendi of this century! You surely know what I'm insinuating! It is they, locked in fierce competition, who imposed their pitiful rules on the world! One is in demise but still ... burbling! The other has risen vehemently and is kicking hard! Blindly ... kicking!

EDGAR (*Lifting his glass*): So far so good. Convoluted a bit ... the introductory phrases of the lecture, but compelling. Compelling. Cheers!

ROLF (*Sharply*): Convoluted?! I'm as straightforward about it as I can be! Our global survival is at stake! Exacerbated by the violent upsurge of nationalistic dogma! And the desperate, often shotgun supported response of the victims! So we must talk about it, no, scream about it. Make our schools, our new generation ... the explosive source of this revelation!

EDGAR: Aren't we doing it?

ROLF: Barely and badly! How much do we teach about the state of communism today? How deeply do we examine the gutter-like state of the doctrine that at one time was to save Mankind from ... impending disaster! And the same applies to Capitalism! Instead of revealing clearly its not so deeply hidden deficiencies, we embrace it with deaf ears! And blindly! Though it carries the seal of destruction in its own gospel! In its sacred belief that it has the ultimate wisdom to resolve all basic human problems! What an aborted way of thinking! What a joke! What a bad joke! No matter how brilliant and caring an individual would be, without a collective effort on a global scale—human misery will continue—hunger, repression, slaughter will stay alive on our Planet! Yes, that's what I preach. The demise of present day Communism! The helplessness of present day Capitalism!

EDGAR: Calm down, my friend. (*Pointing at the people who sit at other tables*) Unless you're looking for an audience. And tell me, what ... cure do you suggest? How do you propose ...

ROLF: To put the brakes on the catastrophe bound glide of our world? As I said before, settled on that course by two evil empires? By suppressing the mega race for the mega profit! By getting rid of the temptation to be power hungry! Corrupt! By giving a boot to the military/industrial brotherhood wherever it pulls its weight! Yes, by kicking the ass of the rocket makers! And the rocket users—the military! By breaking the neck of the military hegemony!

EDGAR: Easier said, than done ...

ROLF (*In a real frenzy now*): By sharing all the riches of this planet! To survive we must share whatever we possess! There must be a balance between the individual and collective needs! We must share what we possess! Not claim the solitary ownership of it! We must share! Share! Share! But that's not all! (*Loudly now*) Ours is a revolutionary age. Our scientific wizards created for us a true wonderland! The ... explosion of our progress, if you want to call it that, is immense, mind boggling! But do we know how to cope with it? No! With each passing day we are more confused! We're blinded by the upside part of it that translated into commercial value makes many of us the rich tyrants of the world! Rulers of those who live by crawling! Masters of the brow beaten! Scourges of the poor! Our ethical standards, morality are in shambles!

EDGAR: Cool it, Rolf! Cool it! You sound like Billy Graham! Are you a Fundamentalist of sorts by any chance?

ROLF: Fundamentalist, me? Edgar, don't be ridiculous!

EDGAR: I touched a sore spot, didn't I? Well, whatever the motivation for the outburst of your passion ... We're here to relax, remember? Enjoy the sunshine ... (*He looks at the sky*) Uh, it's going to rain. (*After a pause*) You said your father was gone in '39. How old were you ... wait, did you know your father?

ROLF (*Smiling bitterly*): Good question. No, I didn't. I was born during the war. By that time he was on the other side. Some months after they ... shoved him into a camp.

EDGAR: Why did that happen?

ROLF: Do you really want to know?

EDGAR: Yes, I do. Unless ...

ROLF: He talked too much. Spat fire against the Nazis, that's for sure. But also made many comments against Stalin. Loudly. Compared him to Hitler. That's what I found out during my trip to the Soviet Union. Two years ago, with some other scholars. We were studying the roots of Communism. Under that guise I was researching my father's disappearance.

EDGAR: That's quite amazing. That you managed to get to the bottom of it. Without being locked in jail! Amazing!

ROLF: I was lucky. One of our Russian translators had gone through a similar experience. He lost his father and his mother for the same reason. They talked too much. And one day after he and I shared a few drinks, he ... confessed his abhorrence of their system. And he helped me to find out about the plight of my parent.

EDGAR: Amazing! Amazing! Don't you think so, Marita?

MARITA: Yes, it is. But if you don't mind I'd rather stay silent on the subject.

EDGAR: Why so? Don't you share our feelings about the horror of the Stalin era?

MARITA: I do. But I must suppress it. I have learned that once you give vent to certain feelings, you can't stop them from staying on the surface. From harrassing you without stop. From strangling you! And when that happens how can you function? No! I had enough emotional turmoil in my life. Not only in recent years, but also when I was a child ...

EDGAR (*Softly*): I understand. I understand. (*After a pause he turns to ROLF*) And your mother? How did she take it all?

ROLF: Well enough. But she was gone when I was five years old. I was brought up by some other members of my family.

EDGAR: Well, well, well … You tasted the bitterest bitters like many of us. I have changed my mind about you. I won't battle you any more. (*In his usual teasing tone*) You're too young for me to wrestle with. And too … strong. (*At the sight of the WAITER who is arriving with another bottle of champagne*) Just on time, Mr. Waiter. We need a good shot of liquor to lift our spirits.

The WAITER opens the bottle, pours the contents into the three empty glasses and exits, silently.

EDGAR: The quietest server I have ever seen. Mr. Tiptoe, I call him. Cheers!

MARITA & ROLF (*Together*): Cheers!

EDGAR: Now the other question. Why are you here? (*Pointing at MARITA*) Because of her?

ROLF: Because of her, yes. When we … bumped into each other, I fell in love on the day we met. That's about it. And to be together, just to relax, we decided to take a trip to the Wonderland! To Florida. And now, we're examining each other more closely. We're trying to determine how long it will last. This affair of ours. Briefly or … for the time of our lives. I'd prefer the second version. Marita though, is less sure of it. She's still … pondering over her previous experience. And …

He can't continue. He looks to MARITA for help. She understands his difficulty and enters into the conversation.

MARITA: Rolf asked me to marry him. I love him too, I think. And that's why I had to refuse. I'm still not sure about it. I was abandoned once. No, twice. But the first time it was so long ago and so strange, that … (*After a pause*) Rolf would like me to be a part of his life in Germany. I don't think I could. For a short while, yes. But to build my home there, my future, no! I couldn't face the people who … (*Louder and stronger*) I couldn't abandon my land! Though I'm only a tiny pebble of it. I couldn't! (*To EDGAR*) Why are you staring at me with such amazement! Surely you understand my upheaval! I'm addicted to my country! I want to hear the breathing, the farting, the laughter of my people!

EDGAR: I understand. I understand.

An image grows before his eyes. He and JADWIGA are in a grungy cellar of a house —we have seen it before—that is in ruin caused by artillery fire. This time the side wall is broken to bits, the moonlight shines strongly, it seems to be right on top of them. EDGAR sits on a broken chair, bent down, his hands covering his face. JADWIGA stands beside him and she whispers:

JADWIGA: It's all finished now, so hide with me! Don't let the Germans imprison you! Don't let them take you to a camp!

EDGAR: I must do what I am told. I'm a soldier. I must go with the others.

JADWIGA: No, Edgar! No! You're a soldier, but also a Jew! If that would come out you'll be shot! Or sent to a concentration camp!

EDGAR: I have to take that risk. I must leave you, Jadwiga.

JADWIGA: No! No! You don't want to be a deserter, but you're deserting me! And the country you were born in. Because once you leave you'll never come back! Even if you survive the camp, you'll never come back! You will join your family. In America! Edgar, we can hide and survive! Edgar, don't leave me! Don't leave me!

EDGAR gets up and walks away. JADWIGA remains, her face masked by excruciating pain and anger. And she whispers:

JADWIGA: Deserter … Deserter …

The image is gone. For a moment they are all silent, though MARITA and ROLF are looking at EDGAR with concern trying to understand what happened to him.

MARITA: Are you alright? You seemed … lost somewhere …

ROLF: You were gone. And in pain. Your face had such a troubled expression.

EDGAR: I must go. I'm feeling a bit … nauseated. (*Pointing to the empty glass*) At my age … too much of that stuff, I guess. (*He calls*) Waiter!

The man materializes almost instantly

WAITER: At your service …

EDGAR: My bill, please.

WAITER (*Handing the bill to him*): Here it is.

EDGAR: You're even faster than I thought. Cash or credit card?

WAITER: It's up to you, sir.

EDGAR: Don't "sir" me. Cash! The less I carry the better. (*He takes out his wallet, removes a number of $10 bills from it and hands them to the WAITER*) Here you are. Your tip is included.

WAITER (*After he counts the money and almost ready to leave*): You are most generous. I thank you from the bottom of my heart.

ROLF: Wait! What about my bill?

WAITER: Oh! It slipped my mind! This gentleman paid it. But if you would want me to calculate your share …

EDGAR: Next time, my dear waiter. Next time (*Pointing at ROLF*) it will be his turn. Now, go … go … go!

WAITER: As you wish, my dear … "sir." But if I may suggest, leave quickly. The weather man sent us a warning. There will be a storm. Or at least a heavy rain. (*He exits*)

EDGAR (*Stands up and addresses his guests*): Please forgive me, but my head is pounding. (*Reading concern on MARITA'S face*) And don't worry how I … connect with my place. My car is on the parking lot. With a driver in it.

MARITA: And our talk? I thought …

EDGAR: Not today. I couldn't go through with it. But I brought you something to read. The story of my young life. I made a copy of it. It's a draft. Clumsy. I'm still working on it. (*He hands it to her, then continues*) I'm on my way. His story shook me up too much. I need some rest. Time to … (*In his usual "comedic" manner and knocking at his head*) expel the disease.

MARITA (*Confused*): What are you talking about?

EDGAR: The yesteryear that clogs my brain, opens up the wounds in my heart. (*Responding to MARITA'S troubled expression*) Don't look at me with such concern. I exaggerate a lot. A bit! I'm a slave to my … crazy way of feeling. And thinking …

MARITA: I will call you tomorrow. May I?

EDGAR: But of course. (*Forcing himself to be humourous*) If there is a tomorrow. Sorry … Sorry … (*He kisses MARITA'S hand, then shakes hands with ROLF*) Good bye. Good bye. (*He takes a step or two away from the table, then stops and addresses ROLF*) One more thing, Rolf. Make an effort to understand her. Look for a compromise. But don't abandon her. Or you will suffer for it till the end of your days. Don't abandon her! Don't abandon her!

Again an image from the past appears to him. He sees JADWIGA in a swimming suit on the beach of the Vistula River. Her hands are on her belly and she whispers:

JADWIGA: And who will take care of me? Deserter! Deserter!

The image disappears rapidly. What we see now is the beginning of a storm. Heavy clouds are hanging over the water, the first drips of rain are falling and a thunderous lightning brightens the sky. Against this landscape we see EDGAR, his face and his body torn with pain. He whispers to himself.

EDGAR: Deserter! Deserter!

Then he collapses on the deck. MARITA and ROLF, momentarily stunned, race to him, bend over him, trying to lift him up. Suddenly JOHNNY appears. He calls softly.

JOHNNY: Mr. Brout … Mr. Brout …

And he sees EDGAR sprawled on the deck, with ROLF and MARITA beside him. JOHNNY yells, runs towards them, kneels beside EDGAR.

JOHNNY: What the hell! What did you do to him!

MARITA: He fainted. Are you his driver? Maybe he needs to be taken to the hospital …

EDGAR (*His eyes opened now, softly*): No, I'm alright. Johnny, take care of me. Johnny, take me home.

JOHNNY lifts him up, gently, and holding him, starts leading him toward the door. EDGAR, his arm around JOHNNY'S neck, whispers:

EDGAR: Deserter … Deserter …

MARITA jerks forward as if those words had some meaning for her.

MARITA: What?

EDGAR (*Whispers softly*): Jadwiga … Deserter … Deserter.

Then blackout.

ACT II, SCENE 4

The deck of EDGAR'S apartment—four days later. The late morning, the weather is warm and sunny. EDGAR, in his pyjamas and a light robe, reclines on a lounge chair. On a small round metal table beside the chair is a half emptied cup of coffee and some remnants of a bran muffin. JOHNNY is in the apartment. He watches EDGAR with concern. Finally he walks out and softly addresses EDGAR.

JOHNNY: D'you want to go to bed?

EDGAR (*Opening his eyes and startled*): To bed? What time is it? Oh, it's so bright ...

JOHNNY: It's past eleven. I settled you in this chair early in the morning. And watched over you. All the time. But when I heard you coughing and snoring, I thought ...

EDGAR (*Completely awake now*): No, no. I don't want to go to bed. I spent enough time in it already. How many days was it? Two, three ...?

JOHNNY: Three days and three nights. But with each passing day you were improving. You did a lot of throwing up the first night. Then ... you forgot about it. Thank God. (*With a wink*) I had a lot of cleaning up to do. Around the bed. And in the bathroom.

EDGAR: It was a hard night for both of us and I am sorry for it. The way I felt—I wanted to scratch out my brain! (*Touching his temple*) It hurt like crazy. And the zoom ...

JOHNNY: Zoom it was! I almost heard it. And surely I saw it. The way you walked. (*Imitating it*) From wall to wall. Grabbing hold of the paintings ... But, you broke nothing. I did my best to catch you just in time. And lead you to the bathroom.

EDGAR: I do thank you for it. You took care of me so well. I don't know what I would have done without you.

JOHNNY (*Sitting down on another chair*): It was not only me. I don't know what I would have done without Ms. Marita. She spent many hours here—during the first day. And the second. A fine woman this friend of yours. (*Giggling*) I would marry her if she were black. I'd be faithful to her. And stand guard around her. So that nobody invades my territory.

EDGAR: And her man? Was he with her? I don't recall ...

JOHNNY: No, she came here on her own. Phoned first. Brought an onion soup for you and me. And salad. Spicy, spicy salad.

EDGAR: I remember it, vaguely. The first couple of days they are so ... unclear. As if they were covered by fog. (*Lifting himself up*) But I'm o.k. now. Ready to start cleaning up my book. (*As if to himself*) I hope she glanced through it. My early life is in that book. (*Then to JOHNNY*) Anybody called?

JOHNNY: Yes, your wife. After I called her. She wanted to know how you are. She said, she was ready to come if you needed her.

EDGAR: And what did you tell her?

JOHNNY: What you instructed me to say when you told me to call her. That you had a bout of your illness and that you would like her to tell your doctor. And that she doesn't need to worry. You're well taken care of, and that you're feeling better. And that you will call her soon. (*Sort of pleadingly*) You will call her, won't you? Today. That will be "soon."

EDGAR: I guess I will. In the evening. No, this afternoon. Who else called? I thought I heard the phone ringing.

JOHNNY: Your doctor. He said you should see the man he told you to see when you're out of sorts. The doctor in Sarasota. And I said to him: "He needs love, not a doctor. That's how I see his sickness. He needs a woman who would take care of him. Not a doctor."

EDGAR (*In his usual teasing manner*): Or a man. Like you. Who needs dollars. That would make me fight my illness with greater vigour. Once there's a cost to it. In U.S. dollars! Which brings me to the crux of the matter. How much do I owe you? For the last few days?

JOHNNY: And the nights. Don't forget that. I've been sleeping here for the last three nights.

EDGAR: How much?

JOHNNY (*Showing it with his fingers*): Zero! I charge you for driving. Not for nursing. I have a special feeling for you Mr. Brout. I treat you as a friend. Who's in pain. So there's no charge for nursing.

EDGAR (*Deeply moved*): What?! You're a crazy fool, Johnny. But I love you for it. Now listen, when I'm o.k. I'm taking you for dinner. A tip top dinner, propped up … by a litre of Scotch! That will give you a chance to tell me more about yourself! About your family! What day is today?

JOHNNY: Tuesday, March the 27th.

EDGAR: Already?! Holy Jesus! How time flies!

JOHNNY: Not Jesus! He's not your master! Holy Moses, that's who you should be turning to. Holy Moses!

They laugh, EDGAR takes a sip of his coffee, munches the rest of the muffin, and says to JOHNNY:

EDGAR: That muffin gives me shivers. Tastes like the one I used to eat when I was a child. No more phone calls?

JOHNNY: No.

EDGAR: Good! (*He gets up*) Oh, I feel so much better today. I'm not dizzy any more. I think I'll have a shower. And after I'm done … you go home.

JOHNNY: You sure?

EDGAR: Sure, I'm sure. (*Making boxing gestures*) You see? I'm in a fighting mood. And that's the best proof I'm out of chains! Disease wise. Don't you dare to contradict me. Or you'll end up …

JOHNNY: Hanging on a chain, I know. And you would say …

EDGAR: Hanging will do you good. To know what life is you need to be in pain!

They burst out laughing, EDGAR is on his way to the bathroom, then, there is a knock at the door. EDGAR who is quite close to it, on his way to the bathroom, opens it. MARITA stands in the doorway.

EDGAR: Marita!

MARITA: Yes, it's me. Are you the doorman? (*Pointing at JOHNNY*) Not him?

EDGAR: That's what I am, for a change. Not a doormat but a doorman. In good shape once again. Ready to face ... I'll be damned: I stink! I was just on my way to take a shower!

MARITA: Oh! Am I too early? I thought ...

EDGAR: Holy Jesus! No, Holy Moses! I just totally forgot! You told me yesterday that you would come here today. At eleven! No, you didn't tell me! It was your day off! You didn't come ...

MARITA: I phoned ...

EDGAR: That's right! You phoned! (*Pointing to JOHNNY*) And talked to him. Johnny, why didn't you remind me that I'm to be dressed up this morning, eh? Expecting a guest? The least you could have done was to shake me up from my snooze! To ...

MARITA: Who cares whether you're dressed up or not? The main thing is—you're better! Have a shower, if you want to. I'll be waiting for you on the deck.

JOHNNY: And I'm going home to see my wife. To get some rest. Nice meeting you, Ms. Marita. See you later, Mr. Brout.

He is about to slip out of the apartment but stops when EDGAR calls to him.

EDGAR: Later, yes. Much later. When the sun's gone. I'll be busy today. And if I need help, this lady will take care of me. Am I right, Marita?

MARITA: I'll be honoured to put you to bed. But to undress you ... that's another story!

They all giggle, then JOHNNY exits and MARITA addresses EDGAR.

MARITA: Have your shower. (*Touching his cheeks*) And shave. Get rid of those needles.

EDGAR: Yes, Ma'am. (*Pointing at the kitchen*) If you want a cup of coffee ...

MARITA: No, thanks. My morning was very rough. I've had three already.

EDGAR: Rough? What happened?

MARITA (*After a pause*): We'll talk about it when we're seated. Please do whatever you need to do. I'll wait patiently. Ah, I read your memoir. It told me a lot about yourself. It moved me, deeply. And it certainly gave me the background for the piece I will write about you. With your permission I may take some quotes from it.

EDGAR: Thank you. I can't tell you how it touches me to hear that you were absorbed by my story. Why is it so—I don't know. But I feel strengthened by it. As a poet would say "Marked by the rays of Glory" Ciao!

He waves his hand to MARITA and races to the bathroom. MARITA slowly walks across the room towards the deck. While walking her eyes catch sight of the photographs of EDGAR'S family set on his desk. She stops, looks at them intensely, picks up one of them, that of ANNA—holds it for a moment, kisses it. Then, her eyes filled with tears, she gently puts the photograph in its place, and steps away from it, on her way to the deck. There, she sits down on the lounge chair, and watches the horizon, her face stern now and marked with bitterness. Then EDGAR appears, dressed lightly—short sleeved shirt, cotton pants, sandals on his feet. He watches her briefly, then he says:

EDGAR: You look drained. What's eating you?

MARITA (*Softly*): Rolf.

EDGAR: Rolf what? Where is he? He never came to see me. When I was ill. Is he ill too? (*Trying to be humourous*) I don't mean, brainwise … (*Then seriously*) Is he ill?

MARITA: He's gone. Back to Europe. That chapter of my life is shut. Tightly. My lover is gone.

EDGAR (*Sitting beside her and trying to comfort her*): But why? What happened?

MARITA: He had his view of life. I had mine. He said to me: "You want me, you follow me." I was ready to compromise but he didn't want to budge. With all his "share, share, share" talk, he thinks of nothing else but himself. And I'm like my sweet mother, a cringing soul. Addicted to suffering … (*After a pause, and getting hold of herself*) It's kind of you to be so drawn to my agony. It helps. I can't tell you how it helps. (*After a brief pause*) Just to change the subject, I'd like to ask you something. What made you fight during the Uprising? It struck me when I read your book. You're a Jew. You lived in Warsaw under a false name. In hiding.

EDGAR (*Who's perplexed by her question*): So?

MARITA: You risked your life. In more ways than one. I've heard stories … Were you ever threatened by those who knew? Was your life in danger?

EDGAR: Yes, it was. A few times. But that didn't matter. I fought to reduce my suffering. To take revenge for the death of my family.

MARITA: That's what I would want to say in my story about you. That patriotism in the true sense is built on suffering. That it is linked most strongly to pain.

EDGAR: I'd go along with that.

MARITA: But you left. You never came back …

EDGAR (*Intensely*): That too had to do with pain! I wanted to live in a new world! Not to live daily under the hammer of pain!

MARITA (*After a pause, avoiding his eyes*): And Teresa? Who was she? There are only a few words devoted to her in your text.

EDGAR (*Smiling gently*): A kid I loved and made love to. My first hearfelt sexual encounter. Her name was different, but I hid it, to protect her. She and I were two examples of the crazy, courageous, gun toting kids …

MARITA: Did you connect with her after the war? Did you make an effort …

EDGAR: Never. Never.

MARITA: Why not?

EDGAR: No answer to that question.

MARITA (*With a somewhat sarcastic smile*): In that case, could I ask you for a glass of wine? Or a vodka if you have any.

EDGAR: What would you prefer, wine or vodka?

MARITA (*Off the chair and sort of dancing*): To imitate you … Vodka! Vodka!

EDGAR (*Also making dancing steps*): To challenge you, a full glass? A full glass?

He grabs hold of her, they dance for a moment or two together, then he swirls her around, lets go of her, and runs quickly to the table, picks up two glasses and pours vodka into them. MARITA follows him, then she says:

MARITA: I feel hot. Would you mind if I take off my dress? (*Responding to the shocked expression in EDGAR'S eyes*) Don't worry! I have my bathing suit on. You have seen me in it before. (*She quickly takes off her blouse and her skirt, and she exclaims:*)

MARITA: I'm undressed! Unchained!

EDGAR (*Eyeing her with admiration*): You look splendid! So … (*Showing it with his hands*) curvaceous! I'm amazed! Amazed!

MARITA (*Spreading out on a sofa bed*): By what, this time?

EDGAR: By how I feel … seeing you. I wish I were younger! I'd make a bid …

MARITA: For my skin or my soul?

EDGAR: For both! If only I had a chance …

MARITA (*Half jokingly, half seriously*): Why don't you give it a try? I mean it, Edgar. (*Then like in a dream*) If you sat beside me and embraced me I would not say no. I would take your hand and I would put it on my breast, to feel … the stirring it would give me. I would let you kiss my lips, caress my loins, to …

EDGAR (*Coming close to her*): Marita, what are you saying? Marita!

MARITA: Make me spread my legs, to let you … put your organ into my moist tube …

EDGAR (*Sitting beside her, in a sweat, and joyously unzipping his pants, ready to make love to her*): Marita … I never thought you would want me … Marita …

MARITA (*In the same tone as before*): To make me fulfill the lust of … vengeance that is boiling in my heart!

EDGAR (*Halting his advance, shocked*): Marita!

MARITA: Vengeance, yes, for the sorrow you have injected into my mother, for the pain you infested her with! And though she is gone and buried, beside the graves of her family …

EDGAR (*Screams*): Marita!

MARITA: I, her daughter and yours … Did you hear me? I'm her daughter and yours …

EDGAR (*Screams even louder*): Marita!

MARITA (*Removing herself from him and now with bitter sarcasm*): Did I play it well, the seduction scene? Did I make you grow with desire? Maybe if you were faster I would have managed to overcome the repulsion, allowed you to pierce into me, which would have made you the ... helpless toy of my revenge! Because after it had happened I would have told you who I am, I would have made you crawl with shame, made you lose your mind, yes, made you the whining slave of my vengeance! (*After a pause*) But as much as I wanted to do it, I couldn't erase from my mind the sorrow that was imprinted on your face when I saw you diverted to the image of your lover, my mother! She appears to you often, doesn't she?! You dream of her, don't you?! You see her, hear her as if she were alive, though she's only cloistered in the hard ribbed cage of your brain! Now let me tell you something you don't know. She went through the same experience as long as she was alive. She saw you, talked to you as if you were before her, and she didn't utter one evil word to me about you! She loved you though you were gone, she died, hoping that she would meet you one day; sometimes she would say to me: "Your father and I will see each other again, and we will live happily, peacefully on the moon. That was our dream. To live on the moon. Or on another planet!" And though she whispered to herself that you were a "deserter," she needed you more than she needed me! And before she died she asked me not to be angry with you, to always remember what your losses were. "Bear in mind," she said, "that he suffered more than any of us! And will suffer to the end of his days! Because he survived and those he loved did not. His father. His mother. His sister. And many other members of his family." So, though I wanted to destroy you, I just couldn't do it! Which makes me a coward! But I couldn't do it!

EDGAR (*After a long pause, his head down, softly*): What should I say? I'm grateful for it. Yes, I am. More than grateful. Relieved that ... (*Then looking at her, gently*) Had you done it, you would have destroyed yourself as well as me. I would have killed myself, possibly. But you would have lived with it, till the end of your days. And most likely detested yourself for it. Vengeance is a two way street. If committed, it makes you feel happy just for a moment. And then, it starts tormenting you. It makes you think of nothing else. It gives you no peace. It torpedoes your life. (*After a pause*) Let me tell you something else. In the book I wrote, there are a few lines about a man called Adam. He was my age. Young. Not a Jew. During the Uprising a soldier like me. One night ... I was returning from a patrol, heading to a cellar, where I slept at night. And when I reached the bottom of the stairs, I saw ...

He stops and an image evolves in front of his eyes. On the same mattress where we saw him making love to JADWIGA—(ACT II, SCENE 3) she is there again but with another man. He's on top of her: What we're witnessing are the last moments of the lovemaking, just before the 'explosion.' EDGAR who sees it, exclaims:

EDGAR: Ah!

ADAM (*Jumping up, recognizing EDGAR and running away*): Don't blame me! She lured me to make love to her! This soft spoken whore! That bitch!

Then JADWIGA lifts herself up. She is dressed, her grubby blouse and skirt are on, and she says in a whisper:

JADWIGA: I was alone. And frightened. I needed help. He promised to stay with me 'till you came back. Then I lost control. I let him make love to me. I ought to be punished for it. But I love only you. Only you …

The image evaporates as quickly as it appeared, superceded by another image. What we see engraved in EDGAR'S mind is a suspended in the air image of the whole BROUT family in 1936 (in Poland), sitting around the table in a splendidly furnished dining room candle lit—observing the passover seder dinner. The family consists of the bearded, grey, 65-year-old GRANDFATHER (his name is JOSEPH), his son, EMIL (Edgar's father), ROSA (Edgar's mother),—they are both in their thirties—his father's sister and her husband (both in their thirties), EDGAR, who is thirteen years old, and his 9-year-old sister, ANNA. All males wear scull caps, the GRANDFATHER is holding in his hand the sacred book of the passover haggadah. And EDGAR hears voices, first of the GRANDFATHER who plays the role of the leader and speaks gravely, then of the rest of them who, as a group emphasize the statements, reciting the words with enjoyment.

GRANDFATHER: You shall not oppress a stranger, for you know the feeling of the stranger, having yourselves been strangers in the Land of Egypt.

ALL OTHERS: Having yourselves been strangers in the Land of Egypt.

GRANDFATHER: When strangers reside with you in your land, you shall not wrong them, you shall love them as yourself.

ALL OTHERS: For you were strangers in the Land of Egypt.

GRANDFATHER: You shall not subvert the rights of a stranger or the orphan.

ALL OTHERS: Remember that you were a stranger and a slave in the Land of Egypt.

The voices fade out, the image disappears. We are back in the condo. EDGAR and MARITA are facing one another.

MARITA (*After a short pause*): And you saw …

EDGAR (*Softly*): What I saw is already gone. Forever. Forever.

MARITA: Bullshit! Bullshit!

EDGAR: Marita!

MARITA: Don't Marita me! I'm not a child to be given your admonitions! But hear this! (*Even more sharply than before*) Were you going to tell me that I'm not your daughter?!

EDGAR (*Softly*): No. How did you arrive at that?

MARITA: I was reading your mind! You spoke of that character from your book! Wasn't it to make me aware of something I didn't know?! That concerned my mother? To put a doubt to my conviction that I am your daughter?!

EDGAR: No. No. (*Then with a gentle smile*) You are my daughter. Lately discovered. The only one I have. Welcome home, my child. Get dressed. And then Johnny will drive us …

MARITA (*Still tense*): I can't. I need to pack. I'm leaving in a few hours …

EDGAR: Is that what you want? To … undo the relationship? To break the bond?

MARITA (*After a moment of silence, softly this time*): No. I don't want to. But I am frightened. I don't want to be bound by another chain …

EDGAR (*Smiling gently*): Chained we are. How we'll deal with it, that's another matter. (*Taking her hand*) Come with me. For a while. To Canada. You'll meet my wife. She won't be shocked, don't worry. She always knew I had a secret cloistered in my heart.

MARITA: Are you sure?

EDGAR: Yes, I am.

MARITA (*Looking into his eyes, softly*): Then I will follow your command. Fulfill your wish.

EDGAR: Then you'll go back, where you came from. To look after your affairs. You'll write to us, often. And then, one day, maybe … I will pray for that. Look forward to it. But don't make me wait too long. Remember, there is a limit to my endurance. I am aging. (*As if reading her mind*) Don't ask me how old I am. No! You should know. I am sixty seven years old.

MARITA (*Lovingly*): I know. I know. I will come back.

EDGAR (*With a happy smile*): As you wish. As you wish.

EDGAR moves quickly to the phone, dials the number, and when the connection is made, he says:

EDGAR: Miriam? It's Edgar, yes. I'm fine. Very fine, thank you. I want you to know that I'm on my way home. Tomorrow. And that a miracle … yes, a miracle brightened my life. I met a woman here, (*He looks at MARITA*) who happens to be my daughter. (*He repeats it more clearly now*) Yes, my daughter. Yes, an unexpected gift from the Creator! A gift from Yesteryear! I will tell you all about it. (*Then smiling in response to MIRIAM'S words*) Yes, I'll have to revise my book. Would you mind if I brought her along? (*Chortling with laughter*) No! No! She's not a phoney! Not modelled on Lolita! (*Then seriously, gently and looking at MARITA*) We'll have a new life together. The three of us. No more games. No treachery. I will live up to it. Take it for granted. I will belong only to you. And to Marita. That's her name. Marita … Thank you, Miriam. Yes, I'll give her your greetings. She sends you just the same. And once you meet the bond between the two of you will be strong. I'm sure of that. You will be close to each other, linger in each other's arms, and share the confusion, the torment that engulfed your lives. (*With a slight gentle smile*) Our lives. Yes, I understand. Have a good time at work. See you soon. Goodbye, Miriam. Your names, they blend so well. Miriam and Marita. Bye. (*He puts the phone down and turns to MARITA*) It's all set. Go and pack. Or if you want Johnny to drive you to the motel, I'll take care of the airplane tickets ...

MARITA: No, thanks. I'd rather walk. There's such a ... turmoil in my head. I need to acquiesce my mind. But, I'll be back soon. And stay overnight if you would want me to. Our last night in Florida. We'll spend it together. (*She quickly puts on her clothes, moves a step or two towards the door. And she says, almost in tears*): Embrace me. Hold me tight. And tell me, it's not a dream. Tell me ...

EDGAR (*Putting his arms around her, softly*): It's all true. Marita ... my daughter ... Marita ...

MARITA (*Responding in kind*): Thank you, my father. My father ...

Then, she is gone. EDGAR walks out on the deck. There is a happy smile on his lips. He puts his hands on the railing and watches the horizon. Once again the image of JADWIGA appears to him. she is in the air, a silhouetted figure against the golden glow of the sunset. EDGAR at her sight whispers:

EDGAR: Are you happy now? I won't see you any more. You and I ... are at peace. Be at peace, Jadwiga. Be at peace. I am on the moon with our daughter. Dancing a tango with Marita.

Then blackout.

Don Rubin

MARION ANDRE: THE PLAYWRIGHT AS WITNESS

In 1984, Canadian director and playwright Marion Andre published a volume of three stories and a play under the collective title, *The Gates*. His first major publication, he introduced the volume with the following lines:

> Born far away, son of
> Jewish people who are
> dead, survivor of the
> Holocaust, I do not
> ask for pity. Only
> for the remembrance
> of the deeds that
> were done.[1]

The three stories in that volume (*The Gates, The Saviour* and *The Leave-Taking*) along with the play *The Aching Heart of Samuel Kleinerman* are all, in fact, remembrances, joyful remembrances of his own family, a family torn apart in the holocaust, painful remembrances of the life they lived in World War II Poland, remembrances of relationships from this time laced with guilt and anguish.

And it is precisely these memories which have continued to obsess Andre in the nearly half century since the war. Yet Andre, in his literary creations about that period, has gone further than just remembrance. Rejecting traditional religious doctrine and only occasionally falling into existential despair, Andre has struggled with quiet dignity to make sense of it all. His works—whether written for stage, television, radio or simply to be read—are an ongoing testimony to his determination to at least come to terms with the inexplicable, to find intellectual strength in personal tragedy and to articulate and bear witness to a dark period in human history through his art.

Obsession is perhaps a more apt word when dealing with Andre's works and it is certainly an appropriate word when looking at Andre's latest play, *Captive of Yesteryear* which appears in this volume for the first time anywhere. The story of a holocaust survivor, an intellectual like Andre, an activist, the play's protagonist, Edgar Brout, is portrayed here as a university professor now living in Canada, Andre's own adopted homeland. In the play, Edgar separates from his wife over a marital infidelity (hers in this case but it is clear from the text that he has not been immune from such things himself), meets a woman more than 20 years his junior who also happens to have been born in Poland and becomes immensely attracted to her. Obsessively returning in his head to the past, by play's end he has come to believe that she is his daughter.

On the surface, it is a straightforward script. Yet looking at it closely one comes to realize that it is, in fact, a play full of subtleties and deeply-imbedded ironies all related to the life of such a man as Edgar, of such a man as Andre. To appreciate this and other equally personal (though not specifically biographical) works by Andre, now retired from his directorial career in Canada but still quite active as a writer, it is perhaps useful to look at the life which served to a very great extent as the inspiration and occasionally as the model for so many of his creations.

Andre was, in fact, not born in Poland but he did grow up there. He was actually born in Le Havre, France on 12 January 1921 while his parents, students at the time, were in that country. His father, Emil Tenenbaum, was a medical student, while his mother was studying to be a pharmacist. After they met at the University of Vienna, Tenenbaum decided to switch into the pharmacy program as well. Upon graduation, they returned to their native Poland and eventually settled in the city of Lvov, the capital of eastern Poland. In 1925, his sister was born.

Tenenbaum, an intellectual, a campaigner for various social causes and an atheist, quickly became one of Lvov's major pharmacists and he and his wife ran a large and important pharmacy in the city. But by night, he was a committed writer and editor. Through the 1930s, he published a weekly magazine, *Counterattack*, which fiercely fought against anti-semitism. He also wrote a novel (*Background*) and a play (*It Started With A Lie*), both intellectually passionate and both published in Lvov in the early thirties. It is clearly from his father that Andre got much of his own social democratic leanings and it was also from his father's activities as head of the Lvov amateur theatre group that Andre found inspiration for his own lifelong professional involvement in theatre.

From almost any point of view, the family was comfortable and cultured and Andre grew up in a privileged home. In 1939, however, everything suddenly changed after the invasion of Poland by Hitler's troops. Soviet forces quickly occupied the eastern part of the country (including Lvov) while German forces took the rest of Poland. The family's property was confiscated but because of the importance of both parent's medical knowledge they were allowed to work in their pharmacy. As well, between 1939 and 1941, Andre was able to attend the University of Lvov taking courses in law as well as studying theatre at the still operating State Conservatory.

By 1941, however, the Nazi's took over the whole of Poland and, for a Jewish family like the Tenenbaums, the situation changed radically. The family was forced to move into the Jewish ghetto and normal work was all but impossible. By the summer of '42, Judaism, never before an issue in young Andre's life, now literally became a matter of life and death.

As he later recalled, "there were pogroms in the ghetto. People were constantly being relocated. We didn't know where they were being sent but the rumours were frightening. We found out later that most ended up in concentration camps like Bergen-Belsen."

My father's contacts in the community, however, helped in many ways. He was still able to operate a small ghetto pharmacy and we all worked there. But people were also needed to work outside the ghetto and my sister and I were lucky enough to get one of these jobs. We worked for a company that gathered scrap metal. We collected it door-to-door from people who lived in the city. We had to pay for it with our own money and then deliver it to a warehouse which sold it to German industry for the war effort. We earned next to nothing but even this little bit obviously helped when we returned to the ghetto each night. And it was obviously a special privilege to be able to leave the ghetto on a daily basis.

We had to wear the yellow star all the time but we also had a badge that had the letters 'WW' on it. This stood for Economically Important. The badge and the job kept us alive and helped us to avoid being relocated. Mostly it was the very young and the very old who were being sent away. But it didn't help my sister. On our way back to the ghetto one evening, we were stopped by SS men because of our yellow stars. They refused to recognize the WW badge. They took all our documents, beat me up and left only with her. We never saw her again. The man who employed us tried to find out what happened. We believe she was raped and then sent off to a concentration camp. In any event, we know that she didn't survive.[2]

It was at that moment that Andre knew he had to get out of Lvov. In the summer of 1942, at the age of 21, he left the city with false documents. They included a Birth Certificate of someone who had apparently only recently died and whose age was similar. The name on the Birth Certificate was Czerniecki, much more Polish, much less recognizably Jewish.

Moving to Warsaw and living life as a non-Jew, Andre, with his parents remaining in the ghetto, struggled to smuggle them out as well. In 1943, he enlisted the aid of a Polish woman—later remembered in his most powerful novel as *Maria B*—and planned to get both parents out of Lvov. Only his mother would come though. His father argued that he couldn't survive outside the ghetto because he looked too Jewish. As well, he wanted to continue working in the small ghetto pharmacy. Andre himself, looking back years later, believed that his father "just couldn't start fighting all over again."[3] Later that year, to no one's surprise the Lvov ghetto was totally expunged and everyone in it, including his father, was sent to a concentration camp. Andre never learned where or how his father died.

Andre himself connected to the Polish Home Army—the underground— and was often used to smuggle messages around the city. The fact that he spoke several languages—Polish, German and English—made him especially valuable. He also fought in the Warsaw Uprising of 1944 "against the regular German Army. I finally had a rifle. I was able at last to shoot the oppressors."[4]

Captured at the end of that battle, he was sent to a prisoner-of-war camp in Germany. Had his captors realized he was Jewish, it would have been to a concentration camp. But this was late in 1944 and the allies were advancing. Just before the war ended, Andre escaped and was picked up by members of the British Army. Because of his language skills, he worked for the British for a time and they repaid him by putting him on a train to France. It was in Paris that he found out that his mother was still alive and, when the war ended, he returned to find her. By late 1945, a new Polish government was being established and those with language skills were needed to work in foreign embassies. From 1946 to 1949 he lived in Amsterdam as part of an official Polish Legation.

But the gradual influence of the Soviet Union in Poland meant that his Jewish socialist background would again be held against him. By 1950 he was back in Warsaw where he began to do documentaries for Polish radio. He also began doing translations of a number of American plays, among them Eugene O'Neill's *The Hairy Ape* and Erskine Caldwell's *Tobacco Road*, the latter staged several times in Poland including once under the direction of Janusz Warminiski at the Atheneum Theatre in Warsaw. Andre also started a small children's theatre in 1953 called Kleks (Spot).

By 1957, with anti-semitism growing once more in Poland, Andre and his mother emigrated to Canada thanks to sponsorship by an uncle, a doctor who had arrived in Canada some years earlier via Italy. It was in Montreal that the 36-year-old Marion Andrzej Czerniecki shortened his Polish middle name to the much more recognizable French form, Andre. In 1988, he legally dropped the Czerniecki. The fact was, by the sixties, the entire Canadian theatre community had come to know him simply as Marion Andre.

It was at this point in his life that he helped establish a drama program for the Protestant School Board of Greater Montreal, directed at McGill University and began writing plays on both radio and television for CBC. He also started two different theatre groups over the next few years—Studio Six in 1957 and the Freelancers in 1958.

In 1967, Canada's centennial year, a number of new theatres opened across the country. In Montreal, the wealthy Bronfman family helped to launch a Jewish Community Centre in honour of the matriarch, Saidye Bronfman. The Centre included a quasi-autonomous, fully-professional theatre. Andre soon found himself its first Artistic Director and he soon achieved a national reputation as a director of serious and literate modern plays from Ibsen to Frisch.

But in 1972, the war returned to plague him again. Deciding to schedule a production of Robert Shaw's post-holocaust drama, *The Man in the Glass Booth*, controversy quickly grew when protests began from some of the Centre's own members about the play's suitability in a Jewish community centre. Though few had read it, the belief was that is was somehow anti-semitic. Andre, of course, believed that he had at least some familiarity with such questions and refused the Board's suggesttion that he cancel the production. As a result, on the eve of the opening, the Board simply pulled the plug and the show was gone. So too was Andre who after five years resigned from the Saidye Bronfman Centre in protest.

Shortly thereafter, Andre, his wife Ina, and their children, left Montreal and its small English language theatre scene and moved to Toronto. In 1973, he decided to begin still another theatre. To be called Theatre Plus, this new company was to be resident in Toronto's municipal theatre building during the months when the city's own company was not operating. That is, Theatre Plus would run each year from May to October, summer months when, traditionally, people's minds went on holiday.

The human mind for Andre, however, was never a thing to send on holiday and Theatre Plus came into being with the stated intent of providing the city of Toronto with a serious theatre during the summer months. No mean feat. Even the well-established Stratford Festival, just over two hours from Toronto, was having to sell itself more as a day in the country than as a serious cultural activity to draw audiences.

In fact, Andre's experiment did succeed and his personal determination turned Theatre Plus into one of the city's most committed and significant theatre groups. Before the first season opened, Theatre Plus had some 1,500 subscribers for productions that included Joe Orton's *Loot* and John Guare's *House of Blue Leaves*. Over the next 13 years under Andre, the company would stage some 40 productions, some of them world premieres, many Canadian premieres of modern European and American plays.

These choices clearly represented Andre's own commitment to a type of theatre in which significant moral issues could be argued. His explorations took him from Wedekind's *Lulu* to Frisch's *The Physicists*, from Trevor Griffith's Marxist parable *Occupations* to Canadian dramatist Michael Cook's most important drama, *The Gayden Chronicles*, from Sternheim's *The Snob* to an original drama about the life of Pushkin.

In several interviews done while he was working as a director, Andre spoke of his belief that theatre had to be "a reflection of the times ... Because I am a political animal, plays that deal with social, political and moral matters of our century have a priority for me."[5] As well, Andre spoke of his own desire to write his own plays, of his "tremendous need to do that."[6]

Andre has generally avoided speaking about his own life publicly but it seems essential not only to get some of those details on the record but also to understand where his works stem from. Andre has, in fact, for most of his life lived in two worlds and his connections to Europe and specifically to the Europe of the holocaust period need to be understood in this way. Such double vision is both his obsession and his strength. It can be seen clearly in such plays as *The Sand* (produced at Toronto's York University in 1979), *Soldat Hans Stumpf* (produced in 1992 at the Man-in-the-Moon Theatre in London, England, under the title *Savage Storm*), *The Aching Heart of Samuel Kleinerman* (produced at Theatre Plus in 1984) and *Captive of Yesteryear*. All reveal aspects of his earlier life and all represent dramatic shatterings of youthful innocence, echoes of which remain to this day with him. These works are, of course, all fictional.

Andre prefers not to write autobiography. The pain is obviously still too great even half a century later. Rather he prefers to keep his grief, pain and anger at a literary distance.

Yet the life and the art are connected. His short play, *The Sand*, focuses around a young man named Marek growing up, like Marion Andre, in Poland during the war. Dealing with the idea of universal justice, here translated as universal indifference, *The Sand* opens with an image of a rabbi giving a sermon about God's implacability, demanding that those who believe must not question. Clearly, this does not apply to Andre himself who has never ceased questioning for even a moment. Andre's own bitterness toward religion is also clear.

Set in an apartment of a Jewish family, the play introduces us to young Marek who spends much of his time watching the war unfold on the street below even as his family discusses death. But what does death really mean? Eventually he learns. A young boy is murdered in the sandbox just below the window. The play ends with Marek's words, "And I couldn't play anymore in the sand."[7] It was a fitting introduction to Andre as a writer.

When he retired from Theatre Plus in 1984 at the age of 63, Andre decided to commit himself to writing full-time. His play *Kleinerman*, staged in 1984, again reveals his basic themes and issues—loss of innocence, the capriciousness of survival, universal guilt, and the need for people to control their own lives. The play indroduces us to a post-war emigré to Canada who tells the audience through dramatized narration the story of the Kleinerman family and how the father's morality and belief in goodness and honesty cost the family an opportunity to be free.

In the years since his retirement, Andre has produced some of his strongest work, work that continues to come closer and closer to personal revelation and, perhaps, even to answers. His most powerful piece to date has been *Maria B*, an extraordinary novel of life in the Warsaw ghetto, of life lived under various aliases outside the ghetto, of a woman who helps people out of a series of very mixed motives. No one, suggests Andre, has totally clean hands. Years later, Maria suddenly turns up once more in the man's life, a situation not unlike that of the young Polish journalist who shows up in the life of Edgar Brout in *Captive of Yesteryear*.

In total, Andre has written more than a dozen television and radio plays, published five stories and a novel, and has written six full-length works for the stage, a short play and a translation/adaption of Carl Sternheim's *The Snob*. Not all these scripts are war-related (one of them, *Glu Glub*, in fact, is a science fiction morality play) but his works are generally tied to the war period and to holocaust themes.

His latest play, *Captive of Yesteryear*, is at once the old-Andre and the new. It reveals such familiar issues as guilt, suffering and the amorality of the universe. The hold of the past on the present is also not new in Andre's work. But as the protagonists in his works get older—here we have a Polish-born professor in his sixties—past and present merge with mind and libido, these elements eventually tear at one another with unaccustomed rage. Andre's characters are also much more active in this play than in many of his earlier works where characters tend to be done unto rather than doing themselves.

As for family, love and commitment, the professor's wife merges in his rage and ravings with his Polish lover of so many years earlier in scenes of infidelity and anger. They had long before agreed not to bring children into this "mad world."[8]

Flashbacks are also more directly integrated into the dramaturgy here than in most of Andre's earlier works. Indeed, in this one play there are no less than ten different flashbacks which reveal an entire second story. In this case, it is the story of Jadwiga, a young, attractive Polish freedom fighter. We see her first as a woman with a rifle who, like Edgar, is fighting for the Polish underground. Edgar dreams of taking a more active vengeance, however, after separation from his parents. Through flashbacks we learn that Jadwiga has gotten pregnant, her desire now simply to be free of the horrors and to dance with him on the moon. We see the violation of Edgar's sister, his determination to hide and to survive, his growing love for Jadwiga and his pledge of love to her. The last flashbacks are of a family Passover seder and Jadwiga against the sunset. The flashbacks bring to the present echoes of love, survival and passion.

There are as well ironies in the work, another hallmark of Andre's growing literary style. Jadwiga's daughter, it seems, had married a Jew. That man's parents too had been destroyed in the war. Like Edgar, he too left Poland but instead of moving to Canada, he moved to South Africa where he spent the rest of his life exploiting others.

Edgar identifies with all the exploited of the world, all the subjugated. His black driver confirms his understanding. "Your race and mine know what pain is … the smell of suffering." And it's the black man who literally holds Edgar up in his darkest moments, urging him to survive. "Live now. Not in the past," says the driver, echoing words spoken earlier by Edgar's wife.

The philosophical centre of the play is, in fact, a debate—a love duel—between Edgar and the slightly younger professor whom the young journalist, Marita, has fallen in love with. A German from Düsseldorf, her current lover's father had served in the Wehrmacht, deserted after "he saw the atrocities" and ended up in a Soviet labour camp.

It's this mating dance for Marita's love between the two scholars which serves as the play's central scene. The battle is at once intellectual and sexual. The World and the Woman. Objective and Subjective. We and Me.

> We're in a mess, … [says Rolf, taking a strong shot at intellectual victory.] Bloodshed, despotism, starvation—these are the features of our global existence. And so little is done about it. We seem to accept this … sickly state of affairs with as little murmur as possible. We lower our heads as an expression of sympathy for the victims, or whisper our … antipathetic slogans. That's about all we're doing.[9]

Are there answers in systems for Andre? Apparently not. Capitalism and communism are seen as equally dangerous approaches to human problem solving. Socialism, perhaps, comes closest but dogma of any kind is not to be trusted. Marita also sees the heavy hand of the past as enemy and suggests that the answer lies in purging it somehow, not letting it in, erasing its horrific images. But that is no answer for either of the professors. Such a position would not only be intellectually wrong but it would certainly be emotionally unaccept-able to Edgar who is, as the play's title suggests, not living in the past by choice but is rather its captive. It's at this point that Edgar's intellectual and emotional tension finally overwhelm him and he collapses. As he later says, "to know what life is you need to be in pain."[10]

Pain then, suffering, for Andre seems the essence of the human condition: the thing we run from, the thing that drives us on. Pain becomes the essential ingredient in individual lives and in societies. And it is there both in the past and the present. Can we live without it? Is death the only real cessation?

By the end of the play, Edgar's physical pain is waning and he discovers that Marita is apparently his own daughter by Jadwiga. Only then, only through the physicalized merging of past and present, a merging brought about by love, does his own guilt and suffering begin to lift. Edgar now knows more about his own past but will this help him to survive any better? Will knowledge help relieve his pain? Anyone's pain? Can we ever be innocent and at peace in this life knowing what we know? This is one of the fascinating questions Andre puts forward in this deceivingly simple play.

As *Captive of Yesteryear* ends, Edgar is recreating a new family—himself now as father, his estranged wife suddenly back by his side, his new and mysterious European daughter. "We'll have a new life together," he says. "The three of us."[11] The play's closing image is of Edgar able to finally look back on his past, able to bury Jadwiga, telling her and all his ghosts that he is finally dancing that tango on the moon, this time with his daughter.

But Andre is too clever to leave us with such a simple ending. We know that this family is more wish than reality. Marita is too bright and too European to remain in such a tortured home with such a tortured couple. Will Edgar's recently abandoned wife really be so welcoming when she fully understands that Edgar is returning home with a daughter by another woman, a woman he also deserted? The sense of a happy future is far from clear.

Like Strindberg who struggled for his entire life to objectify his demons through a series of theatrical creations and quasi-factual autobiographical tales, Marion Andre for the past decade has struggled to objectify his own life through his literary creations. As for justice, his works continue to belie any belief in the concept. As he himself has put it:

I don't believe in divine justice. In any event, that idea is created only by humanity's lack of comprehension of why things happen. Justice is simply a human construct. The enactmant of justice is entirely in human hands.

I've also come to believe that what really controls the world is greed. Not just greed for things but greed for power. And the scale of greed is so immense today that it may be totally beyond the control of any one or any system, even socialism. In this light, the notion of divine control, like divine justice, simply doesn't exist.

I want to believe in the rationality of people but it's difficult to do that given the over-whelming nature of this greed, given this century's cataclysms, events like the holocaust. The holocaust, in fact, may be humanity's ultimate irrationality. Its very immensity is one of the reasons I keep trying to understand it and why I keep trying to give it a place in the ultimate order of things.

In the end, one simply gives up trying to make sense of it because it makes no human sense. It has no meaning. One must simply bear witness to it. It is, in a way, the ultimate proof that there is no such thing as divine justice. But perhaps by bearing witness, one can warn people about the places that unchecked greed can take them. One can tell them that the future will be destruction unless we learn from these mistakes. This need to warn others is a great part of what motivates me to write. As for whether we'll ever learn that we really do need one another, that's another issue and perhaps the ultimate statement in my work. We really do need one another.[12]

Selected Bibliography

Stage:

The Sand. One-act. Published in: *Canadian Theatre Review* 22 (Toronto: York University, Spring 1979). First produced Department of Theatre, York University, 1980.

The Invented Lover. Full-length. Written in collaboration with Martin Bronstein. First published by Playwrights Canada (Toronto: 1982). First produced by Theatre Plus, Toronto, May 1982.

The Snob. A translation and adaptation of the play by Carl Sternheim. First published by Playwrights Canada (Toronto: 1984). First produced by Theatre Plus, Toronto, June 1984.

The Aching Heart of Samuel Kleinerman. Full-length. Published in: *The Gates* (Oakville, Ontario: Mosaic Press, 1984). First produced by Theatre Plus, Toronto, May 1984.

Soldat Hans Stumpf. Full-length. Published in: *Dramatic Voices from England, Canada and New Zealand, Festschrift für Albert-Reiner Glaap*, (Ed. Rurik von Antropoff, Klaus Peter Müller, Berlin: Cornelsen Verlag, 1989). Workshopped under Robin Phillips' direction, Toronto, 1988. First produced by the Man-in-the Moon Theatre in London, England, 1992, under the title *Savage Storm*.

Glu Glub. Full-length science fiction morality play. 1987. Unpublished. Unproduced.

Skinny Dip of an Aging Professor. Full-length. Published in: *Verdict of Fate* (Oakville: Mosaic Press, 1988). Workshopped by the Stratford Festival, 1985.

Captive of Yesteryear. Full-length. Published in: *Inter-Plays: A Festschrift of dramatic writings and criticisms in honour of Albert Reiner Glaap* (Ed. Rolf Althof, Rurik von Antropoff, Klaus Peter Müller, St John's: Breakwater, 1994). Unproduced.

Prose (Novels and Stories):

The Gates, The Saviour and *The Leave-Taking*. Three stories published under the collective title *The Gates*. (Oakville: Mosaic Press, 1984).

The Unique Case of Professor Talentire and *The American Boots*. Two stories published under the collective title *Verdict of Fate*. (Oakville: Mosaic Press, 1988).

Maria B. A novel. (Oakville: Mosaic Press, 1990).

The Battered Man. A novel. In progress.

Television and Radio:

The Scorn of Fate. 60 minutes. Produced on CBC television. 1960.

Recollection. 60 minutes. Produced on CBC television. 1961.

The Value of Fifty. 30 minutes. Produced on CBC-TV and Radio Canada. 1961.

The Two Faces of Love. 30 minutes. Produced on CBC television. 1962.

Confederation of Two. Eight stories on the Inside Quebec series. Produced on CBC television. 1963.

Fate of a Poet. 60 minute dramatization of the trial of Soviet poet Josef Brodsky. Produced on CBC radio. 1964.

French Canadian Prospector. 30 minute documentary. Produced on CBC radio. 1965.

Spanish Civil War. 30 minute documentary. Produced on CBC radio. 1966.

South America. Two-part documentary. Produced on CBC radio. 1966.

Wood Carver. 15 minute film about Charles Butler. Produced on CBC television, 1967.

Notes

[1] Marion Andre Czerniecki, *The Gates* (Oakville: Mosaic Press), 9.

[2.] Marion Andre in conversation with the author. January 1994. Toronto.

[3.] Marion Andre in conversation with the author. January 1994. Toronto.

[4] Marion Andre in conversation with the author. January 1994. Toronto.

[5] Andre as quoted in an article by Richard Horenblas called "Theatre Plus: support adds up," *Toronto Arts News*, May 1982, 1-2.

[6] Horenblas, 1982, 1-2.

[7] Marion Andre, *The Sand*, published in *Canadian Theatre Review* (Toronto: York University, Spring 1979), 94.

[8] Marion Andre, *Captive of Yesteryear*, 15.

[9] Andre, *Captive of Yesteryear*, 36.

[10] Andre, *Captive of Yesteryear*, 43.

[11] Andre, *Captive of Yesteryear*, 49.

[12] Marion Andre in conversation with the author. January 1994. Toronto.

Alan Ayckbourn

SERVICE NOT INCLUDED
(A Play for Television)

CAST

Hall Porter

Jace

Donald

Cathy

Assistant Manager

Hughie

Tony

Coombes

Mrs. Coombes

Neil

Freda

Harris

Mrs. Harris

Warwick

Mrs. Warwick

Riley

1. EXT. GENERAL VIEW OF MAGPIE MANOR HOTEL. (THREE STAR). NIGHT.

(*A converted undistinguished country house. It is winter, about 8:30 pm. Several exterior lights reveal cars parked in forecourt. No sign of people at present except for JACE, a waiter, in white jacket standing on the front steps smoking a cigarette.*)

(*We draw closer to him. A middle-aged forgettable sort of face, generally devoid of expression. We observe him for a moment in the cold clear country night. Car headlights, car arriving, doors slamming, voices. JACE pinches out his cigarette, puts it in his top pocket and goes indoors.*)

2. INT. FOYER. NIGHT.

(*The hotel foyer has a beamed ceiling, thick but worn carpet, fairly impressive staircase and plate glass doors leading, on one side, to the dining room (now marked 'closed') and on the other side, behind a barricade of rubber plants, to the Tudor Bar. A third door leads directly into the ballroom which can also be reached through the bar. A reception desk (deserted) and the HALL PORTER'S desk, complete with room keys and mail rack behind which stands the HALL PORTER himself, elderly, engrossed in the local evening paper. A free-standing sign at the foot of the stairs which reads 'U.B.S. Conference. Fancy Dress Dance. Jane Grey Ballroom.' JACE ambles through the front door, stops by the HALL PORTER and bends the back page of his newspaper to read it.*)

HALL PORTER (*Without looking up*): Raining, is it?

JACE: No.

HALL PORTER: Three nil …

JACE: What?

HALL PORTER: Final score. Three nil.

JACE: To us?

HALL PORTER: You're joking. (*Indicating sign*) Fancy Dress.

JACE: Ah.

HALL PORTER: Fancy Dress.

JACE: Right.

HALL PORTER: Never gets the point of that. Fancy dress. I don't get the point of it.

JACE: No. (*Studying sign*) U.B.S.?

HALL PORTER: Ah. U.B.S. Don't know. (*Slowly*) U.B.S. Don't know what that stands for. They're all going tomorrow morning anyway, thank god. That's all I know. Bloody three o'clock in the morning. Last night. Got their ladies with them tonight. Might be on their best behaviour. Some hope.

JACE: U.B.S. (*He shakes his head.*)

HALL PORTER (*Returning to his paper muttering*): Useless bunch of so and so's. (*DONALD and CATHY come down the stairs. JACE watches them. In fact, as we proceed, we will see only those things that occur within JACE'S vision or hearing. Wherever JACE goes, we go. We catch, like him, snatches of conversation, glimpses of faces and expressions. Unlike us though, whether JACE takes them in or not is another matter. At the moment we are watching DONALD, early forties, stoutish, dressed as a Tyrolean dancer and his wife, CATHY, same age and still attractive dressed as a Spanish dancer. DONALD carries a transparent file filled with close typed foolscap.*)

CATHY (*In mid-argument*): He's not going to want to talk business tonight.

DONALD: He asked me. He's interested …

CATHY: It's ridiculous. He's not going to sit down in the middle of a party and read your report, is he?

DONALD (*Leaving his key at the desk*): Thank you. He's not going to read it. I'm just going to give it to him.

CATHY (*At the doors to the bar*): What's wrong with tomorrow morning, for heaven's sake?

DONALD: He's not here tomorrow morning.

(*CATHY is peering in through the bar doors.*)

CATHY: Neil's not in there. Neither's Freda.

DONALD: We're a bit early.

CATHY: I said we would be. (*Surveying DONALD*) Those trousers still aren't right.

DONALD (*Hitching his trousers*): They're alright.

CATHY: If you'd let me alter them on you …

DONALD (*Calling to HALL PORTER*): Is the bar open?

HALL PORTER: Oh, yes sir. It's open.

DONALD (*Indicating doors*): Well, do you want to—?

Cathy: Might as well. It's freezing out here …

(*DONALD and CATHY go into the bar. JACE wanders to the notice.*)

JACE: Useless bunch of so and so's. (*He nods approvingly.*)

(*An ASSISTANT MANAGER, striped trousers etc. hurries out of the bar.*)

ASSISTENT MANAGER (*With an imperious gesture*): Oy. Oy. (*JACE looks round.*) Customers in there, you know.

JACE: Yes, I'm just going in, yes.

ASSISTANT MANAGER: Well, come on—look lively—come on. (*He marches off.*)

(*JACE, impassive, wanders into the bar.*)

3. INT. TUDOR BAR. NIGHT.

(*Various tables and chairs. The bar itself at one end of the room with usual bar stools with one section corded off for waiters only. HUGHIE, behind the bar, polishing glasses. Assistant barman TONY coming through the service door at the side of it with a crate of light ale. three or four other early evening customers including CATHY and DONALD, who have just sat down at a table for four. Two sets of doors, one curtained to the ballroom and the other to the foyer through which JACE is entering. JACE closes the door and approaches CATHY and DONALD.*)

CATHY: What does he want to see you for, anyway?

JACE: Good evening, sir. Good evening, madam.

(*He adjusts their table mats.*)

DONALD: I've told you—good evening—I want to give him this. What are you having? I mean if the managing director asks to see your ideas, you don't—

CATHY: Vodka and lime.

JACE: Vodka and lime, madam.

DONALD (*Tapping his file*): I have in here what I'm certain are some very good ideas. They could double his sales. Our sales. And if the managing director's secretary phones me especially …

JACE: Excuse me, sir.

DONALD: What?

CATHY: Scotch and water, no ice.

JACE: Scotch and water, no ice.

(*He writes the order on his little notepad.*)

DONALD: If the—(*To JACE*) And don't give me any ice.

CATHY: Well, I hope you're going to put in a word for Neil.

DONALD: Ruins a drink, ice. Neil?

CATHY: Put in a word for him. He could do with it.

(*JACE moves away.*)

DONALD: He can put in his own word.

CATHY: Oh, you're so churlish. Really churlish.

(*JACE, moving to the bar, is out of earshot of DONALD and CATHY and in time to hear the end of HUGHIE'S conversation with TONY.*)

HUGHIE: … forty feet, maybe more.

(*TONY under the bar, lining up the pale ale*)

TONY: Get on. Forty foot?

HUGHIE: Forty. Four—oh. Think about it. (*He nods significantly seeing JACE.*) Good evening to you, squire.

JACE: One scotch and water, one vodka and lime.

(*TONY to JACE from other end of bar*)

TONY: 'Ning.

JACE: 'Ning.

HUGHIE (*To TONY*): And it has been as long as sixty.

TONY: I'd like to see that.

HUGHIE: I've seen it. (*Calling*) Good evening, sir. Good evening, madam.

(*We observe that MR. and MRS. COOMBES have entered. He, as a very large Viking. She as an enormous Rhinemaiden. They are loud, jolly and booming.*)

COOMBES: Good evening, Hughie. (*COOMBES and MRS. COOMBES stand in the centre of the room surveying it.*) The Vikings are here. (*To everyone in the room in turn*) Evening. Good evening. Evening. (*To MRS. COOMBES*) Now then, Peggy, how many are there of us? How many are there going to be? You, me, John, Betty …

MRS. COOMBES: Eight. There's eight.

COOMBES: Eight? More than eight, surely?

MRS. COOMBES: Not counting us.

COOMBES: Ah, not counting us.

MRS. COOMBES: Ten altogether.

COOMBES: Ten altogether. (*Indicating a table*) Well, what about here? Looks alright here.

MRS. COOMBES: Here's fine. Lovely, yes. (*She sits.*)

HUGHIE: Vodka and lime, scotch and water.

(*He puts glasses and water jug on JACE'S tray. JACE returns to DONALD'S and CATHY'S table passing COOMBES who is still surveying the room. DONALD sits studying his report. CATHY sits staring about her, already bored.*)

JACE (*Delivering their drinks*): Here we are, sir.

DONALD: Ah. How much is that?

JACE (*Calculating from his pad*): That's 40—60—77 pence, sir.

DONALD (*Fishing in his pocket*): Right. (*cont ...*)

(*He takes out a small black notebook, hidden in the recesses of his Tyrolean garb, removes the pencil and makes a note in the book. JACE hovers.*)

DONALD (*cont.*): That's alright. I don't want to pay you. I just wanted to know how much it was. Put it on my bill. Room 425.

JACE: 425. Very good, sir.

(*He makes a note on his own pad and moves away.*)

CATHY: Are you going to write everything down all evening?

DONALD: Well, don't sound so surprised about it. I always do, don't I?

(*JACE passes COOMBES who still hasn't sat.*)

COOMBES: Actually, Peggy, I have a notion we might be better off over there, you know. Just a chance of a draught here, don't you think?

MRS. COOMBES (*Rising*): Yes, you could be right. And we'd also be nearer the—er ...

(*They roll across the room. JACE moves ahead of them, clearing chairs from their path.*)

COOMBES: Yes, we are a bit far away here. (*Shouting at the bar*) We're moving over here, Hughie.

HUGHIE: Right sir. Suit yourself.

COOMBES: Yes, this is much better. You see, we're much nearer.

MRS. COOMBES (*To HUGHIE*): We're both very susceptible to draughts, you see.

HUGHIE: Oh, dear ...

(*MR. and MRS. COOMBES arrive at their new table where TONY is waiting, holding a chair for MRS. COOMBES.*)

MRS. COOMBES: Thank you so much.

(*JACE moves away. As he does so, a whole crowd of people enter from the hall—five from COOMBES'S party—Robin Hood, an Arab princess, Henry VIII, Florence Nightingale and Long John Silver. Cries of greetings and mirth from the entire*

COOMBES party. Also MR. and MRS. HARRIS, he pale and lank, she small and sharp featured, both with a novel line in fancy dress. MR. HARRIS is dressed in a wet-suit, goggles on his forehead and a pair of flippers slung round his neck while MRS. HARRIS is a mermaid with discreetly stitched sea shells on her leotard and a cumbersome homemade fish's tail trailing behind her. Also NEIL and FREDA dressed as count dracula and one of his victims respectively. At this moment, from the ballroom next door, the band strikes up. It continues to play more or less constantly from now on. Establish the scene as at present, follow JACE back to the table now occupied by DONALD, CATHY, and FREDA.)

CATHY: And you made that all yourself?

FREDA: Yes.

CATHY: Well, I think that's so clever.

FREDA: Thank you.

CATHY: Really beautifully made.

NEIL (*Greeting JACE*): Ah, good man. Now, we want this same again here …
(*He indicates CATHY and DONALD.*)

CATHY: I'm afraid we rented ours.

NEIL: What was that, Cathy, vodka and lime?

CATHY: I'm hopeless, really hopeless.

NEIL: She looks beautiful. (*Leaning over to CATHY*) Excuse me, Donald—she looks beautiful. (*He kisses her.*)

CATHY (*Pretends to be shocked*): I'll have to dress like this more often.

(*FREDA laughs. DONALD smiles indulgently. JACE stands patiently.*)

NEIL (*To JACE*): Sorry about that, got carried away. Where had we got to … two scotch, that's it.

JACE: Thank you, sir.

NEIL: Well, this is the way to finish a conference, isn't it?

FREDA: What about me?

NEIL: What?

FREDA: Don't I get a drink?

NEIL: Oh. Beg you pardon. Waiter, waiter.

(*JACE returns.*)

FREDA: Thank you. And a large gin and tonic, waiter.

NEIL: Gin and tonic.

FREDA: A large one. Honestly, Neil, you're always doing that.

NEIL: Oy and waiter, I'll have a pint of blood as well.

(*CATHY screams with laughter. JACE smiles palely. It lasts only until he's turned away from them. He heads back to the bar. As he passes their table, HARRIS vainly tries to attract his attention with an ineffectual arm wave. JACE joins TONY at the bar. HUGHIE checks TONY'S laden tray.*)

HUGHIE: Two lagers and lime, two cokes, one gin and bitter lemon, one cider, one double brandy.

(*JACE slides an empty tray along-side TONY'S. Close in on this. Two glasses slammed down on it. Time change: people are now milling in and out from the hall and the ballroom. Cut to JACE on his way from the bar with a laden tray.*)

COOMBES (*As JACE passes*): Waiter, waiter. I must insist you carry this lady upstairs at once and put her to bed. (*Screams of mirth from COOMBES' table. JACE'S pale smile flickers and he continues on his way.*) Chap thinks I'm completely potty.

MRS. COOMBES (*Weak with laughter*): He's quite right.

(*More mirth. MR. HARRIS waves feebly as JACE passes.*)

HARRIS (*Faintly*): Waiter.

MRS. HARRIS (…): Shout at him. Jonathan, for Heaven's sake.

(*JACE unloads his tray on to DONALD's table.*)

FREDA: It all depends what you two got up to before we got here, doesn't it, Cathy?

NEIL: What do you mean? Hardworking conference, eh, Donald?

DONALD: Yes, we've had a very good four days. Some first class speeches. Really first class.

FREDA: What about?

NEIL: Don't ask me. I've been asleep since Tuesday.

FREDA (*Not amused*): Oh, Neil, honestly …

(*CATHY laughs. JACE moves away. He nearly collides with the ASSISTANT MAN-AGER who grabs hold of him and steers him out of the room.*)

3A. INT. FOYER. NIGHT

(*ASSISTANT MANAGER and JACE come from the bar.*)

ASSISTANT MANAGER (*Urgently in JACE'S ear*): I want you to make sure that this gentleman over here is looked after properly, alright?

JACE: Righto.

(*He is steered to a table which contains MR. and MRS. WARWICK, both in conventional evening dress. Both have the appearance of having been hewn from a sheet of metal. They are steely people that glint. With them sits RILEY, a young, balding, pig-faced executive, dressed as a rather chubby Regency beau.*)

ASSISTANT MANAGER: The waiter here will take care of you, sir.

WARWICK: Good. We want a small gin and french, a whisky sour and a campari with soda.

JACE (*Making a note*): Very good, sir.

WARWICK: It would also be very pleasant if you could just wipe over our table before you serve them.

JACE: Sorry about that, sir. Right away.

(*JACE moves towards the bar. The assistant manager follows him.*)

ASSISTANT MANAGER: You must try and keep these tables clean. Wipe them over regularly.

JACE: Right, yes, right.

ASSISTANT MANAGER (*Moving away*): Well, see you do it. See you do it.

(*JACE gives him an expressionless look and starts towards the bar once more. He has to stand aside to allow CATHY and NEIL to pass on their way to the dance floor. Over her shoulder to NEIL CATHY says:*)

CATHY: I don't think I've danced since we were married. I'm warning you. I mean, Donald's hopeless, absolutely hopeless. Bringing a great stack of papers to a party, honestly.

(*NEIL laughs. JACE returns to the bar.*)

3B. INT. BAR. NIGHT

(*JACE comes in and stands waiting for service. Mr. HARRIS is trying his luck with HUGHIE over the heads of those already seated at the bar.*)

HARRIS: Excuse me—could we have—excuse me.

HUGHIE: If you'd like to take a seat, sir, the waiter will be with you in a minute.

HARRIS: Yes, but we've been trying to …

HUGHIE: He'll be with you in a moment, sir.

HARRIS (*Limply*): That's all very well but …

HUGHIE (*Turning to JACE*): Dear oh dear … now then, chief.

JACE: One gin and french, one whisky sour, one campari.

HUGHIE: Gin and french coming up, squire.

(*JACE waits. Two people sitting at the bar vacate their seats. HARRIS, who is still hovering, sees this and beckons eagerly to MRS. HARRIS. She makes her way with slight difficulty owing to her tail and has almost reached him when DONALD and FREDA sit on the stools.*)

MRS. HARRIS: Oh no.

FREDA: Sorry, were these yours?

HARRIS: No, no.

MRS. HARRIS: What do you mean, no. They pushed in.

(*HARRIS drags her back to their table.*)

HARRIS: No they didn't.

MRS. HARRIS: They just pushed in.

HUGHIE (*Delivering gin and french*): Campari, was it?

JACE: And a whisky sour.

DONALD: You don't mind moving here?

FREDA: Not at all.

DONALD: It's just I get a better view of him, you see, I can tell when he's not busy. Keep an eye on him from here.

FREDA: This is fine.

DONALD: Important to catch him at the right moment. (*Winking at her*) Psychological. (*To JACE*) We're moving here, alright?

JACE: Just as you like, sir.

DONALD (*Tapping his file*): No, you see, I've had this little scheme of mine at the back of my mind for some time and I thought, why waste it? What can I lose? I think it's a good one. What's more I thought, I'll take it straight to the top.

FREDA: Best thing.

DONALD: Only way.

(*HUGHIE returns with whisky sour.*)

HUGHIE: Tony, you had that campari out?

(*TONY answers from the other end of bar.*)

TONY: It's finished.

HUGHIE: Well, fetch another one. Fetch another one. (*To JACE*) God give me strength. Won't keep you a moment. (*Speaks to a customer at the far end*) Yes sir?

FREDA: If you do get a chance when you're talking to him ...

DONALD (*Studying his report*): She's made one or two errors in this. I mean, she's corrected them but they show ... what's that, sorry?

FREDA: If you could, you know, put in a word about Neil? I mean, you know, you seem to be in with the people who matter. I'm sure a word from you could make all the difference.

DONALD (*Modestly*): Oh, I don't know.

FREDA: No, it would. They listen to you, Donald, they do. Like you've just said. I mean, it's a knack, isn't it? Getting to know the right people. Neil's friendly but the only people he seems to know are clerks and typists, as far as I can make out. I mean he always behaves like it doesn't matter to him—but I live with him, Donald. I know that really it does. He's been passed over that many times. For promotion. I know he feels it.

DONALD: Well, I'm not responsible for that, I promise you. I've done all I could.

FREDA: Yes, I know, I know, I'm grateful. But now the kids are getting older, it's really getting very difficult. It's not as if he doesn't work hard—he does over-time, everything.

DONALD: I'll do what I can.

FREDA: I know you will. Bless you.

(*HUGHIE arrives with the Campari.*)

HUGHIE: At last. There you go.

JACE: Ta.

(*He starts to move off.*)

DONALD (*Craning his neck*): Is he still talking, can you see?

FREDA: Yes, he's still talking …

(*JACE moves towards WARWICK'S table. His path is suddenly blocked by MRS. HARRIS*)

MRS. HARRIS: Look, excuse me …

(*JACE is trying to get past her*)

JACE: Just a minute madam.

MRS. HARRIS (*Refusing to budge*): No, it isn't just a minute, at all. We've been trying to order a drink here for half an hour …

(*HARRIS is hovering in the background.*)

HARRIS: Millie …

MRS. HARRIS: No, it's not good enough. You're paying enough to stay here, for heaven's sake.

JACE: I'll be with you in one minute, madam.

MRS. HARRIS: No, I'm sorry. I want to order now.

JACE: Excuse me, madam.

MRS. HARRIS: I'm sorry …

HARRIS: Millie …

JACE: Excuse me please, madam.

(*He pushes past her and leaves the bar carrying the drinks for WARWICK'S table.*)

3C. INT. FOYER. NIGHT

(*JACE comes from the bar and goes over to the WARWICKS' table. He puts the tray of drinks down on a convenient chair and wipes the table over. He then sets out the drinks. During this:*)

MRS. WARWICK: I think this is rather a bright way to finish off a conference.

WARWICK: A little light relief.

MRS. WARWICK: Keeps the wives happy too, I imagine. Very bright somebody whoever thought of it.

WARWICK: Me.

MRS.WARWICK (*To JACE*): Thank you. (*To WARWICK*) And it keeps the staff sweet.

WARWICK: Well, the ones that matter, anyway.

MRS. WARWICK (*To RILEY*): You'll have noticed by now, John, my husband never does anything without an ulterior reason.

RILEY (*Smiling*): Oh, I don't know about that, Mrs. Warwick.

MRS.WARWICK: Oh, this is jolly. I rather wish we had dressed up now, don't you darling?

WARWICK: Hardly. Leave it to the people like John here.

MRS. WARWICK: Oh well, John looks divine. Gorgeous. That does so suit you, John.

(*JOHN smirks. JACE moves towards the bar and is met by the HARRIS' who have just come out.*)

JACE: Now, madam …

MRS. HARRIS: No, thank you. We've waited long enough. We're going somewhere else.

HARRIS: Ah, come on, Millie.

MRS. HARRIS: I'm certainly not drinking in this rude hotel. We'll go somewhere else.

HARRIS: I can't go out like this.

MRS. HARRIS: I'm not staying here, that's final.

(*She marches to the hall door. HARRIS follows her reluctantly.*)

HARRIS (*As he goes*): I can't go out like this.

(*JACE goes back into the bar.*)

3D. INT. BAR. NIGHT

(*JACE comes into the bar. He picks up a dirty ash tray and wanders over to the bar counter with it. He takes out his notebook and checks over his orders.*)

FREDA: … Then there's other times, for days on end, he'll just sit there. He won't talk to me, he'll hardly talk to the children. And the only thing I can think of, it must be his work. That's the only conclusion I can come to.

DONALD: Yes. Yes.

FREDA: That's all I can think of …

TONY: Draught lager's off, Hughie.

FREDA: It must be his work …

HUGHIE: Oh no, not again.

FREDA: That's the only conclusion …

TONY: Shall I nip down and change it?

FREDA: That's what it is …

HUGHIE: No. You've too much here. Get him on the phone.

TONY: Who?

HUGHIE: Whatsisname. Grimshaw. He can do something for once. He'll be in that office with his feet up. (*Off down the bar again*) Yes, my dear, what can I get you?

(*TONY moves down the bar to the telephone. JACE does painful mental arithmetic.*)

FREDA: I mean, he is good at his job, isn't he?

(*DONALD is craning again to see WARWICK'S table.*)

DONALD: Oh yes.

FREDA: Well, what is it then? Do they have a down on him or what?

DONALD: I don't think it's that.

FREDA: Well, it beats me. It just beats me. Makes you want to weep sometimes.

(*HUGHIE has moved back up the bar.*)

HUGHIE: What's that, love?

FREDA: Nothing, sorry.

HUGHIE: You don't want to weep in here, love, it's bad for business. Go on, have another of the same.

FREDA: No, thank you.

HUGHIE: Go on. Gin, is it?

FREDA: Well … this is the last one.

HUGHIE: That is the way.

TONY: Not there, Hughie, no reply.

HUGHIE: Jace?

JACE: Eh?

HUGHIE: Could you nip out the front and see if Grimshaw's there?

JACE: Righto.

HUGHIE: Tell him the draught lager's off again.

JACE: Right.

DONALD: I think I'll go over and tackle him in a minute.

(*JACE weaves through the tables and out through the glass doors.*)

4. INT. THE FOYER. NIGHT.

(*JACE looks about for the ASSISTANT MANAGER. MR. and MRS. HARRIS are standing angrily in the hall. JACE passes them without a second glance, goes to the ballroom door and looks in briefly. A burst of louder music. He steps back to allow CATHY out of the ballroom. She passes him and goes swiftly upstairs.*)

HARRIS: Then what are we going to do?

MRS. HARRIS: I've told you what I'm going to do. I'm going to bed.

HARRIS: But it's early.

MRS. HARRIS: I'm sorry. I'm going to bed.

HARRIS: Oh well, suit yourself.

MRS. HARRIS: What are you doing?

HARRIS: I don't know.

MRS. HARRIS: Oh well, suit yourself.

(*MRS. HARRIS stamps off up the stairs. HARRIS hesitates for a second, then marches back in the bar. JACE approaches the HALL PORTER who is now reading a paperback.*)

JACE: Seen Grimshaw?

(*The HALL PORTER indicates behind him with a jerk of his head. JACE moves behind the counter and through the doorway into the small office behind.*)

JACE (*As he goes*): Mr. Grimshaw ...

5. INT. THE SMALL BACK OFFICE. NIGHT.

(*A glimpse of the ASSISTANT MANAGER in his shirt sleeves springing from his chair, snapping off the tv set and grabbing his jacket all in one swift movement.*)

ASSISTANT MANAGER (*Turning to JACE*): Yes?

JACE: Draught lager's off in the Tudor Bar. Hughie says could you change it.

ASSISTANT MANAGER: Can't anyone else do it?

JACE: We're all a bit rushed in there, you see.

ASSISTANT MANAGER (*Straightening himself*): Alright, alright I'll deal with it. I'll deal with it.

(*He pushes past JACE in the doorway.*)

6. INT. THE FOYER. NIGHT.

(*ASSISTANT MANAGER emerging from office followed by JACE*)

ASSISTANT MANAGER: Are the keys in the bar?

JACE: Yes, Mr. Grimshaw.

(*ASSISTANT MANAGER crosses the foyer and goes through the doors into the bar. He passes NEIL who is lurking by the rubber plants, peering into the bar. When the ASSISTANT MANAGER has passed him, NEIL moves forward to get a better view directly through the doors. JACE, who has ambled across the hallway, thus finds NEIL in his path.*)

JACE: Excuse me, sir.

NEIL: Ah. (*He moves aside.*) (*JACE is about to enter the bar.*) Just a minute, just a minute.

JACE: Sir?

(*NEIL draws JACE away by the arm to a point out of view of the bar.*)

NEIL: Could you bring up a bottle of champagne to Room 304?

JACE: Well, if you'd like to ring room service, sir, I'm sure they'll be able to ...

(*NEIL fumbles with his wallet.*)

JACE: We're not really supposed to leave the bar, you see, sir. (*Accepting NEIL's note*) Oh well, thank you sir. I'll see if we can arrange something.

NEIL: 304. Quick as you can.

(*NEIL heads off up the stairs. JACE smooths out the note, slips it in his top pocket and starts back towards the bar. He approaches the WARWICKS' table where DONALD is just introducing himself.*)

DONALD: Excuse me, Mr. Warwick, sir.

WARWICK: Hello.

DONALD: Fawcett, sir.

WARWICK: What?

DONALD: Donald Fawcett, sir. I spoke to your secretary. You said you would very kindly spare me a moment.

WARWICK: Oh good gracious, yes, of course.

DONALD: I hope I'm not in any way ...

WARWICK: No, no.

MRS. WARWICK: Not at all.

WARWICK: Waiter, could we have another chair for Mr. ...

JACE: Sir. (*He retrieves a chair from another table.*)

DONALD: I did mention it to your secretary.

WARWICK: Yes, I do remember. She mentioned it specially.

(*JACE brings the chair to DONALD.*)

DONALD (*To JACE*): Thank you.

MRS.WARWICK: Darling, I can see you're going to want to talk business. I hope you won't think us frightfully rude if we ...

(*She starts to rise. All the men rise. JACE darts around to help her with the chair but RILEY is already there.*)

DONALD: I'm so sorry, I didn't mean to ...

MRS.WARWICK: No, no, we're just going to have one quick dance.

WARWICK: Go ahead, go ahead. (*To DONALD*) Now, let me get you a drink.

DONALD: Oh no—that's ...

WARWICK: What are you drinking?

DONALD: Just a scotch, a small scotch.

WARWICK: A small scotch, waiter. (*Seeing DONALD still awkwardly clutching his file*) Look, do you want to put those down somewhere?

DONALD: Oh, thank you.

(*He looks for somewhere to put them.*)

JACE (*Taking them from him*): I'll put them on here, shall I sir?

(*He planks them on one of the empty chairs.*)

WARWICK: What on earth is it? You look as if you've brought the office to the dance.

DONALD: No, this is my scheme. I mentioned it to your secretary. Just a little idea ... I don't know if she ...

WARWICK: Yes, of course, of course.

(*JACE returns to the bar.*)

7. INT. BAR. NIGHT

(*JACE enters. FREDA, who has had one or two since we last saw her, to HUGHIE as he works:*)

FREDA: I may not look it but I feel it.

HUGHIE: Well, I say you don't look it.

FREDA: You're as young as you feel.

HUGHIE (*Giving her a fresh drink*): There you are, love. (*To JACE*) Lady says she feels sixty-five. (*He laughs.*)

(*FREDA smiles at JACE. JACE gives a pale smile.*)

JACE: Champagne, two glasses please.

HUGHIE (*Calling*): Got more champagne down there, Tony?

TONY: How many?

HUGHIE: One.

JACE: And one small scotch.

HUGHIE: Small scotch coming up.

FREDA: Sounds romantic.

HUGHIE: Eh?

FREDA: Champagne and two glasses.

HUGHIE: Oh yeah. (*Delivering glass to JACE*) Small scotch.

JACE: Ta. (*JACE moves off.*)

FREDA: Long time since I had champagne.

HUGHIE: I'll buy you some, Love, if you'll pay for it.

(*JACE leaves the bar.*)

7A. INT. FOYER. NIGHT

(*JACE comes into the foyer and moves towards the WARWICKS' table with the scotch. He steps aside smartly as COOMBES rumbles past him*)

COOMBES (*To a woman he has in tow*): I'm going to teach you the Viking Tango.

(*JACE arrives at WARWICK'S table. WARWICK is now holding DONALD'S report.*)

WARWICK: You sound as if you've given it a good deal of thought ... I'll certainly read it with great interest. Thank you very much. (*He slips the report back to the chair.*)

DONALD: I mean, you were quoted as saying in our magazine that ...

WARWICK: Suggestions always welcome. Quite right.

DONALD (*Receiving his scotch from JACE*): Thank you.

WARWICK (*To JACE*): I think we might get rid of some of these, don't you? (*He indicates one or two empty glasses.*)

JACE: Yes, sir.

(*He clears and wipes the table.*)

WARWICK: Like your get-up.

DONALD: Thank you.

WARWICK: Dutch, is it?

DONALD (*Uncertainly*): Er … it could be. It could be. It's like it …

7.B INT. BAR. NIGHT.

(*JACE comes in and comes to TONY and HUGHIE at the bar with the empties.*)

HUGHIE (*Repeating TONY'S order*): Two lagers and limes, two cokes, one gin and bitter lemon, one cider and a double brandy.

(*FREDA sits staring into her glass, peeling layers off a beer mat. JACE picks up the tray now waiting for him with champagne in a bucket and two glasses, and leaves the bar.*)

8. INT. FOYER. NIGHT

(*JACE comes out of the bar and goes over to wait for the lift. DONALD is still talking to the WARWICKS.*)

WARWICK: Now, you're based in Manchester, aren't you?

DONALD: No. Edgeware.

WARWICK: Edgeware, that's it. How are things up there? How are you all coping?

DONALD: Oh, very well, very well.

WARWICK: Everybody happy? No-one got any problems?

DONALD: Fine, everyone's fine.

WARWICK: That's what I like to hear.

(*During the above conversation the lift arrives and reveals to JACE a grim-faced HOUSEKEEPER with an armful of towels, keys on her belt. JACE steps inside and the doors close.*)

9. INT. THE LIFT. NIGHT

(*JACE and HOUSEKEEPER standing side by side. HOUSEKEEPER looks at the champagne and then at JACE. JACE looks at her. HOUSEKEEPER looks away, a faint expression of disgust on her face.*)

10. INT. THIRD FLOOR LANDING. NIGHT

JACE emerges from the lift and walks along to 304. He knocks tentatively. A pause. He knocks again. The door opens an inch.

JACE: Champagne, sir.

NEIL (*Opening the door sufficiently to reveal that he has, at least, no shirt on*): Ah, good man. Just a second. Wait.

(*NEIL disappears, pushing the door to. JACE waits. The door is flung open. NEIL stands in dressing gown and socks.*)

11. INT. BEDROOM. NIGHT.

(*Double bedroom with bath. NEIL ushering JACE in.*)

NEIL (*Sotto*): Just put it down here, would you?

(*He clears assorted clothes off the dressing table. As JACE is setting down the tray, the bathroom door opens.*)

CATHY (*Emerging*): Where do you keep you … (*Catching sight of JACE*) Oh my God. (*Bathroom door slams.*)

NEIL: Right, that's all, thank you. (*He ushers JACE to the door.*)

JACE: Thank you, sir.

12. INT. THE LANDING. NIGHT

(*JACE is coming out of 304, NEIL preparing to close the door.*)

JACE: Anything else I can do for you, sir?

NEIL: No, no. (*Sudden thought*) Oh, just a minute. Wait there. Just a minute.

(*JACE stands outside the door.*)

CATHY'S VOICE (*From inside*): Why the hell didn't you tell me there was someone in here?

NEIL'S VOICE: It was only a waiter.

CATHY'S VOICE: I was going to walk in here stark naked.

NEIL'S VOICE: It's alright.

(*The HOUSEKEEPER comes out of 310 along the passage, still clutching her pile of towels and with the briefest of knocks, opens the door of 308 and goes inside.*)

CATHY'S VOICE: What are you doing?

NEIL: I've just got to take care of this chap.

CATHY'S VOICE: I thought you said you'd given him something already.

NEIL'S VOICE: I have. He looks as if he wants more. Just a second.

(*Door opens. NEIL slips another note to JACE.*)

NEIL'S VOICE: Thanks very much.

(*JACE a hint of unexpected surprise in his voice*)

JACE: Oh, thank you, sir.

(*NEIL closes the door. JACE smooths out the note and slips it into his top pocket. The HOUSEKEEPER comes out of 308, closes the door and, with briefest of knocks, opens*) *the door of 306 with her pass key and goes inside. JACE heads the other way along the passage to the main staircase.)*

13. INT. THE FOYER. NIGHT.

(JACE descending the staircase. HALL PORTER continues to read his book. The ASSISTANT MANAGER has just come out of the bar and is helping FREDA across the hall to the front door.)

HALL PORTER: Alright, Mr. Grimshaw?

ASSISTANT MANAGER: Madam's just feeling a little faint, that's all.

(ASSISTANT MANAGER and FREDA go out the front door, FREDA moaning slightly. JACE reaches the bottom of the stairs. HALL PORTER sees him and raises his eyebrows. JACE wanders back towards the door to the bar. The ASSISTANT MANAGER returns hurriedly through the front door.)

ASSISTANT MANAGER (*To HALL PORTER*): Bucket of water, Henry. We need a bucket of water out here quickly, please.

HALL PORTER: Water, righto sir. (*ASSISTANT MANAGER goes out the front door again. HALL PORTER starts across the hall muttering.*) Saturday nights. I don't know why they don't leave a bucket out there permanently.

JACE (*Nodding sagely*): Ah.

HALL PORTER (*Disappearing*): Every bloody Saturday ...

(Coming upstairs from the ballroom are WARWICK, MRS.WARWICK and RILEY who are on the point of leaving the party and in the process of saying goodnight to DONALD.)

WARWICK: Thank you again. It's been most pleasant talking to you. (*Waving DONALD's folder which he carries.*) And I'll certainly study this closely as soon as I've a minute—goodnight.

DONALD: Goodnight. It's been a real ...

MRS.WARWICK, RILEY: Goodnight.

(DONALD goes back into the bar. The WARWICK TRIO pause to speak to JACE.)

WARWICK (*To JACE*): I don't think we've paid for our drinks. Do we pay you?

JACE: Yes, sir. If you like. Just a minute, sir.

(JACE snatches out his pad and pencil and starts his mental arithmetic. WARWICK and CO. cross slowly to the HALL PORTER'S desk, JACE following them.)

WARWICK: Now you see why I always try and avoid these sort of functions, Riley.

RILEY: Quite.

MRS.WARWICK: Poor darling.

WARWICK: I always seem to get saddled with chaps like that.

RILEY: What did he want?

WARWICK: God knows. Wants to re-plan our advertising campaign single handed, as far as I can make out.

MRS.WARWICK: Cheek.

WARWICK (*At the PORTER'S desk*): Do you think we have to break in and steal our own keys?

JACE: Just a moment, sir, I'll get them for you. (*In a confidential tone*) I make it L 5.38 exactly, sir. If you'd care to check that.

(*WARWICK lays DONALD's folder on the counter and reaches for his wallet.*)

WARWICK: No. I made some passing remark in our house magazine a year or so ago. This chap seems to have taken me literally.

(*JACE has gone behind the desk and is now hovering by the keys.*)

JACE: Er … ?

RILEY: 105 and 6.

MRS. WARWICK: That'll teach you.

(*WARWICK has selected a five pound note; finds exact money and now hands this to JACE.*)

WARWICK: Thank you. Are we off then?

MRS. WARWICK: Might as well.

(*The three start for the stairs. JACE holding up the folder WARWICK has left on the desk.*)

JACE: Excuse me, sir, have you forgotten this?

WARWICK (*Turning back*): Oh, I think we can probably survive without that, don't you?

RILEY: I hope so.

WARWICK (*Gesturing to JACE*): Would you find somewhere to …

JACE: Yes, of course, sir.

(*He drops the file into the wastepaper basket behind the desk.*)

WARWICK (*Proceeding up the stairs*): One thing, they all seem fairly happy in their work up in Edgeware.

RILEY: They don't have much to do.

WARWICK: Probably why. Ah well, as soon as we've got Hendon open …

RILEY: Roll on, Hendon.

WARWICK: Quite. (*The three mount the stairs in silence. They pass NEIL coming downstairs alone. JACE meanwhile is checking his money from WARWICK. He aims an inscrutable look at the back of WARWICK'S head. WARWICK'S party meet NEIL on the stairs. NEIL, for a second, looks as if he is about to speak to them but WARWICK starts talking again and NEIL, instead, steps aside.*) I reckon to start about eight. It shouldn't take more than two hours, should it?

RILEY: About two hours, yes.

MRS. WARWICK: Are we going to have lunch there?

RILEY: Yes, I think they're laying that on for us.

(*NEIL reaches the bottom of the stairs and straightens his Dracula costume in the mirror. JACE has tucked away his money and has again crossed to the bar door. Before he can open it, a conga bursts through, led by COOMBES, MRS. COOMBES and PARTY. JACE holds the door again, registering only very mild amusement. The conga snakes through the foyer and heads back to the ballroom through the other door. NEIL joins on the end. JACE watches the dance disappear. CATHY appears at the top of the stairs looking disgruntled. JACE goes back into the bar.*)

14. INT. TUDOR BAR. NIGHT.

(*It is fairly depleted at present. Three or four couples. MR. HARRIS alone in his Frogman's suit sits getting quietly drunk. DONALD, too, sits alone, looking rather pleased with himself. JACE enters from the foyer and crosses to the bar.*)

HUGHIE: You missed the excitement.

(*JACE handing over WARWICK'S bill with the money*)

JACE: What?

HUGHIE (*Cashing it up*): Frankenstein's daughter. You know, sitting here. Fell clean off her stool. Just sitting here and over she goes.

(*JACE shakes his head. CATHY comes in from the foyer.*)

CATHY (*Seeing DONALD*): Oh, there you are.

DONALD: Good dance?

CATHY: Alright. Where's Freda?

DONALD: No idea.

HUGHIE (*Looking at his watch*): Should be stopping in a minute.

TONY: With this band they will. Don't do overtime, do this lot.

HUGHIE: Suits me.

(*JACE wanders over to DONALD and CATHY. DONALD is writing in his notebook.*)

JACE: Can I get you anything, madam?

CATHY: No, thank you.

DONALD: Not just at the moment.

(*JACE starts to clear the table by them. From the ballroom, COOMBES'S party and others return, elated, jolly, full of party spirit. Behind them the band strikes up 'The Queen.' From amongst the group, NEIL comes over and joins CATHY and DONALD.*)

NEIL: Just seen old Patterson.

DONALD: Oh yes.

NEIL: Didn't know he was here. How did you get on then?

DONALD: Oh, he seemed very interested.

NEIL: Good, good. (*To CATHY*) Hallo there.

CATHY: Hallo.

NEIL: Don't I get a smile? (*CATHY smiles a large false smile.*) That's better. Now, a nightcap. One for the stairs, eh? Waiter.

DONALD: Oh no, no.

JACE: Sir?

NEIL: What are you doing there? Writing your diary?

DONALD: No, no. Just writing down what I've spent before I forget.

CATHY: He writes everything down.

NEIL (*To JACE*): Right, we'd like three brandies. You needn't write these down, Don, they're on me.

JACE: Three brandies, sir?

NEIL: Where's Freda?

DONALD: Wasn't she with you?

NEIL: Me? What would she be doing with me? (*He laughs.*)

(*JACE returns to the bar. COOMBES party are now going out with much hilarity.*)

JACE: Three brandies, Hughie.

TONY: Brewery calls on Monday, doesn't it?

HUGHIE: Tuesday.

TONY: We're out of brown very nearly.

HUGHIE: Oh, we'll get through Monday, don't worry.

(*Behind them FREDA has come in.*)

NEIL (*Calling over*): Could you make that four, waiter.

JACE (*Calling*): Four, right sir. (*To HUGHIE*) Another one.

HUGHIE: She's not starting again, is she. (*Delivering the fourth brandy*) There you go.

JACE: Ta.

(*JACE crosses to DONALD'S table.*)

FREDA: Went for a walk. I just went for a walk, that's all.

CATHY: You'll be frozen.

(*JACE serves the brandies.*)

FREDA (*To DONALD*): How did you get on?

DONALD: Alright, I think, alright.

FREDA: Did you manage to—?

DONALD: What?

FREDA: You know. Did you manage to have a word?

DONALD: Oh yes.

NEIL: What about?

FREDA: Never mind. Private.

NEIL: With Warwick?

FREDA: Yes.

NEIL: I hope not about me. I'll slaughter you.

FREDA: Sometimes it's necessary.

NEIL: I'm not starting begging.

FREDA: Maybe not. It's worth reminding people though, isn't it? I think you might at least say thank you to Donald. There was no reason for him to say anything on your behalf.

NEIL: Thank you, Donald.

FREDA: I mean, what does he get out of it?

NEIL: I said, thank you Donald.

DONALD: That's alright.

CATHY: What did he say?

DONALD: When?

CATHY: About Neil.

DONALD: He said he'd look into it.

CATHY: Oh.

NEIL: Can't say fairer than that. Cheers.

FREDA: Cheers.

(*They drink. JACE returns to the bar. Returning tray*)

HUGHIE: Calling it a day, Jace?

JACE: Just about.

HUGHIE: We'll be here for half an hour. See this lot off.

(*JACE moves towards the foyer doors.*)

JACE (*Over his shoulder to HUGHIE*): 'Night.

HUGHIE: 'Night.

TONY: 'Night, Jace.

(*JACE wanders past DONALD'S table. The four are now sitting in silence. The only other occupant left in the bar is Mr. HARRIS, who is sitting glazed in the corner. JACE goes through into the foyer.*)

15. INT. THE FOYER. NIGHT.

(*The HALL PORTER is back behind his desk handing a key to a couple. The ASSIS-TANT MANAGER is holding the front door open to two more who are just leaving.*)

ASSISTANT MANAGER: Mind the step there, madam, it's just a bit slippery.

WOMAN'S VOICE: Is it raining?

ASSISTANT MANAGER: No, no. No rain. We've been very lucky really.

(*He goes out the front door with them. JACE crosses the foyer and goes behind the HALL PORTER'S desk into the back office.*)

HALL PORTER: Home then, Jace?

JACE: Just about.

(*JACE emerges from the small back office. DONALD and CATHY are at the foot of the stairs. NEIL and FREDA are at the desk.*)

NEIL: Probably see you at breakfast.

DONALD: We're off first thing. You may not.

NEIL: Well otherwise, Monday.

DONALD: Monday, yes. 'Night.

NEIL: Goodnight, both.

FREDA AND CATHY: 'Night.

(*CATHY and DONALD start slowly up the stairs.*)

NEIL: Call tomorrow morning?

FREDA: No I'll wake up.

NEIL: We can arrange one.

FREDA: I always wake up. (*NEIL starts for the stairs.*) Have you got the key?

NEIL: Yes, I've got it here. Come on.

FREDA: Good night.

HALL PORTER: Goodnight, madam.

JACE: 'Night.

(*FREDA starts up the stairs. Ahead of her is NEIL and above him again DONALD and CATHY, still climbing separately. JACE buttons his coat, watching them up.*)

HALL PORTER: Go off alright, did it?

JACE: What?

HALL PORTER: The dance.

(*JACE taking out his dog-end and lighting it*)

JACE: Seemed to.

HALL PORTER: No excitements, then?

JACE: When?

HALL PORTER: This evening.

JACE: Not so's you'd notice, no. 'Night.

HALL PORTER: 'Night.

(*JACE walks away as HARRIS emerges unsteadily from the bar, heading for the stairs. JACE passes the foot of the stairs and leaves through a door at the far end of the foyer.*)

Nicole Boireau

"ALL THE WORLD'S A FARCE" IN *SERVICE NOT INCLUDED* BY ALAN AYCKBOURN

An audience in search of an author would be well advised to turn to Alan Ayckbourn. Indeed, the English playwright who is said to fill "more seats than the Bard"[1] and whose works have been translated into twenty-six languages, has been consistently challenging his public since the beginning of his career in 1959. Past master at writing sophisticated comedies, he has a good ear for witty dialogues, a flair for life's little ironies, and enough sympathy for human vulnerability, which he exposes with genuine tact and insight. Alan Ayckbourn, also known as "the Ibsen of Scarborough," has won himself a well-deserved and world-wide reputation in all circles.

The comic spirit reigns supreme in Ayckbourn's polished comedies of middle-class English manners, and *Service Not Included*, a short piece for television, written and broadcast in 1974 to fit in the half-hour slot of a BBC series called *Masquerade*[2], is no exception to the rule, or, should we say more aptly, to the misrule. Ayckbourn sums up what the play was supposed to be: "a waiter's eye view of a dreadful office party." He confesses he was not very satisfied with the result, as the project had to be cut down to size in order to meet financial constraints. Originally written for twenty-four people and thirty-eight sets, the play had to be streamlined to sixteen characters and a dozen, or so, very simplified sets (Watson 82).

Service Not Included describes a fancy-dress dance taking place at the end of a business conference held in a hotel in the country. The wives have come to join their husbands for the party. Jace, the waiter, moves from place to place, taking the orders and serving people. We see what he sees, and hear what he hears. In a way, he operates as the impassive "camera eye" for the spectator. Adultery, alcoholism and human misery seem to be the stuff this little world is made of. The generic features of this semi-farcical bitter-sweet comedy, poised between laughter and despair, inform its world vision.

In all his plays, Ayckbourn theatricalizes human experience in compelling visual terms. In *Service Not Included*, he uses the resources of the filmic technique to the full. The swift-moving camera eye, through Jace's cool gaze, registers minute details, which tie up with snatches of conversation collected here and there, eventually forming a logical and meaningful pattern. The episodic, but firm, structure of the play informs an overall vision, which emerges, little by little, piece after piece, jigsawlike, under the waiter's eyes. Such a structure has much in common with *Between Mouthfuls*, a one-act stage play by Ayckbourn, in which marital infidelities are gradually revealed through interrelated dialogues between couples in a restaurant.[3] Apart from its native fluidity, which can be structurally exploited, as Ayckbourn does in *Service Not Included*, the filmic technique also foregrounds one basic principle of the television medium, whereby the actual idea of "performance" is by-passed and diluted into a "naturalized" framework open to realistic "trompe-l'oeil" treatment. What we get with a stage play is metaphorical stylization, but what we are offered in this television play is metonymical reality.

Ayckbourn seems to hold the positivistic belief that reality can be apprehended, therefore imitated and represented. Ayckbourn's comedies of manners share the stylized artificiality of this very idiosyncratic English genre, but they also provide us with a recognizable context which can be placed on the geographical and social spectrum with utmost precision. In *Service Not Included* the stage directions describe the place as "a converted undistinguished country house" (62). The hotel staff includes three men downstairs (two waiters for bar service and the assistant manager) and a woman housekeeper upstairs for room service. Each member of the staff has a precise function; they are seen while engaged in various practical activities that endow them with credibility as characters. At the beginning of the play, the blasé and bored waiters are idly smoking outside or exchanging comments about the weather. We understand that the stage is set for Carnival as the clients are all arriving in groups of two (husbands and wives) dressed up in various outlandish costumes: Donald, in a Tyrolean outfit, with his wife, Cathy, as a Spanish dancer; Mr. and Mrs. Coombes, respectively as Viking and Rhinemaiden; Neil, as Dracula, and Freda, his wife, as a Dracula victim; Mr. Harris, dressed in a wet suit complete with goggles and flaps, and his wife as a mermaid, with a very cumbersome home-made tail. The Warwick couple, alone, are not dressed up. The hotel management enjoins Jace to treat Mr. Warwick with special consideration, as he obviously is the boss. The hall porter sniggers as they all appear: "They're all going tomorrow morning anyway, thank God" (63). He also imaginatively, and scornfully, construes the "U.B.S. conference" sign at the foot of the stairs as "useless bunch of so and so's" (63).

Ayckbourn introduces rituals in all his plays, in the form of picnics in *Sisterly Feelings* (1978), Christmas and dinner-parties in *Absurd Person Singular* (1972) and *How the Other Half Loves* (1970), Guy Fawkes' explosive celebrations in *Joking Apart* (1978), and family gatherings that all invariably go wrong in *The Norman Conquests* (1973), to name but a few.[4] Ayckbourn relishes those ritualized situations that symbolically celebrate the cycle of life and death, and endlessly reenact the mythic circular pattern of Winter and Spring. The youthful zest of Spring is traditionally considered as being central to the art of comedy. Yet, Ayckbourn's comedies tend to destabilize theories, and *Service Not Included*, again, is no exception. This particular party, the end party of a business conference, meant to celebrate an end and a new beginning, contains all the ingredients of a traditional bacchanalia: dancing, drinking and sex. Drinking and sex preferably with tears, in true Ayckbourn fashion. The three components are also the cornerstone of the dramatic situation.

The fancy-dress situation, naïvely incongruous in itself ("I don't get the point of it" (63), says the worldly-wise hall porter), is made even more so in this play where the characters rarely sustain the role that is supposed to go with the disguise. Indeed, the participants do not masquerade as anything but themselves, their disguises just fulfilling an ornamental function, therefore overemphasizing the triteness of what is said and done. Neil is an exception and lives up to his supposed part, for half a second, when he orders "a pint of blood" (67) with his whisky; so are the Coombes, when announcing themselves: "The Vikings are here" (65), and when Mr. Coombes offers to teach his partner the "Viking tango" (76). Of course, the choice of costumes is deliberate on Ayckbourn's part, as Michael Billington points out: "Neil's Dracula outfit makes the additional point that he is both a bloodsucking parasite and a sexual raver." (Billington 79). On the whole the disguises remain perfunctory and correspond to no particular role-playing, as the characters stick very much to their every-day preoccupations: the Coombes fret over draughts, Donald worries about bills (he makes a note of all his expenses, be they insignificant or not), Cathy and Freda complain about having married workaholics. Dignified appearances are somewhat at odds with personal eccentricities. Ayckbourn thus creates a discrepancy between the conventionally festive occasion and the grim reality that is portrayed.

As Jace takes the orders for drinks, we hear scraps of conversation. Donald, who has an obsessive concern for his career, has brought a report ("a great stack of papers" (69), says Cathy disapprovingly), which he wants to hand in to the big boss, Mr. Warwick, as soon as he can corner him in a private conversation. Cathy enjoins him to put in a good word about Neil, who definitely needs a boost in his career. Freda, Neil's wife, also urges Donald to intercede in her husband's favour, as he only seems to know "clerks and typists" (70). When Donald eventually manages to have a few words with Warwick, he pushes his own project about a new advertising campaign and forgets all about Neil. Very smug below the urbane surface, well-mannered Mr. Warwick listens politely, totally uninterested and rather confused about the exact location of Donald's firm (77). Donald does not say a word about Neil but proudly leaves his report in Mr. Warwick's care before taking his leave. A short while later, the report is dumped on a chair and ends up in the waste-paper basket, going the way of all flesh, like Neil's promotion.

While the Tyrolean dancer is (wrongfully) supposed to give Dracula's career a boost, the latter is dancing with Cathy as a prelude to more intimate exchanges, which Neil plans in the grand style. Indeed, he bribes Jace to take "a bottle of champagne to room 304" (74). A criss-cross pattern rapidly emerges: the trajectory followed by Donald's report, from Donald to Warwick and then to the waste-basket in the bar, ironically crosses that of the drinks. Neil's champagne order and Donald's whisky order are loudly given by Jace to the other waiter at the bar, where Freda (Neil's wife) is tearfully sitting, drowning her despair in gin. On hearing the order of champagne with "two glasses" (76) she comments on the romantic associations that such an order calls forth. Orders and final decisions all converge at the bar, the living heart of the place, where cruel fate is lurking. At the very moment when Neil's professional destiny is sealed, Freda chances to be the innocent witness of an order of champagne destined to "room 304," where her husband is discreetly sneaking for a (very) quick love session with Cathy. This is all taking place while the Coombes are wildly dancing their Viking tango.

Impassive Jace takes the champagne upstairs. He is seen in the lift having to withstand the disapproving gaze of the housekeeper, also going to the third floor with her bunch of keys and a fresh supply of clean towels for every room. As she proceeds down the corridor, entering all the rooms and getting perilously close to "room 304," we briefly follow Jace inside the room; we see him put the tray on the table, catch a glimpse of Neil in his socks and dressing gown, and of Cathy emerging from the bathroom, presumably naked, and rushing back inside, slamming the door. Desperately anxious to give the waiter another tip, Neil asks him to wait outside. Cathy's angry words can be heard through the door, as she takes her lover to task for bribing the waiter a second time. In Ayckbourn's dramatic world, sex is not exactly an exhilarating experience. It is just allowed to rear a very ugly head.

In the quasi-silent sequences of *Service Not Included*, the truth is to be found in the manipulation of the visible. Indeed, the sight of Neil in his dressing-gown and socks haggling over a tip with his flustered mistress casts a somewhat unromantic halo over this adulterous situation. The unheroic bedroom farce episode is given its finishing touches a short while later, when Cathy, all "disgruntled" (81), is asked by her husband if she has had a "good dance" (81), and by Jace if she wants anything. Ayckbourn's wry sense of humour culminates in straightforward cynicism when flippant Neil, who has much in common with Norman, the disastrous conqueror of The Norman Conquests, inquires after his wife:

NEIL: Where's Freda?
DONALD: Wasn't she with you?
NEIL: Me ? What would she be doing with me? (*He laughs.*) (82)

Freda has been indulging in a lonely drinking bout that has made her sick under the insensitive eyes of Hughie, the other waiter, who mercilessly suggests he give her champagne to cheer her up, if she pays for it. Mediocrity is evenly distributed in this little world. The waiter's callousness matches Cathy and Neil's unexciting adulterous capers, and Donald's excessive concern with number one. Ayckbourn stands out as the arch-manipulator of a ruthless world which he pushes to its utmost materialistic limits. Taken one step further on the scale of detachment, the comedy slips into farce; mythic patterns freeze into jokes. Beneficient Carnival turns into nothing more than a second-rate bacchanalia.

As Stuart E. Baker has it: "Like most great farceurs, Ayckbourn is most at home using the pitiless objectivity of farce to dissect the horror, banality and numbing pains of everyday living" (Dukore 27). If laughter and tears go together as the two possible ways of perceiving the same reality, in *Service Not Included* laughter predominates. But, if we do manage to laugh, what do we laugh at exactly? What is the butt of the joke? The truth of the joke probably lies in the telling itself.

Ayckbourn obviously enjoys playing with the material world, which he controls with choreographic precision; in his plays space assumes a thematic as well as a structural function, thus becoming a major determining force in the world vision. In *Service Not Included*, he introduces the right contrapuntal mix of objects: socks, keys, towels, bottles of champagne, beer taps, disguises (Neil straightens his Dracula costume in front of a mirror on his way downstairs). They conspire to build a world from which all sense of transcendence is banished, and the visual quality of which he perversely captures to the full. Each sequence is visually so telling that the overall pictorial effect carries its full weight of metaphysical emptiness. Ayckbourn's concern with the cracks of the middle-class façade is given free expression when the physical world runs wild and turns into a joke. Farce, the pattern-making genre par excellence recycles life into a self-perpetuating mechanism: "farce insists that we laugh at life, however we find it. /.../ farce demands that we treat life as a joke." (Baker 26) Farce, the great organizing principle, freezes experience into patterns: human frailties, exacerbated self-interest, quick and not very enjoyable adulterous sex, make up the common bill of fare of this little microcosm in which we dread to recognize ourselves. Moreover, if the farcical quality of the piece derives from its visual coherence, its real power lies in its sense of recognition. In telling the joke, we have a sudden revelation about the way the world functions. The more outrageous the joke, the more compelling the recognition. Ayckbourn's plays thus foreground the mechanism of comedy, and in doing so they redirect laughter at themselves, at their own visual rhetoric. Wild English humour, ironic fate and an overwhelming sense of absurdity are the founding principles of any farcical comedy.

Service Not Included is stylized enough to represent a sample of ordinary humanity, caught between public desires and private fears. Herbert Blau tells us that "we can hardly think of comedy without laughter, but we have learned to think of laughter without comedy." (Blau 545) Indeed, laughter can feed on itself, as it has consistently been doing since absurdist drama gave a concrete form to "the sense of an ending." In *Service Not Included*, laughter erupts when the reality displayed is too mediocre for words, when the repartee is almost too appropriate to be true. Laughter erupts almost as a suspension of meaning, beyond belief or credibility.

Witty Ayckbourn, the arch-craftsman, is laying bare for us a mechanism devoid of moral purpose. Nothing survives to redeem a world that hides itself from itself, behind a wall of Dutch-made or home-made disguises and marital infidelities. In his *Essay on Comedy*, George Meredith said about Congreve's *The*

Way of the World: "The comedy has no idea in it, beyond the stale one that so the world goes." (Meredith 35) Indeed, "So the world goes" is the fatalistic appraisal of all comedies of manners. Yet, some of them are more corrective and ferocious than others, especially when they explore the margins and transgress the barriers of the socially acceptable, Joe Orton being one of the most representative examples in the second part of the twentieth century.

The little world of *Service Not Included* is not located in the margins; on the contrary, it is made socially acceptable through and through. The (not quite so) festive atmosphere of the pseudo-Carnival challenges no order—if there is any order left to be challenged. No real transgression throws us off balance, no deviant behaviour, no taboo-breaking incestuous revelation. Ayckbourn's realm, in all his plays, is the wide-ranging centre, not the fringes of society. His terrain is the almost stable common-place centre where hardly any tremor can be felt, where the sense of History has come to a standstill, with no bang, only whimpers, in an age commonly known for its moral exhaustion.

Yet, poetic justice strikes. As the title indicates, there is something to be paid for, some time. The stakes of the game are at the same time high and low, depending on who is telling the joke. Donald's report ends up in the waste-paper basket: ironic fate punishes him for pushing himself instead of helping his friend. Donald has no time for Neil's career, and why should he, if all Neil does for himself is hop into bed with his friend's wife? As to Cathy, frustration is all she reaps from her dangerous liaisons; Donald is made the biggest fool of all behind his back. No transcendence, no redemptive force emerges; concurrently, no real vice is stigmatized. Individuals are treated with benevolent detachment, but their little world is shown as potentially nightmarish. Ordinariness contains its own self-perpetuating principle, turning the logic of farce into a nightmare. Ayckbourn's world is a nightmarish farce in which laughter, like love, is doomed.

"I've always thought of comedies as tragedies that have been interrupted" says Ayckbourn (*Plays and Players* 18), reversing Northrop Frye's proposition. Ayckbourn explores the totalitarian madness of both genres, but stops short of tragedy's transcendence and of comedy's rejuvenating principle. His realm is that of dark comedy, the archetypal twentieth-century form that challenges all certainties: "Tragicomedy forces us back uneasily onto our fragile humanity." (Orr 8) The spiralling conga dance at the end of *Service Not Included*, a parodic mythical dance of life and death, tries to fulfill its life-giving function but leaves the spectator on two final questions: what can be done about the void in the centre? Are we not eventually making a feast of ourselves, cannibalizing the totem as the ultimate and only possible sacrificial transgression, just pretending to disrupt the order we have built? If such questions arise from *Service Not Included* the play serves its enlightening purpose.

Despite its obvious limitations, this little television piece contains all the seeds of Ayckbourn's more accomplished works: same characters, similar situations. Lovable Ayckbourn is endlessly juggling with lovable humanity for the spectators' greatest pleasure. Michael Billington sums up Ayckbourn's achievement in *Service Not Included*: "he manages to remind us that our social festivities are often a cover for a good deal of pain and dishonesty." (Billington 79) In its graphic clarity, the play anatomizes the world with true paradoxical efficiency. The comic spirit of postmodernism is desperately calling attention to the entropic centre but also to the need for invigorating values. Carnival is dead, long live Carnival.

Bibliography

Alan Ayckbourn, *Service Not Included*, 1974, published for the first time in this volume.

Alan Ayckbourn, *Confusions*, London: 1977.

Alan Ayckbourn, *The Norman Conquests*, London: 1977.

Alan Ayckbourn, *Three Plays*, London: 1979.

Alan Ayckbourn, *Joking Apart and Other Plays*, London: 1982.

Alan Ayckbourn, *A Cut in the Rates*, in: Rurik von Antropoff und Klaus Peter Müller (Eds.), *Dramatic Voices from England, Canada and New Zealand, Festschrift für Albert-Reiner Glaap*, Berlin, Cornelsen: 1989, 61—69.

"Alan Ayckbourn in Interview," *Plays and Players*, September 1975, 15-19.

Stuart E. Baker, "Ayckbourn and the Tradition of Farce," in: Bernard F. Dukore (Ed.), *Alan Ayckbourn—A Casebook*, New York and London: 1991, 25-40.

Mikhail Bakhtin, *L'oeuvre de François Rabelais*, Paris: 1970.

Michael Billington, *Alan Ayckbourn*, London: 1983.

Herbert Blau, "Comedy since the Absurd," *Modern Drama* 25, 1982, 545-568.

Bernard F. Dukore, *Alan Ayckbourn—A Casebook*, New York and London: 1991.

Northrop Frye, *Anatomy of Criticism*, Princeton: 1973.

Albert-Reiner Glaap, *Alan Ayckbourn. Denkwürdiges und Merkwürdiges. Zum Fünfzigsten Geburtstag*, Reinbek: 1989.

Martin Grotjahn, *Beyond Laughter—Humor and the Subconscious*, New York, Toronto & London: 1966.

W. D. Howarth (Ed.), *Comic Drama—The European Heritage*, London: 1978.

George Meredith, *Essay on Comedy and the Uses of the Comic Spirit*, Archibald Constable and Company, London: 1897.

T.G.A. Nelson, *Comedy—The Theory of Comedy in Literature*, Drama and Cinema, London: 1990.

John Orr, *Tragicomedy and Contemporary Culture*, London: 1991.

Malcolm Page, *File on Ayckbourn*, London: 1989.

J. R. Taylor, *The Second Wave*, London: 1978.

Ian Watson, *Conversations with Alan Ayckbourn*, London: 1981.

Notes

[1]
David Lewis, "An Exchange with Alan Ayckbourn," *International Herald Tribune*, Thursday, 20 September, 1984.

[2]
Ayckbourn has written two television plays; *Service Not Included*, (dir. Herbert Wise), published in this volume and *A Cut in the Rates*, in: Rurik von Antropoff and Klaus Peter Müller (eds.), *Dramatic Voices from England, Canada and New Zealand, Festschrift für Albert-Reiner Glaap* (Berlin, Cornelsen: 1989), 61-69, a twenty-minute comedy, first transmitted by BBC TV Schools, 21 January 1984.

[3]
Between Mouthfuls is one of five one-act plays, *Mother Figure, Drinking Companion, Between Mouthfuls, Gosforth's Fête, A Talk in the Park*, first presented under the general title *Confusions* at the Apollo Theatre, London, in May 1976.

[4]
Dates of first productions at the Library or Stephen Joseph Theatre in Scarborough.

Henry Beissel

WHERE SHALL THE BIRDS FLY?
(ELEGY IV)

"Where can we go on crossing this last border?
Where do birds fly after the final sky?
Where do plants sleep when all the winds have passed?
We write our names in coloured smoke
and we die in this final passage
that olive trees might grow
to mark our place."

Mahmoud Darweesh, *Earth Narrows Before Us*

"My fear is gone now: are my senses mad?
Has the echo returned—is my head whirling?
Who has shaken the prison night from my chest,
and that nightmarish wall? For an age
the blind stovepipe hole has been clogged with dust.
But what's this?
Now it's been split by daylight,
and an echo invites me to escape!"

Khalil Hawi, *The Prisoner*

Everywhere the grass is ravishing
the earth, its roots penetrating the dark
to fetch it into the green morning
where a wind warm as blood blows
the light gently into summer's mouth.
Shadows shrink towards the sun
and at its zenith the mind
must measure its own mystery
against the passionate flesh.

Published in Honour of Albert-Reiner Glaap

The apple trees are suffering
their June drop: fruit flawed perhaps
aborts, the grassgreen matted finish
beads falling, the rags of wilted
blossoms still attached to them
like crippled wings. In the crotch
of cherry branches tent caterpillars
spin sheets of webbing into layered
transparencies from which they crawl
in languid processions to forage
on young leaves. Silk passage
to the veiled rites of pupation.
Butterflies and moths. A fly catcher
balances on a power line by flip
of tail, surveys the morning's buzz
and hum, then tumbles to a swift dive
to reave bug or beetle from the air.

This is the month Hermes rules,
god of thieves and merchants,
messenger of the gods:
what's the news on high?

The rich are robbing you blind
because there's more money
in bullets than in bread
and they've turned the rains now
into vinegar at the stock market
so they can trade the blue
right out of the sky before you
can paint it the colour of blood.
Tell every broker
the stars are not
for sale. Ask them:

where shall the birds fly
after the final sky?

Arid and breathless, Mercury runs
ellipses round the sun, hugging
its orbit so close that lead melts
at the height of day while its one night
a year is cold enough to liquefy air.
For aeons the heavens cratered
the first planet, each asteroid strike
gouging its face till it was battered
into another lunar wasteland.
But for the relentless wind and the grinding waters

but for the frost's crowbar and the crunch of continents,
but for the laser sun and the solvents of life,
the metamorphosis of trees and the slow flameless fire
        in the guts of beasts,
        our blue planet too
        would stare at space
        with the empty eyes
        and the savaged face
        of a violent past
        recording a billion-year
        bombardment, the brutal
        expression of a sky
        forever bent on catastrophe.
        The universe conceals
        its chaos from us
        by strategies it programs
        into our retina, turning
        nuclear holocausts
        into ceremonies of gods
        and music, mathematics
        and colour—until once more
        a meteor strikes
        and buries life's
        most daring travellers
        in a millennium of winters.

Summer solstice is close enough
now for a hatching of ant eggs.
Already the devil's paintbrush
is putting orange touches
to the blue air, and black
leaf beetle larvae are gnawing
away the underside of cottonwood
leaves till only the skeletons
of veins are left trembling
on this young season's breath.
        And I am condemned to wander
        through these woods and fields
        backpacking the skeletons
        of my childhood. Between
        buttercups brimful with golden
        light and the plaintive call
        of catbirds, over the reed-bending
        pond, behind the secretive gestures

of trees, memories hover in search
of a resting-place.

The smell of burning cities, burning flesh
overpowers the pine-scented breeze. I smell fear
and in among aspen leaves I see glittering
stains, always in pairs, small discs shimmering
ovals of light … glasses spectacles frames twisted
pince-nez entangled a whole mound of eye-glasses
shattered and askew reflecting a cracked sun eyeless
burning holes in cedar shadows where eyes running over
with pain and terror—whole galaxies of frightened
eyes glow like foxfire in a cankered world.

> Behind a Bach concert
> in the mind's crimped folds
> an evil magic flips
> the familiar into a flush
> of horror, turning each wood
> stand muscular with beeches
> into Buchenwald, recalling
> the victims in the bluejay's
> screeches, and conjuring up
> a whole summer full of death
> camps for boys and girls.

I hear the howls of men and women
hung from dislocated limbs, swinging
jerking in their sockets I hear shots
bullets thud screaming into flesh
scrupulous not to kill too soon:

> Stand to attention,
> **Schweinehunde**!
> That's what happens
> when you displease
> authority power
> pride with your con-
> duct your convictions
> your frailties your genes.
> Sing, **Judenlümmel**!
> Sing for your life!
> All we want is your
> watches your gold
> teeth your dignity.

Wir werden weitermarschieren …

> Is it true is it true

that we'll march on and on …
bis alles in Scherben fällt …
till all the world lies in ruins
… **und morgen die ganze Welt**
till you and I
are but a charcoal impression
in a future rock formation?

Where do the twisted trees of hatred grow?
In what polluted soil of the heart?
Is it the acid rain of injustice,
the lethal monoxides of fear
or the pesticides of greed
that nurture them?

Does someone else's pain
teach no lessons? What
about your own?

My memories roar with the fire
storms of Hamburg and Dresden,
linger acrid in the smouldering ruins,
of Leningrad and Stalingrad, smell
the macabre sweetness of the smoke
over Birkenau and Belsen—
and now smoke billows over the cities of the Levant:

O Sidon, jewel of Phoenician cities,
you traded the treasures of the earth
and of the sea, your bazaars bargained
for the envy of kings and queens
farther back than Babylon. Homer
sang the praises of your artisans—
but he knew wealth and beauty
are the undoing of men and women
cities and empires: something
craves to destroy what it cannot
possess. You were laid to ashes
by the Philistines and reborn
from the same stone, turned to ruins
by Mongols and by Moslems rebuilt
you were ruled ravaged and restored
by Assyrians Persians Egyptians
Romans Arabs Franks and Ottomans
in the ceaseless tides of history
till now your ancient walls
must endure once more
fire and force of invaders.

Not to dust do we turn
but to ashes. Everything
will burn to ashes.
Everything is born from ashes,
even the inconceivable void
after the final sky.
In another thirty-five sun years
the earth will be a sea
of boiling lava, as our star
burns up its last hydrogen
preparing for the helium flash
that will light the slow fuse
of the final solar pyrotechnics
leaving it a white dwarf
blazing inexorably to cinders.

So the heart is
a fire the sun
ignites in the dark
of carbohydrate tempests
burning us up
in all the colours
the spectrum can mix
between a blinding red
giant and a fugitive
black hole. Solar
flames became flesh
became song in the blood
crucible where life
is freed from slag
and dross to be cast
in the delicate shapes
and patterns of dances,
images, words. Time
in its round-the-clock
laboratory distilled
amino acids into algae,
arthropods, chordates
and worms, each burning
to consume other fires
or be consumed by them
in the advance of flames—
fish, insects, reptiles,
birds and mammals, till
neurons fired in the flesh

its one saving grace: love—
and survival became a ceremony
not a victory:

I love
therefore I am
human.

At summer solstice we used to celebrate
life's pyrotechnics with fireworks of our own:
a giant wheel was rolled flaming into the river
and the night exploded with seedballs of red
shooting-stars and golden rainstorms raging
over song-laden boats and our harmonica
and bonfire hearts dancing garlands of flowers
into a sweeter future. But the cross
that crooked its arms at right angles through
a circle of blood was flexing the muscles
of a reptilian brain crazed and craving
to devour books, cities, innocence and people.
Our summer games turned into gore and thuggery.

At the edge of the pond
a nymph is stretched out
waiting for the sun
to crack its exoskeleton
so that from its thorax
a white-tailed dragonfly
may emerge. Antlions dig
circles in fine-grained soil,
salivate their cocoon snare
at the bottom of the pit
and wait with their poison
to paralyze their prey.
A solitary bee clambers
between pistil and stamen
of a bittersweet, making
its purpleblue petals tremble
softly as the thin sibilance
of mosquitoes drills holes
into the morning for the past
to rush in like a horde of harpies.

Where were you
when they smashed babies
against tree trunks?

I was looking for my childhood

Published in Honour of Albert-Reiner Glaap

when they kicked Jews and Gipsies
       I was playing hide-and-seek
trampled Marxists and homosexuals
       I was going to be a fireman
till every bone snapped and dreams
ran with blood from mouths noses sex ...
       I was learning history
       and sums:

              Multiply the number
              of blind people by
              the number of savages
              and divide by the number
              of innocents: how many
              million corpses do you get?
              The answer is something
              to the power of the power ...

We were Winnitou and Old Shatterhand
when **SS-Scharführer Sommer**
hung young **Untermenschen**
testicles in boiling water
before tightening the cramp
iron to crack the brain pan.

       O Haupt voll Blut und Wunden ...

       Suffering has no season
       and bears no fruit.

Where were you?
       I was discovering Bach
       and wet dreams.

Where was I?
       I was memorizing verbs dates poems:
       amo amas amat amamus ...
       1918 ... 1933 ... 1939 ... **Wer,**
       wenn ich schriee, hörte mich denn ... ?

There were no angels winging goodwill
no omniscient gods watching
SS-Oberscharführer Moll line up
women naked by a pit of fire
to target-practice at the bull's eye
the dark triangle of hair:
he had all the angles covered
with blood ...

What if
I had known?
Would I be here
to bear witness
to the pain
and the shame?

> Lost in the scorched
> and toppled streets
> I was stumbling through
> the ruins of my own
> city not knowing what
> I was looking for what
> I didn't know I was
> looking for
> home.

Home? What home is there
for the eternal wanderer
but a long, dreamless sleep?

> Home is here now
> where memories can get lost
> between summer and northern
> lights, between the shrill
> flight of geese and blackfly-
> infested muskegs, between
> lashes of snow and the warm
> embrace of the Chinook. Here
> you can always find a child-
> hood or two by the shore
> of a lake or on a prairie
> farm a continent and a half
> away from the scene
> of your nightmares.

> Go easy, heart,
> on the sleep of prisoners.
> The past is a cage
> full of pain
> and pitfalls.
> At different times
> different guards
> have the same mugs,
> the same skulls
> in different places
> wear the same masks
> we call faces.

I recognize them
in the censored newsreels
from Chile and Chicago,
Capetown and Kabul,
Seoul, Moscow and Tel Aviv.
Behind them I see the barbed
wire fences that have become
city limits for refugees,
their faces no-man's land
between exile and existence
in the suburbs of history.

O Tyre, mistress of the Mediterranean,
whose thin-spun silk once limned
the pleasures of Cleopatra—you
withstood Shalmanser and Nebuchadnezzar.
You're at the mercy now of those
who have no mercy: they found the pretext
they were seeking to rape you.

Gun barrels roar against
the innocent once more
to exalt a general's ego,
once more tanks thunder
through the cash registers
of arms manufacturers,
crushing the hands
of peasants wresting a home
from the recalcitrant land,
and once more planes
disembowel cities, tearing out
streets, gutting homes, blast-
ing whole families to hell
to swell the bosoms of god's
chosen, the Swiss accounts
of wheelers and dealers
relaxing before breakfast
in a warm bloodbath:

Tyre, Sidon, Damur, Beirut—
the peace of Galilee
is a web of lies. Black
smoke sears and surges
as once above Warsaw
and Cologne—a warning signal
to the heavens that on this planet
we burn all that is human

in the crematoriums
of our messianic fantasies.
Ashes, ashes everywhere.

> Does it matter
> when everything
> is burning
> to ashes, when
> even matter itself is mortal?

Each proton decays
into an anti-electron
seeking to encounter
an electron jointly
to vanish without
a trace in a burst
of gamma rays.

> What place the heart
> where you and I add up
> to zero? What of the mind
> when all the possible worlds
> have run round two or three
> dozen zeros till there is
> nothing left but nothing?

Lend me your ears, fearful
captive reader, I can smell you
as far back as the primal soup,
even under the rain of ashes
drifting through this maple
and spruce forest, even
with my senses mad. I want you
to listen to the sunlight
stalking shadows on moccasined feet
and to the grass converting dung
into blossoms. Watch the bright
pink pouches of the lady's slipper
rise from acid bogs to lure the bumblebee
to push apart the veined lips and enter into
the ancient trade of nectar for pollen.
Insects make the world burst into flower:
the whole spectacle of colours
and the raptures of scent are but to entice
and seduce them—an arabesque of the senses
to embellish survival strategies,
a Bach fugue chasing its own flight
in the cave dwellings of the heart.

This is the month Franklin
perished in the ice
on his passage northwest
where even the wind came
black and ravenous
to the frozen camp
to lick their bones clean.
It is the month Kafka
died, begging his friend
to burn the record
of his nightmare journeys.
They braved the void
and found an end
in their travels.

Energy creates worlds from nothing
in the emptiness which makes movement
possible: space is an invitation to move
to keep a rendezvous with time.
Electrons flashing erratically
at 600 m.p.s. about their core
make stone endure and timber hold,
unleash the wind against mountains
and cast whole continents into the sea,
temper the stars into distances
and enforce a cold and eerie silence
upon a lunar night. They excite
the cell to divide symmetrically,
wrap the velvet flesh around their own
contrivances of blood and bone,
and stir the mind to music and murder.

In the molecular dance of the universe
the hall too dances and the floor spins,
yet we are the dancing-masters
of our destiny.

We are
what we do
with what we are.

Put your ear to the ground
and check your pulse against
the earth's dark heart. Summer
is an invitation to lie naked
in the grass and let the green
fingers of the sun brush all
sorrow from your flesh. The wild

irises unfurl their blue
flags and ants climb through
hedge bindweed into the morning
glories trumpeting the golden
silence of approaching noon into thickets
where deep in the weeds a song
sparrow broods speckled eggs
on a moss-lined nest while its mate
chirps and trills as sprightly
as the light is long.

      A flute, a badinerie,
      a Bach suite—moment
      of sheer joy dancing
      through the open window
      of an improbable

world where at any time
jet fighter planes thousands
of miles away can scream
into your eyes and scare up
memories thousands of years
back in your own childhood:

      Searchlights—bony fingers
      combing the night sky,
      skeletal hands plucking enemy
      planes from a black drone,
      basements sandbagged, stifling
      with the smell of urine and fear,
      air raid shelters, astringent
      taste of damp grit, the short bark
      of anti-aircraft guns, the swift
      downscale glissando of the bomb
      that missed you, and after a heart-
      stopping hesitation the fortissimo
      reaffirmation of your existence
      breaking every window cracking
      every wall for blocks, detonations
      with enough decibels to rupture
      your eardrums and decades later
      still devastate your cochlea.
      The awesome silence that follows
      is ashen, whimpering and sobbing
      with plaster in their hair
      mothers age in seconds, their
      children big-eyed, torn between

terror and adventure, choking
on cement dust and
the incomprehensible
madness of this man-
made apocalypse.

I have been there
and come back.
I have seen
the children
the bombs
didn't miss:

a bundle of bandages wound
immaculately like a fresh mummy
with a single slot for the mouth
where the nurse slips in
the bottle to feed
the napalm-fried infant.

Or the nine-year-old, shredded
by a cluster bomb, both legs
and testicles blown off, looking
at night for his itching feet.

Atura hal junna hissi?
Are my senses mad?

The harpsichord is lost now
in the woodlands of Glengarry
the last chord skimming silver-footed
across a stagnant pond. A flicker
chiselling rapid-fire a dead elm
is gentler than the images
drilling into my heart's core.

A twelve-year-old, skull
and spine broken under the rubble
of her home, her left ear black
and silent, her left eye blind
with blood, her damaged brain dreaming
of life as a ballerina.

Huda, Ahmad, Wafa—
why is it my childhood
memories have Arab names?

Sometimes there are pictures
from Lebanon that bear
names from my childhood:
Klaus, Inge, Lech, Kasis, Mordecai—

You cannot hear me
though I testify
on your behalf.

I heard the general declare: "Why should we
distinguish between civilians
and soldiers? No one can teach us
to be human."—Who said that?

      Heinrich, Jarek, Menachem?
      How to distinguish
      yesterday from today
      when no lessons are learnt?

Suffering is not a function
of numbers, but of pain.

      Is this defenseless city
      Warsaw or Beirut?
      Bombed and shelled
      into a lunar wasteland,
      climax to a **Blitzkrieg**
      against the unarmed,
      last act of the **Götterdämmerung**
      of some deluded **Herrenvolk.**

Joshua fought the battle of Jericho
and the walls came tumbling down.

      Carthago delenda est.

Wir werden ihre Städte ausradieren!

      Is this a true audit
      of history, certified
      by the chartered accountants
      of our aspirations? I know
      the generals ordering food
      and water supplies cut off
      are the same who own shares
      in arms and munitions, but
      are the soldiers the patients
      in the hospitals they shell,
      the teachers in the schools
      they burn? The same puppets
      pulled by the same strings
      of money, slogans and pride
      in this global village theatre
      of profit and loss? Listen:

Of the cities of these people
thou shalt save alive nothing
that breathes: thou shalt
utterly destroy them!

Thus spake Yahweh
in a testament that is holy
only to a species surrendering
any claim to the future.

The cockroach can survive
without mythologies
levels of radiation
that will exterminate us.

Are we to be
executioners
merely
of arithmetic
sentences
the cosmos passes
on all and sundry
predictably
at random?
Marionettes,
you and I,
in a nuclear theatre,
blocked by forces
weak and strong,
gravity and
electromagnetic waves,
destined for the scrapheap
of a preposterous history?
All of us victims
of our own mythologies?

Every child is a future
where a man or a woman
can be free and equal.
Chosen people make terror
reasonable and love
impossible.

Confined to chance
orbits halfway
to the stars
you and I are charged
with self-perpetuating,

like electrons circling
hectically the dead
centre of life, moving
in the emptiness only
an embrace can endure.

In the mountains of the Lebanon
where rivers once fierce have cut
deep valleys tortured to the sea
I hear six-year-old Bandali sing:

Give me back my laughter
give me back my doll
give me back my childhood
give me back my home.

Her childish voice echoes inside me
louder than the banging and bellowing of war.
It carries the burden of its elegy on the back
of pastured slopes, drifts down meandering
streams, lingers in olive orchards or over
the aromatic elegance of cypress trees,
a song looking for deliverance in sacred
groves where a gentler god once raised cedars
majestic from the ground to stand arms out-
stretched to bless the beauty of this land.

Can a jet-fighter pilot
on a supersonic reconnaissance
mission hear the song or
identify the cedars,
smell the eucalyptus?

Our humanity is
an inverse function
of the speed
at which we pass
each other.

The train's whistle sounds wild
and doleful across the apple trees,
like the howl of a wolf desperate
to be heard in another dimension.
It hurtles towards noon oblivious
of the colonies of wild blue phlox
bending to the pressure wave,
of the squirrels mating in the pine
and the tachinid fly that oviposits
behind the head of a caterpillar,

its larvae parasites destined to devour
their host. Again and again the train
howls shuttling drowsy travellers
between a handful of cities spared
the sound of bombs except in the sleep
of those who cannot forget or forgive—

while across an ocean and a half the Hasbani
still carries the last stars downstream,
and grey-haired Mt. Hermon, **Jabal al-shaykh**,
looks eastward waiting for Castor and Pollux
to fetch dawn shivering from faraway deserts.
Westward in the direction of the sea
the night is bleeding into dark
valleys beneath a horizon on fire.

How can you tell
one burning image
from another through
the prism of your tears?
The Warsaw ghetto or
a Palestinian refugee camp?
Photos from a doomsday book:

/ *a group of women, an old man,*
children, their arms raised
in surrender to the uniforms of
gun-toting terror, in their midst
a small girl stunned in her mothers
skirt, a muskrat paralyzed with fear
in a steel trap /

/ *teachers, scientists, artists*
blindfolded, roped together like
camels, stumbling through ruins:
"all of a sudden they are
a bunch of nothings"
the victors' caption reads /

/ *a mother lifts*
her dead child
bloodspattered
to high heaven
with a piercing
wail that should
move the stars/

Is this the way the world ends
—in Warsaw and Treblinka

in a blaze of firestorms and furnaces
incinerating all that is gentle and good
—in Sabra and Shatila
in the glare of magnesium flares
lighting up the night officially
for a massacre of innocents?

> **Atura hal junna hissi?**
> I hear the poet sing
> Khalil's pain I hear
> the shot ring out the shame
> Khalil's pride I hear
> the bullet sever the song
> from the blood of Khalil
> who would not sing
> after the fall of the city
> had driven his senses mad.

Where shall the birds fly
after the final sky?

> Onehundredandsixtythreethousand
> light years ago in the Large
> Magellanic Cloud a giant star
> collapsed under its own gravity
> until its iron core caught
> fire and blew apart, ejecting
> its elements into space
> with enough energy to incinerate
> any nearby solar system
> and seed new ones farther away.
> Among stars birth is
> like death a cataclysm
> without survivors. Only
> onehundredandsixtythreethousand
> light years away is a supernova
> a spectacle to delight the awed
> mind on the threshold of madness.

I lie in the moist grass trying
to banish the ghosts of yesteryear
from the dishevelled circle of clouds
where even a friendly face drifts
too lightly into a grimace. Down
here the grotesque air is green
and the earth's dampness cools
the troubled shades. A spittlebug nymph
is drinking alfalfa upside down

from a plant stalk, converting sap
into a froth cocoon. It has no receptors
for the rush of music skipping
with measured step between blades of grass
and round wildflower stems, impetuous
as some long-repressed need for joy
and affirmation, bursts of strings and brass
chasing each other through baroque tangles
of underbrush till they drop out of hearing
in the somber corridors of the bush.
Are the bees dancing to Bach
among the clover—or is it only
my thoughts, my fancy, this summer
saraband in an alien land?

      A swarm of redpolls puts some colour
      in the hemlock tree. I hoist myself
      into the tall day, leaning on their chatter,
      and scare up a groundhog. Stretched high
      on its hindlegs, it eyes me, rigid
      as a taxidermist's pose, except it cannot
      stop munching. Fat and devious
      it devours the sprouts of peas,
      beans, spinach, the whole gourd family
      buds …—Rage explodes in the dark
      and convoluted spaces of my skull
      and hurls murder into my eyes …
      I take aim, my index finger crooks
      for a trigger —

Is this the passion
that turns Ariel
into a butcher
and makes a mockery
of every Bach chorale?
The alien intruder
threatening our dreams?

      In days of fear gods bless night
      and bombs. In the territories
      of fear an eye calls
      for an eye and the clenched fist
      promises peace and money
      is the measure of our love.

   But you cannot buy the stars
   and if you sell a brother or sister
   you have invested in a holocaust.

The world's battlefields are quagmires
of blood and guts that have sucked
heroes and cowards alike to their foul
deaths, the naive and the fanatic
perishing with their pain in the torture
chambers of history as nations, races
and religions take turns at being victims
and victimizers in orgies of slaughter
and sacrifice madmen organize
to maintain the privileges
of those who have not
earned them.

    Russians Germans Arabs
    and Jews, Christians
    Muslims Fascists—
    all labels tell you
    is the disease:

        xenophobic epilepsy
        ideological elephantiasis
        messianic carcinoma
        the master-race syndrome ...

    Can the sun
    can anything
    save us
    cure us
    from ourselves?

June is the month that lights up
the north from horizon to horizon
stretching the days more than halfway
around the globe, growing galaxies
in the leaves of every tree, hatching
schools of sun in every ocean breaker,
placing a sun on the wing of every bird
and insect, the tip of every reed
and grass, in the belly of every drop
of rain and in the hearts of all
who flounder between fear and fulfillment.

    Skeletons under the skull
    dance in darkness and reach
    for light in the retina.
    I come away with
    only an eye full
    of images:

> *the three-year-old*
> *with her throat cut,*
> *the castrated boy,*
> *women raped, piles*
> *of mutilated bodies,*
> *a bulldozer manoeuvering*
> *with shovel full of corpses*
> *starved till the parched skin*
> *could barely hold the knobbed*
> *bones, harrowed till the mind*
> *could no longer endure living*
> *the pain the living pain of*
> *dying the pain the stars*
> *cannot know the pain ...*

This pain too, like all we know,
joins the procession of memories
that move peristaltically
in the pilgrimage of San Isidro
Goya painted in the Quinta del Sordo
across the scorched landscape of this age.
Enterrar y callar. I cannot
bury them and be silent. I hear
the voices, the endless march
of prisoners and victims—
victims of war, prisoners of lies,
victims of conscience, prisoners
of fear: they drag the chains
of grief and guilt down the blood
tracks across the sands of this century.

> **No business like shoah business.**
> **Shoah business is no business.**

A carnival parade led by the king of fools
surrounded by blind musicians and pious
time servers: they award the peace prize
to a terrorist on a float of booby-traps.
The banner reads: ONLY VIOLENCE CAN PUT AN END
TO VIOLENCE. Black uniforms goose-step faceless
behind a blond doll carrying a pirate's flag and
repeating in a shrill, mechanical voice:

> black is white
> might is right—
> pick your enemy and fight!
> Have your fill
> make your kill—

war is money in the till!
Better dead
than pink or red—
there's no more to be said!

Para eso habéis nacido.
Is that what we were born for?
A cradle made from barbed wire
and in it the torso of a girl
                    singing:

> *give me back my laughter*
> *give me back my doll*
> *give me back my childhood*
> *give me back my home.*

Tears wash the eyes
but they blur the vision.
They make old wounds
burn without washing
the past off your hands.
You can build a house
on the ruins of someone else's,
but you can find no home there.

        Yesterday's Jew is
        today's Palestinian.

                Every refugee camp
                cries out bears witness
                against us—in Pakistan,
                Sri Lanka, Vietnam, Chile
                and Honduras, in Mozambique,
                Namibia and the Sudan,
                in Jordan and Lebanon—
                we've driven millions
                from their homes into
                a world of camps where
                children die of diarrhea
                and the destitute receive
                their dignity as handouts
                in shantytowns. The dream
                of universal brotherhood
                lies shattered in tin can
                shacks and cardboard tents.
                History is wasted
                on a people who survive
                only to inflict their own

persecutions on others
in a single generation.

Not that you fiddle your suffering
from every rooftop makes you human
but that you bury vengeance
in the barbaric caves of your heart.

Beirut is burning.
Palestine's people
are on the move again
looking for home.
Where shall the birds fly
after the final sky?

A dream is burning to the ground
and from the ashes rises the raven
of separation to pitch its caws
across the river where Tammuz' blood
flows still through the valleys of Hasbaya.
The raven flies black and shrill
through fig orchards and pomegranate groves,
its shrieks sharp knives to stab the hearts
of mourners weeping and wailing in red-
roofed villages for the dead who wanted
nothing but a home. Jerusalem, cradle

of three faiths,
and not one gesture
of grace to trade
in Beirut's kidnapping
bazaars against
an innocent victim
or cut the barbed
wire between the two
cities where it's easier
for mountains to meet
than for an eye
to encounter an eye
without shame.

Your shame is my shame
and my shame is your shame.

Reflected ghostly in the window
my eyes stare me in the face,
burning with the shame of being
human. A feisty crow freefalls
from the top of the spruce tree,

a bold black slash across my mouth.
It banks against the cedar-shingled
roof with a scream alarming enough
to scare away the plaintiffs from
my childhood, and plunges headlong
into the bush vanishing between
wildly staggered soft-edged planes
of green and grey on wings wafting
calmly like large pine branches
awash with shade and silence.

       And suddenly the light is
       as golden as the many yellows
       into which van Gogh painted
       his sitters, his flowers,
       his fields. A flock of evening
       grosbeaks flutters into maple trees,
       their white tertiaries flashing
       as they dance from branch to branch
       agitated by a music I cannot hear.
       Perhaps the spheres sing for them
       to make a midsummernight's dream
       come true. A rabbit sits erect
       and scoops up a tall earful
       of this hour's hums and whirs
       whispers rustles and cracks
       trills plashes sighs clicks
       guggles smacks purls and swishes—

Who could've dreamt the bang
that rent a vacuum and smashed
eternal darkness into spacetime
would ever cool down to the temper
of so faint and fragile a music
as orchestrates the balletomania of life.
Who could've dreamt the many worlds
compressed into a sphere of quarks
less than a billionth of an attosecond
old and no bigger than a Mackintosh apple,
a mere bite from which would've contained
all the galaxies and stars, all the nebulae,
gases, quasars and black holes, travelling
time immemorial at the speed of an explosion
away from a centre so small it would've fitted
in the palm of your hand. Who could've dreamt
the sun, the moon and our bluegreen planet

in that dense bubble of catastrophic patterns
of energy—the potential for every possible
reality, including you and me, our struggles,
whether won, lost or ever engaged in, all that
we might have been and will never be, all
the journeys we might have taken plus the one
we do complete, all that packed into one
Hot Big Bang the size of a baseball
that threw billions of universes curved
across billions of light years of space.

> Farewell, unquiet memories,
> the shadows are too slim now
> to sustain you. The sun
> in its zenith lights up
> an inner eye. June is
> the month John Cabot first
> caught sight of this old
> continent, dreaming of jewels,
> spices and gold, aboard a ship
> no larger than a human heart
> and crammed full of worlds
> and dreams wanting to explode
> and hurl galaxies of joy
> into the dark and brutal spaces
> between persecution and war,
> new worlds not waiting for
> discoverers but for creators
> inspired by the possibilities
> of light. Only gods
> can afford to make
> an ass of love.

I emerge from the chrysalis of memory
to reach out across half a century
to touch you, my unknown friend,
and your pain in the camps of death.
And I stretch my hands to reach across
an ocean and a sea to beat the durbakki
drums alongside a young man in a refugee camp
in the mountains of the Levant. Together
we strike up the dabka dance, ancient circle
of lives more enduring than the walls
of cities or the cruel arts of invaders.

> Goldfinches flit through thorn bushes.
> Deep in the forest calypso orchids

bloom magenta, their clusters of stamen
tiny bursts of sunlight in the cool shade.
A pair of sulphur butterflies spiral up
and down about each other, rising higher
and higher till they're dancing on tree tops
and the male abruptly plumps down swift
and bright as a meteor, followed by
the fluttering caprice of the female,
a lotus blossom floating down to her
palpitating mate in the low creeping
grass where a killdeer drags its unbroken
wing with cries of alarm theatrically
away from its nest from its young from
its dupe till it is safe to break free.

Up north in the Truelove Lowlands
on Devon Island musk oxen shed their underfur
among the emerging bluegrass, foxtail and willow
herbs; they stand their desolate frozen ground
against men and wolves shoulder to shoulder
in a dark rosette—a primordial circle
that has kept ice ages and predators at bay.

Rudolf Bader

AN ATTEMPTED FAREWELL
TO UNQUIET MEMORIES

A shattering explosion of words, *"Where Shall the Birds Fly?"* is an awe-inspiring testimony from Henry Beissel's pen. Through the medium of this poem, Beissel, a German-born Canadian poet, playwright, translator, travel-writer and university professor, reveals himself as a true citizen of the world in this century. The elegy is the fourth in a set of twelve projected poems. As part of an entire cycle attempting to take stock of the human condition in various and varying contexts, it takes up a number of themes and poetic patterns already employed in the preceding three elegies.

The first three elegies of the cycle, *"The Ides of March," "April Fools"* and *"May Song and Dance,"* were published in one volume entitled *Season of Blood, a suite of poems* (Oakville: Mosaic Press, 1984). As these titles indicate, each elegy takes one month of the year as an initial focal point and as a general level of reference. *Elegy IV*, accordingly, refers to the month of June.

If we are looking for general themes and patterns carried over from the preceding three elegies, we are first struck by a prevailing sense of duty in the face of human accountability. Can man really grasp the bare essentials of the universe? Do not a great many experiences in the twentieth century point to latent dangers even within seemingly safe concepts of the human situation, sinister threats, unrecognized and perhaps invisible despite their proximity, as the Ides of March were for proud Caesar? Does not the contrast between such threats and dangers to our civilization on the one hand and our scientific claims and cynical self-confidence in our endeavour to understand and explain the universe on the other hand turn us into April fools? All too often in modern history, it appears, our optimistic concepts of human progress, of fertility as symbolized by the season of spring, have been overshadowed by the shocking and sobering experience of violence and destruction, and our May songs and dances have turned into dirges and death rituals. Thus, behind every summer sky, there lurks a catastrophe: "The universe conceals / its chaos from us / by strategies it programs / into our retina [...]" (95).

This view implies a deconstruction of what has traditionally been considered to be the connotations of the adjective "human." As seen through the lens of Beissel's four elegies to date, "human" conveys much more than the state of belonging to the species of **homo sapiens** and possibly being invested with feelings of compassion and a series of altogether pardonable weaknesses: it is turned into a term denoting membership of a highly questionable, selfish, cynical and cruel species, full of the most atrocious potential, violent, perverted and treacherous, yet fully responsible for all the deeds committed because of human intelligence and the human capacity for scientific and artistic achievement. What can our mythologies do for us? What is our task within the cosmos? As Beissel suggestively asks: "Are we to be / executioners / merely / of arithmetic / sentences / the cosmos passes / on all and sundry / predictably / at random?" (108) We are the most outrageous danger not only for creation, but even for ourselves: "Can the sun / can anything / save us / cure us / from ourselves?" (113)

Considering the structural aspects of composition, we can find that this elegy takes over the poetic form of the first three elegies and refines them in the process. Whereas elegies one, two and three were structured in terms of alternating paragraphs or stanzas establishing a sort of dialogue, this elegy increases the number of participants engaged in conversation, as it were, from two to four (marked by four levels of indention alternating at random from paragraph to paragraph). Except for the absence of names of speakers (or theatrical parts), this form invests the poem with a dramatic quality. This effect is enhanced by occasional interjections in other languages, for example German or Latin. Thematically, the text follows what could be called a progression by association, each idea presented immediately leading to another, quite across distances in place and time. This method can be observed at work in several of the quotations to be dealt with in different contexts presently. The last formal aspect worth mentioning in this context is certainly the overall appeal created by the traditional use of the human senses; not only the visual but also other senses, especially smell and hearing, are being appealed to (e.g. 96).

Let us now examine *Elegy IV* more closely: its tone and mood, its wide scope of poetic vision and its thematic preoccupations.

Tone and mood may be found to draw from the elegiac but to transcend it at the same time. The elegiac mood of regret, traditionally looking back in time, is turned towards the future, and our destiny as humans is explored: "Not to dust do we turn / but to ashes. Everything / will burn to ashes." (98) This sets the poet off into further explorations of images connected with ashes, philosophizing by juxtaposition: heat, fire, ignition. The apocalyptic vision seems inevitable: "In another thirty-five sun years / the earth will be a sea / of boiling lava [...]" (98). But then, our commonly accepted concept of history is hardly less bleak:

I was learning history
and sums:

Multiply the number
of blind people by
the number of savages
and divide by the number
of innocents: how many

million corpses do you get?
The answer is something
to the power of the power ... (100)

Dealing with such horrible aspects of humanity at a purely mathematical level is too callous: "Suffering is not a function / of numbers, but of pain." (107) By bringing the horrors down to the level of empathy also implied in the "human," we realize not only the callousness and cynicism but also the arbitrariness of a purely mathematical account of history and thus of the universe, for, after all, "Yesterday's Jew is / today's Palestinian." (115)

The most originally elegiac mood is evoked in the passages expressing eternal sadness and a recurring sense of frustration implied already in the title question. This question, asked in full, "Where shall the birds fly / after the final sky?" three times through the poem (94, 111, 116), takes up the post-apocalyptic vision conjured up elsewhere in the poem and, by means of confrontation, cuts down any grand hopes for eternity: humanity is being confronted with the inevitable, the flight of the human mind is limited to the scope defined by astrophysics. Our choice lies within the scope defined by ourselves, which in turn is defined by our sense of responsibility based on empathy and love: "Does someone else's pain / teach no lessons? What / about your own?" (97) This, the poetic voice implies, is the true meaning of history. Hope lies only where there is love: "I love / therefore I am / human." (99) Love emerges as the **conditio sine qua non** for humanity. "Only gods / can afford to make / an ass of love." (118)

Another image associated with the elegiac mood and evoked in this poem is that of the wanderer. This is stated quite plainly: "And I am condemned to wander / through these woods and fields / backpacking the skeletons / of my childhood." (95) The two most obvious aspects of this state are the ever-increasing burden carried along and a longing for some haven or home. The burden, in this case, is a backpack full of memories, initially memories from childhood, but as we continue on our path through time, additionally laden with adult experience and with lessons learnt from history. Thus, any news of fresh horrors can remind us of these lessons and add to the burden, for example "[...] at any time / jet fighter planes thousands / of miles away can scream / into your eyes and scare up / memories thousands of years / back in your own childhood:" (105) each individual childhood as well as the infancy of humanity. The longing for home, in this case, is futile: "Home? What home is there / for the eternal wanderer / but a long, dreamless sleep?" (101) So the endeavour of the poetic voice to hail farewell to these "unquiet memories" (118) is doomed from the outset. We can never set ourselves free from memories, neither from our individual ones nor from the ones shared by the whole of humanity. We can only hope to come to some sort of peace of mind through commonly accepted terms.

The most ambitious aspect of this poem is certainly its wide scope. It is not merely about a certain part of human experience but simply about the entire creation: the universe, the cosmos; and it probes into this cosmos from different angles and in different dimensions, against which the position of humanity is being measured. In the beginning, physics reign supreme: "Energy creates worlds from nothing / in the emptiness which makes movement / possible: space is an invitation to move / to keep a rendezvous with time." (104) And indeed, the entire text teems with terms and technical expressions from the domain of astrophysics (e.g. 111, 117-118), light years, gravity, elements, space, solar systems, stars, energy, the Big Bang, orbits, aeons, planets, asteroids and such set the pace of the largest dimension. Gradually, terrestrial dimensions come into focus: the crunch of continents, carbohydrate tempests and some sort of lunar wasteland. Only in the next smaller dimension there is a trace of human activity: the history of violence: "The smell of burning cities, burning flesh / overpowers the pine-scented breeze." (96) And, more specifically, there are the memories of the fire storms of the Second World War and of more recent armed conflicts in this world, particularly in the Middle East, and everywhere violence is veiled behind masks that we call faces:

> I recognize them
> in the censored newsreels
> from Chile and Chicago,
> Capetown and Kabul,
> Seoul, Moscow and Tel Aviv.
> Behind them I see the barbed
> wire fences that have become
> city limits for refugees,
> their faces no-man's land
> between exile and existence
> in the suburbs of history. (102)

The history of mankind on this planet is most clearly marked by acts of cruelty and violence. But it is also a history of frustrated endeavour, particularly for those who were trying to accomplish some good deed for the material or spiritual benefit of humanity: explorers, inventors, peace-makers, artists and writers. The poem mentions Franklin, who perished with his expedition in search of the North West Passage between Canada and the polar ice cap. Kafka is mentioned almost in the same breath, the writer who believed in the futility of his writing in the face of the world's nightmares. Both Franklin and Kafka: "They braved the void / and found an end / in their travels." (104) The poetic voice then arrives at the refugee camps around the globe in more recent decades, touching on Pakistan, Sri Lanka, Vietnam, Chile, Honduras, Mozambique, Namibia, Sudan, Jordan and Lebanon (115): this is the result of the scope given to human activity.

Elegy IV, within its wide scope, is preoccupied with a few thematic clusters that recur through the text like leitmotifs. The thematic starting point, as mentioned before, is the month of June with its associations: midsummer night, the longest day of the year, heat of the sun, fire, but also "the month Hermes rules, / god of thieves and merchants, / messenger of the gods" (94). Already at the height of summer, however, "the devil's paintbrush / is putting orange touches / to the blue air" (95), already there are foreshadowings of evil and destruction. After all, the source of all life on our planet, the sun, is itself a ball of fire, fire that may create life and that may consume and destroy. But the season of summer evokes more than that, it is also the fulfillment of promises made in spring: "Summer / is an invitation to lie naked / in the grass and let the green / fingers of the sun brush all / sorrow from your flesh." (104) The sensual aspect of summer is less urgent and pressing than two or three months before, it is seemingly pure enjoyment and a carefree pleasure. Naturally, June is felt to be a very special time in arctic Canada, it is "the month that lights up / the north from horizon to horizon" (113), an idea already explored in depth by Henry Beissel in his play, *Inook and the Sun* (1973).

A further thematic preoccupation emerges from the elegiac view of history, particularly the section of twentieth-century history burdening the memory of the poetic voice. This is the enigma, probed into by various German poets and writers of the 1950s in their attempts at **Vergangenheitsbewältigung** ("coming to terms with the past"): How is it possible for one and the same civilization to produce both a Bach and a Hitler? Even perfection has a double-sided face: the perfection of Bach's music is not quite the same as the perfection reached by the Nazis in their crimes against humanity. Thus, the poem contrasts Bach and Buchenwald (96), chronicles some of the most awful atrocities committed in German concentration camps (e.g. "when they smashed babies / against tree trunks," 99) and, by juxtaposition with childhood innocence, establishes an alternative to the common German guilt complex. The idea of fire and burning, associated with summer heat, is connected through its destructive potential with the theme of the Nazi holocaust, when all that was human was burnt "in the crematoriums / of our messianic fantasies." (103) The contrast between cultural achievement (Bach) and cultural shame (Nazi horrors and other violence) runs through the whole poem. Bach as a leitmotif recurs in the shape of various musical genres (103, 105, 112), thus keeping up the contrastive views of human civilization. This contrast culminates in a scene evoked in the poem where teachers, scientists and artists are blindfolded and roped together like camels and the victors' caption reads, *"all of a sudden they are / a bunch of nothings"* (110): violence emerges as some sort of anti-culture.

A third thematic cluster deals with the question of how to come to terms with modern life, which is so much out of joint, full of futility, wars and atrocious violence in spite of numerous positive achievements. Already when Joshua fought the battle of Jericho the walls came tumbling down (107), and our time seems to believe that only violence can put an end to violence (114). What feelings, moods, reactions, conclusions are adequate today? Hatred would be one reaction that lends itself, but how does it really grow (97)? And more dangerously, where does it lead? Would shame be better (101)? The advantage over hatred would be the communal quality of shame: "Your shame is my shame / and my shame is your shame." (116) Even though the exact shade of our feelings is difficult to define, one lesson to be learnt from all this is the recognition of what really counts within an ethical scale of values. "We are /

what we do / with what we are." (104) This means that our achievements must be measured against our possibilities and our full potential: a plea for an individual sense of responsibility. This sense of responsibility, the true touchstone of humanity in the positive sense, grows through compassion and empathy. The more we know about, feel for and suffer for our fellow humans, the more we feel responsible. "Our humanity is / an inverse function / of the speed / at which we pass / each other." (109) If we pass each other too quickly there is but little chance for communal feelings and common responsibility to develop and the "raven of separation" (116) will hold us in its firm claws. This is the central human message of *Elegy IV*.

To round off my short interpretation, I would like to throw a glance at the Canadian content of the poem. Based on the month of June, it naturally draws from the northern experience of the short summer (e.g. 101), which always has an undertone of **carpe diem** in view of the season's brevity. But also a great deal of imagery drawn from natural beauty (e.g. 103, 111, 112) is based on the overwhelming experience of Nature in the Canadian context. And perhaps there is even a Canadian view of the central issue of the cultural enigma (Bach and Hitler): "The harpsichord is lost now / in the woodlands of Glengarry / the last chord skimming silver-footed / across a stagnant pond." (106) In the context of the New World, recurrence to Bach's music, beneficial though it might be, will not be enough. The Old World confidence in traditional cultural achievements as safeguards of unalienable ethical standards has proved altogether too naïve in the twentieth century, so the New World might find new ways out of the human dilemma; at least there is a small flicker of hope. In terms of Henry Beissel's poem, this hope can perhaps most ardently be harboured under the influence of the brief season of summer in the Canadian north.

Michael Cook

THE GREAT HARVEST EXCURSION

Preamble

In the year of Our Lord, 1908, reports of a record harvest on the Prairies triggered a rash of rumour. Speculation, and reports of high wages calculated to excite the interest of those who, from the Maritimes and Ontario, mostly jobless— either temporarily or permanently, rushed to the wheat fields every year to harvest and thresh the multi million dollar crop, the promise of eight to ten weeks work at two fifty an hour being sufficient to tide them, however meagre- ly, over the winter. Whereas a farmer could plant his crop with a minimum of labour, the harvest itself was highly labour intensive, and thousands of part time labourers were needed to get the crop in before the weather turned.

Canadian Pacific (and others) took the men out for ten dollars. To get back, they had to work a minimum of thirty days, and pay eighteen dollars. Others used the cheap excursion trains to take their families, seek land, and settle—an activity much encouraged by the Provinces, Canadian Pacific, and Ottawa. The wheat crop was rapidly becoming the golden road to the country's prosperity.

To many Maritimers, over the years, the annual harvest excursion had become something of a rite of passage—a journey into manhood fuelled by tales as romantic and heroic as any that graced the opening of the Santa Fe and Oregon trails. For others it was a means of escape, from nagging wives, pregnant girlfriends, a chance to whoop it up until the back breaking work got in the way.

But in 1908 something went wrong.

This play is a fiction. But the facts upon which the fiction is based are not.

Cast

Balladeer

Chorus

Ross
Byrne
Hogan
O'Brien
McLintock
Macintosh

Walsh
Miller

Ancient

Manitoba
Sask(atchewan)
Alberta

Ottawa
CP (Canadian Pacific)

Reporters:
Star
Post
Globe

Robert McGregor
Joyce McGregor
Isabel McGregor
Rory McGregor

Conductor

Victoria

Owner

Constable

ACT I, SCENE 1

The stage is bathed in diffused, dusty golden light. The CHORUS, including the ANCIENT, enter, miming, in slow motion, actions connected with the harvest, raking, stooking, threshing, staggering under sacks of grain. On stage, in his own spotlight, is the BALLADEER. For a few moments, until the action is established, he plays the theme of the worksong—and then begins. The action continues behind him.

BALLADEER: For two fifty a day
from dawn until dusk,
we stook the big sheaves,
part the wheat from the husks,
the chaff sits in our lungs,
dust darkens the sky,
and we do this each year,
God only knows why.

Back home in the East
the ocean is wild,
pays no heed to the heartache
of woman or child,
the merchants sleep easy,

the merchants sleep warm,
while we harvest the sea,
in the eye of the storm.

The prairies, like oceans,
pay no heed to man,
we come here to harvest
as much as we can,
our women and children
wait by the wild shore,
for the money we'll sweep
from the grainary floor ...

The CHORUS stop their action. Call and shout to each other. The BALLADEER plays the theme beneath.

ROSS: Jesus—why the hell do we do this?

BYRNE: 'Tis fear, boy, fear. There's no money at home, so we get driven. Right O'Brien?

HOGAN: Why ask him? Animal. He just comes for beer money and the odd fuck he can't get back home.

O'BRIEN lunges at HOGAN who dodges nimbly amongst the CHORUS making faces.

HOGAN: Can't catch me.

O'BRIEN (*Giving up in disgust*): You'd better make sure I don't then.

MCLINTOCK: Christ—I don't know where you guys get the energy. (*Mimes getting a sack of wheat onto his shoulders.*) This is worse than hauling a trap in a gale.

MACINTOSH: Ye can't drown here boy, that's something.

WALSH: Oh aye, ye just chokes to death in the dust, that's all.

BYRNE:There's a lot of ways to die boy, and at least we get paid for this one. That's why you're here, right Hogan?

HOGAN: I want me brains tested.

O'BRIEN: Are ye sure it's not mine?

HOGAN: Fuck you O'Brien—big as you are ...

He tries to get him but is held back.

WALSH: I minds ye told me ye were giving it up fer Lent.

HOGAN: I did boys, I swear it. (*They all laugh.*) I've got six already fer Christ's sake.

MACINTOSH: So—what's one more mouth to feed?

BYRNE: One more mouth to feed.

HOGAN (*Glum*): Must've happened on Shrove Tuesday. Pancakes make her horny ...

General reaction and laughter ... "Pancakes." The light has been fading throughout ... General comment as they prepare to exit. Spot remains on BALLADEER.

CHORUS: Come on boys, lets pack it in now. Its too dark to see.
        Give us a hand with this then.
        Me stomach feels as if me throat's cut.
        What'll she have tonight ye reckon?
        Stew and doughboys, what else?
        Not again.
        What the hell does she put in them doughboys?
        Dust boy, good prairie dust.
        She's a good Christian woman mind.
        That's why she puts dust in the doughboys. 'Tis what ye
        comes from, and 'tis what ye'll return to.
        I doesn't care what it is ... lets get to it ...

They exit, improvising banter ... in the single spotlight the BALLADEER.

BALLADEER: Two fifty a day
        it passes the time,
        we'll soon earn enough
        to go back down the line,
        pay off the damned merchants,
        buy whisky and flour,
        forget the hard labour
        of every damned hour.

ALL: We'll drink whisky and wine
        as the snow settles in,
        tell tales to the youngsters
        of how its not been,
        from the wheat of the prairies
        to the fish of the sea
        we're God's beasts of burden,
        his harvesters, we ...

A short reprise of the air as the spot fades and he exits. A beat. Flaring yellow light. From the flies, assorted posters drop bearing adverts and promotions exhorting the would be harvesters to go west and participate in the excursion.

MANITOBA: Dammit man, they're a month in front of us again.

SASK: What are you talking about?

MANITOBA: They've already begun cutting in Dakota. Half of our local labour will have gone down there.

SASK: I wouldn't worry about it.

MANITOBA: Why not?

ALBERTA: Haven't you heard? The banks have foreclosed on half the share-croppers in the States, and are forcing the unemployed and the immigrants to work for slave wages. (*A chuckle*) Interesting, isn't it?

SASK (*Exploding*): Interesting! Abusing poor devils with fam ...

ALBERTA (*Cutting in*): Your bleeding heart does you credit, Saskatchewan. (*Innocent*) I was just thinking practically, that's all. (*A beat*) You should try it sometimes. (*MANITOBA laughs.*)

OTTAWA (*Aside to CP*): We have an ally in Alberta. (*CP nods.*) Now gentlemen, if I can call this meeting to ... Naturally, I understand your concerns about this year's harvest, they're mine and CP's as well, but I can assure you that you'll get all the labour you need.

MANITOBA: I hope you're right. The wheat farmers are clamouring like crows.

CP: Alright. Just how many bodies do you need?

SASK: My constituents will need thirty thousand CP. I don't know about anyone else.

MANITOBA: Thirty! You can't have that many. Where the hell is that going to leave me.

ALBERTA (*Smug*): I don't need that many—five, maybe six thousand at most.

MANITOBA: It's not you I'm worried about. But last year that moralistic son of a bitch got half our work force by offering them land deals.

SASK: You could have done it.

MANITOBA: The best of my land was gone and you knew it. So's yours. What are you going to bribe 'em with this year—Artic spur lines.

SASK: Good men can make a living anywhere.

ALBERTA laughs out loud.

MANITOBA: And chickens can scratch the ground too. Christ.

ALBERTA (*Still chuckling*): You're a closet capitalist after all Saskatchewan ... I'm impressed.

SASK (*Stung*): DAMN YOU Alberta ... my situation is different AND YOU KNOW IT ...

CP: Gentlemen, gentlemen, please. There is no problem. You want twenty, thirty, forty thousand then I'll ship 'em to you. For most of them two fifty a day and all found is beyond their wildest dreams—it will be an exodus.

OTTAWA: CP has the right attitude. We just have to fill their heads full of dreams and their eyes full of sky and that will do it.

CP: Exactly.

OTTAWA: CP and I will provide the labour, no matter the cost. And by the way Saskatchewan, I've been told by the Prime Minister to ask you to refrain from sending year end reports detailing, ad nauseum, drought, plagues of gophers, frost and the boredom and hardships experienced by the harvesters. They're your problems, he said.

SASK: He said that?

OTTAWA: Would I lie?

SASK: Laurier stayed in Regina. Once. Overnight. In May. What the hell does he know about the Province, or the Prairies for that matter.

OTTAWA (*Modestly*): He has eyes and ears.

SASK (*Incredulous*): You. God help us all.

OTTAWA (*Steely*): Now you listen. If some damned reporter ever got hold of your negative ideas and ran them as a human interest story you'd scare half of the work force away.

SASK: I tell the truth.

OTTAWA: So what the Devil has truth got to with mythology. In any case, as in every great adventure, the truth becomes tinged with a golden glow when the weary wanderers return home, laden with bounty.

CP: Exactly. What is your work force composed of after all but mighty journey-men who leave their sleeping villages, the out harbours, the rain drenched landscape, to risk all for their country.

SASK: We're not fighting a war.

ALBERTA: He has a point. We are fighting—for our prosperity.

OTTAWA: Exactly. The harvesters come to earn money for the winter—and you, and the country rely upon them to ensure our future. Well—shall we deal with the reporters, CP?

CP goes to the reporters to usher them in.

OTTAWA: And as for you (*To SASK*)—remember what I've said, please.

The reporters come forward.

OTTAWA: Good day, Gentlemen. What can we do for you?

STAR: Can you give us the crop projection for this year?

POST: What's the estimated worth of the harvest?

GLOBE: What's the amount in bushels?

STAR: How many excursionists d'you need?

GLOBE: They're saying this is the biggest year on record. Is that true?

POST: How d'you intend to handle it …

OTTAWA: Please gentlemen—please. A moment.

The politicians rise and huddle in a corner. CP holds the reporters back.

CP: Easy boys, patience now. They'll answer all your questions in A MINUTE. It's all there, on the abacus of their fingers, in the teeming fertility of their brains, as fertile as the prairies that raised 'em.

OTTAWA breaks from the rest.

OTTAWA: You see … Well gentlemen, by common consensus, arrived at by studious computations made by our own highly informed agricultural experts, …

REPORTERS: Oh come on now, sir. Our readers are waiting. You don't have to be one hundred per cent right. Just give us what you have. We need facts—now.

OTTAWA: Quite right sirs, and you'll get them. But don't forget—and this is important, right CP, that the words in which you couch your stories will lead the poor, the oppressed, the immigrant, the lonely, the hungry, to this land of milk and honey.

CP: And I will bring them, of course.

REPORTERS clamour.

OTTAWA: Alright … alright … Our crop is estimated to be in the region of—(*A beat*) one hundred and twenty million bushels.

REPORTERS re-act.

STAR: What would that be worth on today's market?

OTTAWA: How about—eighty five million dollars?

GLOBE: Wow—wait 'till they hear that back East.

POST: How many men will you need, sir?

OTTAWA: What say you gentlemen—forty thousand.

PROVINCES murmur agreement.

STAR: That's not an excursion—that's a migration.

GLOBE: It'll be like moving an army. Come on fellers —we'd better get this one out.

CP: Yes—you'd better … (*He escorts them out all the while exhorting them, sotto voice …*)

Do your best for us boys … Tell your editors—there'll be a lot of advertising revenue this year. No exaggeration can be too far fetched, no estimate too extreme. This harvest is going to be the biggest of all time, in the history of the world.

They exit … He returns.

SASK: It's a lot of people to mobilize. I pray to God the weather holds up.

OTTAWA (*To the others*): There he goes again.

MANITOBA: What's wrong with you man? If we get those numbers the crop will be harvested and threshed in ten weeks. Think positively.

CP: Exactly. It's a challenge, it's exciting. There won't have been anything like this concentration of labour for one specific task since they built the Great Wall of China.

CHORUS MEMBER *enters*: Excuse me sir—there's a delegation of farmers in the ante room.

OTTAWA: Oh dear, no rest for the wicked. I suppose they want to know what we're doing about the work force.

CHORUS MEMBER: They seem a little anxious sir.

OTTAWA: Alright—tell them we'll be with them shortly.

CHORUS MEMBER *exits.*

OTTAWA: Will you talk to them CP?

CP: No, no, no. You don't need me there. I must be off back down the line to the expectant East. I have to organise railway cars, posters, promotions—I've even hired a musician or two to entertain them in the taverns … You there … (*BALLADEER steps from the shadows.*) Give them a verse of the song …

BALLADEER: CP will pay good wages,
    give transportation too,
    provided you all go with him
    and stay the harvest through.
    But if you does get homesick,
    and wants to go back East,
    he won't pay your way back home again,
    and you will miss the feast …

CP: Even got a bit of dialect in there for them you see. Nice touch that … Go on …

BALLADEER: And feasts there'll be in plenty,
    as you whistle in the sun,
    the grain will flow like rivers,
    the mighty threshers hum,
    and as each day is over,
    you will wend your joyful way,
    to the glowing farmhouse kitchen
    for steaks, and mugs of tay.

CP: Good isn't it? A little warning followed by a tantalising glimpse of reality …

SASK (*Under his breath*): Good God.

CP: Here's money for you—keep up the good work.

BALLADEER exits.

CP: Well—I must be off. I'll leave it to you gentlemen to organise the reception in Winnipeg. Oh—Ottawa, a moment. (*He draws him to one side.*) (*Under his breath*) I'd stay with you but I have to make sure my rabble of mythmakers aren't embezzling their allowances—I've hired 'em all—barroom braggarts, rodeo rejects, fired policemen—a motley crew but you know what those Eastern Celts are like—starved for myths in this country. I'll get 'em. You'll see.

OTTAWA: Good man … keep in touch.

CP exits.

SASK: There's something extraordinarily rapacious about that man.

OTTAWA: Nonsense. This country is simply following the same pattern of development as our great neighbour to the South. The ruthless, the greedy, and, yes, the courageous, open it up, and they sell or lease to the honest and hardworking settlers who follow. Historically, it's a very ancient tradition, goes back as far as the Romans and it makes for great and powerful nations. (*Rather pleased with himself*) Well—shall we tackle the farmers gentlemen?

All move to exit except SASKATCHEWAN, who remains looking skywards.

MANITOBA: Are you coming? (*He does not respond.*)

OTTAWA (*Disgusted*): Leave him—he's brooding about the weather again.

ALBERTA (*Laughing*): I don't think so. He's trying to digest your lecture on the glories of capitalism.

They exit. After a beat SASKATCHEWAN slowly follows them. The CHORUS remove table and chairs, then proceed to immediately set up for Act One, Scene Two ...

ACT I, SCENE 2

The CHORUS is set for the bar scene in shadow, a couple of small tables, chairs, bottles and glasses. One group is at the table, another standing, drinking from bottles, two more as onlookers. The BALLADEER covers the activity with the theme for the following song, then sings ...

BALLADEER: It is a truth as old as man,
       the Westward beckons as we scan,
       horizons that collapse and fold,
       a direction only for the bold,
       Cabot and Jacques Cartier,
       the wild vikings in search of prey,
       the Phoenicians and the Greeks as well,
       whale roading down the path to hell ...

A flaring spotlight illuminates the ANCIENT who has been standing, unobserved to one side. The BALLADEER softly plays the air to the song beneath his speech.

ANCIENT: Go west, young man. The eternal cry. To what? The shipwreck of dreams. Who are they, these would-be harvesters, my friends, my enemies, people I've known all my life. Some—boys who've walked the water all their days, a few potato farmers who can turn in any direction and see the boundaries of their space and time, others lice ridden loggers from derelict lumber camps. What do they know—would-be cowboys in search of vanished freedoms. That's if they ever knew what freedom was. Well—they won't get me, not this time. Go west and leave the old alone, go risk your own damned skin and bone.

BALLADEER: Go risk your own damned skin and bone,
       and leave the rest of us alone,
       we're tired of your brawling ways,
       we've journeyed down the restless days,
       we'll sit and die, that's good enough,
       so leave us be, for dying's tough.
       And if you fall along the way,
       please don't expect the old to pray,
       and don't come back, unless you must

>I've been, I know, all comes to dust,
>but as in war, the dream remains,
>though fool's gold proves that hope is
>vain.

He plays the theme under the ANCIENT'S lines

THE ANCIENT: Go west—Go west, the whole damned lot of you, but for the love of God don't come back this time ... I might be caught out in my lies, mightn't I, the ones that fed you over winter nights. I might be caught out as the peddlar of false dreams. I might have to admit, then, to the loss of me own.

The air dies away as the lights rise on the bar scene ... His spot fades as he stares abstractedly into space ... The three CHORUS MEMBERS standing, O'BRIEN, MCLINTOCK, and MACINTOSH, burst into song ...

THE THREE: She'll be coming round the mountain

        when she comes.

        She'll be coming round the mountain ...

O'BRIEN: Wait a minute ... wait a minute ... (*He lurches to the table.*) Are you guys going with us or not?

HOGAN: Don't have much choice, do we fellers? (*WALSH and BYRNE agree.*)

O'BRIEN: Then sing fer the love of Jesus won't ye? (*Spins on the two standing apart*) First time for ye as well is it?

BYREN: Aye. It is.

MCLINTOCK: There's still water dripping from behind their ears ... (*He laughs at his sally.*)

WALSH: No boy ... no ... 'tis just the sight of O'Brien is enough to make 'em wet their pants. (*Both laugh ... O'BRIEN turns on them.*)

O'BRIEN: Ye want a bottle in yer face. Don't get clever with me you bastard.

WALSH: Come on, Come on. Can't ye take a joke. I thought you wanted to sing. Right.

MCLINTOCK: So he did. Come on boys—let's all have it for excursion train ...

In a wild parody of a CONDUCTOR he begins to rush around conducting ... He starts to sing ... "She'll be coming round the mountain" ... After a line or two, he is so outrageous that the others laugh and join in:

>She'll be coming round the mountain
>when she comes.
>She'll be coming round the mountain
>when she comes.
>She'll be coming round the mountain
>coming round the mountain
>coming round the mountain
>when she comes.

MCLINTOCK falls forward across the table laughing. The ANCIENT has been staring out—immobile. Blind Tiresias. O'BRIEN spots him, weaves forward.

O'BRIEN (*Mocking*): What do ye see old man?

WALSH: Indians. Creeping up behind him in the cornfield.

MCLINTOCK: No boy. 'Tis that old farmers wife he had when her old man was feeding the pigs.

O'BRIEN: More like 'twas the pig he had all the time.

Laughter

You're coming again this year aren't ye?

ANCIENT: No, boy, no. It's too late for me I tell you, I'm too old.

O'BRIEN picks him up bodily.

O'BRIEN: Ye don't have to work. Ye can be our mascot, that's all ... what say ye boy?

Laughter and approval

O'BRIEN starts marching him round the room ...:

> You'll be coming round the mountain
> when she comes.
> You'll be coming round the mountain ...
> coming round the mountain when she comes.
> There.

He dumps him into a chair like a sack of straw.

Here old man, have a drink.

He picks up a beer and pours it over his head.

ROSS: What's it really like—out there?

MCLINTOCK: You'll need a six gun.

WALSH: A ten gallon hat ...

O'BRIEN: And a lot of stamina. Right boys?

They agree.

HOGAN: Is it that hard?

O'BRIEN: It better be. (*Laughter*) It's women I'm talking about boy. You'll find 'em naked behind every stook and in every barn. Ukrainians, Eyetaliens, Germans—and they're starved fer it ... why d'ye think he's old before his time ...

The three laugh ... CP enters.

CP: Good evening gentlemen.

ROSS (*Whisper*): Who's that?

HOGAN: The man I think. CP.

CP: I've got good news for you all. The train for the West will be leaving the day after tomorrow.

General reaction and applause

CP: Thank you, thank you all. Those of you who've been before know the drill—but for you eager newcomers—you'll need to get all the gear you need for a three month stay together, enough food for four days on the train and ten dollars—you've got that.

The new hands murmur agreement.

CP: It's amazing, isn't it? A mere ten dollars to get you to the land of your dreams, the land of promise and hope and opportunity.

HOGAN: Is it confirmed what we'll be paid sir?

CP: It is. This year—two fifty an hour (*whistles*) and all found. Comfortable bed and board in the finest barns in the country. I envy you—the bright sun beating down, the golden harvest bending to your arms making the country rich, making you rich. (*Suddenly now*) The train will be leaving at 3:00 tomorrow afternoon. You'll all be there>?

CHORUS of agreement

CP: Good—then the drinks are on me ... set'em up there ... and play my song balladeer ...

BALLADEER: Reprise of "Oh I will pay Good Wages."

Above the following action

Led by MCLINTOCK the CHORUS sporadically join in linking hands with the others. He prances round to form a chain, last of all coming to the ANCIENT who is dragged up in the celebration. The chain swirls and weaves round CP who smiles contentedly, like a paternal godfather ... The lights fade as the song is finished. All exit.

ACT I, SCENE 3

The MCGREGORS. A small table and four chairs. A trunk or two, tops open from which clothes overflow are visible. The family has just finished dinner, and JOYCE is cleaning off the table.

ROBERT (*sighing*): Ah—that's better Joyce. Now that the inner man has been dealt with, we can get on with the packing.

ISABEL: I'm packed.

ROBERT: Aye—but ye've only yerself to worry about girl. I just can't get this pair to appreciate the urgency of it all. We've only two days left.

JOYCE: That's at least the tenth time today ye've said that Robert.

ROBERT: Oh. Is it? It's probably because I'm beginning to detect a certain—lack of enthusiasm lately.

JOYCE: Well—

ROBERT: Och—ye're not getting cold feet at this late stage, are ye?

JOYCE (*Hesitant*): Not really. But Rory and I have been talking ...

RORY: I never wanted to go in the first place. You know that father.

ROBERT: Of course I know that—ye've been whining and moping ever since I proposed the move.

RORY: I just don't think it's the right time, that's all.

ROBERT: Aye well, your still a minor and the law says that I can do ye're thinking for ye—for a bit longer anyway.

RORY sighs in exasperation.

JOYCE: He does have a point Robert. We haven't planned it properly at all. Maybe—if we waited until the spring.

ROBERT (*Stung*): The spring. What would be the point? The crops would be in the ground—there'd be no work but casual labour for months. No, no woman. It's now or never. My mind's made up.

RORY (*Aside to ISABEL*): Stubborn as a mule, as always. (*ISABEL giggles*)

ROBERT: What was that?

ISABEL: Nothing Father—just a little something between us, that's all.

ROBERT (*A disbelieving grunt*): Was it now. (*To JOYCE*) But at least she's packed. She's raring to go.

JOYCE: Och Robert—it's not the same for Isabel. Fergus is waiting for her in Edmonton—she's got a teaching job to go to …

RORY (*Bitter*): And she can't wait to become independant.

ISABEL: That's not fair Rory.

RORY: So …

JOYCE: Now that's enough, you two. I'm agitated enough as it is.

ROBERT: I'm disappointed in ye Joyce. You seemed keen on it when I suggested it.

JOYCE (*Sits*): This might sound silly—

ROBERT: Well …

JOYCE: It's been so depressing around here this year. Hundreds out of work, the weather as dreary as I can remember. It's not that I really wanted to move ye see, but I couldn't find the strength or the will to think it out properly.

ISABEL: You have been looking tired Mother. You try and do too much.

ROBERT (*Brisk*): Nonsense. Your mother's bored. I'm bored. We need a fresh start.

JOYCE (*Pleading for understanding*): But I don't know if I've got the energy for a fresh start again. When ye persuaded me to leave the Highlands—

ROBERT: I didn't persuade ye woman. We were driven, If ye remember.

JOYCE (*Weary*): Oh well, whatever the rights and wrongs of it I don't think I'm up to it again. I'm comfortable now—even if I do complain a bit on occasions—aye and a bit worn too, like this old cardigan. I don't want to be unravelled any more.

RORY: Can't you listen to her father … just for once.

ROBERT: Oh aye, because she's saying what you want to hear.

RORY: It's not that … I'm worried …

JOYCE: I'm sorry.

A Beat.

ISABEL: Come on Rory, give me a hand to do the dishes. (*He hesitates ... urgent*) Come on.

ROBERT: There was no call to say what ye did. I didn't expect it of ye.

JOYCE (*Gentle*): What do you expect of me Robert?

ROBERT (*Takes her hand across the table*): Love, we haven't gone further than the farmers market since we got here, twenty-two years ago. New Glasgow? Ye can't replace the old, but ever since we arrived here, that's what everyone has tried to do—bringing old feuds and quarrels across the Atlantic and planting them before even the fields were put to the plough. I want something different now, space, new voices.

JOYCE (*Indicating the house*): And all this --

ROBERT (*His old self*): It's already on the market. Old McLeod will look after the sale and send the money on to us once we've found a place to stay.

JOYCE (*Laughing*): Old McLeod. Have ye forgotten his motto? In God we trust, all others strictly cash. Aye, and a lot of it finds its way into his large Christian pockets.

ROBERT: He's canny, I grant ye. But honest mind.

JOYCE: I can hardly believe it.

RORY: Neither can I.

ROBERT: What?

JOYCE: That we're really going. Starting from scratch all over again.

ISABEL: You know Father—once he's tamed a space he gets tired of it.

ROBERT: So—what's wrong with a challenge. I tell you the West is vast—beyond imagining—one vast, golden horizon.

RORY: So is the desert.

ROBERT: Don't be ridiculous. Thousands go from here every year to reap the harvest.

JOYCE: Yes—and I know why a lot of them go too—to escape their women and children.

ROBERT: Well—I'm not doing that am I? And we're not going as itinerant labourers. We're going to buy our own land and create our own harvest. Ye just scatter the corn and it grows as you look at it. (*Takes her hand*) Just think of it lass.

ISABEL: He'll really need you out there you know.

RORY: He doesn't really need anyone.

ISABEL: That's not true—is it?

RORY: You won't be watching a horse's backside for eighteen hours a day. *ISABEL laughs.*

ROBERT: Come on lass. To everything there is a season and a time for every purpose under heaven. This is our time Joyce. I feel it ... here.

JOYCE: It's probably heartburn. Ye should stop eating so much salt herring.

ROBERT: Och woman, there's no talking to you at all.

JOYCE: Robert—d'ye mind when ye told me that this was the promised land.

ROBERT: I do. But we only stopped on the edge of it. The future lies beyond … lies west.

JOYCE (*Putting her arms round him*): You're an impossible old dreamer aren't you?

RORY (*Under his breath*): Impossible is right.

ISABEL: Sshh.

ROBERT: Am I—really?

JOYCE: Aye. Ye are. And I've cleaved to ye in everything ye've done and I suppose I must go along with your foolishness now … but Robert—just make certain that we don't fall off the edge, because if we do, I'll never forgive ye … I won't speak to ye until the day I die … (*A little laugh*) And perhaps—not even then.

They all exit. The CHORUS remove the setting. Lights reflect sunset … The BALLADEER emerges into his spot.

BALLADEER: My heart is a swallow
        seeking the sun,
        my heart is the laughter
        of rivers that run,
        my heart is a meadow,
        my heart is a bride,
        my heart is a sailboat
        adrift on the tide.

        My heart is a shadow
        embraced by the night
        my heart is a cry
        in search of the light,
        my heart is—breath
        pursued by the frost,
        my heart is a hunter,
        and the hunter is lost.

He exits as light fades.

ACT I, SCENE 4

The CHORUS enter, laden with boxes, bedding rolls, bags. In the far distance, the whistle of the train. They are hushed, expectant. Some drink openly from bottles. Others sit on their belongings. The Balladeeer emerges to one side.

The whistle of the train … closer

CHORUS individually, hushed.

Here she comes boys, the prairie train,
time to escape the care and the pain.
Time to stop begging,
time to stop strife,
the squalling of children,
the poor nagging wife.
Let the West awake,
let the West beware,
we're Maritimers,
On a tear …

The train whistle. Much closer. The MCGREGORS enter.

JOYCE: Goodness—what a crowd.

ROBERT (*Chuckling*): Just like the old times. Reminds me of the dock at Glasgow.

JOYCE: It does. And if ye remember, I didn't like that either.

Train whistle. On top of them. The CHORUS standing alert.

ROBERT: This is it. Let's stick together now. There'll be a fearful rush. Follow me.

An earsplitting roar as the train pulls into the station. The stage fills with steam … The CHORUS seethe forward. ROBERT and family amongst them. In the confusion CHORUS MEMBERS bring in two or three rows of slat seats. They all settle in their respective places as "the train" pulls out. The rush and roar gives way to the steady rhythm of the train in motion. They sway to the motion (bit too much like Our Town) as the BALLADEER sings …

BALLADEER: Clickety clack, clickety clack,
    you're on your way,
    there's no way back.
    It's good-bye to the wife and child,
    farewell to all the maidens wild,
    gone now the harbour's warning bell,
    the long boats rocking on the swell,
    clickety clack, clickety clack,

    you're on your way,
    there's no way back,
    two thousand miles
    away from home,
    you're on your own,
    you're on your own,
    clickety clack, clickety clack,
    it's too late now,
    there's no way back.

The ANCIENT detaches himself from the CHORUS and moves into his spot … He swigs from a bottle.

ANCIENT: It's not that I wanted to go. I told them. Ten years it's been, dust, drought, hardship, sweat—eighteen hours a day. I don't know why I went so often. It was a kind of need, that's all, stronger than hunger or sex. Like going to war ... escaping to war. The women nagging for money, kids bawling, the only escape the tavern, there to see yerself reflected in someone else's eyes. The same eyes, the same faces, always. After a while, we couldn't even tell each other apart so, when the siren call came every year, in the fall, we went. It's not that it's bad here. It's not that it's good there. It's this country, that's all. The soul starves, the hearth grows dim. Even the churches are small. We praise God in a small voice for fear that He might hear us. (*Suddenly shouting*) Hey—You up there ... can you hear me? (*His voice echoes back to him* ...) HEAR ME, HEAR ME, HEAR ME. See—there's nobody there. Only me. *SWIGS* Journeying. That's all we do isn't it? Whether ye lives on water or the land: Journeying. Escaping into the same place forever.

He stares out into space. The train rattles along. The BALLADEER sings softly ...

BALLADEER: You're on your own,
　　　　　you're on your own,
　　　　　clickety clack,
　　　　　clickety clack,
　　　　　it's too late now,
　　　　　there's no way back ...

Fade sound, light et all.

(End Act One.)

ACT II, SCENE 1

CONDUCTOR: This way Miss ... Excuse me Mr. McGregor, but I found this young lady by herself in the corridor and thought she might like a little company ... (*He looks back in the direction of the CHORUS then again at ROBERT*): If you don't mind that is.

ROBERT: Of course not ... a thousand welcomes ... Miss?

VICTORIA: Victoria McGrath, Sir, from Prince Edward Island. (*She hesitates.*)

ROBERT: Come in girl—we won't bite you.

JOYCE: Whereabouts on the Island, Victoria?

VICTORIA: Tignish—I doubt you'd know it. It's only a small place.

ROBERT: Oh, I know of it. I knew a fiddler from there. A MacNeil. D'ye know of them?

VICTORIA: Oh yes Sir, they're all fine musicians—the whole family.

ROBERT: So I heard. Well, you're a long way from home already. Sit down ... sit down ...

CONDUCTOR: I'll get your luggage Miss. (*He exits.*)

ROBERT: My wife Joyce—my daughter Isabel. Rory, my son.

VICTORIA: I'm pleased to meet you ...

JOYCE: Just make yourself at home Victoria, as best you can on these seats.

VICTORIA: It's better than standing. (*A beat*) It's nice of you to take me in. I'm not used to a crowd like this. (*Proudly*) It's my first time away from home.

JOYCE: I wish I could say the same.

ROBERT: Joyce.

JOYCE: Hush Robert—I'm only teasing. How far are you going, dear?

VICTORIA: Saskatoon. My husband went on in the spring, he's got a job there, in a granary. I wasn't to go until next year, but he's saved enough money to rent a house already.

ROBERT: Ye see Joyce—the land of opportunity.

JOYCE: Yes dear.

CONDUCTOR carrying VICTORIA'S luggage

CONDUCTOR: Your luggage Miss.

Rory springs to help her stow it away.

VICTORIA: (*Shy*) Thank you.

ROBERT: Take this for your trouble ... (*Proffers the CONDUCTOR a coin*).

CONDUCTOR: Oh no sir, I couldn't. It's the very least I could do under the circumstances. It's a help to me—if it wasn't for the presence of a few decent families, like yourselves, I don't know what I'd do on these runs.

JOYCE: You don't mean that you have to handle all this (*Vaguely indicates CHORUS*) by yourself?

CONDUCTOR (*Warming to his theme*): Yes Ma'am. There's just me. You'd think, wouldn't you, that after all the years of running these harvest excursions, the politicians would get me a little help.

JOYCE (*Sympathetic*): I don't know how you cope.

CONDUCTOR: Truth to tell ma'am, I don't. I just let things be and pray for the end of the run. (*Shakes his head*) The crowd gets wilder every year. (*Above him a muffled roar and laughter from the CHORUS.*)

CONDUCTOR: I don't know what it is.

ROBERT: Freedom from care for a few days, aye, and high hopes ...

RORY: ... and a lot of whisky.

ROBERT: Aye, that too. But the way they're going at it, it won't last much longer. (*CHUCKLES*) Then they'll sleep all the way to Winnipeg.

CONDUCTOR: Amen to that sir. Amen.

He exits on another shout of laughter from the CHORUS.

ISABEL: It's a miracle to me where they get the money for it—they've no jobs.

ROBERT: Goodness lass, where have ye been all these years. They get it on credit ... from the merchants.

JOYCE: Why on earth would the merchants lend them money for liquor?

ROBERT: (*As if to a child*) Because—when they get back home with their wages, they'll be no better off than when they left—aye, and their poor souls will be in pawn for another year. (*Looks at his fob watch*). Goodness … look at the time. (*He picks up the Bible.*)

RORY: We're on a train Father.

ROBERT: So. It's the same as a house, except that it's moving. (*Rory expresses exasperation.*) We have a little Bible reading on days of rest Miss.

RORY: A day of rest.

ROBERT: Well, we're not working, are we. (*A beat*) I hope ye don't mind.

VICTORIA: Oh—no. Not at all.

ROBERT (*Thumbing through the pages*): And to what church do ye belong?

VICTORIA: I'm Catholic sir.

ROBERT: I thought so with a name like that. Well, 'tis not your fault I suppose. Some of me own ancestors were before they saw the light.

JOYCE (*Shocked*): Robert. That's not Christian.

ROBERT (*Shrugs*): There's room for all under His bright wings … right Victoria?

VICTORIA: I pray so.

ROBERT (*Flicks another page. Stops*): Ah, here we are. ISABEL … RORY … stop gazing out of the window and pay attention … if you can.

ISABEL (*Innocent*): But we always do.

RORY: Ecclesiastes, by any chance, Father?

ROBERT: And why not? The most sensible prophet of them all.

RORY (*to VICTORIA*): Mind you—Job comes a good second.

ROBERT: But he's not the same. Job asks questions, Ecclesiastes has all the answers.

RORY and ISABEL giggle. Even JOYCE joins in.

ROBERT: Och, laugh away all ye want. Here we are, journeying on to a new world, but there's nothing new under the sun. Neither the world or human nature has changed in five thousand years.

A loud burst of revelry from the CHORUS—dies away.

JOYCE: A pity.

ROBERT (*Annoyed*): I don't know what's got into ye. Well, if ye won't pay attention, I'll read it to myself. (*Mumbles rapidly*) I know that whatsoever God doeth it shall be forever, nothing can be put to it, nor anything taken from it, and God doeth it, that men should hear before him … (*Stops—scans … excited*) This is it. It's what I've just told ye. Listen … That which hath been is now, and that which is to be hath already been … (*Skips a couple of lines—intones with deliberation*) for that which befalleth the sons of man befalleth beasts—as the one dieth, so dieth the others, yea, they have all one breath; so that a man hath no pre-eminence over a beast; for all is vanity, all go into one place; all are of the dust, and all turn to dust again. (*Closes Bible triumphantly*) What do ye think of that?

Another burst of sound from the CHORUS

RORY: We must be listening to the noisiest dust he ever made.

ISABEL: They've not heard father lecturing on the virtue of a few words ...

RORY: From others ...

ROBERT: Ye see the respect in which I'm held Victoria. Honour thy father and mother—it says that in here, but alas, the words fall on barren ground. It all springs from sparing the rod and spoiling the child.

RORY: Hah!

JOYCE (*Hurriedly*): You're so dramatic Robert. I've often wondered why ye didn't go on the stage.

RORY: Playing Macbeth.

ISABEL: One for Rory.

ROBERT (*Stung*): Is it? Now that poor devil was much maligned, and by an English playwright at that, who obviously knew nothing about Scottish history.

JOYCE: I thought we were supposed to leave the past behind Robert—I seem to remember a conversation fairly recently ...

The ANCIENT stumbles out form amongst the CHORUS and lurches unsteadily towares the MCGREGORS ... He stumbles against VICTORIA who gives a little shriek. RORY starts to propel him roughly out ...

RORY: Go on. Get out of here ...

ROBERT: Leave him be Rory ... he seems harmless enough.

ANCIENT sways unsteadily.

ANCIENT: I have seen—I have been—to Hell.

ROBERT (*Amused*): Aye well, we've all seen a bit of that.

ANCIENT: Ye'll see more. More than the mind can compass or the heart sustain. Ye must get off man.

A burst of sound from the CHORUS. It has a different pitch to it—dangerous.

ANCIENT: Ye must get off this train. Take your women. Take everybody.

ROBERT: We won't be getting off this train, old man. The McGregors have never looked back, in war or peace, and we're not about to start now.

RORY (*Quoting Robert*): A good soldier never looks behind—right Mother?

ANCIENT lurches forward and grips ROBERT by the arm. Peers intently into his face.

ANCIENT: It's only this train ye must leave—get the next one, or the next. There's a monster aboard here, evil, devouring. It's caged now, but it's waiting to spring. (*In tears*) Ye must get off.

ROBERT (*Releasing his arm*): Go on now, back to your friends. You're drunk, and tired, and upset. Go and sleep it off and we can talk again in the morning.

JOYCE re-acts. ANCIENT—stumbling off

ANCIENT: I have no friends. And ye don't either. Ye haven't heard 'em. I have …

He disappears amongst the shadowy revellers. A roar as he does so—mocking laughter.

JOYCE: Robert—that man gives me goose bumps. Why did you say he could talk to us again in the morning?

ROBERT: Poor old devil. He's lonely, that's all. Not like the youngsters. He's been before, I imagine, on the excursions, but there's probably nothing back home to keep him so he just comes now, for company. (*Laughs*) Reliving the dreams of his youth.

VICTORIA (*Doubtful*): He seemed to mean what he said.

ROBERT: But what did he say? Beasts. Devouring, waiting to spring. A touch of the demon drink I'd say.

ISABEL: Imaginative though, I'll say that for him. The rhyme of the ancient harvester.

ROBERT: That's good Isabel … very good.

VICTORIA (*Almost to herself*): He had such a sad face, sad eyes.

ISABEL (*Changing the subject*): Look. The sun's going, the lake is on fire.

ROBERT: So it is. The wonder of creation, my girl, the lake is on fire. The pallette of God.

Behind them, a huge roar … a cry of pain from the ANCIENT

ROBERT (*A beat—they've all heard it. Briskly*): I think it's time to give those hooligans some competition, don't you. A good hymn now, might shame them into some sense of sobriety, for ye know that most of them would be like lambs back home.

JOYCE (*Quiet*): Abide with me?

ROBERT: That's appropriate enough. Alright … we've had a sample of their lungpower, now we'll give them a taste of the McGregors—aye and join in Victoria, if ye know it. Altogether then, one, two … three …

They begin to sing, falteringly at first, but gaining in confidence and volume as they progress … RORY doesn't join in at first but ISABEL, using urgent body language, persuades him, reluctantly, to join in:

> Abide with me,
> fast falls the eventide
> the darkness deepens,
> Lord with me abide,
> when other helpers
> fail and comforts flee,
> oh thou who changest not
> abide with me …

The CHORUS have made a distinct retreat during the hymn—one or two … —hesitatingly, have even begun, rather drunkenly, to join in.

ROBERT (*Gleefully*): It's working—listen to that will you … Come on …

They begin the second verse. Raggedly, with increasing volume and fervour, the CHORUS join in:

> Swift to its close
> ebbs out life's little day,
> Earth's joys grown dim,
> its glories pass away
> Change and decay
> in all around I see,
> Oh thou who changest not,
> abide with me …

During this verse, as the volume increases, the lights have begun to fade, in keeping with the sentiment. At the end all are barely perceived shadows … but they remain on stage …

ACT II, SCENE 2

The BALLADEER steps into his spot.

The CHORUS remain in shadow, lit by dim yellow light. The McGregor party are asleep. Some members of the CHORUS are sprawled in various drunken attitudes … Four others are playing cards. The train whistles through the night. At an upper level ALBERTA, MANITOBA, and SASKATCHEWAN are discovered.

ALBERTA: What a night—we've never had an August like this.

MANITOBA: That's true enough.

SASK: I just hope the weather holds up, that's all.

MANITOBA: Oh oh, there he goes again. The prophet of doom.

ALBERTA: There's nothing to be gained by brooding about something that might never happen.

MANITOBA: Exactly. This harvest will be the biggest ever, you'll see.

SASK: When do the harvesters get here?

ALBERTA: The first batch—the day after tomorrow.

SASK: I suppose—if we can get at it soon enough …

MANITOBA: A month from now you'll be complaining about lack of storage space …

ALBERTA: (*Laughs*)

They freeze. Train sound. The card playing members of the CHORUS, their voices unidentified, speak from the flickering gloom.

1ST VOICE: So, what made you come?

ROSS: Kids.

2ND VOICE: Not that I know of.

1ST VOICE: Lucky bastard. I've got four. Will we make as much as they say?

2ND VOICE: Ask him. He's been here before.

3RD VOICE: They promise the earth to get you there … but if something goes wrong …

1ST VOICE: Such as …

2ND VOICE: Could be anything … my deal. You tell him.

4TH VOICE: Frost … or two weeks rain. Can't work then … and when ye does get into the fields it's all rot and mildew.

1ST VOICE: But that's not our fault.

3RD VOICE: No. And it's not theirs either they reckon.

2ND VOICE: Holy Christ. It's no different from home then.

4TH VOICE: Oh—there's good years. This might be one.

1ST VOICE: Might be one? Shit. No different from home.

3RD VOICE: Don't take it so hard son. We—we're always at the mercy of something, or someone. And a change is as good as a rest.

4TH VOICE (*Chuckles*): And ye're in good company. Suffering has to be shared to be enjoyed.

Laughter

1ST VOICE: Is there anything left in the bottle?

2ND VOICE: A smidgin.

1ST VOICE: Then smidgin it here then …

Train sound up and fades … as we move aloft. The light is getting brighter now, as we approach the dawn. ROBERT and JOYCE are awake. ROBERT is rummaging for a small billycan.

ROBERT: I suppose I should make the tea before our hungover friends come to … (*Chuckles*) We got a few of them to sing their prayers though, before they passed out.

JOYCE: I've heard better singing mind.

ROBERT: Tis not the sound but the sentiment lass—God might even be tone deaf for all we know.

JOYCE: Robert …

A member of the CHORUS enters, a would-be settler, also carrying a can.

MILLER: Good morning to ye sir.

ROBERT: Good morning.

MILLER: Miller's the name. George Miller from Truro.

ROBERT: McGregor—New Glasgow. My wife Joyce.

MILLER: Pleased to meet ye ma'am. (*Indicates can*) I'm looking for water … our can is empty.

ROBERT: Already.

MILLER: Has been these two hours. I've a wee bairn back there running a bit of a fever …

ROBERT: That's a terrible oversight on somebody's part. (*He stands.*) We'd better check on our supply right away. How far are ye going?

MILLER: Weyburn—that's in Saskatchewan. We bought a section from the CP agent—seemed somebody died before they had a chance to plant.

ROBERT: Oh well—it's an ill wind. (*Moving towards the CHORUS*) The water is this way—you'll have to tread lightly over a few bodies I'm afraid.

MILLER (*Laughing*): We've got a few of those too—but they seemed harmless enough ...

Train sound ... Cross fade to the three Provinces aloft.

MANITOBA: D'you think the flood of new immigrants coming our way will effect excursion policy Alberta?

ALBERTA: Why should it? As long as new settlements spring up the harvest grows, and as long as it grows we'll need a migrant labour force.

MANITOBA: What if the Maritime economy improves?

ALBERTA (*Laughing*): And what if fish could fly ... no no, they'll always be a subsistence economy, and thousands will clamour to come West every fall. And don't forget, the great advantage of migrant labour is that it isn't, nor can it ever be, organised labour.

MANITOBA: Amen to that.

ALBERTA: The bunkhouse and the workhouse—that creates your ideal beast of bufen, your contented oxen of a labourer, too tired to rebel ... too lonely to think.

SASK: I think I prefer men with more initiative than that.

MANITOBA: He has a point though.

SASK: Oh yes, and it's as old as time. But it's those with initiative who move on after the harvest, buy land, bring their families though God knows by the time CP has finished with them they haven't much left.

MANITOBA: Come on Saskatchewan—he has to get them here somehow.

ALBERTA: And you need the harvesters more than I do, so be practical for once and stop preaching sentiments you don't practice.

SASKATCHEWAN has moved away and stares skywards.

ALBERTA: Now what?

SASK: It's too clear.

MANITOBA (*Joining him*): It is a bit bright.

ALBERTA: It's nothing. It's a fine night that's all.

SASK: You've a different climate Alberta. That clarity promises frost.

MANITOBA: You can't be certain though.

SASK: Who can about anything?

ALBERTA: Thank God there's no whales on the prairies.

SASK (*Surprised*): Why?

ALBERTA: Because if there were, we'd pitch you right down the gullet of one … the biggest we could find.

MANITOBA laughs … a beat … even SASKATCHEWAN chuckles … a luminous white light bathes everything in a bitter moonglow. An ominous sting … fading as the BALLADEER steps into his spot.

BALLADEER: The wonder of the world has gone,
        the promise of the skies awry,
        the distance beckons, siren song,
        but all know that the distance lies.
        once buffalo in their millions roamed
        half hidden in the prairie grass,
        their bones now feed the prairie loam,
        wheat whispers where the herds once passed.

        We follow them, the thundering herds,
        scattered on the endless plains
        awash in stubble now, and dust,
        arthritic, bent, for little gain.
        The hunters are not seen, but they
        still pursue the ancient goal,
        profit from the beasts that prey
        upon the shifting, blowing soil.

        The wheatyard gleams, the horses wait,
        to bring the binders through the gate,
        the buffalo sleep, and pile o'bones
        now houses all the merchants homes
        I cannot help but fear that soon,
        the earth will lift into the gloom
        and disappear into the sky,
        all promise then, and hope awry,
        the crumbling barns, the houses—blind,
        no distance then before, behind,
        the wonder of the world long gone,
        no places left to wander on.

ACT II, SCENE 3

The CHORUS, as before, laying or sitting about in various stages of disorder … The MCGREGORS eating a makeshift breakfast. In shadow the BALLADEER intoning …

BALLADEER: Clickety clack
        clickety clack,
        you're on your own,
        there's no way back …

(*Slowing down to simulate the train coming to a halt*)

        C L I C K E T Y C L A C K

        C L I C K E T Y C L ...... A ...... C ...... K ......

ROBERT: What now I wonder?

RORY: It must have been faster in the days of the canoe.

CONDUCTOR enters.

CONDUCTOR: Sorry folks, there'll be a slight delay. A freight derail up ahead.

ROBERT: How long to clear the track?

CONDUCTOR: They've been at it all night. It'll be another hour or so I guess.

O'BRIEN: What the hell is going on?

CONDUCTOR: Excuse me sir—ladies ... (*He moves behind screen*) A bit of trouble on the line boys ... so you can just sit tight or get off and stretch your legs for a spell.

HOGAN: So who's got legs to stretch?

Some blurred laughter

MCLINTOCK: So where are we?

O'BRIEN moves towards the water tank.

CONDUCTOR: Chalk River—just west of Ottawa.

O'BRIEN (*Throwing a drinking can down in disgust*): There's no damned water left.

WALSH: Since when have ye been interested in water?

O'BRIEN: Since now. Me tongue's got more fur on it than a whore's twat.

HOGAN: Hush man—there's woman can hear ye.

O'BRIEN: So ...

CONDUCTOR (*Hurriedly*):. I'll check the other coaches for you.

MCLINTOCK (*Stops him as he tries to move past*): Just a minute. How many days left to Winnipeg?

CONDUCTOR: Oh—thirty six to forty eight hours ... if we have no more delays. And we'll be taking on fresh water at Fort William.

WALSH: What? That's almost a day away. (*He pushes him backward. ROBERT listens—alert.*)

CONDUCTOR: Boys—I don't make the rules. I don't load the train. I'm one of you—a poor working man. I travel the line and do my job, do as I'm told, and keep me place, if I know what's good for me.

BYRNE: That's true enough boys—it's not his fault.

O'BRIEN: What do you know about anything? Shut up. (*Pushing the CONDUCTOR*) You tell your bosses that Maritimers won't be treated like shit any longer. Have you got that ...(*He pushes him again and he stumbles over a sleeping MEMBER who wakes with a curse and pushes him off. MCLINTOCK senses a bit of sport at the CONDUCTOR'S expense and dashes about to the remainder ...*)

MCLINTOCK: Alright lads, hands off cocks onto socks. Lets get the hell out of here and see if Chalk River has got any real water ...

Aided by O'BRIEN they push, haul and get the remainder ready to get off the train, in the midst of it all making sure the CONDUCTOR is shoved from one to another like a rag doll. ROBERT moves as if to interfere but JOYCE restrains him ...

JOYCE (*Soft*): They're going now Robert.

And indeed they are, laughing, wheezing, coughing, stampeding round the CON-DUCTOR and then off. He dusts himself off and moves to the MCGREGORS.

ROBERT: Are you alright man?

CONDUCTOR (*Chuckles*): Don't worry about it, sir. I'm used to it by now, though I must say this is the wildest bunch I've ever seen. And you can be sure it's not water they're after now.

VICTORIA: Oh no—not another twenty-four hours like the last.

ROBERT: It's alright Victoria—we can hymn them to sleep again.

RORY: I should have gone along to keep them company.

JOYCE (*Shocked*): Rory—you're not serious.

RORY (*Defensive*): A nice draft of cold ale would make me feel a lot better. Two would make the next couple of hours tolerable. (*He spies the ANCIENT coming in.*) Oh no ... He's back.

ANCIENT: You're still here then. Ye never heeded one word I said to ye.

ROBERT: Where else would ye expect us to be? Are ye feeling better now?

ANCIENT: The beast is stirring. l did tell ye.

ROBERT (*Comfortably*): I do believe ye did.

JOYCE: Would ye like a bite to eat? Ye look half starved, poor man. 'Tis only a bite o'bread and cheese, and some cold tea ... but you're welcome.

RORY: Mother—how could you?

JOYCE (*Rummaging and coming up with cheese, bread, and a bottle of cold tea*): A man's a man fer a'that. It's one of your father's favourite sayings.

ISABEL (*Soft—half laughing*): But he does smell, Mother. And Rory has a delicate nose.

ROBERT (*Laughs*): 'Tis the curse of humanity Rory ... we all smell, sooner or later—and once we start manuring those great prairie fields ...

ISABEL: While watching the horse's backside ...

Even VICTORIA laughs at this sally. The ANCIENT is greedily stuffing bread and cheese into his mouth and washing it down with tea ... Crumbs and liquid sputter over his face ... RORY watches him, in disgust.

RORY: This journey is interminable.

CONDUCTOR: Only two days to go, young feller. And, like you, I can't wait for it to be over. (*He exits.*)

ROBERT (*Chuckling*): At this rate of progress our conductor is being optimistic. Oh come on Rory, cheer up. There'll be a few more hours to go after Winnipeg, and then you and I together will build Mother the finest house she's ever had.

The ANCIENT has hunkered down on his heels and appears to be dozing. JOYCE puts away the food.

ISABEL: You make it all sound so easy, Father.

ROBERT: Hush maid. Did you ever hear me say it would be easy? Nothing worthwhile ever is, as ye'll find out soon enough when ye get married.

JOYCE (*Incensed*): So! Marriage hasn't been easy for you, has it? What about me? What makes ye think that living with you has been a joy? Ye reserved your charm and yer manners for ye're courting but once I was bedded—a more stubborn, cantankerous, bullheaded, prideful ...

ISABEL claps, even RORY laughs at this rare dlsplay of intensity.

ROBERT: Alright Joyce, alright. Catalogue me faults, I admit to most of them—although cantankerous seems a bit harsh ...

JOYCE looks as if she will start again but he placates her with a wave of his hand.

ROBERT (*Almost pleading*): Bear with me, love, just one more time. This is exciting, aye, a challenge. And for us, it will be like a second honeymoon. (*JOYCE snorts, ISABEL and VICTORIA giggle.*) Alright then, not with all that implies. But how many men of my age get the chance to start over again, aye, and for the second time in their lives too, to re-create, to make something of substance, rather than live on the tail end of old dreams?

RORY: Everyone being released from jail, I should think.

Even JOYCE laughs at that, but RORY was serious.

ISABEL: Rory—you're incorrigible. Don't you even laugh at your own jokes?

RORY: It wasn't a joke. Somebody had to bring father down to earth, or else he'd take off into the stratosphere.

JOYCE: He's right Isabel. It's not that your Father ever appears to pay heed, on the surface, but I've lived with him long enough to know that a little criticism makes him think twice, and then he'll plan for the worst, even if he doesn't believe it will happen. (*ROBERT starts to protest but she stops him.*) There dear, it's alright. I was only serious, that's all. (*The rest laugh as the lights dim and move up to the platform ...*)

Into his spotlight steps the BALLADEER.

BALLADEER: I wish I were
            gone far from here,
            back where the raven
            and the deer
            vanish in mist
            and appear again
            in a shaft of sunlight
            a cup of rain.

A cup of rain
and golden light
the dreaming fells
an emerald bright
the racing hares
at spring time play
and Mary beckoning
where she lay.

Her breath was
sweet as summer pine,
her hair as thick
as chestnut mane
her body soft
as summer grass
how could I let
such beauty pass?

Twas pain and sorrow
brought me here
far from the raven
and the deer,
and I may
never more be seen
upon the emerald
hills of dream.

His spot fades. Lights to full on MCGREGORS.

ACT II, SCENE 4

Enter SASKATCHEWAN, MANITOBA, ALBERTA, they are obviously agitated.

SASK: You've heard the latest crop estimates?

MANITOBA: I have, unfortunately.

ALBERTA: Not good for you, eh?

SASK: Not good! The damned frost has been ruinous. I should have paid attention to my own instincts, instead of listening to the rest of you.

ALBERTA: Easy now—you can't blame anyone for the weather.

MANITOBA (*Bitterly*): What do you care anyway, Alberta? It won't affect you half as much.

ALBERTA (*Smug*): I'm not exactly thrilled—but thank God, we never did put all our eggs into one golden basket. We can rob Peter to pay Paul, if the worst does come to the worst.

MANITOBA: Stop gloating, it doesn't become you. The only reason you aren't wheat intensive is because the landscape doesn't permit it.

ALBERTA: You could have gone into cattle too, as a back up. If the plains could support millions of buffalo they could also support a few ranches of Herefords.

MANITOBA: That damned Ottawa. Year after year plaguing us to grow wheat, wheat and more wheat.

ALBERTA: You didn't have to listen.

SASK (*Muttering*): Too dry.

MANITOBA: What?

SASK: On top of everything else, it's been too dry. Brittle, everything brittle. One more week of frost …

ALBERTA: It's not as bad as you say Saskatchewan. One touch of winter doesn't mean to say that it's settled in.

MANITOBA: You're right, of course. It was just a warning, that's all, a natural aberration. The rest of the fall will be fine.

SASK (*Gloomy*): And I tell you it won't.

MANITOBA: Well—I predict that it will—Ottawa's right about you at least, you almost pray for disaster. Be positive man—we can still pull in at least three quarters of the original estimate, once the harvesters arrive.

SASK: One half.

MANITOBA: What?

SASK: Don't fool yourself Manitoba. You've seen the fields, (the blight).

MANITOBA: A lot of it's still salvageable.

SASK: For what? Cheap cattle feed. Alberta would like that. Wouldn't you? And then there's the problem of the harvesters. What the devil are we going to do with them all?

ALBERTA: That's easy. Just send 'em back the way they came.

SASK: Use your head, man. Who's going to pay? CP? Ottawa? There's trainload upon trainload out there, backed up between here and Toronto, and they're hungry, without jobs or money.

MANITOBA: My God—I never thought of that.

SASK: That's the trouble. Nobody wants to think.

MANITOBA: Look if, and I'm not prepared yet to admit that it'll be as bad as you say, if we get more than we can handle, we'll just have to pass the responsibility on to Ottawa.

ALBERTA: And he'll just pass it on to CP.

SASK: So—what the hell can he do about it (the wheels are in motion)? We're as much to blame as anybody. No planning. Too much dreaming, too much damned mythology—and too many lies. We've become—practical politicians, gentlemen. (*He begins to laugh. The others look at him in some amazement as we fade them out and return below, to the distant sound of a riotous party—even punctuated by gunfire.*)

ROBERT (*Intense*): Ssh. Listen to that, will you?

Published in Honour of Albert-Reiner Glaap

JOYCE: Sounds like a war.

RORY: It's them alright. They've gone crazy.

ROBERT (*Grim*): Then it's just as well you didn't go for your beer isn't it?

The ANCIENT wakes up with a start. Stands ... runs forward, listening intently. Turns back to them.

ANCIENT: The beast. I told you. I warned you. It's escapes my dreams, IT'S SLIPPED ITS CHAINS. I must go now. If they find me here, they'll kill me. (*Bows with great dignity.*) My thanks to ye ma'am, yes, my deepest thanks. Bread and cheese and cold tea, the accoutrements of kindness. I must go. You're a proud man Mr. McGregor, a good man, but a proud one and ye'll not heed advice from a fool. I trust your pride will stand ye in good stead, and the Good Lord you're so fond of. And you Miss—(*To ISABEL*) even steel bends. The sugar maple cracks and splits when lightning runs. A man is no more than his wants and desires. Bread and cheese and tea ... they feed wants and desires but are not weapons of strength. (*Terribly agitated*) I must go—I would ask God to go with you all but I don't know where He is ... Not any more.

He exits. In the distance, more shooting, whoops, gunfire.

ROBERT: Poor old devil. He's unhinged.

RORY: Mad.

ISABEL: The sugar maple cracks and splits ... what on earth was he talking about.

JOYCE: Well, he's harmless at least, and he means well—I think.

VICTORIA (*Spiritedly*): I think he believes everything he says.

ROBERT: Och Victoria, fools and great men alike suffer from the same affliction. (*He takes out a fob watch and looks at the time.*) I wish they'd get this train moving.

JOYCE (*A beat*): Is anything wrong, Robert?

ROBERT: No, no, no. I'm just anxious to get to our destination. Aye—and the girls are anxious to get to their men I should think.

RORY: And where do I fit in Father?

ROBERT (*Laughing*): You—you're just anxious to prove me wrong—but I doubt I'll give ye the satisfaction.

The two stare at each other as the lights fade.

ACT II, SCENE 5

The BALLADEER is playing a reprise of CP'S song, only now speeding it up until it becomes a jig. HOGAN and BYRNE "square off" and begin to stepdance, each tyring to outdo the other. The rest watch, cheer, jeer, laugh, thump time with bottles and glasses ... the music gets wilder and wilder ... the two desperately try to keep steps in time to the music but finally, the pace is too much and they both collapse, breathless. The BALLADEER stops ... pulls at his glass, and begins to play quietly, under the din, the air to "Farewell to Nova Scotia."

HOGAN: Jesus boy, what were ye trying to do? Kill us both?

BYRNE: Speak for yourself—I'm only a mite out of breath—I could go again in a minute …

The BALLADEER immediately changes back to the original.

BYRNE: No, no, boy—'twas kidding I was …

Laughter as the BALLADEER goes back to the Nova Scotian air.

MCLINTOCK: Which of the two were best boys?

ROSS: I'd say Hogan.

WALSH: No no—Byrne by far.

Shouts of BYRNE. No, no, HOGAN.

MCLINTOCK (*Shouting*): Alright … alright … Shut up now. Listen—(*Noise dies down.*)—We'll put it to a vote. All those in favour of Hogan raise your hands … (*Whatever numbers there are—half plus one MCLINTOCK counts.*) O.K. That's … Now … Those for Byrne … that's … (*Loud cheers*) It's Hogan by one vote. (*Cheers and protests*)

HOGAN (*Shouting*): So—what's me prize?

MCLINTOCK: Why boy—ye gets to buy us all a round.

Cheers and laughter and protests from HOGAN.

OWNER (*Darting forward*): Now boys, are you sure you haven't had enough?

ROSS (*Has been standing with O'BRIEN*): Enough. We've only just started.

OWNER (*Nervous*): But—nobody's paid for anything yet.

WALSH: So what man, we're good for it—and Hogan there has got more than anyone …

They all laugh at the reference to HOGAN'S family

OWNER: Alright then …

O'BRIEN: The bottles man, just bring the bottles …

HOGAN: But --

WALSH: Hold yer whist man …

The owner distributes four or five bottles. After the din, there is an almost uncanny silence. The rest of the CHORUS are watching O'BRIEN and MACINTOSH, as if expecting something. Excitement perhaps—some "fun" at the owner's expense.

OWNER: There you are lads … I'll give you whatever you want—within reason.

O'BRIEN: You will, will ye? And what's yer idea of reason?

WALSH: It's not a reasonable profit that's fer sure. I bet you fixed the tracks so that we'd have to stop here.

Owner protests. O'BRIEN cuts him off.

O'BRIEN: How many of you did it take eh, to wreck that freight train.

OWNER (*Frightened*): That's nonsense boys and you know it. How was I to know you were coming through? You could have been another freight for all I knew.

O'BRIEN: Another freight! So—you admit it.

The rest of the CHORUS are edging closer.

WALSH (*Soft*): It was human cargo you were after Mister. It's excursion time, and you damned well know it.

OWNER: Course I know it's excursion time, but do I know the schedules? This is a small town and trains don't stop here very often ... Hey d'you think Canadian Pacific would bother to talk to me?

WALSH (*Soft to O'BRIEN*): Second time I've heard that line in an hour.

O'BRIEN tips bottle and drinks deeply. Spits it out into OWNER'S face.

O'BRIEN: This whisky is watered ...

A low murmer from the CHORUS as they sense the whole ploy has been to avoid paying anything.

OWNER: No, no, sir ... l can assure you ... it's one hundred per cent ...

WALSH: Rain water.

MCLINTOCK (*Swigs*): My God—you're right—we're being robbed blind—first the railway and now this. There's no end to what they'll do to honest men.

CHORUS response gets louder.

MACINTOSH: Do ye treat all strangers who come to this town like this? Whaddye think we are ... scum?

Angry response from remainder.

O'BRIEN: If he thinks we're scum, then perhaps we should show him how scum behave ... .

The CHORUS approve vociferously.

OWNER (*Shouting*): Boys, there's no water in the whisky, I swear on me mother's grave.

O'BRIEN: Aye—and she probably cursed you for driving her there ... (*Some laughter ... dies swiftly away*) So what are your prices—me dear, honest man?

OWNER (*Consults a tablet hurriedly*): Well—between you all, and with these bottles it comes to ... (*Calculating desperately*) fifteen, twenty-two, thirty-one.

O'BRIEN (*Roaring*): Thirty-one nothing. Are we going to let this crook treat decent maritimers like fucking animals.

Roar of denial about it, the train whistle sounds.

MACINTOSH: Damn—we'd better get back.

O'BRIEN (*To MACINTOSH*): Not before we take something for the voyage. (*Shouting*) Help yourselves lads—Leave no bottle unturned ...

Roars of approval and laughter as they rush around removing bottles, kegs ... The OWNER runs amongst them like a frightened chicken.

OWNER: For the love of God—stop—please ... This is all I have ... I've worked a lifetime for this—I've even been an excursionist, like you. I'm one of you ... please ...

O'BRIEN seizes the cash register … the whistle blows.

O'BRIEN: Catch someone …

He throws it and two catch it before it falls and make off … The OWNER runs to him and flails it at him, uselessly, with his fists …

OWNER: You are an animal. You'll pay for this I'll get the police. We'll track you down …

O'BRIEN punches him savagely in the midriff and shoves him at other MEMBERS of the CHORUS.

O'BRIEN: Get rid of him. Teach him a lesson.

He is submerged and carried off, screaming in pain and fury … as he exits MACIN-TOSH'S voice is heard …

MACINTOSH: Goddamn, he's got a knife. Get the knife!

A scuffle off, then a gurgling scream from the OWNER. The train whistles.

O'BRIEN (*To the couple remaining*): There's two long days to go boys. Don't leave a thing.

They snatch a couple of bottles and rush off. MACINTOSH runs in.

WALSH: Come on, O'Brien, it'll leave without us.

O'BRIEN: No it won't. We're the excursionists, remember. They can't do without us. Go on, man, I'll be with you in a minute.

MACINTOSH exits. O'BRIEN finds half a bottle of liquor on the floor pours it out, then puts a match to it. The train whistles, the flames flicker, swell, roar … the train whistles as we fade to black.

ACT II, SCENE 6

The BALLADEER in his spot … with increasing speed and intensity …

> Clickety clack, clickety clack
> there's no way back
> there's no way back
> two thousand miles away from home
> you're on your own
> you're on your own
> clickety clack, clickety clack
> It's too late now
> there's no way back …

Lights on MCGREGORS the train: MCGREGOR coach. Behind them the CHORUS are drinking, fighting, but there is nothing boisterous about this. The mood is vicious, menacing. O'BRIEN and MACINTOSH huddle together and look intensely in the direction of the MCGREGORS. The ANCIENT tries to slide past them but is thrown back. ROBERT is rummaging through his bags, looking for a weapon, but gives up in disgust.

ROBERT: It's no good. All the tools are in the back of the van. We'd never get through to them.

JOYCE: What on earth are you looking for, Robert?

ROBERT: A wrench, a hammer, anything to make a dent in a couple of those stupid skulls back there.

VICTORIA: D'you really think we're in danger, Mr. McGregor?

ROBERT: I don't know Victoria, to tell ye the truth, but they've gone berserk. That's obvious, and I don't want to take any chances. Rory, my son—let's see if we can wrestle one of these seat slats off.

RORY: What for?

ROBERT (*Exasperated*): Don't you ever listen? To use as a club, ye fool. Come on.

JOYCE: Do you really have to do this Robert?

ROBERT: Yes, Joyce, I do. When they get through fighting each other, they just might look for alternate entertainment.

ISABEL: He means us, Mother.

JOYCE (*Indignant*): They wouldn't dare.

VICTORIA: I don't think so either. (*She doesn't believe this.*) There has to be some God fearing men amongst them, hasn't there?

ISABEL: God lives in communities, Victoria. Apparently he gets lost in the wilderness.

VICTORIA bursts into tears.

JOYCE: Now look what you've done. You're too wilful by far, my girl. (*Goes to VICTORIA*) There, there I'm sure you're right. Ye minds when they were like this before. All we had to do was sing a hymn and they turned into lambs. They respected the Lord, and they respected us. They will again, you'll see ...

ROBERT: I'd dearly love to think you're right Joyce, but then they'd only had a bottle or two. Now they've filled the water tanks with beer and whisky and they don't know who, or what they are. I doubt if they even know where they're going—the very notion of respect for anything or anybody won't enter their stupid minds.

ISABEL: Victoria might be right though, Father. What about the man who made tea with us yesterday morning?

ROBERT: Probably making plans for his own defence. He'd had problems too if you recall ... (*The slat gives way. ROBERT falls back, laughing.*) Good lad, Rory, we've got one ... now, let's get one for you. (*They renew their efforts. VICTORIA is still sniffling. Robert, between exertion*) Will ye stop yer snivelling, girl, that doesn't help anyone. Look in your bag for a hatpin, a needle, anything with a point. Joyce and Isabel ye do the same.

JOYCE: What for, dear?

ROBERT (*EXASPERATED*): For their eyes, woman. Ye canna be raped by a blind man.

JOYCE: Now you're being disgusting.

ROBERT (*Shouting*): I'm trying to prepare ye for the worst, just as ye said, that's all. (*Another slat breaks free.*) There. (*He swings it around.*) Now, if they come, we'll be able to slow 'em down a bit. Most drunkards are cowards, I've observed.

JOYCE has been rummaging in her handbag and comes up with the Book of Common Prayer. ROBERT looks at her in disbelief.

ROBERT: I said find a hatpin, woman. Not a book.

JOYCE (*With great dignity*): Ye know very well what book this is Robert—ye use it every Sunday, and it might calm ye all down to listen to a psalm or two ... Here we are. (*Psalm 59*) Deliver me from my enemies, oh My God: defend me from them that rise up against me. Deliver me from the workers of iniquity, and save me from bloody men, for lo ...

ROBERT (*Breaking in*): Joyce. Joyce. (*She looks at him steadily then continues lip reading, silently, ROBERT shakes her.*) Look, I'm not denying your intentions woman, or the power of the word itself but the Good Lord also helps those who help themselves. (*She continues as before.*) Dammit woman, you are impossible (*He turns to RORY.*) Take the rear (*Towards the CHORUS*) and as for ye Joyce ... ye've made your point. Keep at it, if it makes ye feel more secure ... but I feel more secure with this ... (*Swings slat*) And if they break through, ye might try throwing that good book in their faces, just to find out what kind of a punch the Lord really has.

As the lights dim on them and go up on the politicians JOYCE continues reading as the reporters rush in and bombard the three with questions ...

JOYCE: For lo, they lie await for my soul; the mighty are gathered against me; not for my transgressions nor for my sin, oh Lord. They run and prepare themselves without my fault ...

(*END ACT 2*)

ACT III, SCENE 1

In half shadow, the ANCIENT is discovered. He is lit in such a way that his shadow is enormous—spectral, appearing everywhere. Were it not for his voice, we would have difficulty knowing his true whereabouts. He speaks the following ... BALLADEER plays softly underneath.

THE ANCIENT: It is night now ... Night. Coal black, starless. A cold wind is blowing from the North, across the granite shield, cooling the rump of summer, and we, hurtling into the abyss, are the creatures of night, of dark instinct, masterless men as of old, without a rudder, a Captain even, adrift between destinations. (*A beat*) Between the birth light and the grave, falls the shadow.

ACT III, SCENE 2

Lights blaze. The CHORUS are discovered wildly drunk. O'BRIEN has a rope loosely tied around the ANCIENT'S neck and he is being pulled from one to another a vicious parody of a tug of war. The whistle shrills ... the wheels jolt over converging track then face into background. Others are doing a jig to mouth music, clapping in time, at an impossible speed ...

O'BRIEN: Dance, you old bugger, dance.

HOGAN: Oh leave him be, O'Brien. He's harmless enough.

O'BRIEN: Harmless is it? And him running about from one carriage to another, the old lunatic. It's bad luck he is, he's a jinker and that's a fact. Dance you old coot, before I cut yer legs off.

Amidst jeers, the ANCIENT tries to jig in time, but is pulled off his feet by O'BRIEN. He gets up slowly, painfully and tries again, and again is pulled down.

O'BRIEN: If ye don't do better than that (*A tug*) I'll hang you from the window like an old dishrag.

HOGAN gets to the ANCIENT and takes the rope from his neck. BYRNE and ROSS try to stop him.

BYRNE (*Whisper*): Leave it be boy, fer Christ's sake.

ROSS: 'Tis none of our business.

HOGAN shakes them off.

HOGAN: 'Course it's my business. Have you gone mad O'Brien—abusing old men?

Others protest at this interference.

O'BRIEN: Abusing old men is it? Well yer not wet behind the ears yet, but if ye like, I'll abuse ye too.

He aims a punch at HOGAN who dodges aside and counters with a punch to O'BRIEN'S head. O'BRIEN laughs.

O'BRIEN: There boys, there's the dancer now ... Marquis o' Queensbury rules and all. (*Suddenly kicks HOGAN in the groin who doubles up.*) Take him lads take him and throw him off the train—damned sissy—we've no need of his like in the fields.

MACINTOSH and MCLINTOCK and perhaps another grab him and heave him off stage ... His despairing scream is cut off by the train whistle.

O'BRIEN: Now ye old rat—we can deal with you. (*He grabs the rope and begins to lash him as the ANCIENT cowers.*) that's fer all the lies ye've told in the course o' yer miserable life (*Lash*) and that's fer running in and out of the women's carriage. (*Lash*) Ye'll not go in there again will ye?

ANCIENT: No ... no, I won't. I promise.

O'BRIEN: Well ye might, (*Lash*) fer that's no place for an old wreck like you. It's men they need in there ... (*Shouts of approval*) And, be God, it's men they're going to get—now. (*Lashing furiously*) Dance!

INTER-PLAYS

ROBERT emerges from his half of the coach, carrying the slat.

ROBERT: Leave him alone. (*Flails slat.*) Back up, ye damnable coward.

The CHORUS are hushed, expectant.

O'BRIEN: As—so ye've left yer guardpost Mister McGregor. (*Chuckles*) We thought, me friends and I, that if we tormented this piece of vermin enough (*Kicks* ANCIENT) ye just might decide to interfere on behalf of yer good friend … and ye did.

MACINTOSH and MCLINTOCK start edging behind ROBERT.

MCLINTOCK: Got to hand it to you O'Brien. It worked like a charm.

MACINTOSH: Has a real knowledge of the milk of human kindness O'Brien do.

Laughter

ROBERT: What the devil's the matter with you all. Ye're behaving like animals. Have'ye no shame? I know you Joy Byrne and you Pat Walsh and you Ross. As for you O'Brien, I've never laid eyes on ye before, and thank God for it, but the rest of ye are decent enough men. Stop this nonsense now and calm down. We'll be in Winnipeg in a day—the journey will be over and there'll be work to do.

O'BRIEN: For some there will be. Others might not be so lucky … (A BEAT) alright boys. Now.

MACINTOSH and MCLINTOCK dart forward but ROBERT swings round, stick swinging … they pause.

O'BRIEN: Christ—are ye afraid of a man just because he's carrying a piece of wood … .(*Suddenly pushes the ANCIENT against ROBERT who stumbles and falls to his knees. MACINTOSH and MCLINTOCK rush forward as ROBERT tries to swing at their legs from ground level but MACINTOSH falls across him and pins him down. Others move forward.*)

O'BRIEN: Hold him up now lads, just for me. (*They haul him to a standing position.*) Good enough (*He starts to beat him savagely, methodically.*) Take that Mr. High and mighty McGregor, with yer noble thoughts and deeds. And that. (*He laughs.*) Can ye still hear me. (*Hits again*) Once you're dealt with, it'll be time for a little night music with those prissy women of yours. And it's not hymns we'll be playing. (*ROBERT slumps unconscious but O'BRIEN continues the beating.*) Abide with me—you'll be abiding soon enough I'm thinking.

They cluster towards the shadow of the McGregor half of the coach as ROBERT falls to the floor. The ANCIENT sits on the floor, cradling ROBERT'S head in his arms … as the BALLADEER appears in his spot.

BALLADEER: From the first light
　　　　　　to the dying fall,
　　　　　　there is no hope
　　　　　　death conquers all.
　　　　　　Tugging at the breast we know

there's nowhere but the grave to go
some damned fools pray.

They laugh and hope
but the cord is just a piece of rope
the only thing that spurs us on
is that we just don't know how long
the joker will pay out the line
until he's bored, and calls out "time."

ROBERT stirs and groans ... spot fades.

ANCIENT: What—not dead? Not dead?

In the shadow ... the CHORUS

ANCIENT: It should have been me Robert ... (*He rocks him back and forth*):

There was an old fool from Cape Breton
who not even his mother would bet on
he'd no God and no pride
didn't care if he died,
and if he did, he'd never have let on ...

He begins to laugh, softly, the tears streaming down his face. As the light switches to the McGregorS. The CHORUS menace in background.

RORY: D'you think they've got father?

ISABEL: He's not back. (*A beat*) You'd better take his door Rory.

He pauses, irresolute.

JOYCE: What do you mean ... they've got him? (*A beat*) Och ... I told him. He should never have gone.

VICTORIA (*Hysterical*): That filthy, crazed old man. Why was he more important than us?

ISABEL: A man's a man, for a 'that.

VICTORIA: But what can we do—if they come?

ISABEL: I don't know. Honestly. (*A wry little laugh*) Appeal to their sense of decency?

RORY: You heard what father said ... they don't have any left. Victoria's right. What can we do ... what can I do? If they can take father ... (*An embarassed pause*)

ISABEL: They can take you.

RORY (*Anxious, desperate*): I'll not be much protection for the three of you, you know that. And then what. (*A silence*) Oh God. Don't try to resist them ISABEL ... that way you won't get hurt. If ... No one need know.

ISABEL: I will know.

The CHORUS begins a low pitched, intense humming held under the following ...

ISABEL: Victoria will know. And as for Mother ... i pray to God that nothing happens to her—try and protect her.

The enormity of their circumstance, and fear of what might have happened to ROBERT strike JOYCE like a whirlwind … She cries out:

JOYCE: Robert … Robert …

RORY senses something wrong. Rushes to her, puts his arms round her.

RORY: Hush mother, hush.

JOYCE: Off the edge. I did warn him. You know that Rory. Off the edge. I won't forgive him this time. You and I, Rory, we'll go home.

It's too much for RORY who kneels, arms round her, sobbing.

ISABEL: Give me that plank … (*She snatches it from the ground at his feet and moves towards the entrance as O'BRIEN enters and confronts her. VICTORIA cowers in a corner. The CHORUS crowd behind O'BRIEN.*)

O'BRIEN: You … I thought it would be the boy.

ISABEL: He's too young.

O'BRIEN: You're never too young. For anything. (*Laughter*) Put that down Lassie, I don't want to hurt you. Just a little sport, that's all we need.

ISABEL: Scum. (*She threatens him.*)

O'BRIEN (*Laughs*): I like your spirit. A real chip off the old block … not like Mummy's boy there. I guess it's time he had a little education … (*As the others laugh he makes a rush for ISABEL, and as she swings pulls the plank and her into him and holds her in a vice grip.*) Stop fluttering my little pigeon or I'll have to break your wings. (*He twists her arm …*) Now boys which one shall we take first, inspect the stock.

They circle ISABEL and VICTORIA … the former spits defiance. VICTORIA whimpers.

MACINTOSH: That ones for me … (*Indlcates VICTORIA*)

MCLINTOCK: Me too—Jesus, what a set she's got.

O'BRIEN: Alright missy, show us what you've got. Come on now, make it easy on yourself … (*VIctorla tries a desperate little run but the other two grab her. O'BRIEN shakes his head*) A pity … we'll just have to help you.

VICTORIA screams as one holds her and the other rips her dress.

ISABEL (*Struggling furiously*): Leave her alone, you beasts. (*She manages to bite O'BRIEN'S hand, with a curse he lets her go. She begins to unbutton her dress.*) I dare you to take me … Go on, if you have no shame but leave her alone …There …

She stands defiant.

JOYCE: The edge …the edge …

O'BRIEN: Ye've got spunk girl, fire. I like that. And don't worry, your turn will come … (*A growl of assent*) But ye must understand lassie, that the most exciting thing when ye take a woman against her will is fear … (*Laughs*) … It's the finest cock stiffener in the world, and there's not a man here …

ISABEL (*Spits*): Men!

O'BRIEN (*Unperturbed*): Who doesn't want to take that frightened, pretty plump little rabbit right now. (*ISABEL goes for O'BRIEN'S face with her nails—he holds her and shakes her like a dog.*) We'll deal with you later, when we get a second wind. Hold her boys, hold her hard and if she gets out of hand slap her across the tits—that'll take the wind out of her fine McGregor sails ... (*They grab her.*) I'll take the little one first—but you won't have to wait long ... (*Slaps her across the face.*) because the next best thing after fear is the sight of blood and I'm sore afraid you're going to spill some.

RORY—*snapping out of his self pity and grief:*

RORY: You're not going to hurt anyone ... (*He tries to get to O'BRIEN but is stopped and punched in the stomach and keels over, gagging.*)

JOYCE (*Like a child*): I did warn him. You all know that.

She peers about her at the CHORUS. ISABEL is desperate to keep attention away from her.

ISABEL: Hush Mother ... it's alright. Be quiet now.

A VOICE: Yeah—what are we going to do about the old bidy?

O'BRIEN: It'd be a sin not to give her a chance—for I doubt Mr. McGregor was much interested, being such a good Christian.

An intense silence as O'BRIEN advances on VICTORIA, fixing her with his eyes as he slowly unbuckles his belt. A sudden total blackout ... followed immediately by VICTORIA'S agonised, high pitched scream. A silence. The whistle echoing ... the wheels running ...

ACT III, SCENE 3

The reporters are discovered in separate spotlights. They are filing copy ... cables. Chatter in the background. The BALLADEER stands to one side as newsvendor.

BALLADEER: Read all about it—Italian labourer shot from Maritime excursion train ...

STAR (*Riding over*): The assailants have not yet been identified.

BALLADEER: Excursion train attacked by work gangs at night.

POST (*Riding over*): In retaliation for continual harassment. There are no windows left on the train, the interior is smashed and covered with filth of every description.

BALLADEER: Lone widow defends her home with shotgun ...

GLOBE (*Riding over*): Drives off excursionist drunks, wounding one.

BALLADEER: Three women on train stripped and raped ...

STAR: ... repeatedly claims man, hospitalised at Fort William after being thrown from train.

BALLADEER: Read all about it.

GLOBE: ... dregs of the earth, imported beggars,

STAR: … a mongrel mass of ignorance, crime and superstition …

POST: … totally unfit for the duties of society …

GLOBE: … the decencies of civilised life are totally alien to this ravening horde of Maritimers.

The chattering of the cables increase in speed and intensity. They chant together.

Where were the police? Who is responsible? The police, justice, responsible …

The chattering stops. SASKatchewan, ALBERTA, MANITOBA enter from one side, CP and OTTAWA from the other, accompanied by two policemen. The stage is lit in garish white, slatted with bars as if in a hastily erected stockade. The train whistles.—is heard approaching. The noise is deafening as it pulls into the station. It snorts, stops, expels steam—it fills the stage like a fog. Doors bang but there are no other sounds, no voices. Slowly, painfully, like soldiers returning from the front, the CHORUS enter, carrying the remnants of their belongings. They are dirty, unshaven, blood spattered, ripped and torn. They stumble across the stage and are herded into the barred area by police. Like dumb oxen they offer no resistance … all fight has left them.

MANITOBA: My God.

ALBERTA: Like refugees from a war.

SASK: And one that they created, if the reports are true. Look—here come some of the real victims.

The MCGREGOR party comes slowly into view. ROBERT'S head is swathed in bandages hastily made from somebody's skirt. His arm is in a sling, and he walks with a limp. He is supported by RORY and the ANCIENT. JOYCE walks like a somnambulist, held up and directed by ISABEL and VICTORIA. All three women show signs of their ordeal, but ISABEL in particular shows signs of having been beaten. CP rushes across to them, waving a CONSTABLE to follow. With sidelong glances at the press, he whispers, gesticulates, cajoles. The CONSTABLE begins to escort them from the stage. seeing this, the press rush forward, notebooks in hand but find their way blocked by the second CONSTABLE. Angry gestures prove futile … and their attempts to get round him are blocked, not too gently. The MCGREGOR party exit. The reporters huddle … deprived birds of prey. CP goes to OTTAWA.

OTTAWA: Well?

CP: I've sent them under escort to the hotel. A physician will be in attendance—they can bathe, rest, have their ills attended to. The mayor's wife is arranging for a new wardrobe to be put at the ladies' disposal … at my expense of course.

OTTAWA: That's not what I meant and you damn well know it.

CP: Ah, yes. The other thing. The constable will, of course, once the ladies, once the whole party are sufficiently composed, try and get them to identify the perpetrators of this terrible outrage.

OTTAWA: Try! We have to get someone. Look at those vultures, waiting to pounce. (*Indicates press*)

CP: They're the ones responsible for all this. Printing lies and distortions, inflaming weak imaginations.

OTTAWA: I'm not interested in responsibility. I'm only concerned that we deal with matters as quickly as possible, so that the press and the public will forget the whole wretched incident as quickly as possible.

CP: You're right, of course. But have you stopped to consider that the women might be too distressed to—even wish to discuss it?

OTTAWA: Dammit man, one scapegoat will do. And once you've got him, jail him, gag him, and scatter this lot as far and wide as possible. Out of sight, out of mind.

CP: My sentiments exactly. Ah, the other problems are bearing down upon us.

The three provinces cross to them

OTTAWA: Well gentlemen, this is a sorry mess.

MANITOBA: It is. But it's not much good crying over spilt milk. What do you intend to do about it?

OTTAWA: CP?

CP: As I've just explained to Ottawa, with your co-operation we'll ship this sorry looking rabble out of here with all speed.

SASK: And when does the next train arrive?

CP: Tonight. Then there'll be three every twenty-four hours for the next week … don't worry gentlemen … there'll be twenty thousand men here within days.

SASK (*For once aggressive*): You damned fool—that is the worry.

MANITOBA: What will we do with them all? Can't you cancel a few trains?

CP: Impossible. The tickets are already sold.

SASK: Then give refunds.

CP: I can't do that. They'd lynch us all. We, and that includes you gentlemen, have promised them the earth, if only for a brief period of time, and they're not going to be denied.

SASK: Even if all they find is a desert.

CP: You and your damned gloomy predictions Saskatchewan. They spread like cholera. All you've had is one night of ground frost …

SASK: A killing frost.

CP: Alright. If … and it's a big if, there are too many excursionists then I'll employ them track laying.

SASK: Track laying. They'd get seventy five cents an hour less than they've been led to expect, and by the time you've taken money out for board and blankets they'll have nothing left to get home with. You've just got to change your policy.

CP: The contract they've signed calls for a minimum of thirty days work before they can return on my subsidised fare of eighteen dollars. It's exactly the same as previous years and I see no reason to change it.

SASK: And if they can't get work at all …

OTTAWA: Come now … you're not without resources, any of you. You've got the Salvation Army, the YMCA, Church charities. They'll help in an emergency.

SASK: The emergency is upon us. Or can't you see? (*Indicates CHORUS*)

OTTAWA: Oh that. There'll be no repetition of journeys like that I can assure you. CP has posted armed guards on every following train ...

SASK: Bolting the stable door after the horse has gone.

ALBERTA: At least he's learned from his mistakes.

SASK: Have you? Have I? Have any of us? The poor devils who end up working for the railways for slave wages won't exactly be filling the air with joyful news when they get home ... if they get home. And as for you Ottawa, you'd better start thinking now about your future political strategy.

OTTAWA: I don't understand you.

SASK: Then I'll spell it out. Nobody from the East will ever believe in the great Canadian myth, that there's equal opportunity for all in this Country. It's not a harvest you'll reap, any of us for that matter but a whirlwind. (*To ALBERTA and MANITOBA*) Are you coming to organise our charities or not? (*A beat the exit*)

OTTAWA: That Saskatchewan is nothing but a damned troublesome socialist. For goodness sake, try and keep him away from the press in future.

CP: Don't worry. Meanwhile I'd better try and soothe their feathers ... they look slightly ruffled. (*He calls them*) Gentlemen ... I'm sorry for the time we kept you waitlng but as you must realise, we had a thousand things to attend to ...

PRESS: What's happened to the women? Are they being protected? Where have you taken them? Have there been any arrests ...?

CP holds up his hand.

CP: Both Ottawa and I, and indeed, the representatives of the Province themselves appreciate your desire to speak to the—apparently—abused passengers but, as I'm sure you must realise, the delicate nature of the alleged offences, and respect for the distress that must have occurred—if it did occur—makes it vital that we put their feelings before all else, yet, even our natural desire to bring the offenders to speedy justice, if the rumours are verified. Once they are rested and refreshed, then, and only then, will we proceed with an investigation. Until that time, I beg you to be discreet about the whole affair ... for humanitarian reasons ...

The reporters confer quickly amongst themselves. A slow fade ... All exit in blackout.

ACT III, SCENE 4

The MCGREGORS' hotel. JOYCE is sitting, staring vacantly ahead. VICTORIA and ISABEL have changed and ROBERT'S bandages replaced. He is pacing, limping, slowly. RORY is standing sullen and immobile.

ROBERT: Ye must go, girl. It was horrible, yes, foul beyond imagining, yet it happened. But your whole life is still running ahead of you, and Fergus is a good man. He's strong and kind, and he's waited for ye for over a year now.

Aye, and he's still waiting.(*Isabel doesn't respond. A beat as ROBERT tries another tack*) Won't ye just think of the hundreds of children, many not yet born, who are waiting for ye as a teacher? And ye'll be a good one too.

ISABEL: I am not going to Edmonton.

ROBERT: Why not lass?

RORY: She's right. We should all turn around and go back.

ROBERT (*A little uncertainly*): Haven't I told ye before The McGregors don't turn back, whatever the odds.

ISABEL: I'm not turning back—I'm just changing direction, that's all. Fergus will know about this. (*Bitter*) By now the whole country knows. You're right in one way, Father. Fergus would still marry me despite—all this. (*A beat*) He'd gentle me, ask nothing until I volunteered the information, and if I didn't—he never would.

ROBERT: There you are then.

ISABEL: But the whole world knows. Can't you see? No, I suppose not. I can hear them now, his friends, acquaintances, those he works with, whispering behind their hands as we pass by. "That's his wife, Isabel, you know. The one that was raped, aye, and more than once, by more than one person, on the train." And some would pity him; and some laugh behind his back, and still others wonder whether or not I hadn't enjoyed it—it's the way of men to think like that isn't it? (*A beat*) Do you really think I could do that to him?

ROBERT: Are ye sure it's him ye're thinking about? Is it not yourself?

ISABEL (*Crying out*): I love him. And if I do have any pride or strength left in me, it's because of that love. But it's also because of that that I can't go to him. Understand father, please.

ROBERT (*Sighing*): I don't know if I understand anything any more. But I'll try. (*He sits down wearily.*) Everything is so damned hard … I'm confused … (*Surprised at himself*) I've never been confused in me life before.

RORY: Then why can't we go back? Now. It's not too late. And Isabel doesn't want to go to Edmonton … and I …

ISABEL (*Furious*): Isabel wants to be anonymous. Isabel will change her name. Isabel wants to bury herself in the wilderness and become as inconspicuous as a sparrow.

ROBERT: So—this family is to go on then?

ISABEL: I would wish so.

ROBERT: Mother is not as she was.

ISABEL: None of us are what we were. I'll take care of Mother.

ROBERT: I don't know if I have the strength—or the will.

ISABEL (*Goes to him.*): You can still do it Father. Create a new garden—I'll help. You can even read us Ecclesiastes—I'll listen this time, I promise.

ROBERT (*He raises his head, his eyes full of tears.*): Your poor Mother. He didn't listen, did He, though she cried out. I always knew, in my heart, that when the time came He would avert His gaze. That perhaps, He was never there at all. That's what the old preacher was telling me all that time: "Whatsoever thy hand findeth to do, do it with thy might; for there is no work, nor device, nor knowledge, nor wisdom, in the grave, whither thou goest."

ISABEL (*Soft*): He also said, a living dog is better than a dead lion.

ROBERT: Then ye listened, after all. (*A beat*)

ISABEL: Father—we need you now ... more than ever.

ROBERT: A living dog ... Aye. Then I suppose we'll have to try one more time, won't we? Och Victoria—I was so wrapped up in meself I'd forgotten ye. What will ye be doing?

VICTORIA: I'm going to him. I have to see if he understands. I have to trust him.

ISABEL: It will take a long time.

VICTORIA: I know ... But ... (*Struggles for words*) It's not just the pain, the hideous memories—it's as if my whole self has been violated Isabel ... and my soul is in pieces. I need him to make me whole again.

ROBERT: I'm not sure I know what ye're talking about either ... well, if it doesn't work out as ye wish, ye must come to us for a spell, wherever we are.

ISABEL: We'll write.

VICTORIA: Yes, we will.

CP enters discreetly.

CP: Ladies ... Gentlemen ... I trust that everyone is feeling a little better, somewhat refreshed. (*A pause. No response*) Your wants have been catered to? (*An uncomfortable pause*) Well, if everything is fine ... (*Another pause*) It's just that—I have been asked, by various authorities—(*Quite nervous*) I don't really know how to approach this.

ISABEL: Then don't.

CP: What?

ISABEL: I know what you've come for.

CP: Really.

ISABEL: You want to ask us if we wish to identify the men who attacked us. Really though, you're hoping that we don't.

CP: My dear lady, I know you are distraught, but that is a preposterous assumption.

ISABEL: It is, isn't it? Well, you can put your mind at rest, aye, and those of your political friends. None of us have any intention of identifying anyone. (*With increasing anger*) We're not going to feed sensationalism, the bawdy gossip of taverns, the prurient minds of prissy old maids. If you gave me a gun and asked me to shoot them I'd gladly do so, without a flicker of conscience, but you won't do that and anything less is unthinkable. By pleading drunkenness, temporary insanity, even compliance from us, they'd probably receive nothing but the applause of every frustrated male in the country. No. They can carry my scorn and hatred with them to the grave. They will never have the satisfaction of becoming heroes to their kin, or gain notoriety at any trial. They won't even have the satisfaction of repeating their exploits to their friends, for without public exposure and almost certain exoneration there can be nothing but shame in the telling—a cankerous wound in the memory.

A pause

CP: Well—I can see that your mind is made up. And, to be frank with you, I'm in total sympathy with your position. I agree, shooting or hanging would be their just deserts but I'm afraid, knowing our justice system, that even a jail term would be unlikely—particularly with so many ... Well, obviously, you understand. And ... now sir, to more pleasant matters. You wish to travel to Saskatchewan. I understand. I am authorised to tell you that the best available land is now at Swift Current and we are prepared ...

ROBERT: We'll travel to Swift Current.

CP: Good. I'll make sure you get a private coach, at our expense of course ...

ROBERT: No thank you. We'll pay our own way. We need neither charity or sympathy.

CP: Oh Sir. If only there were more settlers like you. At the very least then, allow me to telegraph our agent and tell him you're coming. That way, we can speed up the acquisition process for you.

ROBERT (*Angry*): Didn't you understand me, sir? We will arrive in exactly the same position as anyone else seeking land. There will be no cables.

CP: As you wish. (*He turns to go—pauses*) I must say that, as a family, you have excited my profound admiration. You have treated this whole unfortunate incident with great courage, and restraint, and circumspection. Remarkable.

He exits.

ISABEL: Thank you for that, Father.

ROBERT: Taking anything from him would contaminate us for life. Will you be travelling part way with us Victoria?

VICTORIA: No. Thank you anyway. Like you, I must make my own way now. The Lord is my shepherd, I shall not want.

She stares steadily at ROBERT. Visibly moved, he turns away. ISABEL goes to her. They embrace.

ROBERT (*Blowing his nose loudly*): Rory ... go help your Mother.

RORY goes to her, lifts her gently and begins to lead her off.

ROBERT: I was too hard on him Isabel, wasn't I? He's his mother's son, too gentle by far for this land, but then, she'll need all the gentling she can get now ... (*A beat hesitant*) You think, Isabel, that you and I can build upon this—together?

ISABEL: Yes. In praise of God and for the love of man.

ROBERT: In defiance of Him now I'm thinking. And as for the rest—oh well. Time has its ways. (*They move to exit.*) Good bye Victoria.

ISABEL and VICTORIA embrace ... then she and ROBERT exit. VICTORIA surveys her space, tears in her eyes then falls to her knees and begins to pray as the lights fade.

ACT III, SCENE 5

The CHORUS discovered in the stockade. They sit, stand, sullen and resentful. O'BRIEN prowls amongst them like a caged lion. The BALLADEER:

BALLADEER: (*A slow mocking reprise of the CP song 2nd verse*)

> And feasts there'll be in plenty
> as you whistle in the sun,
> the grain will flow like rivers,
> the mighty threshers hum,
> and as each day is over
> you will wend your joyful way
> to the glowing farmhouse kitchen
> for steaks, and mugs of tay ...

The ANCIENT shuffles forward.

CONSTABLE: All right you lot, get your gear together. Who the hell are you ... what are you doing here?

ANCIENT: Oh nothing sir, I just came to work, that's all. That's what we leave home for ye see. To work ... to labour. To forget.

O'BRIEN seizes upon the diversion.

O'BRIEN: My God boys, look. It's the old Jinker himself.

CONSTABLE: The what?

O'BRIEN: Bad cess to him. If I could get me hands on him.

Moves as if to do so, held back by MACINTOSH

CONSTABLE: What's he done?

O'BRIEN: Done. He's the one started it. All of it. Back there in Nova Scotia, egging everyone on, filling the youngsters full of booze, bragging of all the women he'd taken. I bet it was him and his cronies did all that stuff on the train.

CONSTABLE: Where are they?

O'BRIEN: Ain't seen 'em since we got here, eh lads. Must've been moved on. I thought he'd gone too, the dirty old bugger. They had to kick him out of the ladies carriage the very first night ... isn't that right?

The CHORUS begin too, to see a way out, and some mumble their assent.

"True. Right enough."

A train whistle ... very loud ... in the station. CP hurries in. The train whistle.

CP: That's their train. I want them out of here ... now.

CONSTABLE: A moment, sir.

He draws CP to one side and whispers, indicating the ANCIENT who stands confused, not knowing what is happening.

O'BRIEN (*Intense*): Did ye mind that? We're gone. All of us. Now fer God's sake keep yer mouths shut. It's all over.

CP (*Turns and looks at ANCIENT*): Him! Oh well, he'll do I suppose. (*The train whistles.*) Now get that rabble out of here.

CONSTABLE: It'll be a pleasure ... we don't want their kind hanging around Winnipeg.

He opens the stockade door. Light change reflects the action.

CONSTABLE: Alright you lot. The train's over there. Get moving.

The train whistles. The station begins to fill with steam. There's a moment of disbelief and then in concert, whooping and jostling. The CHORUS rush off. BYRNE and WALSH hesitate a moment ... MACINTOSH turns ... Urges them on. They run after the others. The train whistles ... The ANCIENT Slowly begins to follow them ... CONSTABLE grabs him ...

CONSTABLE: Where d'you think you're going?

ANCIENT: With them. I belong with them. I came with them. I must follow them.

CONSTABLE: Get back in there.

He pushes him back into the stockade. The bars return at full. A roar of steam and thunder as the train pulls out.

CONSTABLE: He seems an unlikely villain, sir, I must say.

CP: Villainy has a lot of faces, Constable. And yon fellow has a lean and hungry look.

CONSTABLE: What's that, sir?

CP: Never mind Constable ... In any case, our Cassius is better off than the other ruffians.

CONSTABLE: Sir?

CP: There's little or no harvest where they're going which means no money, no food. They'll lay my tracks or starve and wait for the winter to kill 'em off. There's more than one way to skin a cat. Come with me now, there's another train due in twenty minutes—I think I'll dump that lot in Regina and let them deal with 'em. I've owed Saskatchewan one for a long time.

Chuckling he exits with the CONSTABLE. The train sounds recede into the distance. The lights fade save for a two bar spot. The ANCIENT stands, as if with one hand on each bar. BALLADEER plays softly in background.

ANCIENT: Gone. All gone. I could have gone too, with the McGregors ... they asked me out of kindness, but what should an old fool do with his falling days. I'd always remind them—pining and misery. So I came back to my own ... Not that I've ever been one of them, but I am a part of their history and pain, their violent stupidities, their occasional little dreams and loves, the false hopes that flicker, like glow worms in the dark as time travellers, we drift across oceans, continents, without direction or purpose as the night, like life, opens bleakly before us, shuts bleakly behind as we wait for the hangman to reel in the cord.

He slides down the bars.

This is as good a place to wait, as any.

The BALLADEER half lit:

BALLADEER: I wish I were
> gone far from here
> back where the raven
> and the deer
> vanish in mist
> and appear again
> in a shaft of sunlight,
> a cup of rain.
>
> A cup of rain and golden light,
> the dreaming fells
> all emerald bright
> the racing hares
> at springtime play
> and Mary beckoning
> where she lay.
>
> Her breath was sweet
> as summer pine,
> her hair as thick
> as chestnut mane,
> her body soft
> as summer grass
> how could I let
> such beauty pass?
>
> 'Twas pain and sorrow
> brought me here,
> far from the raven
> and the deer,
> and I may
> never more be seen
> upon the emerald
> hills of dream.

ANCIENT stares out.

ANCIENT: This is as good a place to wait, as any.

He begins to laugh, and cry. The lights fade.

Wolfgang Klooss

"WHEAT IS EMPIRE"
MICHAEL COOK'S *THE GREAT HARVEST EXCURSION* AND THE DRAMA OF THE MARITIMES

When Canada's most influential newspaper, the Toronto *Globe*, concluded in an article of 10 December 1856 that Canadians "[were] looking for new worlds to conquer"[1] this reflected as much the nationalist spirit of the pre-Confederation era[2] as it corresponded to the political creed that Canada's fate depended essentially on territorial expansion. A few years later, this vision was substantiated by journalist and poet Charles Mair[3] who captured the Canadian imagination with the slogan "wheat is empire."[4] Mair, one of the most radical spokesmen of *Canada First* and the *Expansionist Movement*[5], thus not only expressed the general conviction that Britain's future in North America rested largely on the agricultural potential of the Canadian West, but deliberately employed a terminology which signalled notions of extensive territory, rule and dominance as well as exploitation, subordination and control.[6]

At the turn of the century, most of the expansionists' dreams have come true. Due to the completion of the transcontinental railway in 1885 and the destruction of the old order in the West, i.e. the change of the Canadian Prairies from a Native economy based on the fur trade and the buffalo hunt to a farming industry, the Federal Government in accordance with the Provinces of Manitoba, Saskatchewan and Alberta[7] fosters massive immigration from Europe and Eastern Canada in order to prolong a steadily increasing crop production. In the years between 1911 and 1913, for instance, more than a million immigrants[8] arrive in Canada, many of whom settle in the Western regions. Regardless of these impressive numbers, labour is, however, still in great demand, especially during the harvest season, and it cannot come as a surprise that the Prairies even attract large numbers of migrants from Ontario and the Maritimes, where impoverished communities are only too eager to follow the lures of the "Golden West." At a wage rate of $ 2.50 per hour, they lend themselves as cheap labour force to a highly capitalist crop industry which promises record harvests and a personal share in the country's prosperity.

Usually exempted from historiographical accounts, this widely neglected chapter in Canadian history has become a story of erasure which is, however, brought to light again in Michael Cook's drama *The Great Harvest Excursion*. As Cook points out in the preamble to his play:

In the Year of Our Lord, 1908, reports of a record harvest on the Prairies triggered a rash of rumour, speculations, and reports of high wages, calculated to excite the interest of those who, from the Maritimes and Ontario, mostly jobless—either temporarily or permanently, rushed to the wheat fields every year to harvest and thresh the multi million dollar crop, the promise of eight to ten weeks work [...] being sufficient to tide them, however meagrely, over the winter. Whereas a farmer could plant his crop with a minimum of labour, the harvest itself was highly labour intensive, and thousands of part time labourers were needed to get the crop in before the weather turned.[9]

Originally conceived as Cook's contribution to the 1987 Stratford Festival[10], *The Great Harvest Excursion*, due to production costs[11], has, unfortunately, never been put on stage, nor has the text become available in print. The following discussion therefore aims at a contextual reading of the most prominent features of a play which deserves not only to be rescued from obscurity but which is among the few recent works of a playwright who is generally considered Newfoundland's most authentic stage voice.[12]

Born in Fulham, London, of Anglo-Irish parents in 1933, Michael Cook experiences manual labour and a 12-year service in the British army that takes him to Korea, Japan, Europe, Malaya and Singapore before he enroles in a three-year drama course at Nottingham University. In 1966 he writes his first radio plays. It is also the year when Cook leaves England for Canada where he settles in St. John's, Newfoundland. As he recollects twelve years later:

All I know is that I love theatre with a passion. It's life and
breath to me. [...]
Some men are born at home.
Others spend all their lives in search of it.
I spent thirty-four years looking for one.
When I came to Newfoundland I found it. [...]
I know I shall have to leave it spasmodically, but I'll always come
back. It is the source of my imagination and the seat of any joy I
have ever found.[13]

Interestingly enough, Michael Cook chooses one of Canada's remotest regions for his home. He feels as much attracted by the overwhelming presence of the sea, as he is impressed by the spiritual strength and physical endurance with which Newfoundland's fishermen try to resist a hostile environment and social hardships. In his own words, Newfoundland was always a "survival culture," it "remained an outpost [...], became a place for the dispossessed: [...] the nature of the environment determined that it was more important to depend upon [the] neighbours than it was to keep old animosities alive."[14]

In this way, playwright Michael Cook establishes a close kinship with the most prolific poet of the Maritimes, E.J. Pratt (1882-1964), whose evolutionary visions and deterministic view of nature are recorded in such epic works as *The Roosevelt and the Antinoe* (1930), *The Titanic* (1935), or historical long poems like *Brébeuf and His Brethren* (1940) and *Towards the Last Spike* (1952).[15] Accordingly,

Pratt's psychological reading of the Newfoundland landscape has informed many of Cook's plays. This is particularly true of *Jacob's Wake* (1975)[16] which concludes his Newfoundland trilogy, a series of plays that also comprises *Colour the Flesh the Colour of Dust* (1972) and *The Head, Guts and Soundbone Dance* (1973). At the same time, Cook is fascinated by the idioms of a culture that is deeply rooted in mythology and finds its expression in folklore and highly ritualistic rites. His Anglo-Irish background makes him particularly sensitive to a "communality of place and tongue unique in North America."[17]

When Cook arrives in St. John's, Newfoundland's cultural heritage is seriously endangered though. The Liberal government under Premier Joseph Smallwood has enacted a resettlement programme,

> whereby fishermen and their families from no longer viable outposts of Newfoundland [are] able to begin new lives in areas such as Placentia Bay and other more active centres on the south coast. Resettlement had soon begun after the Second World War, at the time when Newfoundland finally joined Confederation (1949), but its most active period was from the mid-sixties to the mid-seventies.[18]

In Cook's understanding, this policy means "an assault upon a traditional way of life unparalleled since the enforced evictions from Ireland, Scotland, and England that had brought so many settlers to the Maritimes."[19] For him, Newfoundlanders [leave] behind not only

> noble, high-steepled wooden churches, built by their own hands. They [leave] behind their sense of identification and place and community. They [leave] behind the bones of their ancestors. They [leave] behind their history.[20]

This sense of cultural deprivation and lost identity inscribed so deeply into many stories of migration, accounts for both Cook's "almost reflex sympathy for any underdog"[21] as well as his paramount concern for historical drama, "to which he says he returns in order to reactivate his own original experiences."[22] Subsequently, Cook develops a thematic scope which echos many of the political and social issues emerging in the theatrical productions of the *Mummers' Troupe*, Newfoundland's first professional company to concentrate solely on local and indigenous material. Whereas the *Mummers' Troupe*, which was founded in St. John's in 1971, adheres to the practice of collective, politicized theatre, using Paul Thompson's *Theatre Passe Muraille* with its touring productions as a role model,[23] Cook, on the other hand, refrains from activist forms of dramatic entertainment. Instead, he strongly subscribes to Shavian and Brechtian theatrical conventions as well as to the Theatre of the Absurd. This deliberate reference to traditional European modes of drama may explain why Cook becomes nationally known in Canadian theatre within a very short time and why his works are quickly staged in Canada's major playhouses. Moreover, it serves as an explanation for his delight in "large casts [...] colour and excitement [...] movement and light,"[24] or as he points out: "I like lots of things happening on stage [...]." [25]

Notwithstanding Cook's immediate success on a national level, his dramatic reconstructions and theatrical treatments of history deal so strongly with Maritime subject matters that his oeuvre has been rightly placed in the context of regional drama which registers a particular concern for the documentary form[26] and renders the most typical variant of Canadian theatre in the latter half of the 1960s and the following decade, until it loses some of its original momentum during the 1980s. Even more so, Cook's works "are more suffused with the atmosphere and spirit of Canadian regional life than most plays written in Canada."[27] In this regard, he lives up to Northrop Frye's dictum that the "question of identity is primarily a cultural and imaginative question [and that] the question of Canadian identity, so far as it affects the creative imagination, is not a 'Canadian' question at all, but a regional question."[28]

Moreover, as indicated above, for Cook the meaning of region extends beyond the boundaries of mere physical geography. Instead, it opens itself up to the artist's visions, turns landscape into mindscape, creates spaces for specific metaphors and characters, becomes foremost a territory of social anxiety and psychological encounters. Similarly, Saskatchewan's Ken Mitchell[29] or Alberta-born George Ryga argue that

today's drama to a large extent concerns itself with the vanishing landscape. The fisherman working depleted waters […] the Nova Scotian family leaving its ancestral fields […] the Indian torn between two worlds—these seem to be paramount sources of concern, and content matter of contemporary plays. Certainly these are critical regions of social anxiety. But what is the larger contribution we are instinctively making? Perhaps we are defining the more visible details of a canvas on which our national hopes and frustrations are enacted. Perhaps we are doing what our earlier theatre should have done but failed in undertaking—recording in a human way the agonies and triumphs of yet another transition when nature or economics beat us back and alter the course of our destiny as a people.[30]

Since Cook shares these views on the nature and function of contemporary Canadian drama, it can hardly come as a surprise that Ryga's statement reads like a commissioned introduction to *The Great Harvest Excursion* which is probably one of the plays which Cook had on his mind when he confessed in 1978: "I have about six plays in my head that are waiting to be written, though God knows when they'll get done or if they'll see the light of day."[31]

Although *The Great Harvest Excursion* has not seen the light of the stage, it has at least been delivered from the mind of the author. Again Michael Cook returns to historical drama, again he selects a story from "the last human frontier"[32] and demonstrates his artistic commitment to issues of social, political and anthropological concern.

As the title suggests, most of the dramatic action takes place on a train of the *Canadian Pacific* which is on its way from the rain-drenched landscape of the Atlantic shores in Nova Scotia to the "land of milk and honey" (I,1, 132) in the West. The railway carriage serves as an enclosed space within which two major sets of characters indulge in a common obsession: "wheat" is the magic word that has caught their imagination and determines their lives. Whereas Canada's political and public voices, i.e. the Federal Government which is represented by a character named "Ottawa," the Provinces which appear as "Alberta," "Manitoba" and "Saskatchewan", the transcontinental railway companies which are personified by "CP," or the press which figures as "Star," "Post" and "Globe" have merely an interest in rapid economic growth and large turnovers, the two travelling parties stand for the human side of this enterprise. On the one hand, they are portrayed as a group of rather stock-like male figures of either Scottish or Irish decent, who have been recruited as an itinerant labour force to serve in the great harvest, on the other, they are conceived as individualised members of the McGregor family who dream of "something different, space, new voices." They are eager "to buy [their] own land and create [their] own harvest." (I,3, 139) The McGregors are accompanied by Victoria McGrath, a young woman from Prince Edward Island who has never been away from home, but now wants to meet her husband in Saskatoon. They are the true protagonists of this three-act drama which also introduces a balladeer and a chorus who, similar to the "Spokesman" character in Cook's Newfoundland trilogy, open and close nearly all of the 15 scenes, thus providing an epic frame for what happens on stage. In addition, the playwright employs a few supporting characters, namely a train conductor, bar owner and two police constables, as well as a *dramatis persona* of allegorical proportions. It is the either visual, verbal or spiritual presence of the "Ancient" which supplies *The Great Harvest Excursion* with a specific countertext that undercuts the actual plot from its very beginning so that the reader/spectator becomes immediately sensitive to the human tragedy that will evolve during the course of the following events.

In the opening scenes, Cook acquaints his audience with the political and economic mechanisms at work in the crop industry as well as the ideological means that are mandatory for the construction of what Ottawa terms "great and powerful nations." According to Ottawa,

> this country is simply following the same pattern of development as our great neighbour to the South. The ruthless, the greedy, and yes, the courageous, open it up, and they sell or lease to the honest and hardworking settlers who follow. Historically, it's a very ancient tradition, goes back as far as the Romans [...]. (I,1, 133)

The representative of Federal Canada gives, of course, just a "lecture on the glories of capitalism" (I,1, 134) as Alberta remarks with a tone of conspiracy. Subsequently, the human dignity of the workmen from the Maritimes is never acknowledged, instead the O'Briens, Rosses, McLintocks, Hogans, Walshs or Macintoshs are reduced to a necessary means of production which guarantees "for our prosperity." (Alberta, I,1, 131) In order to have them fulfill their designated roles "we just have to fill their heads full of dreams and their eyes full of sky and that will do it." (Ottawa, I,1, 130) Later, Robert McGregor tells his family that "the West is vast—beyond imagining—one vast golden horizon." (I,3, 139). He does not know yet that he only echos CP's propagandistic voice which captures the west as "the land of promise and hope and opportunity." (I,2, 137)

These are only two out of many textual references which signal the importance that Cook's play ascribes to myth as a specific form of discourse in the identity formation of a country. As far as Canada, or by the same token the United States, are concerned, myth is strongly associated with the geographical notion of West.

> West is the direction of the open, the possible, adventure, expansion, growth the self. West is the margin on which we stand. It is our future, the uninvented world. European explorers sailed west across the ocean to a new world. Horace Greeley spoke the famous words "Go west, young man," and western expansion as the best expression of possibility became established as the central North American myth. [...] The Canadian Prairies are the last stronghold of the discourse of west, the last place where the myth of open possibilty has a quotidian function. [...] on the Canadian Prairies, people identify themselves very strongly as Westerners. [...] And political dialogue, both in the press and in ordinary conversation maintains the distinction. The West consists of good guys, always oppressed by an older, more decadent and Cynical East.[33]

While Cook, on the one hand, uses the North American myth of the West as an ideological setting for *The Great Harvest Excursion*, he, on the other, deconstructs its implications by a plot which shows how little space the vastness of the Plains offers to those who have nothing to give but themselves. The Maritimers are string puppets in a game, whose rules are entirely defined by economic and political interests. They represent the underdogs in a country which looks West, without ever acknowledging what is beyond East. Among the caricatures of institutionalised power, it is only Saskatchewan, who gives second thoughts to the social injustice encoded in regional difference. He even shows some sympathy for the cause of the poor and becomes increasingly aware of the ideological traps inherent in mythmaking.

> MANITOBA: What if the Maritime economy improves?
>
> ALBERTA: (*Laughing*) And what if fish could fly ... no no, they'll always be a subsistence economy, and thousands will clamour to come West every fall. And don't forget, the great advantage of migrant labour is that it isn't, nor can it ever be, organised labour. [...] your contented oxen of a labourer, too tired to rebel ... too lonely to think.
>
> SASK: I think I prefer men with more initiative than that. [...] it's those with intiative who move on after the harvest, buy land, bring their families though God knows by the time CP has finished with them they haven't much left. (II,2, 149)

When the weather does not hold and CP's enthusiastic prediction that "this harvest is going to be the biggest of all time, in the history of the world" (I,1, 132) proves completely mistaken, Saskatchewan not only considers the consequences for the itinerant workers, but also takes responsibility.

SASK: And then there's the problem of the harvesters. What the devil are we going to do with them all? [...] There's trainload upon trainload out there, backed up between here and Toronto, and they're hungry, without jobs or money.

MANITOBA: My God—I never thought of that.

SASK: That's the trouble. Nobody wants to think. [...] We're as much to blame as anybody. No planning. Too much dreaming, too much damned mythology—and too many lies. We've become practical politicians, gentlemen. (II,4, 155)

In contrasting the cynicism typical of Ottawa, CP, Manitoba and Alberta, with Saskatchewan's concern for the human side of labour, Cook puts his play into an additional political and historical perspective. Although the Liberals were in power in 1908, the year in which *The Great Harvest Excursion* takes place, co-operative tendencies have always been so strong in Saskatchewan that this Prairie province in 1944 elected North America's first Socialist government.[34]

How strongly Cook challenges the notion of West becomes evident, when *The Great Harvest Excursion* reaches its climax. The Ancient's mysterious forebodings—"There's a monster aboard here, evil, devouring. It's caged now, but it's waiting to spring" (II,1, 145)—eventually come true. Treated like herds of cattle, the harvesters engage in heavy drinking and fights before they begin to stampede. When the train has to make an unexpected halt, they escape from their cage, beat up a bar owner, plunder his stocks and set the building on fire. Now that the "beast [has] SLIPPED ITS CHAINS" (II,4, 156), the Ancient himself falls prey to its appetite, and if it were not for McGregor's brave intervention, the raging gang would probably knock this "jinker" (III,5, 173) to death. Instead, they turn to McGregor's family and Victoria McGrath. At this point, the audience is well prepared for a scene, which requires no further comment. Joyce McGregor and her daughter Isabel, together with Victoria, become the victims of violent harassment and sexual abuse. Neither Joyce's trust in God, nor her husband's attempt to fight back, or Isabel's laconic conclusion that "God lives in communities [and] apparently [...] gets lost in the wilderness" (II,6, 160), can spare Cook's protagonists the dreadful experience of bodily harm and humiliation. Canada's political institutions, of course, deny any responsibility for the drama. Ottawa and CP make just a few sardonic comments. They need a scapegoat, who can live up to the expectations of a decadent press that is longing for sensational stories. When O'Brien, one of the men involved in the crime, blames the disaster on the Ancient's "stories" about his adventures during previous harvest excursions, CP turns and approvingly looks at the scapegoat: "Him! Oh well, he'll do I suppose." (III,5, 174) The train can continue its journey out West and with it the harvesters disappear out of sight. Left behind on his own, the Ancient bids his farewell with a philosophical statement on the hardships of life, whereby his extensive usage of metaphors reflects some of the poetic quality that belongs to the trademarks of Cook's dramatic language:[35]

[...] Not that I've ever been one of them, but I am part of their history and pain, their violent stupidities, their occasional little dreams and loves, the false hopes that flicker, like glow worms in the dark as time travellers, we drift across oceans, continents, without direction or purpose as the night, like life, opens bleakly before us, shuts bleakly behind as we wait for the hangman to reel in the cord. (III,5,174-175)

Like in many of his previous plays, Cook, in *The Great Harvest Excursion*, again portrays the cruelties of men toward each other. He "recognizes a viciously destructive side to the populace, an appetite for senseless violence."[36] Moreover, he shows that a savage environment creates savage behaviour, or, as Brian Parker argues with respect to the final message in *Colour the Flesh the Colour of Dust*: "[…] just being alive, mere existence, is man's basic value; [this] also relates to the idea recurrent in Cook's drama, that feelings of humanity may be weekness in a savage environment […]."[37] The environment presented in *The Great Harvest Excursion* is, first of all, a product of the human nature. It emerges as a social landscape, filled with stories of appropriation, exploitation and control. In other words, Cook's play re-enacts a much neglected chapter of colonial history in North America. For a change, it is not the conquest of Western Canada's Native population which is under scrutiny, but, in reverse of geographical directions, the exploitation of the very Eastern provinces by Western interests. At the same time, Cook uses the colonial encounter to disclose a ruthless and barbaric self that is usually covered under the normative codes of civilisation and progress.[38]

Regarding the contents of the play, the process of civilisation, and with it the notion of "possibility", one of the prime ideological stimulants for Canadian westward expansion, are identical with destruction and death, the final possibility. Cook's Maritimers remain purely a labour force, they never manage to overcome their designated roles as servants who lend themselves to the construction of empires without ever sharing the profits, or, as Saskatchewan bitterly puts it: "Nobody from the East will ever believe in the great Canadian myth, that there's equal opportunity for all in this Country." (III,3,169)

In addition to the deconstruction of the Myth of the West, *The Great Harvest Excursion* does away with another legend. Whereas

to many Maritimers, over the years, the annual harvest excursion had become something of a rite of passage—a journey into manhood fuelled by tales as romantic and heroic as any that graced the opening of the Santa Fe and Oregon trails (Preamble 126).

Cook converts romance into nightmare. Thereby, he counters the male concept of initiation, which conceives the "journey into manhood" as a conquest of the female body. Since this conquest implies the appropriation of formerly unknown territory, "heroic tales" about initiation are essentially stories of the frontier. In this way, Cook's deconstructive approach towards the Myth of the West is paralleled by his attempt to demythologize the practice of male rites in a frontier society.

Although *The Great Harvest Excursion* depicts a rather gloomy world, Cook's play is not an entirely pessimistic piece of drama. It should not go unnoticed that Robert and Joyce McGregor, together with their children Isabel and Rory, form a permanent moral stronghold in the midst of a social wilderness void of ethical bonds. They exhibit a spiritual strength throughout the play, which, despite of their incredible humiliations, is unmatched by any of the other characters. While Joyce remains seriously scarred and Rory wants to return to the East, it is especially Isabel and her father, who regain their energy. Nothing will ever be the same for them, yet they manage to look forward again and keep their goal in sight:

RORY: Then why can't we go back. Now. It's not too late. And Isabel doesn't want to go to Edmonton ... and I

ISABEL (*Furious*): Isabel wants to be anonymous. Isabel will change her name. Isabel wants to bury herself in the wilderness and become as inconspicuous as a sparrow.

ROBERT: So—this family is to go on then?

ISABEL: I would wish so.

ROBERT: Mother is not as she was.

ISABEL: None of us are what we were. [...]

ROBERT: I don't know if I have the strength—or the will.

ISABEL: (*Goes to him.*) You can still do it Father. Create a new garden—I'll hel [...]

ROBERT: [...] Then I suppose we'll have to try one more time, won't we? (III,4, 170,171)

Subsequently, the balladeer's repetitive song lines: "It's too late now/there's no way back," loose not only the meaning of doom, on the contrary, for the McGregors, they open the road to the future. This is only made possible, because neither of them has been deprived of his dignity. Now, that they can continue the journey, *The Great Harvest Excursion* becomes yet another version of the ultimate Canadian story, which is the story of survival.

Notes

[1] Quoted after Doug Owram, Promise of Eden. *The Canadian Expansionist Movement and the Idea of the West* (Toronto: University of Toronto Press, 1980), 47; cf. also Doug Owram, "Reluctant Hinterland," in: Larry Pratt, Garth Stevenson (Eds.), *Western Separatism. The Myths, Realities and Dangers* (Edmonton: University of Alberta Press, 1981), 45-64.

[2] *The British North America Act* was enacted by the British Parliament on 29 March 1867. It provided for the confederation of the Province of Canada, i.e. Ontario and Quebec, Nova Scotia and New Brunswick into a federal state with a parliamentary system modelled on that of Britain. Subsequently, Canada gained Dominion status.

[3] Charles Mair is the author of *Dreamland and Other Poems* (1868), *Tecumseh: A Drama* (1886), *Through the MacKenzie Basin: A Narrative of the Athabaska and Peace River Treaty Expedition of 1899* (1908).

[4] Quoted after Owram, Promise of Eden, 127.

[5] The *Canada First Group* was founded in 1868 by George Taylor Denison, Robert J. Haliburton, William Foster, Henry J. Morgan and Charles Mair who promoted an imperialist ideology which envisaged Canada as a new stronghold within Britain's empire.

[6] Cf. *The New Shorter Oxford English Dictionary* (Oxford: Clarendon Press, 1993), 809, *s.v.* "empire."

[7] Manitoba had joined the Confederation in 1870, Saskatchewan and Alberta followed in 1905.

[8] Cf. Hans Braun, Barbara Schartz, "Die Bevölkerung," in: Hans Braun, Wolfgang Klooss (Eds.), *Kanada. Eine interdisziplinäre Einführung* (Trier: WVT-Verlag, 1992), 60-75, 61.

[9] Michael Cook, *The Great Harvest Excursion*. Playscript, dated 26 May, 1987, preamble.

[10] The Stratford Festival was initiated by businessman Tom Patterson in 1952-53. Its first artistic director was Tyrone Guthrie who served in this function from 1953-1955. The Stratford Festival has had a major influence on the development of Canadian theatre. Cf. Richard Horenblas, "The Stratford and Shaw Festivals," in: Anton Wagner (Ed.), *Contemporary Canadian Theatre. New World Visions* (Toronto: Simon and Pierre, 1985), 148-158.

[11] Michael Cook in a letter to the editors of this volume.

[12] All subsequent references to *The Great Harvest Excursion* are based on the playscript as published in this volume. Despite the fact that David French is a native of Newfoundland who has gained international acclaim as one of Canada's established playwrights, the majority of his works does not bear the emotional affinity to the Maritimes which has become a trademark of Cook's dramatic oeuvre. This applies even to French's play *1949* (1988) which centres on Newfoundland's entry into Confederation.

[13] "Michael Cook," in: Geraldine Anthony (Ed.), *Stage Voices. Twelve Canadian Playwrights Talk about Their Lives and Work* (Toronto: Doubleday, 1978), 207-232, 228.

[14]
Michael Cook, "Culture as Caricature. Reflections on a Continuing Obsession: Newfoundland," *Canadian Literature* 100 (1984), 72-78, 72.

[15]
Cf. for example Sandra Djwa, *E.J. Pratt: The Evolutionary Vision* (Vancouver: Copp Clark, 1974); Susan Gingell (Ed.), *E.J. Pratt on His Life and Poetry* (Toronto: University of Toronto Press, 1983).

[16]
Cf. Anthony (Ed.), *Stage Voices*, 227.

[17]
Cook, "Culture as Caricature," 72.

[18]
Richard Perkyns, "Michael Cook, *The Head, Guts and Soundbone Dance*. An Introduction," in: Perkyns (Ed.), *Major Plays of the Canadian Theatre 1934-1984* (Toronto: Irwin Publishing, 1984) 444-448, 444.

[19]
Cook, "Culture as Caricature," 73.

[20]
Cook, "Culture as Caricature," 73.

[21]
Brian Parker, "On the Edge: Michael Cook's Newfoundland Trilogy," *Canadian Literature* 85 (1980), 22-41, 22.

[22]
Parker, "On the Edge," 23.

[23]
Cf. Diane Bessai, "The Regionalism of Canadian Drama," *Canadian Literature* 85 (1980), 7-20, es 16; Terrie Goldie, "Newfoundland," in: Wagner (Ed.), *Contemporary Canadian Theatre*, 96-100, es 97, 98; Renate Usmiani, "The Alternate Theatre Movement," in: Wagner (Ed.), *Contemporary Canadian Theatre*, 49-59, es 53, 54.

[24]
Anthony (Ed.), *Stage Voices*, 228.

[25]
Anthony (Ed.), *Stage Voices*, 227.

[26]
Cf. Bessai, "The Regionalism of Canadian Drama," 12.

[27]
Perkyns, "Introduction," in: Perkyns (Ed.), *Major Plays*, 1-17, 1.

[28]
Northrop Frye, *The Bush Garden: Essays on the Canadian Imagination* (Toronto: House of Anansi, 1971), i, ii.

[29]
Cf. Robert Wallace, Cynthia Zimmerman, *The Work: Conversations with English-Canadian Playwrights* (Toronto: Coach House Press, 1982), es 92.

[30]
George Ryga, "Contemporary Theatre and Its Language," *Canadian Theatre Review* 14 (1977), 9.

[31]
Anthony (Ed.), *Stage Voices*, 228.

[32]
Quoted after Parker, "On the Edge," 23.

[33]
David Arnason, "The Prairies: Site of a Discourse About the Meaning of West;" typescript (1993), 16 p, 4-5.

[34]
Another, more specific, historical reference point is Prime Minister Wilfried Laurier's visit to Regina, which is mentioned earlier in the play. (See, I, 1, 130, 131).

35
Cook has not only acknowledged this observation, but even confessed that "a lot of the central ideas from [his] plays come from lines in poetry. [His] poetry." (Anthony (Ed.), *Stage Voices*, 222.)

36
Parker, "On the Edge," 25.

37
Parker, "On the Edge," 27.

38
Some of these apprehensions are reminiscent of Joseph Conrad's seminal work on colonialism, *Heart of Darkness* (1899), where storyteller Marlow comments his discovery of Kurtz with the words: "[…] the wilderness had found him out early and had taken on him a terrible vengeance […] it had whispered to him things about himself which he did not know […]." (Joseph Conrad, *Heart of Darkness* (Harmondsworth: Penguin Books, 1973; repr. 1974), 83. Cf. also Wolfgang Klooss, "Die Metaphorik des Kolonialismus. Joseph Conrad's *Heart of Darkness* als Problem literarischer Wirklichkeitserfassung um die Jahrhundertwende," *Germanisch-Romanische Monatsschrift* NF 31:1 (1981), 74-92.

David French

MEMOIR
(Chapter 1)

When Esau French married Sarah Patience Earle on May 18, 1892, my grandfather was twenty-nine, my grandmother, twenty-two. Sarah's family lived close by in Country Road. When she was two years old, her father, William, had drowned on the *Huntsman* and her mother, Tryphena, married James Mercer.

The following year Esau and Sarah's first child was born: Edith. For as long as my grandfather lived Edith would always remain his favorite, though she would die at the age of thirty-three in a tragic car accident, on the very day his grandson, fifty-eight years later, would set a play called *Salt-Water Moon*. Over the next seventeen years there were five more children: Will, Minnie, Eliza, Edgar, and Doris. Edgar was my father, a name he never liked and couldn't pronounce. In later years he still transposed the d and g, making it Egdar. All his life my father was known by his middle name, Garfield or simply Gar.

I remember an autumn day in the late 1960s. By that time my parents had sold the house on Dufferin Street, the last home they would ever own in Toronto, and built a house at Alcona Beach, Lake Simcoe, where so many of my early summers had been spent.

I took the bus up from the city that day, the air so clear you could see for miles, the country flat and brown and already touched by that distinctive autumn stillness. I found my father in the backyard, raking leaves that crunched underfoot like cellophane.

'You'll get a kick out of this,' he said, his blue eyes full of humour.

'What?'

'I was raking the leaves,' he said, 'when all of a sudden I heard someone calling my name: "Gar! Gar! Gar!" I looked around, but there wasn't a soul in sight. Then I heard it again: "Gar! Gar!" So I set down the rake and went around the house, walked around all four sides of her. I t'ought someone was playing a trick. Then I heard it the t'ird time: "Gar! Gar!" And I looked up, and there was this goddamned big black crow perched on the limb of that Scotch pine, crying, "Caw! Caw!"

We both laughed at his expense.

'I can get you a hearing-aid,' I said, finally. 'A friend of mine sells them.' He could've used a pair of prescription glasses as well, but he was far too vain for that. The image he had of himself refused to accomodate such human frailties.

'All right, my son,' he said, the humour draining from his eyes, 'there's no call to make fun. One of these days you might be afflicted yourself, and then we'll see how much you likes it.'

'Oh, come on.'

Disgruntled, he went on raking the leaves. He didn't mind poking fun at himself, my father, but it rankled him to the core if he thought someone else was doing it.

Originally Coley's Point had been Cold East Point, but over time the phonetic corruption became its legitimate name. In Newfoundland there are places whose desolate beauty makes the breath catch in your throat, and yet Coley's Point, the outport I was born in, has little to recommend it. In fact, it's rather austere and unprepossessing, a splinter of rock, almost a geological afterthought, that juts into Conception Bay, next to Bay Roberts.

The Frenches, like the Earls, had come from the West of England, Thomas Hardy country. For as long as anyone could remember our family had lived on the same postage stamp of rock. When Esau took his new bride to live with him, the floor of the house consisted simply of gravel. Every Saturday evening the men would sweep out the old gravel and bring pails of fresh stones up from the beach. There was no stove, just a fireplace whose hearth could accomodate a dozen people seated on a bench. Esau and Sarah's first three children were born in that house, but it was torn down before Eliza was born in 1903, and replaced by the house my own father was born in, and later his own children. The new house stood in the lee of a cliff, with a narrow road running in front of it. From the road you could spit into the blue waters of Conception Bay.

My grandmother had a garden she wouldn't let anyone enter. There were peonies out front, roses, bleeding-hearts, and honeysuckle. The honeysuckle clung to the sides of the house, and when the windows were left open on a summer night, the scent of honeysuckle would drift sweetly through the rooms.

The house consisted of two storeys. On the first floor you had a kitchen, store-room, a bedroom, parlour, and back porch. On the second floor, three more bedrooms. I remember there was a cedar chest on the second floor landing. My grandmother kept her good linen in it. That chest had once belonged to my grandfather's brother, Jacob. Years before Jacob French had been part of a seven man crew that had sailed to the West Indies with a load of salt cod, and on the return voyage they put into Bermuda to pick up a cargo of molasses and rum. All the crew came down with malaria. Four of the men died, including Jacob, and were buried at sea, sewn into canvas sheets and weighed down with pig-iron. And when the cedar chest belonging to Jacob was sent to Coley's Point, my grandparents found it still contained some of his clothes. But mostly it was filled with coconuts, souvenirs he was bringing home from that ill-fated voyage.

My grandfather, who died two years before I was born, had a reputation as a man you crossed at your own peril. In *Leaving Home* Mary describes Jacob's father to her son, Ben: 'He'd hurl you t'rough the window one minute and brush the glass off you the next.' That line captured the two warring sides of my grandfather who could erupt into sudden violence and wax sentimental just as quickly. It was a side of the man he passed on to his youngest son.

In 1980 I stood on a road in Coley's Point—my first visit home in thirty-five years—and listened to an old-timer recall my grandfather. The old gentleman had perfected the art of perpetual motion: every part of his body was alive and in constant motion. He wore a baseball cap whose peak he'd switch in the telling of the story, so that one second the peak faced forward, the next it tipped down on the back of his neck like a Jockey. It was a hot July day, and he danced around the road in the sunlight, delighted to be recalling an event from the distant past as though it had happened last week.

'Oh, he was some hard case, Esau was. One time he wanted to build a stone fence, so he hired me and Bobby Gooseney. We was just boys. Esau had this old wooden wheelbarrow he was fond of. It had iron wheels, and he loaned it to us to get the rocks up from the beach. I had the barrow all loaded, when one of the wheels dropped off and the rocks capsized. Suddenly a coconut struck me on the back of me head. Esau was standing up on the road pitching coconuts down at us like cannonballs. Well, sir, Bobby and me, we took off as fast as our legs would carry us, with Esau chasing after us, shaking his fist. He caught us somewhere up by Long Beach Pond. "What's you running away for, b'ys?" he says. He was smiling. "Come on, now. Come back to the house. Sarah'll make youse both a cup of tay." Christ, you didn't know from one minute to the next what he'd do.'

I have a photograph of Esau in middle age, posed in a rocker, looking more than slightly uncomfortable. He wears a black suit, fedora, and high starched collar and tie. The starched collar must have been just for the occasion, because he always insisted Sarah cut the collars off his shirts. His neck, being thick and short, the collars always chafed him under the chin. His face is strong and handsome, though stolid, the upper lip hidden by a neatly-trimmed brown mustache. In his eyes is a fierce unyielding quality that I've always associated with birds of prey, and it's that implacable look in his eyes, more than anything, that gives his face its forbidding cast. To have those eyes fix on you must have been intimidating, to say the least. It's no wonder that grown men would step off the road if they saw him coming.

My grandmother was the opposite. In another picture I have of them, Sarah stands in the garden beside her husband, her head cocked to one side in an attitude I remember from the years she lived with us in Toronto, her face wistful, even ingratiating, as though somehow she had to compensate for the fierceness of the man beside her, who gazes sternly at the camera in his white shirt and braces, his large big-knuckled hands dangling in front of him like a gunfighter.

In *Salt-Water Moon*, chronologically the first play in the Mercer quartet, the young Jacob Mercer returns to Coley's Point one night in the summer of 1926, determined against all odds to win back his former sweetheart, Mary Snow, the girl he'd abandoned the year before. In the course of the play we discover why Jacob fled the island the previous summer. And his reason had to do with his witnessing his father's humiliation at the hands of a local merchant. And his belief that his own fate was mirrored in what happened on the merchant's porch that summer.

The event that I wove into the dramatic fabric of the play actually happened. Unlike Jacob, however, my father never witnessed it. It occurred sometime between 1896 and 1900—Esau and Sarah had two children by this time, Edith and Will—but the shame that Esau suffered would forever live in my father's imagination, though it happened at least ten years before his birth in 1908. In no small way, it may have accounted for the depth of my father's compassion for the underdog.

In those days a fisherman like Esau would go into collar the first of May, meaning he would sign on as a member of a fishing crew. The month of May would usually be spent readying the schooner and gear for the voyage to Labrador. In the fall of the year the crew would come out of collar at the end of October—the termination of the six months of employment. The schooner would then be moored for the winter.

A man could either ship, which meant he worked for wages, or he could ship as a shareman, meaning he would receive a share of the catch, one half of which went to the skipper, the other to be divided amongst the sharemen. Esau decided to work for wages, which became his downfall, because later on it left him totally at the mercy of the local merchant who had bankrolled the voyage.

In early June the schooner sailed off for Labrador. But not long after putting out from Bay Roberts, it encountered a storm, so Skipper Will Dawe put into Harbour Grace, intending to wait out the bad weather. When the storm persisted, Skipper Will hired a horse and dray to take him back to Coley's Point, figuring he could wait just as well in the comfort of his own home. He left Esau in charge of the men.

The days passed, with no change in the weather. The crew could do little except sweep and clean. Towards the end of the second week the wind slackened off, and in the morning the men performed their duties and had breakfast. Then they went below to rest.

Esau stretched out on his bunk, fully-clothed. He wasn't aware that Skipper Will had returned until he heard his voice and saw him standing at the foot of his bunk.

'So this is what you do behind my back, eh, Esau?'

Esau stood up.

'I did no harm behind your back,' he said crossly. 'We all got up and had our breakfast. There was not'ing else to do, so we came below.'

The argument continued until both men were on the deck, the rest of the crew now watching. Esau knew he was being singled out unfairly, the skipper not wanting to rebuke the sharemen. Which is why Esau refused to back down.

Finally, the skipper lost his temper.

'Go below, Esau,' he shouted, 'and get in the bunk!'

'And that I wunt.'

'Go below, I said, and get in the bunk!'

'No, I wunt.'

There was silence on the deck as the skipper glanced around at the men. No one ever dared question his authority.

Skipper Will nodded to one of the crew, Jake Dawe.

'Jake,' he said, 'take the punt and fetch the constable.'

Jake didn't move.

'Do as I say, Jake. Take the punt and fetch the constable.'

Still, Jake wouldn't move.

'No odds, Jake,' said Esau. 'I'll go below.'

And for the rest of the day Esau lay on his bunk, his fierce eyes staring at nothing, until Skipper Will said it was time to get up. If he hadn't gone below that morning, both he and Jake Dawe would have spent six months in the Harbour Grace jail.

The fishing was poor that summer, and when Skipper Will sailed home early in the fall, the local merchant, Lewis Dawe, was furious. So in an all too human way, he looked around for a scapegoat. There was little he could do to the sharemen, who as soon as they tidied up their traps, were released from collar to seek other work. Not so the man who had shipped for wages, who still had to work off the alloted days of his indenture. And so Lewis Dawe focused his rage on Esau French, the one member of the crew who had disobeyed the skipper that trip.

Legally, Esau was obliged to perform whatever task the merchant gave him, and as punishment, Lewis Dawe marched Esau up to his house in Country Road and brought out a small hardwood cradle that had belonged to one of his children. And he ordered Esau to sit on the porch and rock the cradle. And every day thereafter, rain or shine, Esau would show up on Lewis Dawe's front porch, and in plain view of the passing locals, some of whom stared, some of whom looked away, would sit there from morning till dark, his foot making that small gentle motion on the rocker of the empty cradle, until two months had passed and he came out of collar.

I remember the silence in the room when my father finished telling me that story. We were sitting across the table from each other, in the sunporch of my apartment on Brunswick Avenue, on a lovely spring afternoon, two years before he died. He had never before recounted that story to anyone, and I could understand why. The fury that made his eyes glitter seemed to charge the very air we breathed. At that moment he could have driven his fist through the wall and I wouldn't have flinched.

He could barely look at me, his eyes flicking from walls to ceiling to floor, until finally he scraped back his chair and stepped to the window. In the backyard a breeze was stirring the branches of the maple tree, the room so silent I could hear the dry soft whisper of leaves.

He still had on his old grey fedora, tipped high on his forehead, and the brim of it hid his face as he gazed at the back of the houses on Borden Street. I remember he stood there a long time, staring at nothing, the way his father must have stared at nothing but his own thoughts that day on this bunk in Harbour Grace, over ninety years before.

What it had cost my father to share that story was a measure of the friendship that by this time had developed between us. A friendship that had deepened in the days following *Leaving Home*, a play in which, ironically, I'd portrayed him rather harshly, though honestly, I thought. He'd never said much about the play, except that he liked it. But one day, years later, we were strolling quietly along Bloor Street, his eyes as usual sucking up every ounce of life in his path, when suddenly he halted and slapped his hand on my shoulder, pinning me to the spot.

'You know that play, *Leaving Home*?' he said.

I nodded.

'That's about me and my father, isn't it?'

For a moment I thought he was kidding. But he took a step backward and looked at me in a way that would brook no contradiction. It was as if the thought had just occurred to him, as if he'd just been struck by a shining insight that seemed to surprise him, seemed to make him happy.

'Yeah,' I said, finally. 'Yeah, it is.'

Konrad Groß

FATHER AND SON: DAVID FRENCH'S *MEMOIR*

"*Leaving Home* ... is set in the fifties and smacks of autobiography. Its young man, Ben, sounds very like the author as a young victim of an impossible father. Such public accusation is too often more satisfactory to the writer than the viewer, but not so in *Leaving Home*," wrote theatre critic Herbert Whittacker in *The Globe and Mail* May 17, 1972 on the premiere of French's first stage play at the Tarragon Theatre Toronto.[1] French confirmed the autobiographical element, although he warned that the play was only "emotionally," "not exactly factually autobiographical"[2] and that the characters were "not carbon copies" of real people.[3] He also admitted that for years he had tried to write about his family, but to no avail, and that in writing *Leaving Home* he attempted to vent his anger and frustrations towards his family.[4] He even spoke of the therapeutic value of the play in which he obviously cast himself in the role of Ben who decides to escape a bullying father. One critic, R.W. Bevis, felt *Leaving Home* to be "seriously marred by a failure of authorial sympathy for the pater familias, Jacob Mercer ... the play is so 'loaded' against Jacob that it becomes impossible to take his side, difficult even to take him seriously... here the scales are constantly weighed in favour of one side, and hence the drama suffers."[5] Obviously, viewers and most reviewers must have felt differently, for *Leaving Home* enjoyed a tremendous success across Canada and was to become "the most produced play in Canadian literature."[6] Evidently the play must have held a kind of public spell which left its mark on the theatre scene and helped Canadian drama to be accepted in Canada.[7] A large part of the play's fascination undoubtedly comes from the relationship between father and son(s) and the conception of a father who is a more complex character than Bevis' view suggests. It is true that Jacob Mercer is to blame for much that is happening in the Mercer family. His unbridled temper that has him fly into a rage even at the slightest turn, his impatience to listen to anyone except to himself and his notion of the tough male for which he sees himself as a model make a working relationship with his sons almost impossible. As a kind of self-protection he builds up a self-image, which he derives from a harsh Newfoundland childhood and a working class background, that of a tough man in an even tougher world. It is this image with which he justifies his harsh treatment of Ben as an initiation into real life. It also allows him to assume the role of the strong father who believes he deserves complete filial submission for having provided for his family fairly well under the circumstances. One of the reasons for Bevis' impression of an unfair treatment of the father is that Jacob is an overpowering presence in the play and that in comparison Ben has fairly little to say. Yet, sympathy with Jacob is never completely withheld. For Jacob's verbal strategies, his love of exaggeration and his telling of fictions, result partly at least from a social inferiority complex and reveal a highly vulnerable character. Some of these fictions which help him to preserve his self-image are occasionally corrected by his wife Mary, while others are kept alive by the family, for example that of the father's role as the breadwinner. The revelation that it was Ben's money that kept the family financially afloat when Jacob was laid up for half a year after an accident is a blow to his self-respect. The ending of the play presents a different father who for the first time is able to depart from his role of the paternal lawgiver and to admit that he is desperately in need of his family. For the first time he does not give a command, but begs a favour, when he asks Ben not to leave: "We never seen eye to eye in most cases, but we'm still a family. We've got to stick together. All we got in this world is the family—and it's breaking up, Ben."[8] But despite Ben's insight that mother and sons made the father "feel like an outsider all these years"[9] the gap between Jacob and Ben is too deep to be bridged. It is in keeping with the changed image of the father that the mother should have the last say in the play. Her reminiscences of a story from the past show another side of her husband whom she married because of his sense of justice and social compassion. The final image is that of a father who for all his coaxing and bullying is a highly vulnerable person deserving his wife's declaration of loyalty. In the context of this very mixed father figure the title of the play means two things: not merely the departure of the sons, but the earlier departure of Jacob from poverty-ridden Newfoundland for Toronto, where he remains a stranger and an exile.

In *Of the Fields, Lately* (1973) Ben after an absence of two years returns home to attend his aunt's funeral. Against his former assertion of his individuality he begins to develop a new understanding of the father-son relationship, or in French's own words, he "comes to realize how profound an impact his father had on him and how profound an impact he had on this father." This time he decides to leave "home to save his father," not to save himself.[10] Chronologically these two plays stand at the end of the so-called Mercer tetralogy. After an interlude of works with different subjects French felt compelled to return once again to the Mercer family, this time turning the clock back to Jacob's wooing of Mary in 1926 (*Salt-Water Moon* 1985) and the blending of the Mercer family history with Newfoundland's entry into confederation in his play *1949* (1989). The early Mercer plays with their central focus on the faultlines running between father and sons immediately recall Eugene O'Neill's classic autobiographical play *Long Day's Journey into Night* or Arthur Miller's *All My Sons* and *Death of a Salesman*. But whereas O'Neill's and Miller's plays live from the exposure of their father figures who are more or less guilty of the mishaps that befall the younger generation, French's plays plead increasingly for understanding. Edward Mullaly in a review of the first two Mercer plays was right to say that *Of the Fields, Lately* "will not only allow French to free himself from his father, but also from Arthur Miller."[11] Although *Leaving Home* and *Of the Fields, Lately* end with the insight into the deep rift between the generations, the story of father and sons is basically one of loving antagonism. Much of the underlying sympathy for the father surfaces from the fact that the Mercer plays link the personal story to the concept of Jacob as a *homo sociologicus* whose roles and attitudes are shaped by his social background, not merely by his temper. The generation gap is tied to history and opportunities. Bill and Ben Mercer have all the opportunities their parents had not. Jacob's awareness of this and his memories of his family's social victimization in Newfoundland are the source of his sensitivity to class and social injustice. Naturally, in the two latest Mercer plays French appears to do justice to the figure of the father as a social individual. Jacob's feeling of social victimization forms the background for *Salt-Water Moon* , where the audience willingly sides with the social underdog whose vitality, wit, shrewdness, and persistence help him to beat his wealthy competitor Jerome McKenzie out of the field and to win the hand of Mary Snow. With his gift of the gab he pulls all the strings of persuasion, and his success remains a live memory in later skirmishes with his wife. While the initial Mercer plays show Jacob as a father figure with bruises, *Salt-Water Moon* is a comedy with the father-to-be as a hero triumphant.

In an interview in 1982 French told Cynthia Zimmerman of his plans to continue with the Mercer history. He even mentioned the possibility of writing five Mercer plays,[12] yet it seems that with *1949* he has exhausted the family history. In *1949* the figure of the father no longer is important and the private issue has given way to the political issue of Newfoundland's linkage with Canada.

French's as yet unpublished memoir indicates that he may feel to have arrived at a point in his artistic career when he should attempt an autobiographical summing-up. Born in 1939, he may still appear to not be old enough to publish the story of his past. As a rule writers are not driven to promote their market value by exposing their private lives in autobiographies to the public gaze. In contrast to pop stars who keep their image in the public limelight where the wheel of fortune and marketing metes out success or failure (one need to think only of pop singer Bob Geldorf's memoir *Is That It?* of 1985 in which he constructed an image of sinner and saint) writers tend to look back upon their past when they have reached a sort of completion.

James Olney describes the "shift from attention ... from the life to the self" as a major constituent element of the modern autobiography.[13] Every autobiography is a reconstruction of the self and an assessment of those formative forces, persons, and events which have left their imprint on the autobiographer's character. Thus, autobiographies are matters of selection, choice of focus, and perspective. Benjamin Franklin and Jean-Jacques Rousseau, the well-known fathers of the modern autobiography, mark two of the extremes between which many modern autobiographies are situated. While Franklin sets himself as an example of the successful bourgeois and public person by tracing decisive factors in the story of his education, Rousseau exposes the shortcomings of his upbringing which have made him what he is.[14] The discrepancy between these two autobiographical archetypes can be pinned down to the dichotomy of success - failure, virtue - guilt, example - self-justification, confidence - doubt, identity assured - shaken identity, public focus - private focus, and autobiographical - confession. Without wanting to stretch alignments too far, the initial chapter of French's memoir seems to justify its assignment to the confession type. Without knowledge of the whole book, however, my impression can be only provisional and possibly requires future corrections.

We find one clue for French's confessional impetus at the end of the initial chapter, where he concedes to have portrayed his father in *Leaving Home* "rather harshly."[15] It is also revealing that the only plays mentioned at the beginning are *Leaving Home* and *Salt-Water Moon*, the two plays in which the shift from Jacob Mercer's portrait of a defeated old man to that of a triumphant young person becomes most obvious. What one can glean from a first reading of the memoir then is a sense of guilt driving the narrator to keep his own person in the background and to focus on relevant ingredients of the physical, mental, and social environment of father and grandfather. What emerges at the end is not so much a revelation of the self, but the son's growth of understanding for his father and a story of reconciliation to which French had already given artistic expression. At the close of the chapter French tells us of his father's surprising reaction to *Leaving Home*. Years after he had seen the play, his father takes it to be about himself and his father. This is an astounding response which the playwright had not expected. His father's identification with Ben universalizes French's very personal experience of the father-son relationship indicating that the father had also been a victim and finally understood the son. This ironic twist comes like an epiphany which makes the reconciliation complete and the surprise ending an homage to the father.

This is the chief reason why the father, not the son is at the centre of the recollection which does not start with the naive formula of the narrator's own birth and childhood. Unlike many modern autobiographies the memoir is not so much concerned with the autobiographer's identity, but with that of his father's. By taking us back to the grandparents' marriage in 1892 and the birth of the children, among them his father Edgar, French turns this part of the memoir also into a story of fathers and sons. From this documented information on the grandparents' history the chapter leaps straight to a personally remembered event in the late sixties illustrating the father's character. Called by all the family simply by his nickname Gar, Edgar mistakes a crow's cries for somebody calling him by his name. Realising his mistake he can laugh at himself, but is resentful of his son's advice of getting a hearing aid. This introduction of the father as a character who finds it hard "to accomodate such human frailties" (188) is slightly reminiscent of Jacob Mercer's pose of the strong man in *Leaving Home*.

This episode closes the first part of chapter 1, which is structured very carefully. Its four sections highlight events which are intended to explain why the father was what he was. They also mirror the growth of the author's understanding. At times we feel that French casts an almost naturalistic network around the story when he talks about the influence of character and place. Thus, the second part commences with a reference to place, first to Coley's Point in Newfoundland, where French and his father were born, then to England, from where the grandparents had come. Here it is tacitly assumed that both places have shaped the family destiny and the character of both grandfather and father in particular:

> In Newfoundland there are places whose desolate beauty makes the breath catch in your throat, and yet Coley's Point, the outport I was born in, has little to recommend it. In fact, it's rather austere and unprepossessing, a splinter of rock, almost a geological afterthought, that juts into Conception Bay, next to Bay Roberts. (189)

The tacit implication that an austere environment generates austere characters is intensified by the reference to the Thomas Hardy country as the grandparents' place of origin. As no other details are given, we are immediately reminded of the role of circumstance and fate in the lives of characters in Hardy's fiction. The death of French's great-grandfather and a great-uncle at sea reinforce the impression of man as a victim of external circumstances. Section 3 then shifts our attention from the impact of a harsh physical environment to that of an unequal society. It contains the memory of an episode which French has worked into *Salt-Water Moon* and which appears as a key to his father's personality. It was an incident in which his grandfather Esau was deeply humiliated by a local merchant for whom he had worked as part of a fishing crew and who after a poor fishing season had condemned him to work off the remaining two months of his indenture by doing the useless job of rocking an empty cradle in full public view. Although the event occurred before Edgar French's birth, the story left a deep scar on the son and, in French's words, "may have accounted for the depth of my father's compassion for the underdog." (191) French learned of this incident long after the first two Mercer plays and this knowledge obviously brought about that changed image of the father which we encounter in *Salt-Water Moon*. The sharing of that story with the son was the final proof of the friendship that ironically enough seems to have developed because of Edgar's surprising reaction to *Leaving Home*. Hence it is only right that the author introduces his father's voice to record that crucial story.

In almost naturalist fashion the physical and social environment serves to explain character, for the grandfather's characterization seems to be in agreement with the harsh natural environment. A foto of the grandfather even invites the observer's comparison with nature:

> In his eyes is a fierce unyielding quality that I've always associated with birds of prey, and it's that implacable look in his eyes, more than anything, that gives his face its forbidding cast. To have those eyes fix on you must have been intimidating, to say the least. It's no wonder that grown men would step off the road if they saw him coming. (190)

From this kind of description we can guess the grandfather's powerful influence over his son of which we get an inkling in *Leaving Home*, where Jacob Mercer is reminded of his father's unflinching resistance to his courting of a Catholic girl. It would be wrong, however, to assign simply a deterministic outlook to French's memoir. Victimization is certainly an important, though not exclusive feature of this chapter. It is true that one character trait, which plays a decisive role in Jacob Mercer's portrait, is passed on from grandfather to father, yet in contrast to the absurd naturalist reduction of human nature French presents a mixed picture which he sums up with Mary's characterization of father and grandfather to Ben: "He'd hurl you t'rough the window one minute and brush the glass off you the next" (189). The bleak picture is further toned down in section 2. After the description of the austere nature of Coley's Point the reader's attention is directed to the grandparents' first house whose gravel floor attests to poor living conditions. The bleak impression is then relieved by the description of the spacious second home with the grandmother's splendid flower garden.

In this context the role of females deserves a comment. The initial chapter is clearly dominated by male characters. At the beginning Esau's marriage with the grandmother, Sarah, and the tragic death of their first daughter, Edith, in a car accident are mentioned. Females then recede into the background: section 1 focuses on Edgar, section 2 and 3 on Esau, and the final section again on Edgar. Of French's mother there is not one word, and the grandmother is permitted to surface only to offset the harsh image of the grandfather:

> My grandmother was the opposite. In another picture I have of them, Sarah stands in the garden beside her husband, her head cocked to one side in an attitude I remember from the years she lived with us in Toronto, her face wistful, even ingratiating, as though somehow she had to compensate for the fierceness of the man beside her, who gazes sternly at the camera in his white shirt and braces, his large big-knuckled hands dangling in front of him like a gunfighter. (190)

It remains to be seen from the rest of French's memoir, if Estelle C. Jelinek's view can be retained that male autobiographers generally focus on their mothers, whereas female writers attach great emphasis to their fathers.[16] In consideration of chapter 1 and the portrayal of female characters in the autobiographical Mercer plays this is a rather doubtful statement. Equally doubtful is Jelinek's view that as a rule men's autobiography is characterized by "orderliness" of design, while women's prefers fragmentary and disjunctive form. It is hard to believe that women's autobiography follows no design and that its disorganised appearance mirrors the "multidimensionality of women's social roles." According to Jelinek, female autobiographies are often interrupted by anecdotes, portraits of people, quoted letters etc.[17] Yet orderliness and lack of order are also questionable categories which should be also connected to time and culture, not only to gender. In the case of French's memoir one could argue that chapter I employs no strict chronological sequence and that its dual time scheme is typical of the autobiographical (male or female) quest which hovers between the now and then and assesses the past from a present perspective. French progresses by moving back and forth in time and by linking documented facts with personal anecdotes, stories heard, memories, and the scrutiny of fotos. His associative method is better suited to the unravelling of his father's personality as the prime intention than a chronological proceeding with its lesser demands on emotional involvement.

Autobiographies tend to string events together into a meaningful whole. At the beginning of French's memoir we encounter, however, a strange linkage between two events which are not causally related: the death of his Aunt Edith in a car accident at the age of thirty-three which occurred on the very day French, "fifty-eight years later, would set a play called *Salt-Water Moon*." (1) At first sight this connection does not make sense. It seems purely arbitrary and accidental, unless there is a concealed meaning which could be summed up as a development from death to hope. It may not be too daring to suggest even a religious reading by explaining the connection as a sign of God. French admitted in an interview to becoming more and more religious, and the Biblical references in the titles of his early Mercer plays show that the possibility of a Christian understanding would not be too far-fetched.[18] Confessions are generally concerned with feelings of guilt and aim at the restoration of an individual to some state of innocence or healing. French in the first chapter of his memoir achieves this in his development from a state of estrangement to one of friendship and reconciliation between father and son. While the early Mercer plays can be termed as declarations of French's independence and the defence of the son's self against paternal encroachments, the start of the memoir is a kind of the son's return to the father whose formerly overpowering figure is no longer remembered as a threat.

Bibliography

Geraldine Anthony, Ed., *Stage Voices: Twelve Canadian Playwrights Talk about Their Lives and Work* (Toronto: 1978).

R.W. Bevis, "Sins of the Fathers," *Canadian Literature* 59, Winter, 1974.

L.W. Conolly, Ed., *Canadian Drama and the Critics* (Vancouver: 1987).

David French, *Leaving Home*, New Drama 7, (Don Mills, ON: 1980).

Albert-Reiner Glaap, "Familiendrama, Romanze, Komödie: Zu den Dramen von David French," in: Glaap, Ed., *Das englisch-kanadische Drama, (Düsseldorf: 1992).*

Estelle C. Jelinek, "Introduction: Women's Autobiography and the Male Tradition," in Jelinek, Ed., *Women's Autobiography. Essays in Criticism* (Bloomington: 1986).

Werner Loch, "Benjamin Franklin und Jean-Jacques Rousseau - zur politischen Bildung des bürgerlichen Subjekts," *Geschichte in Wissenschaft und Unterrich: 29, 1989.*

James Olney, "Autobiography and the Cultural Moment: A Thematic, Historical, and Bibliographical Introduction," in: Olney, Ed., *Autobiography, Essays Theoretical and Critical* (Princeton: 1980).

Robert Wallace and Cynthia Zimmerman, Eds., *The Work. Conversations with English-Canadian Playwrights* (Toronto: 1982).

Notes

[1] In: L. W. Conolly (Ed)., *Canadian Drama and the Critics* (Vancouver: 1987), 88.

[2] In: Robert Wallace and Cynthia Zimmermann, (Eds.), *The Work, Conversations with English-Canadian Playwrights* (Toronto: 1982), 305.

[3] In: Geraldine Anthony (Ed.), *Stage Voices: Twelve Canadian Playwrights Talk about Their Lives and Work* (Toronto: 1978), 241-247, here 242.

[4] Wallace, Zimmerman 1982, 306.

[5] R. W. Bevis, "Sins of the Fathers," *Canadian Literature* 59, Winter 1974, 106-108, here 106f.

[6] Wallace, Zimmerman, 1982, 305.

[7] Albert-Reiner Glaap, "Familiendrama, Romanze, Komödie: Zu den Dramen von David French," in: Glaap (Ed.), *Das englisch-kanadische Drama* (Düsseldorf: 1992), 229.

[8] David French, *Leaving Home*, New Drama 7 (Don Mills, ON.: 1980), 101.

[9] French 1980, 95.

[10] Wallace, Zimmerman 1982, 306-307.

[11] In: Conolly 1987, 132.

[12] Wallace, Zimmerman 1982, 308.

[13] James Olney, "Autobiography and the Cultural Moment: A Thematic, Historical, and Bibliographical Introduction," in: Olney (Ed.), *Autobiography. Essays Theoretical and Critical* (Princeton: 1980), 3-27, here 19.

[14] Werner Loch, "Benjamin Franklin und Jean-Jacques Rousseau - zur politischen Bildung des bürgerlichen Subjekts," *Geschichte in Wissenschaft und Unterricht* 29, 1989, 420-434.

[15] All quotes in the text from the first chapter of the *Memoir* published in this volume.

[16] Estelle C. Jelinek, "Introduction: Women's Autobiography and the Male Tradition," in: Jelinek (Ed.), *Women's Autobiography, Essays in Criticism* (Bloomington: 1986), 1-20, here 12.

[17] Jelinek, 1986, here 16 f.

[18] See Walace, Zimmerman 1982, 307. For the Biblical references of the titles see ibid., 307 and Glaap 1992, 230, 233.

Linda Griffiths

THE RED SPRAY CAN
(from: SPIRAL WOMAN)

Cosmology: There was once a time in the City, when all the theatres were run by warring clans. Each clan had its chieftain, or Director, each clan its warriors, hangers on, and hopeful members—also called actors, playwrights and designers. These are stories of Trish, an underground actress and clan member of ever-beleaguered, Dirty Theatre. At the time this story begins, the theatre is fighting the gathering darkness as Trish is struggling with the forces of clan loyalty.

TRISH, the actress, speaks:

About a week before we opened the play, someone asked the Director of the Dirty Theatre when we were being called for rehearsal. He said, "I can't rehearse tomorrow, I'll probably be in jail." Anyone else would have taken this with grains of salt like piles of sand, but I felt the familiar clutch, and immediately went to the rescue. No one wanted to ask, 'Why?' at such an obvious lead, with the person dying to be asked, but I seem to have no desire to squash someone who just wants attention. My guts clench, and I give it. So everyone kind of ignored him, and I asked, "What's this about you going to jail?" He had that twitchy quality again, a kind of heroin addict shake that went right to the bones. To my knowledge he'd never been a heroin addict but that didn't stop the shaking. I hoped he wasn't going to blow again. It had been hard enough to calm down that night before meeting the Writer. The Writer was beginning to get a little bored with the constant crisis, was beginning to suggest that the survival of this or any play wasn't of earth shattering consequence. After all, no one even went to the Dirty Theatre any more, certainly not anyone who counted. It was a job, that was understandable, even interesting, but it couldn't possibly be as important as, say, writing. There was no permanence, no immortality. No Novel to stand on bookshelves, to be looked up in the library. No Novel to be rediscovered years later and declared a piece of genius. How could I tell a man with his sense of reality about the gathering darkness? How could I tell him that we were keeping the theatre doors open, so that when the shadow powers got really strong there would be a place for people to go? An energy source, imperfect as it was, dedicated to freedom and anarchy? How could I tell him I actually believed that the energy of the plays rose up and out into the stratosphere, strengthening the powers that would fight darkness, repression and genocide? I couldn't.

So I asked the Director, "What's this about you going to jail?"

His bloodshot eyes turned to me. "The theatre's out of money, nobody seems to understand that. I go to the bank manager on my fucking knees every week, begging him to give us a little more time. We owe money all over town, we don't answer the phone anymore, so if anyone wants tickets, we're fucked. We've been overdrawn for four months. We lend people stuff and they steal it, we let them use our space for nothing and then they bad mouth us all over town. Do you know how many lights we've lost? People come with garbage bags and fill them with our costumes, they use our van, then leave it with no gas. We're empty. The accountant fainted on the street yesterday, we're going to lose him, he has trouble with his ears and he's having a nervous breakdown. Today I went to the bank ready to crawl again and the guy said, "No way, that's it, it's over, no more money." So tomorrow I'm going to the Council offices with a can of red spray paint and if they don't give us enough cash to open the show, I'm going to spray their newly painted walls with, "Money for Artists not Bureaucrats" and I won't stop shouting till they call the cops and drag me away." This was clearly a situation for the pipes.

"I'm going with you," was all I said. Then I worked it out.

The problem was that the Director could be very eloquent with a few beers in him and a joint but it was a late night thing, or at least a late afternoon thing. The appointment was at nine fifteen the next morning. These meetings were never held where or when we felt comfortable, on the theatre's time and turf, they were always held with us blinking in the sunlight, having worked till eleven and drunk till three. What of it? Did they finish at five and go home to sleep? No, they had a few to calm them down from the day, that's for sure. But no matter, I had to get the Director in some kind of shape to talk to the Council, because, as a female warrior, I was hoping to get away without bloodshed. Even without red paint on the walls. Even without the police. I figured the police part was just bragging, I wasn't as gullible as all that, but still, I could see it had to be part of the stakes if we were to save the theatre. Again. If I could kick-start the Director into eloquence at nine fifteen in the morning and sober, then we had a chance.

We worked out our strategy late into the night. We were to get up at seven, so we would be at least awake when the meeting started. We would bathe, he would shave, at least. We were to meet for breakfast because that was another way we always lost, they always had a good breakfast in them, and we never did. We argued about the angles. In many ways the Dirty Theatre was indefensible, in many ways it was a charitable institution. Why were we always broke? The answer to that was too complicated for a poor actress, I'd never been able to figure it out. It had something to do with the money rules never fitting the clan. It had to do with the clan never accepting anybody else's rules.

That night I slept alone, calling the Writer, my voice trembling with excitement and the smell of battle. I tried to be calm, not wanting him to think I was indulging in cheap dramatics. "I have a meeting early tomorrow, yes, have to save the theatre, shouldn't take too long, see you after rehearsal""

It was a dry awful morning. The reason for the adventure seemed incomprehensible. Did we actually think they would give us money? What was our argument? That we were worthy and we needed it? I tried to cover the bags under my eyes with a pale pink make-up stick, it was important that I look good. My hair stuck out sideways in an odd pattern that looked vaguely Egyptian, and I had a big stain on the white suit I had planned to wow them with. Jail. What do you wear to go to jail? We had worked it out that I would be the one to talk to the press. The press indeed. What press? What jail? What money? What goddam cunnihoping asshole of a pee stained hopeless dump of a theatre?

We met for breakfast, the Director was there on time but nothing felt right. There's something about putting on a tie when you don't mean it. Kind of obscene. How could we be who we were if we were on time? We looked like old people dressed up as schoolkids. It was too early for breakfast and I could feel the diarrhea starting.

"Have you got the spray paint?" I wasn't sure if I wanted him to have it, but otherwise where were the stakes?

"No, I forgot it."

Forgot it? Forgot it? I should have known then, I should have known what kind of a clan this was. You forgot your axe, you forgot your sword, you forgot the cause itself? We're fighting the gathering darkness and you forget the spray paint? Was I, a mere woman, a mere actress the only one ready, the only one desiring death? I did desire death. Looking at the Director, a man the world thought rushed toward death at every opportunity, I knew his life forces were stronger than mine. He wanted to live, and I would rather have died this morning than face another opening night, than face the Writer as we grew apart, than face poverty and aging and being alone. I would rather have died in some battle against the darkness. That is how I knew the darkness was about to win. Because I desired death.

We paid the bill and I made him go across the street to the hardware store and buy some spray paint. He came back, looking a little more energized, with a small paper bag sticking out of his left hand jacket pocket. Our security, our defence, our stakes.

I thought of the theatre offices as we walked down the cool grey halls of the Council, full of smiling people and modern art. I thought of the smell of old vomit that clung to the filthy carpeting, of the ashes in the air. We weren't fooling anybody. What had we come here to do?

In the office was a nice man with kind blue eyes in a suit. I had been warned that he wouldn't exactly look like the enemy but I felt all of the energy drain away. What were we so mad about? What was the big deal? Theatre was so puny, so tiny, so miniscule in the big world, why would smart people even bother? And besides, we were being helped, this nice man had already given us a certain amount of money, wasn't it unreasonable to ask for more? But we were there to be unreasonable. I sat primly in the chair, hoping not to hurt the nice man's feelings.

The Director's voice was shaking, his hands clenched, his bent little body and little stick arms smoked cigarettes. "We need five thousand dollars tomorrow or the theatre goes under."

I half expected him to hold the spray can to the nice man's face, but not yet, we both knew it was there. You could see the expression on the nice man's face, these artists, always so volatile, turning every problem into a big crisis.

"Could you give me a few details, how has this happened?"

"It's happened because when you make policies you steal our ideas. We get a good idea and do it badly, then the nice theatres steal it, and do it well. Then you take the idea, and hand out money for people who want to use the idea. Except we don't fit in the criteria to get money for the idea we thought of in the first place, because once you guys have put it through your bureaucracy, we don't qualify for some stupid reason. We give money to some vermin infested group to do whatever they want for three weeks. We don't give them a lot because we don't have a lot. Then the show goes well for a change, everybody likes it. But there's no money for big fancy publicity because meanwhile we're giving money to other vermin infested groups. Everybody gets pissed off. The next year, that group, not so vermin infested any more, goes to one of the fancy dan theatres and gets the show produced again. We don't get any money for what we lost producing it in the first place. Then the Council comes along, looks at the nice new production and gives the fancy dan theatre money because they're doing such good work. What do we get? A kick in the ass because we didn't make money on the original production. I've got playwrights on my doorstep starving to death, I'm giving them money out of my pocket, you're giving yourselves money to paint your offices and get new stationary. I'm not coming here with my fucking tail between my legs. We're rich. You see that? We're rich. We could sell the building now, pay all the debts, take a chunk for each of us and be on our way, but you know what you wouldn't have then? You wouldn't have a place for the artists of this city to sleep and fuck each other and borrow money. There'd be no place to put on their plays even if they aren't that good this time, because maybe they'll be good next time. Somewhere dedicated to the possibility of failure. Risks, you want to talk about risks? I'll shove risks up your ass, so don't treat us like failures, you smug asshole, we haven't done anything wrong. That's what I've finally figured out, all this time I thought I'd done something wrong. You need us, even though you shit on us."

"I've never shit on you," said the nice man. "I think I should call someone else in to hear all this."

We were both shaking, but I was fairly pleased, he wasn't as good as he was in the bar, but he wasn't bad either. I was racing through my mind for the points the Director had failed to make. I had to keep him as honest as possible. I had to be the one that mentioned the many faults of the Clan. Or at least explain the reasons why these faults were so universally condemned and obvious. We sat silent, trying not to dissipate the energy. I didn't know how much the Director had left. It was nine thirty in the morning.

Another man entered, clearly the nice man had dragged him away from his office, telling him something was about to blow and he'd better be there. This man settled in his chair, crossed his legs and said, "Now what seems to be the problem?" My eyes went to the spray paint. Was that the only solution?

Once more, the Director said hoarsely, "We need five thousand dollars by tomorrow or the theatre goes down."

"And how did you get yourselves in this situation?"

I thought of the paper flowers filling the theatre. I heard my voice cry out as if from a great distance.

"The artists are going to rise up, take to the streets, they'll come in buses outside your building, there'll be no logic. Bad artists or good artists, pretentious ones, and humble ones, covered in paint, old hamburgers, smoking dope, with stacks and piles of paper poetry plays books, carrying instruments, wailing voices, they'll cry with such abandon from their tiny dirty rooms. Look at us, look at us, we live we write we play we sing we dance, we have lives that are reflections of our many torments. We think with our stomachs, we drink with our minds, we feel we feel, it's right to be us, to be here, look at us, we're here. Some of us are nice and some of us aren't. We're here we're here we're here. They'll come in their weird clothing, thinking only of themselves and the next note, next show, the next blob of paint. They'll have no pity. They'll smother you in ugly colours, oppress you with limp images, deafen you with the screeching noises of a thousand harpies, they'll mime you to death, they'll performance art you into the ground, they'll come naked, puking, whining, bleeding, and finally kill you with boredom. Not because you're the enemy, we know you're not the enemy, but are you our friends? We are not accidents, we actually know our purpose. Even the Dirty Theatre is not an accident. We are not the salvation of the world, but we aren't accidents either."

"You need to write this down in a report."

I was breathless, in another world, watching the artists rise up from their shamed place. It was amazing that the Director could be coherent, we were leaving the reality of the men so quickly. He even replied, "We don't have the time or staff to write reports, we don't have a fancy office, every penny we have goes into losing money."

The nice man spread his hands so the palms were upward, in a Buddha like gesture, either in prayer or sacrifice to the gods of futility. "We're feeling the squeeze as much as you, who would you have us cut, so we can give the money to you?"

Turn on your friends. Name names. Save yourself. The Director started to jerk and twist, but he bravely said, "No one. I don't think you should cut anyone."

"But that's not possible."

"I know you've just gotten a sum of money and that we don't qualify for it."

"You want us to change the criteria just for you?"

"Yes."

"Do you know how many people are calling for that money? We are your supporters, it's easy to rail at us because we're here in the office, but there's nothing we can do. We're more vulnerable than you think. And we don't have five thousand dollars."

We both thought of the spray can, but it wasn't right, we were too tired, it didn't make sense. The nice man's face was beaming, the electricity was tangible, but impotent. It was exciting. That's all, exciting. We would tell versions of it to our wives, lovers, friends. Maybe the Writer would understand if I made it very entertaining and was careful not to repeat myself. He hated that.

My stomach was like one of those old wringer washers full of acid, slurpy sounds were coming out of it, as the coffee met the eggs met the bacon met the beer from last night and the chemicals slurshed it all around. Slurp slurp euurp, eeoheu slurp slurp slurp.

"First of all, you should write all this down in a report, then we'll have another meeting. For now, all we can do is call your bank manager and try to convince him not to cut you off. Let's make an appointment."

Dully we shook hands, patting each other on the back that this scintillating exchange had taken place. Dangerous and everything. Had we ever had a dialogue. In the corridor outside I looked at the Director, expecting to see the pasty death mask I'd seen so often. But his eyes were shining. At that moment I realized he'd known all along that the five thousand dollars was impossible. He had set the stakes in a hope that it would be different, but underneath had known he could only rattle the cage. It was a clan leader's decision, not to be completely honest with me, to use my innocence to appeal to the nice men, but there had been too many decisions like it. You could never tell what was true. The excitement was still there, pounding away stupidly, even though there was nothing left to be excited about. It wasn't true to say he'd lied to me, after all, he had wanted to win. He wanted someone to talk to besides the warring chieftains who waited for him to lay down the motto and give up. After all, I was just an actress and he was the leader. The tears I shed in the washroom were the tears of an eternal innocent. A fucking fool.

I didn't know that one day there would be no Council, that the nice men in suits would be gone, replaced by machines with even less sense of style. The conscience we appealed to would be gone, what would be left is nothing. Nothing nothing. No Council, no money anywhere. Only the gathering darkness, with its stupidity and lack of grace. The gathering darkness, weeding out the deadwood. Like me? Like the Director? Like the Dirty Theatre? They called the dismantling of the Council 'devolution,' like 'demolition,' like 'destruction.' Like the end.

Albert Rau

TRISH AND THE FAIRY TALE
OF THE DIRTY THEATRE

> To this end, I urge you to ignore any and all dissenters who will tell you
> that the outrageous stories of the early days at Theatre Passe Muraille—and
> at the other barrier-breaking theatres of the same generation—are idle
> gossip or bar talk. They're wrong. Those stories and memories of theatre
> without walls are the lifeblood of alternate theatre.[1]

Linda Griffiths is a Canadian woman playwright and one of the outstanding
representatives of the country's alternate theatre movement and of collective
creation in particular. She started out working with collectives at 25th Street
Theatre in Saskatoon and her name is closely connected with Theatre Passe
Muraille in Toronto. She began as an actress, but since then has developed into
a dramatist of her own right, yet without abandoning the first.[2] Her contribution
to this festschrift is the story *The Red Spray Can*, taken from her one-person play
Spiral Woman and the Dirty Theatre, a monologue she performed for the first time
in a workshop at *Theatre Passe Muraille* in May 1993.[3] In this play, Trish, an
underground actress, is confined to bed suffering from a mysterious illness and
with all her "housemates" deserting her, she finds herself left alone in a "giant
bed," reviewing her life at a "mythic place, the ever beleaguered Dirty Theatre."[4]

It is winter and fiercely cold outside and through "a huge window, framed
in fantastic flowers" (SW 2) snow and the blue sky can be seen. In these
surroundings Trish is reminded of the winter, when the rehearsals and performance of what they then called the "Paradise Play" took place. Trish's stories and
memories revolve around this period at the Dirty Theatre and in her recollec-
tions of the events of that time she allows an insight into a throbbing, intensive
and often chaotic life at the alternate theatres, yet nevertheless suggesting that
they are the homes of "the real theatre" as opposed to "the boring bourgeois
theatres in the city, where theatre life, brawling thing that it was, could never
live and breathe in their neat prissy spaces" (SW 4).

When the story of *The Red Spray Can* begins, there is only one week left
before the opening of the new play and the theatre is, as so often, suffering from
a chronic problem, a shortage of money.[5]. Trish believes that this "had to do
with the clan never accepting anybody else's rules" (RSC 203), or with the
alternate theatres constantly and as Eugene Benson and L.W. Conolly express
it "deliberately opposing established values and norms of society."[6] These

young theatres have always faced problems financing themselves and having to cope with high mortgages for the buildings they played in and they have often worked on a tight budget, ever so often operating on the verge of bankruptcy. Nevertheless, they have always stuck to their revolutionary ideas of making "real theatre," dealing with Canadian themes, close to the people of this young country.

Although alternate theatres, like other theatres too, have been supported by the Canada Council, they have also always felt dependent on them. How to qualify for financial assistance if the theatre and its plays are regarded as a risk, financially and artistically, and are not considered to meet the required "international standards?" When facing a meeting with members of the Council Trish feels the opposition of the "we," that is the always dirty, drunk, drugged, volatile, unreasonable, always broke and only dirty language using artists, against the "they," that is the clean, straightforward and correct bureaucrats of the council. In addition, but not least important are the press and the critics. Only a good review of a new play means financial support and can save a theatre. "We" are always on the weak side, at a disadvantage, facing a situation as if being cross-examined, because the meetings with the members of the council "were never held where or when we felt comfortable, on the theatre's time and turf, they were always held with us blinking in the sunlight, having worked till eleven and drunk till three." (RSC 203) Thus, the only defence they can think of is an irrational and futile attack with a red spray can, the weapon of demonstrators against the establishment: "Money for Artists not for Bureaucrats"(RSC 203). Although these "nice men" are not the enemy, they do not seem to know what theatre is all about, they simply lack understanding, not allowing any real "dialogue." Nevertheless there is no doubt that they are vital and indispensable for the promotion of theatre life in Canada:

> I didn't know that one day there would be no Council, that the nice men in suits would be gone, replaced by machines with even less sense of style. The conscience we appealed to would be gone, what would be left is nothing. Nothing nothing. No Council, no money anywhere [...] They called the dismantling of the Council 'devolution,' like 'demolition,' like 'destruction.' Like the end. (RSC 207)

Despite this sometimes hopeless situation, Trish is convinced that "In many ways the dirty theatre was indefensible, in many ways a charitable institution" (RSC 203) because it has been a refuge, a home and a family to young Canadian writers, offering them a chance to produce plays that deal with Canadian topics as opposed to the many imported plays staged in the big theatres. She even sees them dedicated to develop a distinct Canadian theatre and identity, almost placing them in the range of heroes for the country, rather than classifying them as irresponsible "accidents" or even "failures:"

> The country was a vast unpolished gem of a place, under the thumb of cowardice within and Landlords without. We had a mission-build up the strength within, stop sucking up to the Landlords without and we'd have

---

a country to be proud of, great art, great community, great parties. Or so the Elder Chieftain taught us to believe.

All the theatre clans had been involved in the great mission. You began with a belief that the country was good. Better than good. Less racist, less materialistic, less violent, less snotty. Nicer. Better than anyone else's country. (SW 8)

Although a unit of its own, the story *The Red Spray Can* has nevertheless to be placed into the context of the whole play of *Spiral Woman and the Dirty Theatre*. Trish is no doubt talking about *O.D. On Paradise*, a play written by Linda Griffiths in close collaboration with Patrick Brymer and she makes many references to real people and to actual events and places. The audience might, for example, recognize Clarke Rogers as the director or Paul Thompson as the Elder Chieftain. There is even a real counterpart to the spider woman critic with her international standards who is viciously and silently waiting for a chance to catch the artists in her web in order "to crush the freaks" (SW 4). Trish remembers that this woman "was a stranger to the Country" (SW 31), but "I know now that she is in us, deeply in the clan, a poison we've carried with us, of fear and doubt." (SW 30, 31) The world première of *O.D. on Paradise* took place on February 19, 1982 at 25th Street Theatre, Saskatoon, where Linda Griffiths played the part of "the shy and unlucky Joan" (SW 6) and its Toronto première was staged on January 15, 1983 at Theatre Passe Muraille.[7] Even the so-called strawberry-tea incident, when the police were called in because critics had suspected that marihuana was being smoked on stage, is a recorded fact. This all clearly suggests that the play deals with the early to mid-eighties, yet, a closer look shows that the play deviates from the historically correct events and rather reveals that real facts and events are interwoven and blended with fictional things.

The story is structured along the evolution of the "Paradise Play," however, it is not clear how much time passes in the play, nor is there a precise reference to when is present or when is past. Linda Griffiths was at the same time involved in the creation of her play *Jessica*,[8] the dramatization of an autobiographical account of a Métis woman's life. Thus, there are frequent references to characters appearing in *The Book of Jessica*, such as the native country singer or the girl living in the theatre[9]. In addition, characters from earlier plays, such as the Billies, reminding of *Billy the Kid* and *Billy Bishop goes to War* show that reality and fantasy have been blended. The references to the Spiral Woman in the title and in the introductory stage directions, in particular, show the important influence the play *Jessica* and what she then learned about the mythology of the Métis has had on Linda Griffiths. Sometimes during the play, "especially when the story centers on her mysterious illness, [Trish] moves her body in a spiral motion, as if trying to unwind her body from within" (SW 2). It reminds of the crucial situation, when Linda Griffiths was accepted by the Indian community, became an integral part and experienced a moment of shared mythology:

Grateful for the pink skirt, I relaxed and was asked to dance. But it was the fiddle music that did it. People began step-dancing in circles, feet jumping and pounding, arms limp to their sides. Something stirred my blood in a familiar way. My feet couldn't keep still. It was the demon fiddler, who was Scots, who was Irish, who was French, who was Cree. I saw pictures of wind-swept moors, heard the ocean, felt the desire to run screaming down hills with a standard in my hand. Soon it was time to leave, and the group rose from the table, but the fiddler was too strong. I began to dance all by myself at the edge of the crowd, as Maria and her family watched and laughed. People were watching, but I didn't care. I was no longer the oppressor, I danced away the oppressor.[10]

The play is not simply a realistic account of events and stories centering on the rehearsals and staging of the "Paradise Play" at Theatre Passe Muraille, but it is rather an allegorical play, a parable that borders on a satire, about the ethics and aims of the alternate theatre movement and its people, the actors, directors and dramaturges and about the actress Trish, who is caught right in the centre of it. The beginning of the "cosmology" of her play: "There was once a time in the City" (RSC 202), already identifies it at once as a fairy tale and Linda Griffiths herself argues "When you tell a story it becomes fiction."[11] And for her there is no difference between fairy tales and reality. When asked what in particular attracted her to this genre she said:

In fairy tales, whether you're a writer or an actress, there have always been good parts for women. When I was growing up, they were the only stories I read where women had adventures! In fairy tales, the females carry the burden of the story: the narrative goes through the woman ... And they had good parts! When I realized that fairy tales actually came out of a spiritual tradition, a shared mythological tradition which is also a psychological tradition, I finally stopped feeling ashamed ... many things that have happened to me have been fairy tale-ish (and nightmare-ish) in combination, sometimes in balance.[12]

No wonder that it is Trish, who tells the story and guides the audience, allowing only her point of view. Only once the point of view shifts to an observer narrator: "The actress and clanswoman who is now bedridden with a mysterious illness, was running around getting in between people, trying to appease, cajole, defend" (SW 21). It is also she, who acts as the uniting force and the driving power in this play and it is she, who takes the initiative, who feels the "familiar clutch" to save the theatre from the gathering darkness, from oppression, from being closed down, from state control and from bankruptcy and again it is she, who finally initiates the harmonic reunion and the experience of a "cosmic moment," of spiritualism at the end of the play.

Linda Griffiths places the story into the ancient past of the Celts, thus relating to a mythology that forms a common ground for the many Scottish immigrants. By describing the theatre groups as clans the notion of fighting and the smell of battle comes up, depicting the clan members as warriors who fight for the few resources available, an impression that is emphasized by the sometimes aggressive language used in the play. They stick together to survive: "Brute loyalty became the credo" (SW 4). But the hierarchical and patriarchal structure of the clans also press Trish into the familiar cliché of a woman's role. She has to fill the female side of the clan, she only has to be pretty, not to fight and allow the decisions to be taken by the men.

One of the trademarks of alternate theatres, and the Theatre Passe Muraille, in particular, is collective creation and the intention "to demythologize the dramatist, the director, and even the individual actor."[13] Linda Griffiths describes herself as an actor-writer and this duality with its inevitable changes and "transformations" from one role to another[14] and the conflicts and "contradictions" inherent in this double identity appear as a major theme in her works and also in *Spiral Woman and the Dirty Theatre*. Trish is constantly arguing with a nameless Writer, because he is searching for the perfect sentence, when she herself proclaims that real theatre is a process not a product. Their conflict culminates when the Writer transforms into a snake, speaking with a split tongue and threatening to intrude into the "paradise" of the actor-theatre. For Trish "the printed word is really a betrayal of the real power of oral story telling" (SW 5,6). She always defends the collective process of theatre against "a Writer who knew less than nothing about the bloody theatre" (SW 5). Only when the clan members, together with other clans, unite on the stage and experience a common spirituality in front of the spider woman critic, only then is the snake silent. Right at this moment it seems as if Trish incorporates more than just the actress of the theatre and the narrator of the story, but that she is rather even both writer and actor at the same time, only as a writer feeling to be a traitor to the actors and to real theatre. Here, Linda Griffiths' own conflict with the for her contradictory roles of writer and/ or actor becomes transparent: "And I still don't know if that's right for me, to cross to one or the other sides of the actor-writer line."[15] Trish's name, the short form of Patricia and the female form of Patrick, perhaps even suggests a symbiosis and constant transformation of actress and writer, male and female.

Is *Spiral Woman and the Dirty Theatre* what Linda Griffiths herself would consider a typical play? It undoubtedly deals with her background, with collective creations and with alternate theatres and has her work as its subject. Moreover, as an insider, Linda Griffiths serves as a first hand source of information about this theatre movement and of places such as the Theatre Passe Muraille, in particular. However, as suggested in the introductory quotation, it would be totally misleading to confine the play to this one theatre or even only to the alternate theatres. Linda Griffiths has rather created a play that on the one hand stands for and symbolizes the problems, worries and fears of these theatres, but on the other hand also stresses their aims and achievements for the development of professional drama in Canada.

The play is set in the mid-eighties and was basically also written at that time, yet the difficulties to be overcome as an artist in Canada, perhaps of experimental theatre in particular, can also be felt by young theatre groups today.[16] The play expresses a certain anger, perhaps intended to rouse people up and to stir their conscience. Although Griffiths maintains that this play is mere fiction, it is common knowledge that fairy tales also contain a grain of truth. It reminds the reader of what she expressed in the interview with Judith Rudakoff, namely that she prefers "political analysis without journalism ... And that sense of wanting to take things from real life comes from my experience with Paul Thompson's creative process."[17]

Spiral Woman and the Dirty Theatre is also a very personal play, where she turns her inside out, where she deals with her basic conflicts and philosophies and which deals with her dominant themes of transformation and duality, contradiction and balance, a concept that underlies all existence: light and dark, male and female, night and day, reality and fantasy, weak and powerful and for her, in particular, writer and actor or vice versa or both. In the fusion of reality and fantasy, Trish experiences a process of self-discovery, of reviewing and coming to grips with this time at the theatre. If related to Linda Griffiths' biography, it almost appears as a stock taking of her theatrical career, something akin to an interim report of her development to both an actor and a writer. Needless to say that the development has not come to an end yet.

All characters of Griffithss plays are in some kind of a crisis, "driven towards something that will alleviate their pain or confusion."[18] Trish is suffering from a mysterious illness, she constantly wants to escape the Dirty Theatre and wants to run away to some lonely place, or even to another theatre, torn between her role as a writer and as an actor, also constantly struggling with her clan loyalty. But she stays, attracted by the spell of the theatre and the play's immanent "energies." At the end of the play the illness is still there, she is still searching, but she has found a certain kind of salvation. The experience of the "cosmic moment," of transformation and spirituality have given her a feeling of opening up, of merging into a community, of having found a shared mythology, of having unwound her "locked mind" in a spiral dance. At the end Trish knows what the spell she was looking for is all about, it is transformation and "change." She has earned herself this ending.

At the end of the play, the theatre people are dispersed and their place is closed, suggesting failure, even having failed their mission, their country. This play is certainly written in defence of the ethics and aims of alternate theatres and of the process of collective creation in particular. But the play also reveals crucial aspects and elements of Linda Griffiths' philosophy, her concept of duality and balance and the need for spirituality, for a shared mythology, without which there is no survival. The processes of collective creation or collaboration have not ended with her writing her own plays, because a workshop process is only another form of collaboration, providing the writer-actor or actor-writer Linda Griffiths with the necessary feedback: "That contact with a live audience is a very special thing, and it's something that I truly love."[19] Therefore, one is really curious to see, what the final version of *Spiral Woman and the Dirty Theatre* will look like.

Notes

[1]
Judith Rudakoff (Ed.), *Dangerous Traditions*, A Passe Muraille Anthology (Winnipeg: 1992), p. x.

[2]
Cf. Diane Bessai, *The Canadian Dramatist, Vol. Two, Playwrights of Collective Creation* (Toronto: 1992), 217.

[3]
This play has not been published yet and for this article Linda Griffiths was so kind as to provide a photocopy of the workshop version: Linda Griffiths, *Spiral Woman and the Dirty Theatre*, "First Draft," Patty Ney, Chris Banks and Ass., Toronto July 24, 1993. Page references to the manuscript of the first draft are indicated SW; references to *The Red Spray Can* are accordingly indicated RSC, page numbers there refer to this volume.

[4]
In a letter to the editors of this publication, Linda Griffiths gives a few introductory sentences to the story *The Red Spray Can*. In a telephone conversation, conducted on February 14, 1994, she also mentioned the fact that it is not sure yet, when this play will be performed next.

[5]
In my conversation with Linda Griffiths she pointed out that she chose this story, because it comprises a unit of its own, but also focuses on a serious problem young theatres and artists are facing in Canada in general.

[6]
Eugene Benson/ L.W. Conolly, *English-Canadian Theatre* (Toronto: 1987), 85.

[7]
Rudakoff 1992, 148.

[8]
Linda Griffiths/ Maria Campbell, *The Book of Jessica*, (Toronto: 1989).

[9]
Griffiths/ Campbell 1989, 93.

[10]
Griffiths/ Campbell 1989, 22 f.

[11]
She stressed this fact in the above mentioned conversation.

[12]
Judith Rudakoff/ Rita Much, *Fair Play*, 12 Women Speak (Toronto: 1990), 20.

[13]
Benson/ Conolly 1987, 86 f.

[14]
Rudakoff/ Much 1990, 16.

[15]
Rudakoff/ Much 1990, 26.

[16]
In my telephone conversation with Linda Griffiths she mentioned that she would even like to apply this to the world of theatre and artists in Canada in general.

[17]
Rudakoff/ Much 1990, 17.

[18]
Rudakoff/ Much 1990, 22.

[19]
Rudakoff/ Much 1990, 26.

Kristjana Gunnars

FORGED LETTERS

One day, not so long ago, my story began. It has no ending, but then nothing ever ends. It is a picture. If I look into those eyes, how do I know what eyes he has looked into? What am I looking at? If he looks back in real life, what is he looking at? So far there is no real life. Only a picture, as I say. The first thing I did when I came here was to look out the window. I confuse these views. One city is much like another. All hotel rooms are high up, all views look out on flat roofs and shopping squares. I could see West Georgia Street and an office building with seventy windows to choose between. There was a light on in every one, and people at desks.

I do not remember the airplane ride. Airplane rides resemble each other. I confuse the people I sit beside on different journeys. Sometimes I confuse them deliberately. Those who sit beside me are pictures. Not moving pictures, not the cinema. I am thinking of polaroid shots, the kind that develop instantly. I begin to ask ontological questions: what is such a picture "in itself?" I did not phrase this question myself. There is more to a picture than what you see.

I do remember Vancouver Airport, however. I am always glad to walk outside without a coat on for the first time. I make my home in a very cold place. You cannot walk outside without a coat on where I live. That is a moment I do not forget: stepping out of the airport. Usually it is overcast. Today the sun was shining. Whenever I come to Vancouver I begin to doubt existence. It appears that what I see does not in fact exist. I do not know why I have this feeling. I will not linger on it, but it is a serious doubt. The pictures become the cinema and I am always watching. I go around and through the cinema, but it is always on and I am always looking at it. I cannot stop looking at these moving pictures. Every conscious moment.

Pictures may affect you as much as life does. In some ways there is no difference between the two. I know this; if you believe a picture is real, then it is. I have also come to doubt the existence of a difference between pictures and reality. Pictures are in reality; they also reflect on the reality they are in. They reflect on themselves more than real life does. Real life may not be reflective at all.

It happened that I was hungry when I arrived at this hotel. I suppose the plane left before breakfast and I slept through coffee service on board. That may be why I forget the air trip. But I went downstairs for lunch. It was past three in the afternoon and the restaurant was empty except for one other customer.

Since we were both off-schedule people, we began to talk. After a while we were joined by a third. I found I was sitting with two Cypriots who called themselves Greeks. Some large Cypriot happening was taking place in Vancouver, the details of which went by me. Nor did I learn the names of my acquaintances. Both were men in their late thirties. One was casual and wore glasses. The other was formal and bore a pocket watch on a chain.

That picture evaded me, as pictures do. Empirically speaking, I had no basis from which to judge my acquaintances. Neither scientific evidence nor experience. How could I know what they said was even said? How could I tell they were what they said they were? "Why don't you call yourselves Cypriots instead of Greeks?" I ended up asking. "So we will not be mistaken for Turks," the formal one with the watch chain said. He was smiling through the corners of his mouth.

The rhetoric of such pictures also evades me. How is it possible to narrate such indecisive occurrences? Events which may not even be real events? Physically these two men were there. They spoke, I heard voices and received information. But external to their physical appearance in the picture, I could not determine their essence.

Existentially speaking, there was also this to consider. A picture, such as this one of two Greeks and a Dane at a coffee table in Vancouver, in a restaurant otherwise deserted, can never be created over. Once it crystallizes and once it dissolves. There are no recurrences. I have to narrate this uniqueness, and the problem becomes aesthetic. How is it possible, within narration, to create an advent that is new only once? How can the image itself be transcended as it occurs within the parameters of English rhetoric?

In the case of the two Cypriots, call them Mr. S with the watch chain and Mr. M with the glasses, you acquire your identity from your allegiance, not from what you are. Or, you are your allegiance. The Greek allegiance in Cyprus is comprised of nearly eighty percent of the population of the island. Yet in Athens their dialect is scorned. Even though the Greek Cypriots speak a purer Homeric Greek than the mainlanders do. According to legend, Greek Cypriots are descended from the Achaeans. They are if they think they are. Mr. S and Mr. M cannot be transformed from this page, because they are their allegiance and allegiance is transparent. They must remain weightless. Yet I did ask about the Homeric tradition, once we were on the subject. "Do you cover your bodies with olive oil?" I said. Mr. M with the glasses assured me, "it will come back." For this comment he took off his glasses.

Naturally they did have some weight, physically speaking. Mr. M was changing his allegiance to Canada, so he was not so much a Greek. He had become a citizen. This made his identity less specific. So we recede backwards through specificity into non-reality. Or, we cannot escape the deictic language that requires us to prove our point.

It was cold in the restaurant. In Vancouver buildings are not heated to suit the human body. By this time it was raining hard and I bought an umbrella. This I took up to my room, for I expected to need it later when going out with my brother. The references contained in such simple actions are immediate. You may infer that it was raining in Vancouver since I bought an umbrella. Also that it does not rain where I live. It is these references that give events their status. You may also infer that there were Cypriots in the cafe because of an unidentified Cypriot cultural event that was about to take place. I cannot say how many of these people were now present in Vancouver. And numbers are only meaningful within their context. There is no meaning without a hypothetical framework. You would therefore be unable to perceive the importance of twenty or of twenty hundred Cypriots in Vancouver unless I told you how many of them there are in Canada, and how many in Cyprus.

These contingencies also have much to do with time. How am I to present a chronological narrative when I am not sure time is chronological in the first place? Reality is necessarily tautological, and so is time. So I am at liberty to divulge that I was to run into Mr. S and Mr. M again in the future. Each such encounter is a funeral of contingencies, giving rise to further contingencies. But at this point I had only encountered them in a cafe. Let them remain faceless for now.

I took my umbrella to my room, as I say, after picking up a message for me at the desk. It was about what I should do in Vancouver tomorrow. Yet this schedule I had acquired was only a moot point in a host of developments over the next few days. It occurred to me the Indian restaurant my brother and I had planned to go to that evening was closed for political reasons. It concerned the owner's relation to an Air India disaster. It did not occur to me, as it might have, that the Cyprus conflict was also being acted out in Vancouver.

As evening descended, the offices across from me were deserted one by one. At last there was only one window remaining with a person inside. This picture became an object of concern as I waited for my brother. Why was this man alone in that large building? Was he working late? Perhaps he was in trouble. Or he was having an affair, because a woman showed up in his room. Such speculations have a kind of fatality about them. Let the disorder of never having chosen return. When you choose a solution you classify the unclassifiable.

That evening we went to Gastown. It was dark and still raining. It was not the Gastown of earlier years when I lived in Vancouver. Streets were now cobblestoned and the atmosphere was more Gothic. We parked the car at the edge of a pier somewhere. Or is it Toronto I am thinking of? In Toronto I also parked a car on the water's edge. One city, as I say, is much like another. We did not seek out our Indian restaurant right away, but wandered about the streets in talk. It was a long time since we had met. The sights were new to me, the pictures had been changed. The dark smell of the rain beating down, the weak lamplights along the sidewalks, the black air, these cannot be rendered in language. The pictures became, through our interference, experience. As experience, what I saw became invisible. Let me just say it was a pleasure. The rain, especially.

So as we dined in the dark red and close room of our Indian restaurant, which was not the one the police had closed earlier in the week, for political reasons, I thought I detected yet a third Cypriot. Through the corner of my eye. Let me call him Mr. Q. He was short, stocky and dark, and had the smile I was beginning to associate with Cypriots. It is a smile that must remain undefined in language. But it served as a referent for what was now becoming an uncomfortable feeling in my bones. We spoke about Cyprus, my brother and I, necessarily. The adherence in one's mind of a dominant image dictates one's victimization. I wanted to focus on the phenomenon I was encountering on my first day. The events that were presently crystallizing were doing so at what seemed a great distance. This is not an advent that can be discussed with any precision. It is a sense of an encroachment.

On the exterior, or on the surface, we return to the language of **scientia**. Receding point by point, we come to A.D. 45. At that time Paul and Barnabas introduced Christianity to Cyprus. This fact signals a categorical encroachment as well. I was, in another voice, hankering after a primitive integration of sensations. Christianity gave Greek Cypriots a unity against the Turks. That has been the function of Christianity in Europe since the beginning. To unify against the Turks.

We spent several hours in that room. What we talked about passed on into something integrative, as spurious as the pictures that cannot transcend onto the page. To express our conversation again would require a descent into the primitive arena of pure memory. All that has passed since that evening would necessarily be discarded. But it is not possible to reduce time to an essence that has been erased.

I am therefore at an impasse in this narrative. That is perhaps an ending of a kind. We ended by walking through Gastown once again. The streets were as deserted as before; we seemed to find ourselves in a ghost town. The corners of the buildings appeared to me unnecessarily sharp. The few lights glowing in a window or two gave a threatening light, as if passing judgement on the stark gloom outside. Our footsteps echoed; we were silent. Across the street I noticed Mr. Q rushing on his way.

That night, at about three in the morning, I was in a manner disarmed. I went to sleep as soon as I got back to my room. I had been dreaming. I even remember my dream very well. Dreams are countless and they adjourn in a way once the dreamer awakes. But mine was vivid. I had been dreaming about a certain Kharadj tax. This was levied on infidels in Cyprus in return for tolerance towards Islam. This tax passed from one hand to another in my dream in the form of a black box. A tin box, probably, with some gold inscriptions. A slip of paper came with it containing the word "AIDS" and an arrow pointing to the box. That is all.

At this point the whole hotel resounded with a spinning fire alarm. It was a rude awakening. I dizzily tore into my clothes, bare feet in my shoes, and went into the hall. Other hotel guests were opening their doors looking confusedly at one another. All were reluctant to head down the stairs. How could we be sure the fire alarm was real? It could be false. That moment, as I was deciding what to do next, was a small eternity. I had also seen pictures of hotels turned into flaming infernos. Against possibilities and uncertainties, I was alone. Scientifically speaking, we are alone at such moments.

It was during this brief solitude that the door across the hall from me opened and a dark figure stepped out. I could not hide my amazement, for I found myself looking into the eyes of Mr. Q. He showed no sign of recognition. I realized I had no evidence for thinking he was a Cypriot. But proof can be far more ephemeral than statements or names or numbers. He bore the culture, in an insistent way; something I recognized in opposition to another culture, my culture for example. We did not go down the stairs. We were left, as I said, looking at each other. Framed by the door.

Rolf Althof

KRISTJANA GUNNARS'S ALTERNATIVE REALITIES: THE PAGE AS STAGE FOR NARRATIVE PARADOXES

Kristjana Gunnars was already an established poet,[1] when she published her first novel entitled *The Prowler*[2] in 1989. This novel is basically concerned with the I-narrator's childhood in Iceland, Denmark and North America.[3] It also includes reflections on the possibilities of narrating stories which clearly mark the text as postmodern.[4] The book aims to shatter conventions but also to tell a story. The questioned literary conventions, however, make it difficult for reader and critic alike to find a vantage point from which to discuss *The Prowler*. While a well-known principle of structured learning is to move from the known to the unknown, the act of prowling in itself already seems to constitute the opposite of structure. Thus it should not be surprising to a reader, but is so nevertheless, that this book is not paginated. Despite this refusal to follow convention, another form of subdivision is provided in the numbers 1-167 for the short chapters of *The Prowler*. This rather external first observation forces any reader into the process of prowling even before he or she has really begun to read the book.

Logic and convention have it that since Aristotle stated that every story is a whole and has a beginning, a middle and an end,[5] we usually begin discussing literary texts from the beginning, by which page number one is meant. *The Prowler*, however, offers several possibilities for a first close look. As far as the chronology of the narrated childhood is concerned, one could begin with chapter 152 where the fate of the paternal grandmother is told, or with the very end, with chapter(s) 166 (and 167 in order to include the mother of the I-narrator) because in these last two chapters of the book the I-narrator's parents come to Iceland before the narrator's birth: "My parents where on that ship."(167), while at the same time the paradox of the chronological beginning of the story at the end of the book is also reflected with regard to narrating stories:

> It must be possible after all to find a beginning to any story. Even if it is
> arbitrary. I have been thinking that there is an actual beginning to this story
> and that a story should end with its origins. It is necessary to conceive of
> time running backwards. (166)

Time running backwards and the beginning at the end of a book necessitates prowling on the part of the reader, or, as Moss puts it: "In some ways, perhaps, it is a novel to be re-read rather than read;…"[6]

Any reader who has reached this beginning at the end has already read the text once, and in the course of this reading was informed not only about the childhood and life of the I-narrator but also about dozens of other, narrative problems. He has, for example, been told rather early on that the end of a story is contained in its beginning and that the I-narrator does not want his story to have any direction, but rather regards it as a growing plant, getting bigger but not moving anywhere.(cf. 24) Following the theories the book adheres to, the reader can identify this seed-like growing as a more or less circular development said to be a female way of writing as opposed to the rather linear, male, concept of development.[7] The image of prowling seems to be particularly apt as it offers the chance to combine both principles. The prowler may move in any direction he chooses. He is therefore the ideal reader for a story that has 'no direction'(cf. 24). Moreover prowling is an end in itself and as an image works on various levels. It is an end in itself because the reader prowling through or in the story, i. e. reading and re-reading it, is putting together the pieces of a jigsaw puzzle and thus enters into a communication with the writer. This is paradoxical in at least two ways: on the one hand because the reader 'creates' the text, or his version of it, as much as the author and thus is the text's author, and on the other hand because: "The prowler does not know he already has what is being sought." (110)

The image of prowling, however, is not limited to the process of reading. It is also used literally within the narration of the I-narrator's childhood since she and her sister are warned that a prowler is about in Rungsted in Denmark (57). This possibly historical prowler is transformed into the I-narrator's image of his potential activities and then generalized:

There are, I have come to understand, prowlers everywhere. They prowl about, looking for dialogue. They look for threads.

I do not want to shirk the responsibility of joining in the search for threads. I know there are a few, but it is in the nature of things that the threads be kept out of sight. Or be only barely discernible. Yet they are quite obvious.

The text admits: this is how I am sewn together. (74)

This passage is in itself a paradox by stating that the threads of the story, the story-line, are kept out of sight and are obvious. The passage can be linked to another chapter in the book quoting James Joyce's statement: 'The reader wants to steal from the text' and refuting it by saying "It is a relief not to have such rules. To play such games. Hide and seek. Not to have rules perhaps means you are free to steal from yourself. Finally." (59) Stealing from oneself refers to the autobiographical aspect of this novel. It is strongly connected to memory. While the author memorizes bits and pieces of her own childhood, changing and transforming these into the childhood of the I-narrator, author as well as I-narrator prowl about in fragments of memory. The development of the narrator's life, which the text deliberately calls "God's story" (119)—thus being able to pretend: "It is not my story. The author is unknown. I am the reader." (119)—allows for the further extention of the prowler image to the writer:

> The writer is a prowler in a given story that emerges in time. The writer reports on incidents. There are no protagonists in the given story. Any subject is a contrived subject. The point of view is uncertain. The writer is necessarily part of the story. (120)

If the writer is herself part of the story which reader and writer puzzle together the next paradox arises: it can no longer be the author who is in control of the text, it must be the text itself which decides on what is being written and how: "The text is the writer's prison. The words will not take the writer into themselves. The author is therefore locked out of the book." (93)

What even the text has to acknowledge, are certain facts for which there are no alternatives—not even paradoxical ones—if narration is to be possible at all, even though a hint at the potential paradox is also given: "The story knows the pattern is given. There are some things it cannot change. It would like to be free to rewrite itself. To surpass itself." (95) Viewed from another perspective even this desire of the text to 'surpass itself' is successful. As John Moss comments:

> The Prowler violates the conventions of story-telling which dictate that the story knows where it's going, even if the reader doesn't. It is many stories each with its own centre some only a few words, none more than a few pages. [8]

These stories often take on an aphoristic quality and frequently use poetic imagery; both also characteristics of Gunnars' other novels. Using the plural here means that *Zero Hour*[9] is also regarded as a novel, although—perhaps due to its highly autobiographical content—it does not place itself within any genre.[10] The title *Zero Hour* does not refer in any way to the point in time which, in European history and literature, is usually associated with zero hour i. e. the end of World War II.[11] Instead it is another paradox meant on the one hand to provide an image for death and on the other the central symbol for the feeling of the bereaved for the whole book. The paradox as an image for death is: "*There is no zero on the clock. To get to zero, you have to step outside of time.*" (122). The central narrative paradox Gunnars had to solve in *Zero Hour* was the seemingly impossible task of writing about the personal grief inherent in the death of her beloved father in such a way that would allow the reader to take an interest and become emotionally involved, but at the same time of avoiding an excess of sentiment about the dying process of her father. Gunnars' way of dealing with the paradox lies in employing the same structure and patterns she used in *The Prowler*. The account of the deterioration of her father's condition is interspersed with reminiscences of mountain-hikes with friends, memories of occasions on which she joined her father on walks or in other activities, and the descriptions of the Gateway City to the West, i.e. Winnipeg, as the place where she retreats to after her father's death. While this specific way of alternating threads in the story enables the reader (and perhaps the author as well) to come to terms with the emotions involved in the portrayed process, there is also the matter-of-fact style of the book that renders the involved emotions readable. One model for this may be seen in Roland Barthes' *Le degree zero de l'ecriture*,[12] an intertextual reference the text itself makes.[13] In his review "Away from zero" Stephen Scobie has paralleled exerpts from Roland Barthes' text with quotations from *Zero Hour*, thus attempting to show that Gunnars successfully employs 'ground zero writing' because: "[...] she searches for a style so clean, so pure, so ascetic that it will exclude any hint of sweetness."[14] Following Barthes, Scobie calls this matter-of-fact style innocent. Thus *Zero Hour* is innocent of the sentimentality the book itself criticizes:

> Certain human experiences are made to come out sentimental. Birth and death are sweetened.
>
> Yet I can sense in the hollow cavity of my chest that birth and death are not sweet. They are awful. They wipe you away, everything you were up to that moment. There is a great loss and a great unknown: an uncertainty the human mind must be unable to cope with. You are disappearing. You want to scream. You know nothing will ever be the same and everything you know is unalterably lost. (17)

This total loss is encapsulated in a number of images most of which have to do with zero. The loss is compared with the mushroom cloud of an H-bomb which has fallen, an odometer that goes berserk and has to be pushed back to zero (cf. 18), the century is labelled the century of the countdown (cf. 33) and Gunnars has the idea that we could paginate our books in the same way, counting them down to the end. The room she rents after her father's death is also completely empty, thus has 'zero' furniture (cf. 27). While she is attending to her father in a Portland hospital, her bank account moves to zero (cf. 41) and the strain of experiencing the dying process of her father makes her soul reach "rock bottom [...] ground zero" (98). But at least as important as the imagery used and the reflections present in *Zero Hour* is the presentation of a death which is allowed to happen with dignity. Though at times the perfectly functioning social networks of understanding doctors, nurses, neighbours and above all family seem rather idealistic, the portrayed way to die is one everyone would wish for, especially in an age which still has the tendency to shut dying people away in hospitals.

In 1992 Kristjana Gunnars published *The Substance of Forgetting*,[15] which, depending on the way *Zero Hour* is regarded, is either her third or her second novel. The book begins with a quotation from Julia Kristeva explaining that all networks of possible meaning are arbitrary, and then embeds the whole story it tells in the intertextual context of W.B. Yeats' poem *"The Lake Isle of Innisfree."* The beginning of this poem—the first stanza and the first two lines of the second stanza—are printed at the beginning of *The Substance of Forgetting* and the first two lines of the second stanza are repeated at the very end. In between, the novel takes the reader home in the literal sense:

> I am thinking home is where you choose to forget and choose to remember at the same time. Nothing hinders your choices. Nothing forces you to remember and nothing forces you to forget. There is no reason to repress

any memory. There is no reason to hold it up against the daylight either. (125)

This time Gunnars ends with the end and not with the beginning but she nevertheless evokes a circular image with the double quotation from Yeats and retains her typical style of writing. Life at home, the home being a cottage in the hills above Woodlake, is again one of the storylines in this book. Another is the relationship between the English-Canadian I-narrator and the Quebecois Jules, who have met in a town in the American Midwest from where the I-narrator will go to Minneapolis and Jules to Montreal. Setting up this relationship—although only hinted at a few times—of course takes place against the topical political background: "*What does English Canada want?* No one asked the question but it was in the air. English Canada wants the presence of French Canada. [...] *What does French Canada want?* A kiss. A stolen kiss and separation." (48) These lines are as much a comment on the latest developments in Canadian political history,[16] as they are on the (two) protagonist(s): "His mouth on mine. A meeting of languages. Unofficial bilingualism. We are defined by our desires, by what we want." (48) Paradoxical implication this time is the impossibility to fulfill the desires of both Canadas. At the same time this question is closely connected to the question of the further development of Canada as a nation—or more precisely three nations—and thus the question of alternative realities comes into view, for example the alternative reality of what would happen if Quebec really were to separate. The novel, having repeated one of the questions already posed in *The Prowler*—"Shall I fill in all the details? Or shall I let the reader imagine them all? Who should write this book, me or my reader?" (16)—proceeds in its reflections on narrative technique and the possibility of discussing alternative realities. Next to the reflections on psychoanalyst theory connected to Jacques Lacan, who provides one framework for *The Substance of Forgetting* much like Roland Barthes for *Zero Hour*, the possibility of an alternative reality is another narrative paradox Gunnars shows at work:

> Lives we could have led but did not choose. Choices we did not make. The alternate paths. That what we choose is real only because we choose it. Perhaps what we have not chosen is even more real. [...] There are official stories and then there are unofficial stories. Sometimes we break through the official story. We escape into an alternate story. Just for a while. (71)

While the idea of the existence of an official story in whose subtext an unofficial story would provide another, perhaps even better, reading of the text(s) was already present in *The Prowler* (cf. 47), Gunnars now takes memory as a means to narrate alternative realities. One example she chooses is an oncoming train while Jules and the I-narrator are walking along the railway tracks. The imagination of what the situation could be like if there were a train and if this train were to kill the two lovers is repeated with several alterations and modifications. Moreover, this episode is connected to a light shining through the curtains of the room in which Jules and the I-narrator spend a night. This image is also repeatedly narrated with modifications. Such alternative realities are paradoxical from the point of view of the narration of a linear, chronological 'true' sequence of events. They are, however, quite in line with processes of memorizing and forgetting. While memory is in a way only possible through repetition, the counterbalancing process of forgetting always presents the memory with slight alterations, brought about by forgetting. While unaltered repetitions would be a real strain on the reader, modified repetitions do not lead to strain, but to recognition and consequently reflection on possible alternatives. If existence only comes with the written word as the text stipulates: "Is reality determined by words on paper? If that is true then what I write is real. What I write exists. Unless it is written it does not exist. It never happened." (100) Alternative realities can only exist, if they are incorporated in the text. Therefore a linear, chronological narrative is impossible and only circular ways of writing enable the unfolding of such realities:

> I do not think there will be enough repetitions to develop a technique. There are only circles and every circle strikes you as new. You do not remember having done this before. I looked at Jules' windblown profile and did not remember having done this before. Just precisely this. I was thinking it is not possible that this combination will ever crystallize again either. It is a solitary moment. All alone in its immensity. (89, 90)

While *The Substance of Forgetting* amongst other things concerns itself with the narration of alternative realities, these and the solitary moment mentioned in the last quotation are also some of the concerns of the short story *"Forged Letters"* published for the first time in this volume. In 1992 Kristjana Gunnars published a collection of short stories entitled *The Guest House and Other Stories*.[17] When reviewing *The Substance of Forgetting* and *The Guest House and Other Stories* for Books in Canada, Daniel Jones wrote:

> In *The Guest House*, her second collection of stories, Gunnars explores literary terrain very different from that of her novels. In some ways the stories fail in comparison. If the novels could be classified as postmodernist, the stories are definitely modernist in their orientation and execution. Simple and straight-forward in tone and structure, the stories concern themselves with characters struggling against harsh and isolated environments.[18]

"Forged Letters" provides what Jones was looking for in *The Guest House*. Already the title allows for speculation about the presented reality. It, too, definitely encompasses alternative realities. What is 'staged' begins as an ironical comment on the form of short stories since these are often open ended: "One day, not so long ago, my story began. It has no ending, but then nothing ever ends."[19] At first the by now familiar idea of alternative realities is presented this time in the dichotomy between two people looking at each other without any security of having perceived the same reality. A day ago the I-narrator arrived at Vancouver airport in order to meet her brother. She remembers people who sat beside her on the plane in the form of pictures and is trying to decipher potential subtexts by asking the Kantian "in itself" question about pictures.

"What is such a picture in itself? [...] There is more to a picture than what you see."(215) The once again paradoxical conclusion she draws is that pictures are at the same time real and non-real, they are reality and reflect reality. To turn pictures into an existing reality for the writer means to change them into text and make them appear on the 'stage of the page.'[20] Therefore, when the narrator meets two Greek Cypriots she has to 'forge letters' calling them Mr. M and Mr. S, and a third person later on Mr. Q in order to represent the picture in what to her constitutes the real existence, the written text. While giving reality to the existing perceived pictures requires naming them—an echo of *The Prowler*: "Only that which is named is able to live in language." (52)—the missing background or framework against which to measure the encounter also poses a problem. "That picture evaded me, as pictures do. Empirically speaking I had no basis from which to judge my aquaintances." (216) The necessity for the I-narrator to acquire further knowledge, in particular so as to solve the problem why Cypriots call themselves Greeks, to which Mr. M and Mr. S give the obvious answer: in order to be distinguished from the Turks, leads to the narrator's reflection on yet another narrative paradox. If reality presents time chronologic-ally and events happen only once, it is true that: "There are no recurrences. I have to narrate this uniqueness and the problem becomes aesthetic. How is it possible within narration, to create an advent that is new only once?"(216) At first it seems that the text does not find an answer to this problem, nor is this possible, because the very act of presenting a written text, allows one—as long as texts are published in the form of books—to leaf back and re-read the story. While prowling is possible and essential to certain forms of narrative, the one-dimensional chronology of reality cannot be achieved by narrative means. The problem is brought into focus again after the I-narrator has stated that she cannot provide the hypothetical framework which alone would make the encounter with two Cypriots in Vancouver meaningful, i. e. by providing a context. (Cf. 217) The way out of this dilemma which the short story takes is to open up another paradox, by challenging our usual perception of reality and replacing it with an alternative reality:

> How am I to present a chronological narrative when I am not sure time is chronological in the first place? Reality is necessarily tautological, and so is time. So I am at liberty to divulge that I was to run into Mr. S and Mr. M again in the future. Each such encounter is a funeral of contingencies, giving rise to further contingencies. (217)

The idea that reality and time are tautological is mirrored not only in the fact that the I-narrator foreshadows the future or that she walks through Gastown twice (cf. 217 and 218) or even meets Mr. Q three times (cf. 218, 219), but also in the recurring reflections on imagery. This short story in itself thus tries to prove the alternative reality that time is not chronological: "The story [...] may seem a little strange to you. It is supposed to be strange and the narrative is supposed to backtrack and curl in on itself, so to speak."[21] The frequent usage of alternative realities and of paradoxes are both cases in point.

When Gunnars describes the evening in Vancouver she once more employs these means:

> The dark smell of the rain beating down, the weak lamplights along the sidewalks, the black air, these cannot be rendered in language. The pictures became, through our interference, experience. As experience, what I saw became invisible." (217)

Here images are created and the synaesthetic description of the **dark smell** of the rain **beating down** together with the adjectives weak and black lend strength and atmosphere to these images, while the short story simultaneously professes not to be able to express the images. Moreover, describing them as experiences doubles the paradox because not only has the unexpressible been expressed,[22] but also it is stipulated that that which has just been forged into letters is invisible.

With *"Forged Letters"* the paradoxes do not only refer to questions of narrative. It should not go unnoticed that this short story intersperses several stories just as Gunnars' novels do. Apart from reflections on narrative possibilities and the I-narrator's meeting with her brother, there is of course also the problem of the Cypriots. This is a meaningful cultural subtext extending the paradox to culture. Just as it is paradoxical that a Cypriot living in Cyprus should refer to himself as a Greek or a Turk and thus becomes a 'hyphenated' Cypriot, this implicitly poses the question whether hyphenated Canadians are not also a paradox. This is in particular true with regard to the fact that Kristjana Gunnars in her novels, and in this short story, has definitely written postmodern multicultural stories. All the multicultural components are mentioned, whether they are Iceland, Denmark, the United States, or Cyprus, or the English-Canadian I-narrator or the French-Canadian Jules in *The Substance of Forgetting* or—**primus inter pares**—Canada as such. But it is the task of the reader to reflect on and to hold out against the paradoxes. On the stage of the page the narrative paradoxes of the form find their alternative paradoxical reality in the multicultural existence of the protagonists.[23]

Notes

1

Cf. Kristjana Gunnars, *Settlement Poems I* (Winnipeg: Turnstone Press, 1980); Kristjana Gunnars, *Settlement Poems II* (Winnipeg: Turnstone Press, 1980); Kristjana Gunnars, *Wake-Pick Poems* (Toronto: Anansi, 1981); Kristjana Gunnars, *The Night Workers of Ragnarök* (Toronto/Victoria: Press Porcepic, 1985); Kristjana Gunnars, *Carnival of Longing* (Winnipeg:, Turnstone Press 1990). Her two poems "wakepick I" and "changeling VIII" are included in *The New Oxford Book of Canadian Verse in English*, chosen and with an introduction by Margaret Atwood (Toronto, London, New York, OUP: 1982), 453-455.

2

Kristjana Gunnars, *The Prowler* (Red Deer: Red Deer College Press, 1989). All further references to this book are incorporated into the text, giving the number of the chapter in brackets.

3

Cf. Gardar Baldvinsson, "Cold War," *Canadian Literature*, Winter 1992, no. 135, 157, 158. Dayv James-French's review "Past and Present" in *Books in Canada*, vol. XVIII, no 6, August/September 1989, 35 is hardly worth reading, as it—despite its brevity—clearly indicates the superficiality with which the reviewer skimmed over the novel.

4

Cf. John Moss, "Postmodern Prowl," *Canadian Forum*, Vol. LXIX No 792, September 1990, 30, 31.

5

Cf. Aristoteles, *Poetik* (Stuttgart, 1961), 33, 34.

6

Moss, 1990, 31.

7

Cf. Moss, 1990, 30.

8

Moss, 1990, 30.

9

Kristjana Gunnars, *Zero Hour*, (Red Deer: Red Deer College Press 1991). All further references to and quotations from this text indicate the page numbers in brackets.

10

Cf. Elisabeth Anthony, "Eros by Any Other Name:" "Writing out her grief she gives us 'a story that is not a story, a novel that is not a novel, a poem not longer a poem,' a heterogenous form she explored effectively in her previous book *The Prowler*," *Books in Canada*, vol. XX, no. 6, September 1991, 36.

11

Cf. Rolf Althof, "Le temps des ideologies (1933-1945)" in: Annick Benoit-Dusausoy et Guy Fontaine (Eds.) *Lettres Européennes Histoire de la Litterature Européenne* (Paris: Hachette, 1992), 811-854, here 854.

12

Cf. Roland Barthes, *Le degree zero de l'ecriture* (Paris: Du Seuil, 1953).

13

Cf. Gunnars, *Zero Hour*, 10. In all her novels Gunnars frequently uses intertextual references to European and American novels, poems, plays, fairy tales, other non-fictional texts and scientific theories. These references merit an in-depth analysis which is way beyond the aim of this article.

14

Stephen Scobie "Away from Zero," *Canadian Literature*, Winter 1992, no. 135, 194-196, here 194.

15

Kristjana Gunnars, *The Substance of Forgetting* (Red Deer: Red Deer College Press, 1992). All further references to and quotations from this text indicate the page numbers in brackets.

16
Cf. Rudolf Woller, "Nach dem gescheiterten Referendum - Ratloses Kanada," *Canada Journal*, vol 11, Nr. 1/2, Jan./Feb. 1993, 9, 10.

17
Kristjana Gunnars, *The Guest House and Other Stories* (Concord: Anansi, 1992).

18
Daniel Jones, "Filling In the Details," *Books in Canada*, vol. XXII, no. 1, February 1993, 45.

19
Kristjana Gunnars, *"Forged Letters,"* as published in this volume. All further page references given in brackets are to this edition.

20
For the 'origin' of this metaphor cf. *Zero Hour*, 76: "I have seen the blank page referred to as a stage. All that happens on the stage is theatre. Writing is a play. Words are actors, props, singers, dancers."

21
Kristjana Gunnars in a letter to the editors July 29, 1992.

22
Cf. *"Forged Letters"* 217: "When you choose a solution you classify the unclassifiable."

23
In a way this text also succeeds in realizing the desire expressed in *The Prowler* (cf. 95) to surpass itself: The very last image of *"Forged Letters"* has the I-narrator meet Mr. Q, recognize a difference in culture and end with the words: "We were left, as I said, looking at each other. Framed by the door" (219). This ending offers not only the coming-full-circle-reference back to the beginning, but apparently also a narrated 'solitary moment,' a 'uniqueness.' Framed by the door, the I-narrator and Mr. Q are static, are kept in suspension, are caught immobile in a picture. Thus for the briefest of moments all gaps are bridged, all paradoxes resolved. Cf. the similar technique in Timothy Findley *The Wars* (Toronto: 1997), 190, 191.

Roger Hall

THE dream FACTORY
(A Play for Radio)

Cast

Benny
Male Voice
Bert
Marvin Landor
Carol
Miss Claymore
Vance
Miss Hernandez
Fritz Schulman
Thelma
Miss Arnold
Cop
Miss Castella
Psychiatrist

BENNY: You say I'm an old man. Nearing death. Am I frightened of it? Listen: I'm a writer. The only annoying thing about death is when I go I'll be thinking: "Hey, I won't be able to write about this." Know who was always my hero? P. G. Wodehouse. Oh, not for his writing, sure he had something. Good stories. Great lyrics. No. P. G. Wodehouse was still writing, still typing his stuff, right into his nineties. I always vowed that's what I wanted to do. Well! I've made it. Which is why I can tell you what I'm about to tell you. When I was in my thirties, that was the peak of my production. Not my **best** stuff. But I sure churned it out. I was a writer in Hollywood. I was **the** writer in Hollywood. But how many people remember the name Benny Lee nowadays?

Fade up FX bevy of old fashioned typewriters

BERT: Hey Fellers!

Typewriters stop.

VOICE: What gem is it this time, Bert?

BERT: How does this sound? Harlow's trapped by snow in the Alaskan cabin. Been there days. No one for miles. No food. She's desperate. Door opens. Gable. Six months' beard. Unrecognizable. Staggers. Exhausted. Bleeding from some Grizzly attack.

VOICE: Even grizzlier if he was attacked by Harlow.

Male laughter

BERT: Yeah, yeah. She helps him onto the bunk.

Whistles

BERT: Rips open his shirt to tend to his wounds—even though it's forty below the guy hasn't got a singlet on—and sees—

BENNY: The medallion she gave to her man two years ago.

BERT (*Surprised and hurt*): Yeah! Yeah, Benny. Like it?

BENNY: I always have.

BERT: So you think I shouldn't—

BENNY: Bert. It's a good ending. Always has been. Always will be.

VOICES: That's right./Great ending./Not a Dr.y seat in the house.

BENNY: Bert! With any luck your name won't appear on the Credits!

Laughter

LANDOR: Why are you men not writing?

Stunned silence

BENNY: Script conference, Mr. Landor.

LANDOR: I watch you sometimes. Sometimes you guys don't write a word for ten minutes at a time. You're writers. Paid to write. So write. How's it going Benny?

BENNY: Eleven hunDr.ed and forty-three words, Mr. Landor.

LANDOR (*To the others*): See! That's writing!

Typewriters resume.

Fade, hold under briefly, fade out

BENNY (*To us as narrator*): Marvin Landor. Biggest producer in Hollywood. The most powerful man in Hollywood. Walk out on Landor, and you walked out on Hollywood—he saw to that. He had the Midas touch—everything he touched turned to excrement. **Then** to gold. Marvin Landor! In New Jersey he was brought up as Hymie Schwarz. Now you're not going to believe all this. But it happened. (*Reminiscent*) Hollywood in the thirties. We writers were in one big room. Like it was a newspaper set. In fact it was. It was a factory. Mass production. Write a picture for x, y and zee. Then maybe zee Dr.ops out so you have to change it to suit w. Producers with brains the size of ants' eggs lectured you on story structure. OK, I was coining it. No other reason for being out there. I'd had coupla stage plays. Coupla thrillers. The twist at the end, that's what made them. So they brought me out West. I was also coining it in other ways . Hollywood was a hot town. In every sense. I'm talking sex. Like commitment was still being there in the morning. Married, single, it made no difference. It was in the air. This stuff I'm giving you now is exposition, back-story. I'm telling you: I was seeing a lot of broads.

Back in time

CAROL: Oh Benny!!!!!!

BENNY: Norma!!!

CAROL (*Indignant*): Carol!

BENNY: Carol! Only teasing. How about I get us some more wine from the fridg—

CAROL: You have to go, Benny. My husband will be home (*Fade*) any second now, and he's got———

BENNY (*To us*): But this story's about Marvin Landor. Marvin was the type of guy told you what he wanted, you gave it to him, he wanted something else. It made no difference to the paycheck, but he got no feelings. You slaved away, did some nice dialogue, hint of sub-text—nothing subtle—and he trampled on it. After a while you got to realise it didn't matter, you could use the stuff again in something else. I tell you, long before the rest of the world, writers discovered re-cycling.

Each day, Marvin'd look into the writers' room accompanied by his latest (*Coughs*) secretary.

VOICE: He's comin', boys!

FX typewriters start up.

LANDOR: Mornin' boys.

BOYS: Mornin' Mr. Landor.

LANDOR: Like you all to meet Miss Claymore.

BOYS: Mornin' Miss Claymore.

LANDOR: Benny. Benny's my star writer Miss Claymore.

CLAYMORE (*Quite warmly*): Hi.

BENNY (*To us*): Marvin Landor liked to measure things.

LANDOR: How's it going today, Benny?

BENNY: This morning, one thousand four hunDr.ed and fifty nine words.

LANDOR: Great. See what I mean, Miss Claymore? Hear that, boys?

BOYS: We hear it, Mr. Landor.

LANDOR: Got that, Miss Claymore?

CLAYMORE: Got that Marv—Mr. Landor.

BENNY (*to us*): He once checked my total. I watched his finger dot every word, and his mouth outlined every number to see if I had it right. As it happened, I'd under-estimated so he was even happier. Thought he had the extra words for nothing. (*Aloud*) Want to read some, Mr. Landor?

LANDOR: No, no, no. Whose working on the Leroy McGuire script?

VANCE: I am Mr. Landor.

LANDOR: Vance. McGuire needs more than you're givin' him. He needs meat. He needs jealousy. How did I put it Miss Claymore?

CLAYMORE (*Reading*): "I want the hero eaten alive with jealousy like the darkie who went nuts over a handkerchief."

LANDOR: Know the one, Vance?

VANCE: I know the one.

LANDOR: What man doesn't feel crazy, thinking someone's shtupping his wife. Leroy wants to do some acting in this film. He's got to jealousy in his correspondence acting lessons, I don't know—jealousy makes a good story. More meat, Vance.

VANCE: Anything you say Mr. Landor. More jealousy.

LANDOR: That's it boys. I gotta be runnin'. Time is money. Time is money.

BENNY (*To us*): He said it like he coined it himself.

LANDOR: Keep it up, boys!

BOYS: So long Mr. Landor.

BENNY (*To us*): That's how it went. Every day. Though he'd call in different time of day to keep us on our toes. Sheesh! (*i. e. pathetic subterfuge*) Most of the time we were writin' formula stuff. I put in some of my own ideas to the studio, but got nowhere. Until one morning …

LANDOR: Morning boys!

BOYS: Morning Mr. Landor.

LANDOR: Like you to meet Miss Hernandez.

BOYS: Morning Miss Hernandez.

LANDOR: How's it going Benny?

BENNY: Nine hunDr.ed—

LANDOR: Forget that script you're on. Give it to Bert to finish--

BENNY: But—

LANDOR: Your story line.

BENNY: Yes?

LANDOR: Erm … er … (*Snaps fingers*) Miss Hernandez.

HERNANDEZ (*Reads stiltedly*): "The Amethyst ring, a story about passion, power and lust. Vincent Guardia, a wealth—"

LANDOR: I just needed the title Miss Hernandez. I like it, the Studio Board likes it. Approval to go-ahead.

BENNY: Thank you Mr. Landor.

LANDOR: We'll give it to Spencer, Katherine, Clark, and Bette.

BENNY (*To us*): This was fantastic. Great cast, great story if I do say so. I mean we were talking Oscar potential.

LANDOR: We're talking Oscar potential. I must run. Busy, busy.

BENNY: Sure Mr. Landor. Thanks.

LANDOR: Appointment with the psycho-analyst. (*Almost a boast*) I'm ... being psychoanalysed Benny.

BENNY: So who isn't? (*To us*) Everyone was into psycho-analysis. I went myself a few times.

LANDOR: You go to psychoanalysis?

BENNY: I've been.

LANDOR: We're paying you too much.

HERNANDEZ: Want me to make a note of that, Mr. Landor?

LANDOR: It was a joke. Kinda. So Á who did you go to?

BENNY: Schulman. Fritz Schulman.

LANDOR: That's the guy. (*Mock German accent*) "So, vat did you Dr.im las night?" That the guy?

BENNY: That's the guy. (*To us*) That's what he always asked me ... It went something like this:

FRITZ: So! Benny. Vot did you Dr.im last night? The orchestra again?

BENNY: I'm conducting. Carnegie Hall. Sold right out. It's my own composition they've come to hear. And the goddammed strings take no notice. Take no notice of my notes, my conducting. And ...

FRITZ: Take your time.

BENNY: No matter what I do, they refuse to... and I think the tuba rebelled. I'm not sure ...

PSYCH: Take your time.

BENNY (*To us*): "Take your time!" At 15 bucks an hour. It Dr.ove me crazy. Which was the opposite of what it was supposed to be doing. After a few sessions of this, Fritz then took **his** time making comments.

FRITZ: I detect anger. I sense impatience. Impatience with those who interpret your work. Give anger a holiday. Be tolerant of others.

BENNY (*To us*): Silly old fool. The best relief I got was from his wife. She said "Take your time," too, for a quite different reason. So I reduced the treatment from him; and I increased it from her.

THELMA: Benny, Benny, Benny!!!

BENNY: Oh God, Thelma you're wonderful. A roll in the sack's worth ten sessions with your old man.

THELMA: I can believe it. He sees patients all the time. Yet **he's** the weird one. When we make love, I have to fake that I like it best when he pretends he's—

FX front door opening

THELMA: Oh my God, it's him. It's Fritz. He's back from Chicago early!

FRITZ (*As if approaching upstairs*): Thelma? Thelma! Are you in the ...

THELMA (*Over above*): Get out the window!

BENNY: Too late.

FX beDr.oom door opening

FRITZ (*Now close to us*): ... beDr.oom?

Silence

BENNY: Dr. Schulman. I can explain everything.

FRITZ: Oh?

BENNY: I'm screwing your wife.

FRITZ: So I see. Stay there.

FX steps running down staircase

THELMA: Oh my God, he's going to his office.

FRITZ (*From stairs*): Don't go. Stay there.

BENNY (*Relaxing and amused*): What's he going for—my file!

THELMA: A gun! He keeps a gun in his desk.

BENNY: Oh my God! He's going to shoot them off.

THELMA: Out the window!

BENNY: I knew it'd happen to me one day.

THELMA: Out the window!

BENNY (*Now frightened*): Oh my God!

THELMA: There's a tree by the window.

BENNY: What about you—he's not going to kill you, is he? (*To us*) I retained a touch of gallantry even in extremes.

THELMA: NO! I'll be OK—

BENNY: One of my socks—one of my socks is miss—

THELMA: GO!!!!

FX BENNY'S exertions climbing down tree. Snapping of branches; panicky breathing etc.

FRITZ (*Shouting*): I know you're there!

A couple of shots. Bullets whizz past close to BENNY.

BENNY: It wasn't until I was round the corner I could get my breath. And get Dr.essed. All except one sock.

It all ended reasonably civilised. Thelma got a black eye and a warning next time he'd fire at her; I got the bill, paid it, and that seemed to be the end of it. Thelma told me later Fritz's temper flared up but quickly died away. And she told me Fritz's little love-making quirk. Course, it put an end to my psycho-analysis sessions. And Thelma had to come round to my place. But sometimes I wished I could go back. Find out what made me tick. I mean, to a writer it's all material isn't it. Anyway, the material I was interested in was The Amethyst Ring. I was so keen I even worked on it at home.

FX typing

FX phone

BENNY (*Irritated*): Tch!

Picks up phone

THELMA: Benny?

BENNY: Thelma.

THELMA: You haven't called for a while, Benny.

BENNY: It's work, Thelma. Work. I'm writing this script.

THELMA: Don't give me that. You never write at home. You boasted about it. You write on company time only; you **said**—

BENNY: **Now** I'm writing at home. This is something special. Right now I'm at white heat.

THELMA: You used to be at white heat for me.

BENNY: I know Baby. I'll call you soon as I can. Truly.

THELMA: Promise?

BENNY: Promise.

FX ringing off

BENNY: I worked on that sucker every moment I could. So it wasn't long before one day in the morning at the factory...

typing "The sheet of the bed is pulled back ... she finds ... the amethyst ring ... shock ... she knows she has been duped ... Look of horror on Bette's face—the whole thing as a set-up." What a twist, no one'll see it comin'. (*Types*) "FADE ... THE END"

FX lights cigarette

BENNY: Now if that don't win an Oscar ... OK Oscar **nomination**. (*Aloud*) 'THE END' boys. I just typed 'THE END.'

VANCE: The most beautiful word in da English language.

VOICE: One of your best, Benny?

BENNY: It always is. That's it. Taking the rest of the day off.

VOICE: He's comin'.

FX typewriters starting

LANDOR: Morning boys.

BOYS: Morning Mr.. Landor.

LANDOR: I want you to meet Miss Arnold.

BOYS: Morning Miss Arnold.

LANDOR: Benny, Benny! Where are you off to?

BENNY: Here's the script, Marvin. This is a humdinger. Finished it. Now, the old creative juices Dr.ied up—Takin' the rest of the day off.

LANDOR: The rest of the day off! It's not eleven in the a. m. yet.

BENNY: I've been working night and day, Mr. Landor.

LANDOR: Give it to Miss Arnold, here. Miss Arnold. What have we got arrived today?

ARNOLD: Arabian Mirage. Pirate Plunder. Tarzan's Jungle Conquest. Hellbent for Texas.

LANDOR: Any one there appeal to you, Benny?

BENNY: They're all equally attractive, Mr. Landor.

LANDOR: Give him "Tarzan," Miss Arnold. Ideal for someone hails from New York. That's a jungle, isn't it. Hey? (*Chuckles*)

Sycophantic chuckles from the other writers

LANDOR (*Confidentially*): Oh. Benny. Fritz Schulman. I told you he wants to analyse my dreams.

BENNY (*Still sulking*): Yeah.

LANDOR: And sometimes, I don't have dreams. When I go to sleep, I go out like a light, know what I mean?

BENNY (*To us*): He said "Go out like a light" like he coined it himself.

LANDOR: And I'm a busy man. Busy, busy.

BENNY: Nobody could deny that, Mr. Landor.

LANDOR: If I don't dream, I should make one up. Otherwise the session's a waste of time, waste of money. I have no time to make up a dream.

BENNY: So where do I come in?

LANDOR: Where you come in is write some dreams for me.

BENNY (*To us*): Was he serious? (*Aloud*) You want me to make up dreams for you!

LANDOR: You're the writer. You make up the dreams.

BENNY (*To us*): He was serious. (*Aloud*) Not in studio time, Mr. Landor?

LANDOR: Sure, sure. Fit it in with Tarzan.

BENNY: Not in my contract, Mr. Landor.

LANDOR: When's you're contract up for renewal, Benny?

BENNY (*Resigned*): OK … I'll write you some dreams. (*To us*) The cheap skate. (*Aloud*) Can you give me any idea what the … er … problem was?

LANDOR: Huh?

BENNY: Er why you … er went to Fritz in the first place?

LANDOR: 'Cos every other producer in Hollywood was going, that's why!

BENNY: Any particular themes—that you dream about?

LANDOR: For Chrissake, you're the writer. Just get on and write them. (*Fade*) See you tomorrow.

BENNY (*To us*): So there it was. Me, Benny Lee, writing dreams for Hollywood producer included in the budget for some Jungle epic. This needed thinking about. I went home. On the way home from the studio that night, I did something no one does in Hollywood—**I walked**.

FX Footsteps. Traffic. Background.

BENNY: Listen, when some character in a novel says, or in a play says "**I had a dream last night**", I switch off. dreams are too easy. No boundaries, no limitations, no rules. You can write anything. Like cartoons. Those guys can dream up anything. The four unities, there ain't **no** unities. Have the hero sliced up in a bacon slicer and instantly re-form himself and carry on with the chase. But about 17th and Vine I had a thought. **What if I gave him *my* dreams!!!!** A) I wouldn't have to write them and B) (And B was the bit that appealed) And B: I'd be the one being analysed. At the studio expense. The idea was so exciting I—

FX squeal of brakes and loud blast of motor horn

COP: Hey! What the F-

BENNY: Sorry officer.

COP: You mad, buddy?

BENNY: Screenwriter.

COP: Oh. OK. On your way.

BENNY: That night I made a phone call. I had to pretend I was interested in a certain lady again …

FX phone ringing at end of line

THELMA: Hallo?

BENNY: Benny.

THELMA (*Gasps*): Benny! I never believed you'd call me.

BENNY: Thelma. I can't go on like this—I have to see you again.

THELMA: Oh Benny!

BENNY: Can you get away?

THELMA: I must go. Fritz has just—

FX burrrrr of phone receiver placed down

BENNY (*To us*): But that night Thelma managed to get round to my place.

THELMA: Oh Benny.

BENNY: Thelma. Was it as great for you as it was for me?

THELMA: Oh Benny.

BENNY: You're a gorgeous woman, you know that?

THELMA: So you said.

BENNY: Hey, never noticed this before. On your thigh. Birth mark is it? Kind of cute. It's shaped like a …

THELMA: Like a bell. That's what Fritz says.

BENNY: Ding dong. Tell me … does Fritz still record all his sessions? With his patients?

THELMA: I think so. He never discusses work with me.

BENNY: Do you know where he keeps the tapes?

THELMA: Ye-es. But …

BENNY: I'm doing a script. About a character undergoing analysis.

THELMA: Oh Benny is it one of your thrillers? A murderer?

BENNY: Mmmmm. I can't say. But I want the real thing.

THELMA: Which ... patient—do you want the tapes of?

BENNY: Marvin Landor.

THELMA (*InDr.awn breath*): Marvin Landor!

BENNY: The same.

THELMA: But he's not a murderer. Is he?

BENNY: He is of scripts.

THELMA: It'll be risky.

BENNY: But you'll try?

Slight pause

THELMA: I'll try.

BENNY: Mmmmmmmmm, it's time I took a closer look at this little bell of yours. (*fade*) Oh yes, now I see ...

THELMA: Oh Benny.

BENNY (*To us*): That night I had another dream. I typed it out and gave it to Landor. His ant-sized brain managed to get some of it right when he talked to Schuman.

THELMA: Here's the tape, Benny. Only I gotta get it back tonight.

BENNY: Sure, sure. (*To us*) My hands were trembling I could hardly thread the reels. I sat back to listen to myself being analysed.

Tape

FRITZ: So. How are ve today?

LANDOR: Busy, busy.

FRITZ: So tell me about this "busy busy".

BENNY (*Aloud*): Tch! Who wants to know busy busy. Get to the dream.

FX *sound of tape fast forwarded*

Tape

LANDOR: And then they're painting my mural on the side of the studio. Only they're botching it up. Not doing what I tell 'em. It's **my** mural!

FRITZ: Ya? Vot does the mural portray?

LANDOR: A Biblical epic. Only it's stories not in the Bible. Stories that should have been in the Bible. Stories I made up. That's all I can remember of the dream.

FRITZ: So. You think the person, this designer of murals, this writer of epics, is really you? The real you?

BENNY (*To us over the tape*): Fritz thought he knew who it was. But only I knew he was talking about me—

FRITZ: I think they represent how you see yourself. I think these are signs of a wilful person. A person who thinks he is superior to those who are above him—

LANDOR: No one is above Marvin Landor.

FRITZ: I'm not necessarily talking about the high-powered executive situation. Emotional relationships perhaps. Parental—child. Mother—son. Father—daughter. Do you ever have a sense of using people?

LANDOR: "Using people!" Course I use people! That's my job.

FRITZ: Again, I'm talking maybe relationships—you get into a relationship for what you can get, not for what you can give.

Tape stops abruptly.

BENNY: Had enough of this crapola!

THELMA: Gee! That's the first time I've ever heard Fritz at work. Amazing. Just from a dream, Fritz could tell Marvin used people and thinks he is superior—

BENNY: Yeah, yeah. Thanks for the tape. I'll give you a call—

THELMA (*Hurt*): Benny! Usually you pour me a Manhattan. Put some swing on the gramaphone ... and ...

BENNY: Oh ... sure sure ... yeah yeah.

Swing music. Faint and hold under

BENNY (*To us*): I was thinking to hell with my dreams. Who needs those comments even if someone else was paying for it. I was thinking it would be more interesting if I did as he suggested and made up some dreams for Marvin Landor. First ... I just made up a dream ... any old garbage ... and, in the fullness of time ... heard it back on the tape ...

Tape

LANDOR: I had this dream.

FRITZ: Gut.

LANDOR: I was in a field.

FRITZ: Take your time.

LANDOR: And I couldn't pick a flower. Fruit everywhere. I couldn't pluck it from the tree.

FRITZ: Ya.

LANDOR: And then Eve appeared.

FRITZ: Eve?

LANDOR: Of Adam and Eve! First couple in showbiz.

FRITZ (*A little laugh*): Ho. A liddle joke. How did Eve appear?

LANDOR: How do you expect? Naked!

FRITZ: So, what did you and Eve do?

LANDOR: We went to the movies.

FRITZ: Movies! With Eve?

LANDOR: Yes.

FRITZ: Was she naked?

LANDOR: Yes. Nobody in the audience turned a hair.

FRITZ: What did you see?

LANDOR: It was the Garden of Eden.

FRITZ: And then?

LANDOR: We became part of the movie. We were in the garden. Only now I was with Eve I could pick the flowers. Pick the fruit. We made love. Right there on the screen.

FRITZ: Ya?

LANDOR: Except … no, I can't remember.

FRITZ: Take your time.

LANDOR: Stop saying that! Time is money. I tell you the dream. You tell me what it means. That's a take. I get outta here. I mean, Jesus where is this getting us?

FRITZ: U-huh.

LANDOR: What do ya mean, Uhuh?

FRITZ: What do you think I mean?

BENNY (*To us*): And so on and so forth until another fifteen bucks was in the little Kraut's bank account. I thought I could play it along for a while longer; Landor'd get bored with it all soon enough. I would have been content to leave at that until a few mornings later …

VOICE: He's comin' boys.

FX typing starts up

LANDOR: Morning boys.

BOYS: Mornin' Mr. Landor.

LANDOR: Good news Benny. "The Amethyst Ring." Going right ahead.

BENNY: That's great.

LANDOR: Cast all settled. They love it; they love it. Shooting schedule'll be ready any day. Miss Castella?

CASTELLA: Toisday.

LANDOR: Toisday—Thursday. (*Louder*) Keep up the good work, boys.

BENNY (*Confidentially*): Another dream for you Mr. Landor.

LANDOR (*As if glancing through it*): Hm … uhuh. Eve again? You're obsessed with Eve.

BENNY: No Marvin, you're obsessed with Eve. That's the whole point. You got to have some obsession for him to get his teeth into. I mean that's something, isn't it? Having the first woman in the world. Not only that. Having it over the first man in the world.

LANDOR: Yeah well I guess. Yeah, I like that.

BENNY: One in the eye for God.

LANDOR: One in the eye for God.

BENNY (*To us*): So Eve survived. Jeez I'd done enough re-writes for the guy, I didn't want to start on re-writing his **dreams**! Meanwhile things were going great with "The Amethyst Ring." I used to go down and see the rushes. Everyone liked it. Cast, crew, they were impressed. Hell I mean they were treating me, a writer, with respect! Then one day just as Landor was leaving the Factory he came back to me.

LANDOR: So Benny how's the Western comin' along?

BENNY (*To us*): He'd forgotten he'd given me Tarzan. It was going terrible. But that was something you could never admit to Landor. (*Aloud*) It's going OK, Mr. Landor.

CASTELLA: How many woids today?

LANDOR: I ask the questions Miss Castella. Oh, Benny, by the way. "The Amethyst Ring".

BENNY: Yes Mr. Landor?

LANDOR: I changed the ending.

BENNY (*To us*): He changed the ending. **He changed the ending!** The ending with the twist. The ending that turned everything on its head. Changing it was like saying "Oh, by the way, Oedipus doesn't marry his mother after all." There went my respect. There went my Oscar. Marvin Landor was a murderer. It was that night I had my plan. How I would get my revenge on him.

FX typing

BENNY (*To us*): My instrument would be the dreams. A series of dreams that would lead him inevitably to his doom … I typed them up, took them to work, kept them in a folder all ready to dole them out one for each session. I gave him the first one the next day. It was to contain elements of the first but with a new development with each dream …

Tape

LANDOR: In this dream, Eve …

FRITZ: Eve again? For you this is a long-term relationship.

LANDOR: Hey?

FRITZ: I'm sorry. It's just that—well, Mr. Landor, you are notorious … famous! for your success with women.

LANDOR: I guess I am.

FRITZ: Even other people's women.

LANDOR: I'm not responsible for what they do.

FRITZ: You were telling me about Eve.

LANDOR: Yeah. This time we were in a room.

FRITZ: You were making love again?

LANDOR: Yeah, and there was a tree at the window. The Tree of Knowledge …tap tapping at the window. And I noticed Eve had a birth mark.

FRITZ: Eve with a birth mark! She shouldn't even have a navel.

LANDOR: There shouldn't have been rooms or movies, but there were.

FRITZ: Vere did you see this birthmark?

LANDOR: In her beDr.oom.

FRITZ: I meant vereabouts on her body?

LANDOR: Oh. Sure. Inside of her thigh.

FRITZ: Really!! (*Slight pause*) Vot … shape voss the birthmark?

LANDOR: I don't remember.

FRITZ: No such thing as not remembering.

LANDOR: He didn't write th(at)—ahem—I don't remember. Or I didn't see it properly.

BENNY (*To us*): The next dream was more specific.

Tape

LANDOR: The birthmark on the inside of her thigh was shaped …

FRITZ: Ya?

LANDOR: Like a bell.

Sharp inDr.awn breath from Fritz

BENNY (*To us*): I expect you're getting the picture. Fritz was getting a good idea who Eve was. Each day I was going to provide just a bit more information. Marvin didn't have a clue what it was Dr.iving to. I had the sequence of dreams Dr.awn up. On my desk all ready. One day I went down with a fever. Couldn't go into work. Told Miss Castella—she seemed to be lasting longer than most of them—she should pick it up from my desk. I waited eagerly to hear the tape.

THELMA: I brought the tape, Benny. Could I listen to this one? You haven't been letting me listen to them lately.

BENNY: Thelma!

THELMA: OK. That's the last tape you get from me.

BENNY: OK, OK. But don't be upset at what you hear. I'm not responsible for whatever that megalomaniac might say.

THELMA: I know that.

BENNY: We'll fast forward the preliminaries.

FX tape going fast. Then:

LANDOR: Then, as she is halfway across the river, a croc slithers into the river heading straight to her. Nothing it seems would save her.

BENNY (*Over the tape*): What the hell!

Tape

LANDOR: Then, with a piercing Odle odle oiiiiii, Tarzan leaps into the river beside her, plunges his knife into the croc's eyes.

FX noise of switch. Tape comes to abrupt halt.

BENNY: That dumb broad Castella!

THELMA: Gee, Benny! That dream was almost like a movie.

BENNY (*To us*): How little she knew. Landor had to pay. Had to pay for killing my movie script. But, of course, the criminal had to get away with it. I reckoned the next dream would set a few things in motion. Immediate motion. (*Aloud to THELMA*) Thelma. I think you should spend a few days out of town.

THELMA: Out of town!!!!!

BENNY: And don't tell Fritz were you're going.

THELMA: But why Benny? Are you in danger?

BENNY: No but you are. In the next couple of days. Don't ask questions. Trust me. Make any excuse you can; just go and leave a note. But put several states between you and Fritz for the next coupla weeks.

THELMA: Oh Benny. Are you sure it's necessary?

BENNY (*Fade*): I'm absolutely sure, Thelma.

LANDOR: Morning boys!

BOYS: Morning Mr. Landor.

LANDOR: Like you to meet Miss Zabritski.

BOYS: Morning Miss Zabritski.

LANDOR: She may be dumb, but she ain't Polish!

Laughter from the boys

BENNY (*Confidentially*): Here's your next dream Mr. Landor.

LANDOR (*Off hand*): Er yeah. Look, I'm so busy. I might send Miss Zabritski in my place.

BENNY: Miss Zabritski!

LANDOR: Me, Miss Zabritski. What's the difference—it'll be the same dream. Or maybe I'll cancel. I'm thinking of quitting anyway.

BENNY: Don't do that, don't do that. Look, stick with it, Mr. Landor. I know Fritz. You think nothing's happening, then woosh out it comes—he tells you things about yourself you never even suspected. It could change your life.

LANDOR: … Ok. Can't go today. Maybe tomorrow. Hey, we got the ending of "The Amethyst Ring" in the can. Want to see the rushes?

BENNY: I'll wait. Surprise me. Here. Your dream. (*To us*) Well. It all went according to plan. The way it turned out it was some weeks before I could get the tape; the one I wanted.

Tape

FRITZ: And then what happened?

LANDOR: We made love.

FRITZ: As always.

LANDOR: Not quite as always. This time it was weird; because she told me the only guys who satisfied her—

FRITZ: How could she have had other guys, she was Eve there were no other guys.

LANDOR: I was there, wasn't I? So presumably others had been around as well. This is what she told me. If I wanted to satisfy her I had to pretend I was ... (*Mutters*) God help me, Benny

FRITZ: What?

LANDOR: ... had to pretend I ... a buck rabbit.

Silence, then rather heavy breathing from Fritz.

LANDOR: What's up, Doc?

FRITZ (*Slowly*): A ... buck ... rabbit ...?

LANDOR: Yeah. Twitch my nose a lot, make a squeaking noise—

FRITZ: You've been screwing my wife!

LANDOR: What!

FRITZ: The tree by the window, the birth mark—where it is, its shape!—the rabbit!!!! You've been coming here, laughing at me, now boasting that you've been having my wife!

LANDOR: Hey. Wait a minute. I've never met your wife, let alone —

FRITZ: I don't believe you. You're not telling me dreams at all!

LANDOR: Look, there's some mistake—put that thing down—don't shoot—

Tape stops.

BENNY: But he did. (*Chuckles*) Yeah. Shot old Marvin. Big headlines. Most powerful figure in Hollywood shot dead. And there was no doubt who did it, so there was poor old Fritzy out of the way. Well ... all that was long time ago. Yeah ...a long time ago ...

PSYCHIATRIST: What did Thelma do?

BENNY: Thelma. Thelma was suspicious, but she never found out I was writing Marvin's dreams for him. So? Perfect crime. Wouldn't you say, Doc?

PSYCHIATRIST: You got away with it.

BENNY: I got away with it.

PSYCHIATRIST: So ... why do you think you've ended up here? The Scott Fitzgerald Rehabilitation Centre.

BENNY: 'Cos the Betty Ford Foundation was full.

PSYCHIATRIST: You know what I'm saying.

BENNY: You're saying, if I got away with it, why end up on the booze?

PSYCHIATRIST: You must have a theory.

BENNY: No theory, Doc. I know for a fact. It was "The Amethyst Ring."

PSYCHIATRIST: Highly successful film as I recall.

BENNY: Oh yes indeed. It won several Oscars. Including Best Screenplay.

PSYCHIATRIST: That must have made you very happ—

BENNY: The writing credit went to Marvin Landor. They gave him the Oscar posthumously.

PSYCHIATRIST: I see.

BENNY: Yeah. All my years of writing, I never got an Oscar. (It's) Come to haunt me in my old age—Marvin got the last laugh. I keep wishing it was **me** shot the bastard. (*Pause*) Well? What d'ya think?

Slight pause

PSYCHIATRIST: I think, Benny, you're the biggest liar I ever met in my life.

BENNY: Is that what you think?

PSYCHIATRIST: I do.

BENNY: Well, I did tell you. I wanted to keep on writing right till the end.

The end.

Janice Probert-Gromüller

ROGER HALL: PUTTING THE NEW IN NEW ZEALAND DRAMA

In May 1992, at Professor Glaap's invitation, Roger Hall gave a lecture at the Heinrich Heine University in Düsseldorf, Germany on how he became a playwright. His advice to aspiring dramatists reflects his own modest, practical approach. "If you're going to write, then write. Never wait until you are 'inspired'; it doesn't work like that. Sit down and write. You have to put in the hours. Writing is sheer hard work." *The Dream Factory*, a play for radio, contains echoes of a similar sentiment:

> LANDOR: Your're writers. Paid to write. So write. How's it going Benny?
>
> BENNY: Eleven hundred and forty-three words, Mr. Landor.
>
> LANDOR: (*To the others*) See! That's writing! (231)

But there the similarity ends. Roger Hall has indeed written a great many words but, unlike Benny, in a multiplicity of styles ranging from full length comedies and dramas, one-act plays for adults, one-act plays and stories for children, pantomimes, full length musicals, television comedy and drama series, magazine articles, stage revues and film reviews. His works are both numerous and various, unlike the stereotype, industrial mass production churned out by the Hollywood "Dream Factory" of the thirties.

The idea of becoming a writer had always appealed to him and, on emigrating to New Zealand in 1958 at the age of 19, he began his "apprenticeship" by regularly writing home to his family and friends in England and filling exercise books with short stories and reviews of every film he saw. Four years later at Wellington Teachers' College he contributed further book and film reviews together with many stories, humorous articles and poetry to the college magazine, in addition to writing and performing in his own stage revues. He started writing and acting for television in comedy shows, and also had four plays screened on television. But it was with his first stage play written at the age of 35, that he achieved spectacular success, the play performing to sell-out seasons throughout the country. This play, which was first staged at the Circa Theatre in Wellington on 11 August 1976, was called *Glide Time*[1] and was based on his own experience as a junior office clerk in the State Insurance Office when he had first arrived in New Zealand.

In contrast to the crude, escapist, sensationalist titles of Mr. Landor's "Dream Factory"—The Amethyst Ring, Arabian Mirage, Pirate Plunder, Tarzan's Jungle Conquest, Hellbent for Texas (cf. 233, 237)—Roger Hall chooses his titles from an everyday stock of topical phrases and buzz words. *Glide Time* (1976), *Middle Age Spread* (1977)[2], *Fifty-Fifty* (1981),[3] *Hot Water* (1982),[4] *Multiple Choice* (1983),[5] *The Share Club* (1987),[6] *Conjugal Rites* (1990)[7] these expressions all belong to the area of normal, everyday life and are the titles of some of his most successful stage plays. They also reflect the subject matter which centres around very ordinary, mostly middle class people getting on with their lives as best they can.

Middle Age Spread examines the doubts and disillusions in the lives of three middle class middle-aged New Zealanders; *Fifty Fifty* looks at the havoc redundancy, unemployment and stifled self-fulfillment can cause in the average family; *Hot Water* takes a sidelong peek at the stresses involved in family gatherings; *Multiple Choice* delves into the pros and cons of compulsory state education and debates the meaning of education while *Conjugal Rites* portrays the threadbare rituals and the strains in a long-standing, worn-out, middle class marriage. Yet all these plays with their weighty undertones have something very much in common with the clichéd superficiality of *The Dream Factory* and that something is central to Roger Hall's talent as a playwright. They are all comedies which exhibit his exceptional gift for making people laugh. They paint a portrait of the times by combining elements of humour, satire and farce to help us look steadily and clearly through the social facade, through the character masks even very ordinary people make for themselves and deep into the beliefs, wishes, dreams and feelings of the average human soul. In many ways *The Dream Factory* is a Hollywood-type distortion of Roger Hall's own business of creating, if not dreams, then illusions on stage. It is a hilariously wry comment on the world of the writer while at the same time illustrating many of the features which have made his own works so successful and popular.

Most noticeably, it sheds light on the contradictions he sees in being a writer. Writing is both routine hard work and creative inspiration. In *State of the Play* (1978)[8], the character of Peter Dingwall, "a once successful playwright" (121), expresses a similar opinion. When asked if he enjoys being a writer he replies, "It's very like being a jet pilot. Half an hour of excitement and five hours of boredom every day. Getting ideas is exciting, the rest is just hard slog. Driven by we know not what."(132)

We are left in no doubt about what is driving Benny and his pronouncements on where he finds his ideas correspond to Roger Hall's practice. "It's all material, isn't it?" Indeed it is; from the disagreement about the choice of new office curtains in *Glide Time* to a bad bout of flu in *Conjugal Rites*, everything which forms part of everyday life is necessarily important. For Roger Hall's plays are about very ordinary people with normal everyday concerns. "Everyone's the dramatic type"(130), says Dingwall during his weekend course on writing. "There's something in everyone that can be used. One characteristic that can be drawn on, developed." (130) Hall's everyday characters, just like the real people behind the Hollywood clichés, have to master the problems and crises in their lives and ward off the "grizzly" (231) bear attacks of commonplace misunderstandings, mundane disappointments or predictable, routine family jealousies and tragedies which pose such a threat to their happiness. They defend themselves with as much resiliance and ingenuity as Benny does when Mr. Landor tramples all over his creative insticts. When the going gets tough in the suburban jungle, people still find a way of getting on with their daily routine. After the shattering revelations—the real world equivalent of the "story about passion, power and lust" (233) in The Amethyst Ring—which emerge during the course of the dinner party in *Middle Age Spread*, the nice, well-meaning, well-off, middle-aged, middle class hosts close the door on their guests and sit down wearily.

ELIZABETH: What do we do now?

COLIN: What we do, Elizabeth, is the dishes. (82)

The great attraction for audiences watching Roger Hall's plays is that they see and recognize themselves on stage and laugh, not only at the comic situations and witty dialogue, but also at their own foibles. This was one of the success-bringing, innovative factors in *Glide Time*. Until then, New Zealand theatre had drawn its material principally from standard British literary sources. For the first time, Roger Hall put contemporary New Zealanders on the stage. The audiences were thrilled when they recognized themselves. They found themselves irresistible. Landor's line expressing the tingle of excitement he feels on going to a psychiatrist says exactly what the theatregoer experiences when watching a Roger Hall play. "(*Almost a boast*) I'm...being psychoanalysed, Benny." (234)

By making the audience laugh at themselves Roger Hall is also making a wry, social comment. But although the audience laughs, he never laughs or pokes fun at his characters. They are not criticized but portrayed with tolerance, sensitivity and fellow feeling. All his characters have their own subjective, valid points of view and as such represent a cross section of society's viewpoints. His method is to concentrate on an individual example which reflects basic, general themes and concerns within society as a whole; a feature which also makes his work attractive to audiences outside New Zealand. He is no moral arbiter. He offers no blueprints for a better world. His characters portray people as they really are with all their strengths and weaknesses. They are in the process of living out, and in some cases outliving, their dreams of a good life. They are exasperated in their efforts by the practicalities of everyday life. Like Landor they can barely find time to dream, unlike him they cannot delegate the responsibility. Roger Hall is at his very best when he is presenting people rather than issues. It is interesting to note that *Multiple Choice* is one of his least produced plays. It is a debate in which issues connected with education are presented and discussed from a variety of angles by a variety of characters. Critics and audiences alike tend to get engrossed more with the issues than with the play.

Benny writes in terms of pure Hollywood, Roger Hall in terms of pure theatre; a quality which is admired by both actors and directors. The dialogue rings very true to character—even the Hollywood stereotypes in *The Dream*

Factory have the ring of truth about them—providing marvellous parts for actors. He has a very fine ear not only for what people say but also for what they leave unsaid; thus creating dramatic space in which actions can speak louder than words. Although *The Dream Factory* abounds with examples of this technique, here is nevertheless a sample from another play and television series called *Conjugal Rites*. Barry, a dentist and Gen(evieve), his successful, career-woman wife, have just returned home from a restaurant where they have celebrated their twenty first wedding anniversary.

> *Gen is already in bed. Hearing Barry coming towards the room, she plumps up the pillows. Looks very attractive.*
>
> BARRY: (*Enters—maybe wearing old dressing gown—carrying a plate of sandwiches. Sees the way Gen is.*) Ah.
>
> GEN: Barry!
>
> BARRY: I said that place never gives you enough to eat.
>
> GEN: Well ... it's cheese and pickle ... or me. I advise you to choose carefully.
>
> BARRY: Right. Yes. Er ... am I allowed them afterwards ...? Or should I put a bit of Glad Wrap [= cling film] over them?
>
> GEN: I'll put Glad Wrap over you ... (I, 316)

Comedy depends on a tight structure for its comic effect. *The Dream Factory* is a cameo example of the way Roger Hall interlocks and interweaves scenes and episodes to create comedy. In the radio play he also incorporates other techniques which he uses to great effect in his stage plays and writing for television. The plot and the storyline are often underscored by leitmotifs. In *The Dream Factory* the typewriter, the tape recorder, orchestrated silences and fading techniques form a structural thread throughout the piece, punctuating, dividing up and pacing the action. In the theatre or on television visual elements perform similar functions: a raincoat and a railway book are expertly used in *Middle Age Spread*; in the classic farce *Hot Water* a bikini and a trout are adroitly used to create maximum pandemonium; the antique vase and the stereo in *Fifty-Fifty* represent the last remnants of any value left after a marriage and family break down, and in the television version of *Conjugal Rites* there are close-ups of the family dog out walkies with his owners giving vent to his own private thoughts on their behaviour.

Roger Hall is also very adept at drawing his characters together in the most appropriate setting. Where better to exhibit the strains and stresses within a family than cooping them up together in an out-of-the-way, family, lakeside holiday home? Where better to illustrate the break up of a family than in the family flat as it is gradually being emptied of all its contents as family members and complete strangers arrive to take away everything but one last chair? In his early plays Roger Hall tended to follow Dingwall's "handy hints" on construction. "Have a main plot and a subplot; first act clear, last act short, everywhere interest; ... have the main character at a turning point in his life ... but delay the climax to the end." (134) It seems unlikely that he will ever completely agree with Benny about "The four unities, there ain't no four unities." (238) but he does experiment with dramatic form not allowing himself to be bound by convention. In *Middle Age Spread* the main frame of the action is a dinner party which the hosts felt obliged to give but to which none of the guests really wanted to go. This dinner is interrupted by a series of flashbacks each getting closer in time to the events of the evening and each revealing something more about the past of those at the dinner party. In the final scene the events of the past are exposed and put an end to the evening. *Multiple Choice* also experiments with form. The play sets out the arguments for and against compulsory education. Each point of view is as valid in its own way as any other and this balance is reflected in the division of the play into two long acts consisting of sixteen and fifteen scenes each. The term act is used very loosely to denote a division of the play. The complexity of the issues is also mirrored in the structure, particularly towards the climax of the play when the school board has to decide whether Paul must return to school or not. At this point in the action the scenes are blended to show what is happening simultaneously.

"Benny: ...] Vance I did something no one does in Hollywood—I walked." (237) In his own quiet and unassuming way Roger Hall is just as unconventional. When a student in Düsseldorf asked him if emigrating to New Zealand as a young man had influenced his work as a playwright he replied that it was like looking at the world through a new pair of eyes. In theatrical terms he is equally willing to take a fresh look at things or approach them in an unexpected or unusual way. He owes his first big success with *Glide Time* to his willingness to break with tradition. This aspect of his work—no "writin' formula stuff" (233) for him—is in keeping with his own spirit of independence. He has twice left New Zealand for a prolonged stay abroad. In 1982 he spent a year, which was later extended to sixteen months, travelling with his family through the USA in a mobile home and then visiting his family in England. Ten years later, in 1992, he and his family took another year away from home but this time travelling around Europe. Actors and directors welcome the fact that he is also unconventional when it comes to rehearsing his plays. He fully accepts that "the fresh eyes of a director and a cast provide another essential hurdle for the play to surmount before there can be an opening performance."[9] Not only is he willing to attend rehearsals and listen to other ideas but he is also prepared to rewrite or delete passages. In *State of the Play* he allowed Anthony Taylor, the director of the 1978 production at the Downstage Theatre in Wellington, to make two major alterations. The first was to delay Dingwall's conflict with a course participant called Neil; the second to delete the bizarre revelation that Neil is a transvestite. "One reason that I like Tony Taylor as a director is that his theatrical instinct knows very shrewdly what changes need to be made." (170) Roger Hall's fairness in giving credit to other people's talents is also to the fore in the "Author's Note" to *Middle Age Spread* where he openly acknowledges Michael Haigh's contribution who suggested showing "a sequence of slides together with appropriate music" (7) to cover up long pauses during each scene change. "This device worked brilliantly and added another dimension to the play." (7) In the same author's note he also mentions the debt he owes to Dave Smith.

"The line about the Labour Party and sleeping sickness, which gets one of the biggest laughs in the play, was originally devised by Dave Smith whom I thank for permission for its use." (7) What a contrast to Marvin Landor who says time is money "like he coined it himself." (233)

Roger Hall's distinctive inclination to do the unexpected is also evident in the endings of his plays. He is a master of "The ending with the twist. The ending that turned everything on its head." (242) In *Glide Time* it is the offstage character, present on stage only through his untidy, totally disorganized desk, who gets the much prized promotion. In *The Share Club* the most unlikely collection of people get caught up in a wave of investment fever and form a neighbourhood share club. Their amateurish efforts to make some easy money seem doomed to failure as they get sidetracked by other more personal considerations. But for one of them at least, the bank employee Garth, the unpredictable happens. Only with hindsight is this the most predictably unpredictable outcome of all. The ending of *Multiple Choice* also contains a twist that no one sees coming. It is not the arguments of the parents or the educational experts—all behaving very childishly—that tip the balance in deciding whether the schoolboy, Paul, should return to school but the boy's own very mature speech on his own behalf.

The audience at a Roger Hall play not only watches but also experiences the twist in the end of the story. They come to be entertained, to see a comedy, a piece of theatrical illusion, to laugh at the witty remarks and the comic situations. They only gradually realise that they have been enticed into a hall of mirrors, that they are laughing at themselves and at their own comic distortions, pulling funny faces and behaving in the most extraordinary ways, seeing themselves from unusual angles. Like Fritz Schulman it suddenly dawns on them: "You're not telling me dreams at all!" (245) Amidst all the unexpected developments there is, however, one thing his audiences have come to expect and rely on; skillfully crafted, highly entertaining plays, full of keenly observed social detail which present us with a "sparkling, hilarious portait of our time"[10] viewed from new perspectives.

Notes

1
Roger Hall, *Glide Time* (New Zealand Play Scripts, Victoria University Press: 1984). All page references given in brackets are to the editions mentioned in the notes or to this volume.

2
Roger Hall, *Middle Age Spread* (New Zealand Play Scripts, Victoria University Press: 1985.)

3
Roger Hall, *Fifty-Fifty* (Price Milburn with Victoria University Press: 1981).

4
Roger Hall, *Hot Water* (New Zealand Play Scripts, Price Milburn with Victoria University Press: 1983.)

5
Roger Hall, *Multiple Choice* (London: Casarotto Company Ltd.: 1984).

6
Roger Hall, *The Share Club* (New Zealand Play Scripts, Victoria University Press: 1988).

7
Roger Hall, *Conjugal Rites*, 17 page typescript, also (Samuel French Inc.: 1990).

8
Roger Hall, *State of the Play*, in: Rurik von Antropoff, Klaus Peter Müller (Eds.) *Dramatic Voices from England, Canada and New Zealand; Festschrift für Albert-Reiner Glaap* (Cornelsen: 1989), 121-169.

9
Roger Hall, Reflections on the Transvestite Sequence in: *Festschrift für Albert-Reiner Glaap*, 1989, 170.

10
Publisher's Note in *The Share Club* (New Zealand Play Scripts, Victoria University Press: 1988), reverse cover.

Ronald Harwood

STARRING LAURENCE OLIVIER

Disappointment, like everything else, requires training, Edward Lands discovered. His resilience was often remarked on and he suspected he must have received the training early in life. An incident from youth, unexpectedly remembered, confirmed the conceit; the memory mattered to him and, therefore, lingered.

Edward, who only began to write when well into his twenties, had first been driven by a desire to be an actor. He was born in Cape Town which is six thousand miles from the centre of things so he knew little of the English theatre, but he loved performing in the local Eisteddfaud (recitation, mime and sight-reading), in school plays (Tranio in *The Taming of the Shrew*), and with local amateur companies (The Bell Hop in *Room Service*). His other passion was for films and film stars, his especial favourites being Tyrone Power and Laird Cregar. His ambitions were vague; thoughts of escaping to London had not yet become his daily obsession. A push was needed, no more than a nudge; a door to be opened a crack to allow him to behold a treasure store more richly endowed than Aladdin's cave: his for the asking.

Edward exercised no judgment, his parents no control over what he should or should not see; he had no one to guide his taste and he had no innate critical faculty. His earliest memory of the cinema was of being taken, aged six perhaps, by his mother to the Odeon, Sea Point, to see *The Mark of Zorro* with Tyrone Power (his mother's favourite actor; secretly, she wanted Edward to look like him and thus encouraged the use of Brylcreem). Afterwards, emerging from the pleasure-dome, Edward asked, 'Now can we go and see the actors?' 'How d'you mean?' asked his mother. 'Can we go round the back and watch the actors come out?' A lengthy, tortuous explanation followed: the actors were on celluloid, they lived in Hollywood, they weren't real. 'Not real?' He was desolate.

The revelation did not discourage the increasing frequency of his visits to the local cinemas, or bioscopes as they were called, but created a vague distrust of what appeared on the screen as though, because the actors weren't real, they lacked respectability. And his enjoyment was further marred by always emerging from the dark of the Marine or the Odeon or the Adelphi—where he devoured the Three Stooges, Abbott and Costello, Leon Errol, Edgar 'Slowburn' Kennedy, Pete Smith Specialities, George Formby, Johnny Weismuller and the Goddess of Improper Thoughts, Rita Hayworth—into the piercing African sun with a blinding headache. He loved the entertainment but he wished he had never been told that the actors were on celluloid; he wished the headaches would cease.

School outings to the cinema were rare. Most of Edward's contemporaries detested the idea because invariably they were taken to what were called 'heavy' films, and always in the afternoon when the beach or the tennis-courts beckoned. But Edward, indiscriminate as ever, welcomed any opportunity to sit in the dark, to be bombarded by the gigantic images, to emerge painfully into the sun. Predictably, the school arranged a visit to *Hamlet* starring Laurence Olivier.

The moment the film began Edward took the first steps on his road to Damascus. There, in the darkened and almost empty cinema, seated beside noisy iconoclasts, he was blinded by the light. The story, the film, the actor convulsed him, and his life was never the same again. In those hours Edward's aspirations were born. And his obsessions.

He received the plot as a detective thriller, terrified by the ghost, burning to know if the King was guilty or not of murder, exulting in the play scene, willing Hamlet to kill Claudius in prayer, recoiling at the treachery of the poisoned foil, desolate at the death of the prince. These were the hooks that grappled his twelve-year-old imagination to the drama. And the film itself led him along winding corridors, up twisting stairs, high atop the battlements casting shadows over the troubled sea below, into the graveyard with its surfeit of bones, allowing him to glimpse a tender and tragic landscape. Of the actor: Edward had been kidnapped, like Hamlet, by a pirate, bewitched by a daring magician who plucked his spells from the mysterious air of Elsinore, and took possession of the boy's mind.

Afterwards, Edward broke away from the school party, cut down a side street to the beach, tramped across the rough, sea-shell sand to a favourite outcrop of rock where he sat and gazed out at the horizon, the final image of the film—Hamlet dead, carried by four captains, head lolling backwards—still burning in his eyes. He made two discoveries: he had wet himself, and he had no headache.

He saw the film six times. His sister bought him records with extracts from the soundtrack and each day, after school, the boy played them, lying full length on the floor, sticking his head under the radiogram, near to the speaker, to be as close as possible to the source of that magical sound. In a very few months he had read the whole play more than a dozen times, and before his thirteenth birthday he knew word perfect the part of Hamlet.

There was, too, the other obsession: he was determined som-how to prove the actor real. Edward's existence was transformed by a new and mighty charge. From England he received monthly a magazine called *Theatre World*, studied and memorised every cast list, gazed with longing at the photographs which adorned its pages and when in the school play he was cast as Sergius Saranoff in Shaw's *Arms and the Man*, his mother modelled his costume from the one his idol had worn at the Old Vic.

Some boys collected stamps; others matchboxes or cigarette cards or marbles. Edward's mania was to catch up on all the films the sorcerer had appeared in, to visit Agincourt and Trafalgar and Netherfield Park. (And indeed for longer than was decent Edward thought that Aldous Huxley was the author of *Pride and Prejudice*.) But was the actor real? Was he? Did he exist? Did he sleep at night and go to the lavatory? Was he real?

A news item in the *Cape Times* gave promise of final proof. A ship carrying the actor and the Old Vic Company, the report said, would dock in Cape Town before continuing their journey to Australia. The actor would come ashore to record an interview for the South African Broadcasting Corporation.

Come ashore. Set foot. Be.

The resourcefulness of the desperate knows no bounds. For some unexplained reason the actor wanted no fuss; the exact date and time of the recording was not to be announced. But in small towns secrets cannot be kept for long. A friend of a cousin of a brother of a friend of an uncle of a friend who actually worked for the Corporation revealed the vital information. Edward played truant from school. It rained that day and he took shelter under the portico of the Alhambra Theatre which was opposite the entrance to Broadcasting House. He hid his satchel beneath his school blazer and waited, in his hands a piece of paper which was quickly sodden, and his Conway fountain pen in readiness for the autograph, watching the doorway as Hamlet watched for the Ghost. He was soon drenched. He waited and waited, but no sign. Noon passed, one o'clock, two. By three he was shivering and hungry. He could bear it no longer. He crossed the street and walked into the building, but he was terrified: what would he do if he met the actor face to face? What would he say? Would any sound come from his mouth at all? ('O that this too, too solid flesh would melt.') He approached the commissionaire behind the desk.

'Yes, sonny?'

'Has Sir Laurence Olivier come out yet?'

'Who?'

'Sir Laurence Olivier.'

The man consulted a list. 'Yes,' he said. 'He's gone.'

'When? When?' demanded Edward overtaken by panic and beginning to cry with awful disappointment. 'I've been standing out there all morning,' he continued to fight his tears, 'he couldn't have come without my seeing him. He couldn't. When did he leave? When?' 'Yesterday,' said the man.

Liesel Hermes

ON FIRST READING RONALD HARWOOD'S *STARRING LAURENCE OLIVIER*[1]

How does it feel when some colleagues assign you a short story by an author you are not familiar with and give you a homework: "Write an appreciation of this text. Take into account its topic, structure, characteristics, literary relevance, and merits of the author. Do not write more than X pages. Your essay should be handed in by ..." That was exactly the situation I found myself in when I agreed to contribute to this *festschrift*. After assigning similar tasks to my own students for years, all of a sudden I found myself in the student's position. I had been given the photocopy of a text by an author I had not come across before and a written assignment, for which I had an approximate number of lines and a certain period of time.

For several semesters I had experimented with my own students in literature classes in order to find out how they go about reading and preparing a literary text at home, how they deal with it in class and respond to the teacher's stimuli, how they react to a variety of student groupings in class as well as other students' individual readings of the same text, and what they actually learn in the course of a semester. In other words, the process of my students' reception of the literary texts I asked them to read, prepare and discuss or analyse in writing, had been the focus of my academic teaching interests for some time. Therefore I have decided to play the rôle of one of my students and to document my own process of reading and understanding Harwood's short story.

The title states a very familiar name: Laurence Olivier, a byword for theatre and film acting of the very highest quality. One can easily arrive at the conclusion that the story to come must have something to do with films and acting and/or centre round the figure of the title, especially with the subtitle of the collection in mind: *Adventures in the film trade*. I started to read the text, writing down in the margin whatever ideas, thoughts, associations came to my mind as I went along. The first word, "disappointment" seems to hint at a crucial incident in the central character's life: "Disappointment ... requires training ..." (254). There is an ironic semantic gap between "disappointment" and "training." Moreover, the present tense makes clear that Edward Lands has experienced this feeling as a pervading factor of his life, if privately or professionally, seems to be of no relevance at this point. The "incident from youth" and his "memory" (254) alert the reader to the fact that the story to follow will be an event of his adolescence which still has a considerable emotional impact on him.

Edward is a writer who, earlier in his life, wanted to be an actor. His place of birth, Cape Town in South Africa, is characterized as being far away from "the centre of things." (254) Its position is therefore marked by a deficit in Edward's eyes: London, it seems, is the cultural hub of the world so that Cape Town has no cultural identity of its own but looks to London for its own standards, fashions and guidelines. As an Englishman (this is suggested by his name) living in South Africa Edward seems to be painfully aware of his position far from the centre, as far as his cultural contacts and education go, otherwise his thoughts of "escaping to London" would not, in due course, become an "obsession" (254).

It is here for the first time that another short story comes to mind: Willa Cather's "Paul's Case."[2] Paul, the central character, is so much intoxicated by musical and theatrical performances and the world of illusion they create that he is fully absorbed by his dreams. Whereas his day-to-day life at school as well as at home leave him dissatisfied and with a constant feeling of being misunderstood by his teachers and father, his zest for life is realized only in the vicinity of artists and actors whom he even follows to their hotels, an "exotic, a tropical world of shiny, glistening surfaces,"[3] as they are characterized by the narrator.

Edward has likewise been captured by his passion "for films and film stars" (254). Uncritically, he avidly takes in whatever is shown in the cinemas: Hollywood films with their typical heroes and heroines or whatever comes from London and has the stamp of British authenticity and, in Edward's eyes, quality. The "pleasure-dome" (254), a metaphor for the cinema that offers the splendours and delights of an illusionary world to Edward, of course recalls Samuel T. Colerigde's "Kubla Khan."[4] Edward is avid to see the actors he has admired on the screen and longs to be in physical touch with them just like Paul. The disillusioning sense that the film offers a world of make-believe that is fundamentally different from the theatre in that it is two-dimensional and endlessly repeatable comes as a shock to the young boy. He has been so completely taken in by the semblance of reality the film screen suggests that the celluloid is reality to him. The revelation of its true mode of existence proves painful.

One cannot help going back to Plato's *Republic (Politeia)*, where in book VII the author offers the Allegory of the Cave.[5] Plato here tries to delineate the process of recognition, from mere perception to knowledge. Human beings are sitting in a cave, tied up so that they cannot move, looking at the rear wall of the cave on which they perceive moving shadows which they, knowing no better, take to be real objects. Once they have been freed and are able to turn round and see the entrance of the cave, they perceive that they only saw shadows, not real things. This may prove so shocking that they want to revert to their previous state of being tied up, or they set off for the entrance of the cave, proceed into the real world of light and the concomitant ability to perceive things as they are, however they can perceive only concrete objects not their abstract concepts.

At this point in the narrative, Edward does not want to be enlightened and hates being "told that the actors were on celluloid" (255). He prefers illusion and therefore cannot be deterred from going on to seek his personal pleasure in the fake world of his film heroes' make-believe.

It is with the usual "indiscriminate" (255) and uncritical enthusisam, that he welcomes the opportunity to see *Hamlet* starring Laurence Olivier. It is a common experience for pupils that, ironically, "school outings to the cinema" (255) always have didactic aims that ususally clash with pupils' interests and preferences and, normally, are bound to be followed up by all kinds of unpleasant compulsory tasks that leave no room for the pupils' individual receptions and their imagination. Accordingly, the effect of the film is lost on his culturally illiterate class-mates ("noisy iconoclasts", 255). To Edward, however, this experience, like all the previous ones, comes as a welcome opportunity to escape from reality, which is here again associated with the sun, as opposed to the wished-for darkness, the cave, with its "gigantic images" of illusion (255).

Paradoxically enough, *Hamlet* eventually proves to be a blinding light (cf. 255) or revelation that changes his life entirely. Edward is "on his road to Damascus" (255), just like Paulus or rather Saulus in the *Acts of the Apostles*,[6] who has a sudden visionary experience, a direct revelation of Jesus and is given a vocation. Within the literary tradition this experience can be regarded as an epiphany in the Joycean sense. To Edward, Olivier's *Hamlet* is reality.

Edward's reception of the film *Hamlet* as a "detective thriller" (255) testifies to the immediacy of the film's impact, but also the boy's faculty of giving himself wholly up to the illusion that is assailing him. Of course James Thurber's short story "The Macbeth Murder Mystery"[7] comes to mind, in which an American lady likewise reads *Macbeth* as a thriller, believes that she has found the murderer in the end and is ironically encouraged by the first-person narrator to go on to solve the mystery of *Hamlet*, too. Are the two victims of profound misunderstandings, due to their own superficiality of character, or is their naive reception only one of a multitude of possible readings of a literary text that can be adapted, changed, and deepened on further text analysis? Edward as a twelve-year-old boy is in my opinion wholly justified in taking the action to be real or at least as a mirror of real life and responding accordingly.[8]

What seems important in the present context is that Edward is totally oblivious of the school's educational objectives and abandons himself to the entertainment, lets himself be carried away by Olivier's personification of *Hamlet*: He is "terrified, [...] burning to know, [...] recoiling, [...] desolate" (255), all testifying to a passionate abandon to the action that has "bewitched" him (255): Edward is spell-bound.

This experience has a profound impact on his personality. It can be looked upon as a serious step towards adulthood, as an experience of initiation: Edward leaves his class-mates, seeks an isolated spot by the sea in order to fully empathize with the dead hero at the end of the film. Looking at the horizon from his vantage point, makes it all the easier for him of course, to recapture the final atmospheric moments of the film drama.

It is here that Edward reacts differently from Paul. Whereas Paul, who from the start had no desire to become an actor himself,[9] is wholly absorbed by the more superficial dazzling world of glitter, flashiness and splendour, which is in complete opposition to the drabness and dreariness of his ordinary world of "respectable beds, common food, kitchen odours, ugly sleeping chamber, cold bath-room,"[10] Edward's desire is "to prove the actor real" (255). His idea of solving the problem of the illusionary film world is to make it become more real for him in the person of the actor who, as he knows, does exist. Again, this desire is called an "obsession" (255), the typical youthful capacity of abandoning oneself wholly to an idea. Edward is setting off towards the entrance of the cave.

To Edward, the conflict between the image of Olivier as Hamlet and his real being as an ordinary human person becomes the focus of his existence: "Did he sleep at night and go to the lavatory? Was he real?" (256) It acquires an existential dimension, as if his own identity were dependent on it, and the story, which so far was more or less the description of a boy's youthful obsession with the cinema and its somewhat doubtful educational benefits now acquires dramatic impact, when Edward tries everything in order to actually catch a glimpse of Laurence Olivier in person. The brief drama of playing truant from school, waiting for hours in a drenching rain in order to see the real man, can be interpreted as the result of the unusual single-mindedness and perseverance the boy evinces in order to prove to himself that reality prevails over illusion.

Ironically, the last line of the story comes as a punch line: Laurence Olivier, Edward learns, does in fact exist as a human being. But his ardent wish to verify it for himself by asking him for an autograph will remain unfulfilled. Edward is too late. The brief dramatic development comes to an abrupt end and leaves the reader at a loss as to how Edward, the twelve-year-old boy, will react to this blow. The reader can only revert to the beginning of the story, i.e. a time more than ten years later, at which Edward has long overcome the tragic event of his youth and is able to see it with detachment as one step towards adulthood, which eventually leads to his ability to cope with disappointments.

Following this first reading of the text, I became involved in a more and more fascinating process of getting deeper insight into the fictional character and the psychological core of the story. I located the video cassette of *Hamlet*,[11] watched it and tried successfully to empathize with the young Edward Lands and the profound impact Olivier's acting made on him. Hamlet's deep depression, his inactivity and failure to take the initiative make a lasting impression on the young boy and leave him awed. A young man's doubts about himself are convincingly personified here.

Next, I borrowed Harwood's short story collection *One. Day. Interior.*, from which the text is taken, from the library. This collection, the only one the author has published so far, is somewhat unusual in that it is a cycle of stories, and Edward Lands is the central character of all of them, thus constituting a unifying element. The stories portray him as a young man who is trying to make a career for himself by writing film scripts and has pleasant and unpleasant encounters with other people from the film trade, Europeans as well as Americans. However, even though the stories are linked by one character this does not preclude reading them individually. Each is a thematically self-contained unit.

Finding out more about the author was the next step. The climax of this process was having tea with Ronald Harwood at his home, certainly a memorable event. By that time, I had thought so much about his story that I was able to offer a summary sketch of my thoughts, impressions and discovery of literary allusions for him to comment on as a critical author. That he largley confirmed my ideas was a rewarding experience. It was of greater relevance, however, that he talked about his own youth and the wealth of autobiographical details in this story, which had of necessity escaped me. Of paramount importance is the fact that he was born in Cape Town and only left it for England at the age of 17. Therefore he was in a unique position to write about how it feels to be far away from the "centre of things" (254)or "lifeline", as he put it then, geographically away from the cultural influence of London, however close he felt to it inwardly. He commented about the influence British and American films can have on a boy on the verge of adolescence, of the impact they made on his psyche, on the problems of identity that ensue, on the "obsession" with the problem of the degree to which illusion and reality can clash. To Harwood, London, so far away, was the hub of life, and he strongly identified with whatever came from there in the way of films. The detail that Edward learnt Hamlet's part, as played and recorded by Olivier, by heart with all the cuts Olivier made himself, is wholly autobiographical. Harwood himself still conveyed his enthusiasm for the theatre and Olivier's art of acting. To him, he said, Olivier at the time of his boyhood was more real than reality, so that for some time his inner conflict between illusion and reality seemed to carry him away in the direction of illusion. That is a typical experience of adolescence and the process of growing awareness of the clash and attempts to solve the conflict in one's own life, i.e. setting off towards the entrance of the cave, is bound to be painful.

My reception of this story thus proved to be a lenghty process, consisting of a number of steps that each led individually to deeper awareness of the central message of the text. Reading it for the first time already had brought home to me a wealth of associations, proof not only that intertextuality can create patterns of significance in a text and serve as a guideline for analysis, but also that our previous knowledge or "world knowledge" guides the process of reading and can determine its direction. Reading *Starring Laurence Olivier* as part of a cycle of stories was an enriching experience but did not fundamentally change my reading of it. Watching *Hamlet* made a great impact on me and helped me empathize with the central character of the story. Rereading "Paul's Case" put both "cases" into perspective for me, afforded a better understanding of Paul's character as well as of Edward's, and made me aware of the profound differences in the ways both authors cope with the process of writing about adolescence. Listening to Ronald Harwood's account of his adolescent life in Cape Town was fascinating and confirmed my character analysis. Going back to the *New Testament* as well as Plato's *Republic* and the Allegory of the Cave finally brought about another change in perspective and the recognition of how human perception and knowledge are acquired by adolescents in a laborious process.

Last but not least, stylistic devices in this text should be briefly mentioned. Quite apart from the melodious rhythmic flow of the prose (Harwood admitted to being deeply influenced by the language of the *Old Testament*), there are subtle lexical repetitons like "obsession," "light," "sun," "dark." "Disappointment" is the first word and one of the last ones of the story. Words like "bewitch, magical, magician, sorcerer" also help give better insight into Edward's psyche.

What is the outcome? What is the result? My reading and analysin *Starring Laurence Olivier* was influenced and determined by a series of factors, internal as well as external; both categories were of equal relevance and all the factors contributed to my better understanding of the text. The central character finds himself in a tormenting conflict between illusion and reality, in other words: the dark world of the cinema, two-dimensional pictures of celluloid or the cave with its shadows, and the real world, the light which can be painful to the eyes and the mind. Edward strives to overcome the conflict and arrive at a better recognition of reality, however hard the process of enlightenment with its dramatic development at the end may be. He strives for personal as well as for a cultural identity. From the safe distance of more than ten years later Edward is able to put his experience into perspective and judge it from a more mature point of view. However, this does not take anything away from the impact of the original experience and its painfulness.

Finally: there cannot be a cut-and-dried result. Each reading of a literary text offers new insights, modifies previous approaches and evaluations. My experience with this story was what my students have sometimes told me: Reading a story is a never-ending story itself.*

Notes

[1]
First published in: Ronald Harwood, *One. Day. Interior. Adventures in the film trade* (London: 1978), 77-80. All page numbers in brackets refer to the respective pages in the present volume.

[2]
Willa Cather, "Paul's Case," in: *Five Stories* (New York: 1956), 149-174.

[3]
Cather, 155.

[4]
Samuel Taylor Coleridge, "Kubla Khan," in: Sir Arthur Quiller-Couch (Ed.), *The Oxford Book of English Verse 1250-1918* (Oxford: repr. 1961), 668-670.

[5]
Platon. *Politeia*. Sämtliche Werke Bd. 3. (Reinbeck: Rowohlt 1958), 68-310, here 224 f.

[6]
Acts of the Apostles, chapter 9.

[7]
James Thurber, "The Macbeth Murder Mystery" in: *The Thurber Carnival* (Harmondsworth: repr. 1972), 83-86.

[8]
It seems worth noting in this context that in Willy Russell's comedy *Educating Rita* the eponymous herione, a 26-year old hairdresser, who is taking courses at the Open University, reports to her Tutor Frank that she has been to see *Macbeth* on stage. Her reception is just as naive and simplistic as Edward's. She takes the tragedy at face-value. (Harlow 1985, scene 6, 38-42. Longman Study Texts).

[9]
Cather, 162.

[10]
Cather, 155-56.

[11]
Hamlet. Laurence Olivier and an All Star Cast. Rank Home Video. P.O. Box 70, Great West Road, Brentford, Middlesex TW8 9HR, England (ISBN 5 014861 305520).

* I am grateful to Dr. Virginia Teichmann who checked my text with the native speaker's competence and helped me clarify my own thoughts.

James Reaney

SLEIGH WITHOUT BELLS: A GHOST STORY ABOUT THE DONNELLYS

Preface

This Puppet Play is written for for FOUR puppeteers, a MUSICIAN, and a TECHNICIAN, visible to audience in an environment which hides very little of its artifice from the pre-show viewers arriving—in the case of the premiere run in London, Ontario, crowds of public and high school students. Five perform- ances at the local Art Gallery had adults mixed with children, and a preview had college students with children. The style of presentation was suggested by the way local kids play with their Barbie dolls and cut-out paper dolls; they hold them in one hand and shake them for moments of passion; their toy wagons contain doll furniture for interior scenes. Sometimes, a white sheet lit with a flashlight from behind shows shadow puppets of roughly cut cardboard. In the workshop preliminary I stapled actual photographs of the Donnellys to sticks of wood, but in production, David Smith Marionettes and Rag & Bone Puppet Company provided semi-Bunraki portrait dolls with a big spectrum of simpler figures for crowd scenes and minor characters. John Donnelly, for example, was seen only as a lighted lantern with a hand attached to it. There were various sizes of sleighs and carts, as well as puppet figures, to suggest distance and nearness. In effect the set boiled down to three or four tables on castors. Stage Left upstage stood the Donnelly Homestead Wagon which opens out to reveal their kitchen with stove pipe, stove, chimney on a section of roof. On a wagon upstage Right we had the door of this kitchen plus a window.

Downstage centre was the MAIN TABLE with puppets all ready. Under- neath it waiting for use were Ephraim's sleigh, Crowd Cutouts, Deer, Bird, River (blue transparent streamer) and a miniature lantern for Ephraim's sleigh. Also visible were a white sheet for snow blizzard and silhouette effects as well as a large swatch of artificial green turf for the spring sequence at the end of the play. Most of the puppets had heads modelled on photographs of the historical characters. This gave the iconic mesmerizing effect I desired of undertakers' ghosts. Mr. and Mrs. Donnelly, as well as their children and servants, were dressed neatly as pins, with particular elegance for court appearances. This, of course, was one thing that drove their enemies crazy. James Carroll, on the other hand, is a pretty wild looking customer but for court appearances he tidied up. The "false" Donnelly puppets should give the craftsman the chance for Grand Guignol monsters although my fury here was restrained by budget and they became, very satisfyingly, just a hat on a stick or—whatever suggestive prop was available. Actually, I now recall that the False Donnelly puppets were modelled on Punch and Judy hand puppets with clubs which they used freely. On downstage Left, the musician's synthesizer and collection of sound effects stands ready—the actors enter with him and the technician, the house lights darken and two company members wave a white sheet lit from behind across which a shadow sleigh (sleigh bells ringing) journeys from Perth County into Biddulph Township during a resounding blizzard. The white sheet shakes in the whistling wind. The horses for the sleigh, big chunky Percherons, were purchased at a toy shop.

CAST

Young Man on Sleigh (Ephraim Flummerfelt)
Hawk
Deer
River
Vigilante Constable Carroll
Sparks
Lantern
Mrs. Judith Donnelly
Mr. James Donnelly
Bridget Donnelly (Niece of the Donnellys)
Theresa Connors
Michael's Ghost
John Donnelly
Patrick Ryder
Father Connolly
Clerk
Lawyer McDiarmid
Magistrate Casey
Chorus
False Mrs. Donnelly
False Mr. Donnelly
False John Donnelly
A Voice
Police Chief
Choir

Priest

Mr. Darcy

Mrs. Darcy

Schoolmaster Panton

Maria Panton, nee Keefe

James Keefe

Undertaker Mudie

Prologue

A white semi-transparent curtain begins to shake with the howling wind of a blizzard. In silhouette, we see a cut-out sleigh drawn by two horses, another horse tethered at the back, a young man in heavy fur coat driving. We hear the sleigh bells at a distance then close-up. For a moment, we glimpse a man—JOHN DONNELLY—waving a LAN-TERN at the stranger in the sleigh. His shadow is gigantic. Momentarily, we glimpse a log house, some barns, an orchard. Then, he vanishes, lost in the blizzard.

YOUNG MAN ON SLEIGH: Whoa! Keep your lantern alight, sir. I've come a long way down from Perth County and I'm lost in this storm.

Turning around, he makes another try at the house, but fails to find it.

YOUNG MAN: Where the devil has the man with the house and the lantern gone to? Is there nothing there by the orchard?

Stepping in front of the silhouette curtain, he holds a flashlight which lights up his face.

YOUNG MAN: My mother and father said goodbye to me as I started out on my journey. I was to take this mare and the seed grain to my uncle in Southwold Township and something else secret. What township am I in? (*Only the storm & the waving silhouette curtain reply.*) My father warned me not to go down through the Irish settlement, but I appear to have got into the settlement of disappearing houses and vanishing lanterns. Holloa there!

HAWK: I was the hawk that watched him make his first mistake from my tree. He chose the road I wanted him to take, not the safe one his mother and father, good Protestant souls, sagely advised.

DEER: We were the deer whose antlers he glimpsed in the swamp bottom. We could smell him and his sweaty horses.

RIVER: I was the river that last week knocked out the bridge he should have used so that he would lose his way and find the place he was most afraid of.

YOUNG MAN: At the tavern where I managed to stop for water and feed they would not tell me my way and ... (*The sleigh bells abruptly stop ringing.*)

VIGILANTE CONSTABLE: I cut the bells off his sleigh. Strangers are not welcome this month of February in our settlement. We have work to do they might interrupt.

SCENE 1
THE ARREST

YOUNG MAN: Guten Abend. My name is Ephraim Flummerfelt. In the early spring of 1887, why I was sleighing south of Perth County on my way to Elgin County and I lost my way.

SPARKS: We were the sparks of light in the log house windows that came up to him thick beside each other with green doors that did not answer his knock.

EPHRAIM (YOUNG MAN): I was desperate for shelter. Hungry. Why did I leave the tavern? (*A chord of music, supernatural, terrifying*)

LANTERN: Do you know where you're going, sir?

EPHRAIM: I'm lost, friend. How many more miles is it to Southwold?

LANTERN: Southwold? Another whole day's sleighing, sir. Come into our yard and we'll put you up for the night, horses and all.

The white sheet is tucked away: EPHRAIM stands in front of a log house, knocks on a door.

EPHRAIM: He and his brother took care of the horses for me. (*The log house opens out to reveal a kitchen.*) First they let me into their father and mother's house. There was a tall woman standing by the stove and a shorter man across from her. She was the tallest old woman or young, I ever seen. Six foot four. Taller than a man. There was one young woman sewing, and another baking.

MRS. DONNELLY: You've been on a long journey, young fellow.

EPHRAIM: I wondered how she knew it was a long journey. My hands were so cold. I couldn't get myself unbuttoned from my bearskin coat.

MRS. DONNELLY: Mr. Donnelly, help me unbutton his coat till we get a look at him.

MR. DONNELLY: Look at him shivering, Mrs. Donnelly. He's stiffer with cold than I am with rheumatics. (*In a routine protracted for comic effect, the two tragic figures out of legend uncoat what turns out to be a blond young man, frozen and totally innocent, tabula rasa for the fierce slate pencils of tragedy in Biddulph township. EPHRAIM and his puppet equivalent are look-alikes.*)

MRS. DONNELLY: Bridget, dear one, hurry up with those tea biscuits you're baking and boil the water for tea.

BRIDGET DONNELLY (*Niece of the DONNELLYS*): Theresa, my hands are all floury, could you pump the water for the tea, dear?

As the DONNELLY parents rub and chafe and tug and sweep and brush the traveller into shape, we should see BRIDGET using a rolling pin, and then THERESA take a pail, open the kitchen door on the other wagon (—it's a back door—) fight against the howling wind which knocks over EPHRAIM, shut door behind her. Then pumping sounds heard from outside, opens door to re-enter, wind knocks down young man again, door closes. Next kettle is put on stove, biscuits put in oven. All this very stylized. underneath the following dialogue, we should hear the kettle coming to a boil.

MRS. DONNELLY: There now, young sir, warm yourself by the stove. James, give him your chair.

EPHRAIM: Oh no, I can stand by it, Mrs? It's rude to ask people their names, I know, but mine's Ephraim Flummerfelt from Logan Township up near, um Got Willen, Mitchell. Nearer Moncton, actually. (*The kettle climaxes to its highest whistle, steam spouting out as the old man and woman rise from either side of the stove and say:*)

MR. DONNELLY: James Donnelly.

MRS. DONNELLY: Judith Donnelly.

From stretching out his hands to warm them over the stove, the young fellow whirls about, makes for his coat, and faints with a muffled scream.

MR. DONNELLY: And it's rude to ask people their names I know, but mine's Ephraim Flummerfelt from Logan Township up near, um Got Willen, Mitchell.

MRS. DONNELLY: Well, at least he only fainted when he heard who we were. Bridget, get a pail of water pumped fresh and we'll try to bring him round, this young Protestant, a Methodist you can tell by his nose … so scared of an old woman and an old man.

BRIDGET: Theresa, darling, could you pump us a fresh pail of water. I'm about to take out the tea biscuits from the oven. Oh, the poor fellow, he's out like a light.

THERESA CONNORS: Ah, it's a pail of snow I'll get him. It's solid ice to the pump like a skating rink only I've got no skates.

Again the opened door, wind! Wind on, off, on as THERESA returns with snow. She sprinkles it over his face. BRIDGET comes over with a tea biscuit. He begins to revive. THERESA bends over him with a cup of tea. There is a silence.

EPHRAIM: I came to and looked up into their faces. (*Pause*) Whether it was the tea or the biscuits or the fact that the girl was sewing a handkerchief edged in black with tiny little delicate stitches so tiny they made me want to marry her, Catholic Papist though she very probably was—I never desired union with a woman so much as I did that moment. (*Pause*) I marvelled that the Donnellys weren't like what I'd been told.

DONNELLYS (*To us*): Ah, sure, as my son Michael once wrote to the paper.

MICHAEL'S GHOST: What you all don't know is I was murdered just a month ago down in Waterford. (*He emerges from the roof of the log house, sits on the chimney.*) Stabbed in the groin by a perfect stranger in the tavern there. Sure I was waked on the big four poster bed where he'll sleep with my father tonight just under a week ago, and my spirit still wakes here for I died unconfessed. So I sit on the roof here near the chimney where it's warm. What my mother and father remember me writing is when our enemies slandered us in the London Free Press, and I wrote in saying: "You call us the Donnelly tribe. Well, we're not a tribe. And there's two sides to every story."

THERESA: Ah, smell the smoke would you?

BRIDGET: The wind's baffling the smoke down the chimney, it won't draw at all. (*The ghost stands up.*)

MRS. DONNELLY: Dear God, it's better at drawing now. (*Repeat. Make this a comic routine.*)

MR. DONNELLY: Judith, it is only a fantasy you have.

MRS. DONNELLY: That's our son, Michael is walking on the roof. Sure, where else would his poor soul go when they didn't give him a chance to say his prayers.

MR. DONNELLY: Don't talk of it, Judith. Surely, our prayers count for something.

We hear someone walking on the roof. We watch MICHAEL DONNELLY'S ghost, after some walking back & forth, he vanishes.

EPHRAIM (*Rising and addressing us*): You see my parents had been told that the Donnellys were ugly, misshapen creatures like Cain and the Devil rolled into one. But I never saw better behaved, polite, generous souls. We spent the rest of the evening with tea, biscuits, and some pork fried up for me since I was hungrier than tea biscuits, and when the clock struck nine, why it was time for bed, since, like us at home, they rise at four o'clock to milk cows and feed pigs. I slept like a top. Got up about a quarter to four to obey a call of nature. Lit a candle, crept through the quiet house with them still sleeping—pictures on the walls, with one big difference—candle in a red glass cup beneath one of them, just like my parents' house when I'd been led to expect no doors except maybe a bit of sacking and no glass in the windows. (*Pause*) We at my father's house have no candles guttering below pictures of sacred hearts. Wondered why the sons hadn't come in yet, but then I recollected they were at a wedding dance at the Keefe's and—they'd still be dancing. John, the man with the lantern, had stayed home. He was still asleep. Opened the door, no wind. (*Pause, turns about buttoning up his trousers. A red glare lights the sky.*) It's a bit early for the dawn, isn't it? (*Two men appear, a farmer—Pat RYDER and JAMES CARROLL whom we've met before cutting off EPHRAIM's sleigh bells.*)

VIGILANTE (*CARROLL*): It is not the dawn, stranger. Have you up I could for indecent exposure. Pat Ryder's barns are burning and I discover Donnelly's sons have been at a dance all night, a likely story but supported by respectable liars—wake up the old man and the old woman. Pat Ryder says they burnt down his barns. I've a warrant here for the arrest of (*Loudly*) Judith and James Donnelly.

EPHRAIM: Are you insane, man? Get out. I shall not disturb their sleep with such a heap of tommy rot. Get out!

VIGILANTE: Perhaps you'd like to be charged with them? (*They scuffle. Again a puppet routine.*)

MRS. DONNELLY (*Sticking head out of window*): Don't waste your time talking to that blackguard. Bridget! Bridget!! Get you up, put on your cloak and your winter boots. Take this note over to Mr. William Hodgins—Protestant Line, just at the back of our farm. Tell them we need bail money fast or we'll be dragged through the Main Street of Lucan handcuffed to the lock-up.

BRIDGET: Oh, Aunt Judith, never! (*Runs off.*)

JOHN: Mother, he's after arresting you and Father for burning down Grouchy Ryder's barn.

MRS. DONNELLY: Is he now. Mr. Donnelly, put on your go-to-mass suit for we're likely to make public appearances today. (*Both appear well dressed and hatted, well aware that they're supposed to be demons in rags.*)

MR. DONNELLY: This is false arrest, Mr. Carroll. If it's law you want, we'll give it to you.

CARROLL: And I suppose, Jim, you're after telling me that you'll bring that feeble-minded niece of yours …

MRS. DONNELLY: Feeble minded, sir? Sir, she's bright as a penny and at least doesn't have the epileptic fits your poor soul is wracked with, Mr. Carroll.

CARROLL: Where is she? Bridget Donnelly, come with your uncle and aunt in my sleigh and make your usual alibi for these old thieves and barn-burners. (*Pause*)

MRS. DONNELLY: What you don't know is that I've sent her on an errand to our neighbour's at the back. But we have two other people who stayed with us last night. (*A howl of despair from CARROLL*)

THERESA CONNORS: Sir, Mr. Constable Carroll or whoever. Last night Mrs. Donnelly never left the house. She slept between me and Bridget.

EPHRAIM: Constable, Mr. Donnelly was not out of the house last night. I slept on the outside of a four poster bed shoved up against the wall, with his son John between us.

CARROLL: Son of a bitch, they've as good an alibi as the sons.

RYDER: Carroll, if you've got me into a malicious arrest charge —did they not burn down my barns ?

MRS. DONNELLY: I'm over sixty, Mr. Ryder, rheumatic, and not a great navigator of four foot snowdrifts. What brain-worm has got into you?

MR. DONNELLY: Pat Ryder. We never never have quarrelled with you for all the forty years we've neighboured. Why there's no fence between that field the Maloneys left us and your field you bought from Flannery.

MRS. DONNELLY: Why, Patrick Ryder. I shall tell you who burnt down your barns. Carroll here— had them burnt down to provoke you against us. Is that not so, Jimmy Carroll?

CARROLL (*Pause*): You old lying bitch. You burnt them and I shall prove it on you. (*Loud!*) Jim Donnelly, is that your name? I have here magistrate's warrants charging you with burning down the barns of Patrick Ryder on (*Pause*), in early morning of and setting bail at $ 500.

MRS. DONNELLY: On when, Mr. Carroll?

CARROLL (*Pause*): Will no one provide me with a calendar? (*Searching pockets*)

JOHN (*Looking at the warrant*): Jim Carroll, you've got the date right here on your warrant. The night of January the 14th. Then my brothers' names are scratched out here. They were supposed to burn the barns down last evening, but your matches were wet. So, now, it has to be my parents ?

CARROLL (*Howls and stamps*): And a warrant for the arrest of Judith and James Donnelly here on charge of conspiring with her husband to burn down the barns of Patrick Ryder.

MRS. DONNELLY (*Pause*): When? (*Laughing*) Last night? (*Bending down to catch his averted eyes.*)

CARROLL *signals RYDER to bring up a sleigh. CARROLL draws a gun and the DONNELLYS with THERESA help themselves up unto his sleigh.*

MR. DONNELLY: Where are we off to ?

CARROLL: To justice at last.

MR. DONNELLY: Well, sir, I have a right to know or it will go ill with you when we launch our lawsuit for malicious arrest. (*Pause*) When you were a scholar at the school here—my wife fed you, remember.

PAT RYDER (*Pause. Sotto voice.*): Lock-up at Lucan, Jim.

CARROLL: Handcuff her! Handcuff him!

We hear the clink of the handcuffs as he throws them up in the air, then offers RYDER a pair.

MRS. DONNELLY: One moment, please. At what amount is my bail set?

CARROLL: Same as your husband's.

MRS. DONNELLY (*Looking at the warrant CARROLL holds out to her*): That must be the highest bail ever set for an old woman and old man in this county.

CARROLL: Hands!

JOHN: Don't you dare handcuff my mother.

CARROLL: Do you have her bail then?

JOHN (*Pause*): No. What family has 1,000 dollars on their premises?

BRIDGET (*From a distance*): Wait, Constable Carroll. Tell him not to handcuff them. I've got the (*Pause as she comes closer, falling at the feet of CARROLL with a letter which he reluctantly opens.*)

CARROLL: But this is only a blank note at hand—my handbook says I can demand the bail in cash. Let's go.

The two vigilantes drive their sleigh away with all the DONNELLY party barely climbed into it. JOHN "swings" farewell to them and to FLUMMERFELT who with his sleigh (hitched up during above) pursues the other sleigh down the Chapel line past St. Patrick's church and right turn on highway four up to Lucan.

JOHN: Here Mr. Flummerfelt. Here's another set of bells for those they cut off your sleigh. Are you off to Southwold now?

EPHRAIM: Oh no, Mr. Donnelly. It just so happens—it's a great secret—that I have a thousand dollars in gold coins on my person.

JOHN: Don't tell that to many, or you'll find yourself stretched dead on the road.

EPHRAIM: That's why I'm really going down to my uncle's place to pay off a debt that has to be paid in gold. But they can wait. I thought I'd lend it to your parents to get them out of those handcuffs.

JOHN (*Pause*): My Father in Heaven, Mr. Flummerfelt. You have a kind heart with love in it. God speed you. You see—we have so few friends lately.

The LANTERN gets smaller, the bells fade away and we focus instead on the slowly appearing Main Street of Lucan. Using a 19th century photo, string cut-outs of buildings on west side of Main Street in 1880. This should extend from post office to Bernard Stanley's great mansion, now Haskett funeral home. A puppet feature could be manipulated cloth smoke issuing from scores of houses and stores as Lucan arise. A stage coach goes whizzing by. A train whistle.

SCENE 2
LUCAN

MANIPULATORS	Lucan, sweet spot, thy memory twines,
(four part	Around my heart I bind thee still.
harmony)	E'en while I write a street lamp shines
	Beside the lock-up near the mill.
	Tho' fire and torch around thee burn
	Tho' lawless bands at midnight rove,
	My fondest thoughts still to thee turn,
	Thy grassy lanes will calm my love.

CONSTABLE CARROLL'S sleigh parades the handcuffed DONNELLYS now forced to stand up and down in front of a fast gathering crowd. Sound of same muttering:

Barn burners. He's caught them red-handed at last.

FLUMMERFELT jams his sleigh across the street thus stopping the public humiliation.

CARROLL: Behold the barn burners!

EPHRAIM: Constable Carroll, I have the bail money.

CARROLL: I'll believe it when I see it.

EPHRAIM: I have it in a money belt I keep for safety between my legs here.

CARROLL takes out a set of balances. turning his back to us, FLUMMERFELT takes the money out.

PATRICK RYDER: Remember to get a receipt from your friends here, Flummerfelt.

EPHRAIM: Take off their handcuffs, please.

CARROLL: Not so fast. You are 10 scruples short, Flummerfelt.

EPHRAIM: Are you adjusted to Troy weight? (*Pause, as he examines the balances.*)

MRS. DONNELLY: Never. Never adjusted to Troy weight. Hell weight is all our Jim Carroll knows.

EPHRAIM: Then, some of the coins have slipped down into my stockings. (*He takes off his boots, socks and comes up with three coins. Still the balance is not right.*) I think I know where the last coin is. Pardon me, while I visit the hotel over there.

CARROLL: What in hell's name are you up to Flummerfelt?

EPHRAIM: Well, the best way to keep gold clean according to my father is to swallow it a piece at a time. I swallowed a dirty piece of gold dollar last night. I'll just use their latrine here and pass it. See you shortly. (*Exit. Returns with coin which he throws to CARROLL who catches it.*)

RYDER (*Pause*): Take them off.

CARROLL gives him a key and walks sulking away. RYDER frees the DONNELLYS.

CARROLL: You're due at the council chambers two p. m., you.

The DONNELLYS limber up their arms, helped by their young friends. Drawing a full size democrat (demi-cart) behind him, a stage hand stops at upstage centre. Town bell strikes noon.

SCENE 3
THE DEMI-CART

MR. DONNELLY: Mr. Flummerfelt, will you join us at Maclean's Hotel for dinner? We have an appointment with Lawyer McDiarmid at one. My wife and I wish to show our thanks for all you've done for us. In some small way. (*They promenade to hotel. At centre upstage we note a demi-cart with a stage hand asleep in it.*)

EPHRAIM: Mr. and Mrs. Donnelly, may, um Gott Willen, I—ask you a few questions?

MR. DONNELLY: Ask away.

EPHRAIM: I couldn't help but note that you lack a personal buggy or cart to get around in. Do your sons ever drive you in theirs?

MRS. DONNELLY: Our son William does, yes. He farms over at Whalen's Corners and keeps the best stallion in the Province.

MR. DONNELLY: Lord Byron. Out of Oliver Mowat into Lady Byron.

EPHRAIM: Yes. My uncle has a colt out of Lord Byron into—well, not a well known mare but she did win the cup at Glencoe last fall—Wilhelmina!

MR. DONNELLY: Last September, we did have a fine demi-cart. Made at Maloney's here in town before he was burnt out. That one's the twin of it. (*Touches the demi-cart. A clock strikes twelve.*)

MRS. DONNELLY: We were playing cards on Sunday.

EPHRAIM: Cards on Sunday?

MRS. DONNELLY: Our church allows that after 12 noon if you've been to mass, Mr. Flummerfelt. (*A whirlwind with thunder gathers sudden intensity.*)

EPHRAIM: Um Gott Willen, what then?

BRIDGET: I said to my uncle James—Uncle James there's a tempest outside— look at the buggy for it's all outlined in blue light.

A YOUNG STAGE HAND asleep as usual in the cart, leaps out and runs towards us as lightning strikes the vehicle, its various parts flying up & away. The church wagon opens up, PRIEST emerges. Crowd kneels before him.

FATHER CONNOLLY: My friends, was not this event of last Sunday a sign from Heaven? Lightning strikes this family's only wagon! After this, how can this difficult family stay a day longer in the parish?

Crowd murmur. The church snaps shut. MR. DONNELLY, so neatly dressed for court, walks over to the place where lightning struck. He is outlined in blue light. Thunder. He looks straight up and shakes his fist at the heavens. Pause. Music. Sudden shift to Lucan council chambers.

Taped sound of pen scratch up & underneath.

SCENE 4
INCENDIARISM

CLERK: Lucan January 22nd, 1880. Council Chamber Patrick Ryder versus James Donnelly and Juldith Donnelly. Incendiarism.

The DONNELLYs and their LAWYER, McDIARMID. PATRICK RYDER enters with MAGISTRATE CASEY, a fanatic vigilante.

CARROLL (*With staff*): Oyez, oyez, the court is in session.

CLERK: Will all those present rise.

After the J.P. sits down, people in court sit down.

CASEY (*From a handbook*): Patrick Ryder versus James Donnelly. Patrick Ryder versus Judith Donnelly who are called-uh-charged with incendiarism. The prisoners are called.

CARROLL: James Donnelly. (*Pounding gavel with timidity, then more thunderously*)

CASEY: To answer to their names.

MR. DONNELLY (*Rising*): I am James Donnelly.

J.P. CASEY: How plead you, James Donnelly?

MR. DONNELLY: Not guilty.

CONSTABLE: Judith Donnelly.

MRS. DONNELLY (*Rising*): I am Judith Donnelly.

CASEY: And how plead you, Judith Donnelly with regard to the charge that you helped your husband burn down Patrick Ryder's barns on the night of January the 15th?

MRS. DONNELLY: Not guilty.

CASEY: First witness for the prosecution called.

CONSTABLE (*Beating floor with staff*): Patrick Ryder!

CLERK (*Under the CLERK'S narration penscrape*): Herein, the Prosecutor—Justice of the Peace William Casey—asked for an adjournment to procure witnesses.

MR. and MRS. DONNELLY: No adjournment, Mr. McDiarmid.

LAWYER McDIARMID: Your honour, we object to any adjournment.

PATRICK RYDER: We have not had, your honour, sufficient time—notice to procure witnesses to prove our case.

CASEY: How long an adjournment do you need for the sake of Heaven?

PATRICK RYDER: Five days or four viz Tuesday January 27th next—say, at where?

CASEY (*Pause*): Oh, variety is the spice of existence. Sure these old rascals have never been to Granton. (*Indicates where it is on courtroom map.*) The Huron Hotel!

LAWYER McDIARMID: Not unless my clients are given an extension of their bail.

CARROLL, RYDER, and CASEY look at each other.

CASEY: On condition they do not attempt to leave the township. (*Music.*) Court adjourned.

CLERK: Everybody rise.

CARROLL: Court adjourned.

SCENE 5
A TRIP TO ST. MARYS

EPHRAIM: After I had driven Mr. and Mrs. Donnelly home Theresa came running out and asked if I would take her to St. Marys where she had a week's sewing and dressmaking lined up. (*Two big panels can be revolved to show. Name of paper on one side: Its DONNELLY comments on other.*) In St. Marys we found that they had two papers-- the Argus and the Journal. Outside their offices they had news placards. On one placard, that for the Argus paper it said: Extirpate The Brutes. On the other, for the Journal, it said: They Were A Family Of Ishmaelites. Theresa—this newspaper says that the Donnellys are animals and should be—destroyed.

THERESA: Oh, Ephraim Flummerfelt, there's many agree—those who are their enemies you see.

EPHRAIM: And the other newspaper says—I can't understand why it talks of them as if they were dead. As if they had suffered from prejudice. I understand that.

THERESA: Oh, Mr. Flummerfelt—everyone keeps saying that something terrible's going to happen to the Donnellys some day.

EPHRAIM: "Some day." But the newspaper placard says: "They were a"—were? (*THERESA laughing and floating away, occasionally after she has disappeared behind the pro-DONNELLY placard peeking out at him and laughing. Sometimes she is a large THERESA (maybe just the head), sometimes she is even tinier than her puppet version. A crackling sound of flames, outcries, weeping, a confused babel of voices. Led by THERESA for the DONNELLYS and CARROLL against them, we have the following fighting match:*)

I love them / I hate them.

As if by magic the handpuppets illustrating CARROLL'S point of view appear from behind his "extirpate" placard. His version of MR. and MRS. DONNELLY is Sesame Street crossed with David Lynch: THERESA'S version is that already established.

Not half bad.	They're the terrors of the township. Get them out of Biddulph!
They were all right if you left them alone, but no one ever left them alone.	They cut the tongues out of horses.
Never! They loved horses. Cut the tongues out of lying men, yes. Never horses.	She taught them how to! Old Mrs. Donnelly.

CARROLL (*Holding up his versions of MR. and MRS. DONNELLY.*): Yes, Mike Donnelly, there are two sides to every story. The old man killed a cousin of mine, murdered him in 1857 at a logging bee. (*The FALSE DONNELLY puppets are two dimensional caricatures.*)

MR. DONNELLY: It was an unlucky stroke given in liquor.

CHORUS *led by*   Donnelly squatted on Bill Farrell's land,
CARROLL: Just laughed when ordered to pay,
                      Then with iron bar struck Farrell dead
                      At a logging bee one day.

MR. DONNELLY: It was a wooden handspike, not an iron bar. It was manslaughter, not murder. Why did I get off with seven years in the Kingston Penitentiary instead of being hanged if it was murder?

CARROLL: Well, we got you at last, Jim. Justice will out!

MR. DONNELLY: I fear the punishment of my God more than anything man can do to me, Carroll.

EPHRAIM: Why does he keep talking as if Mr. Donnelly is dead?

CARROLL: And now listen to her!

CHORUS: So hurry to your homes, good folks,
               Lock doors and windows tight,
               And pray for dawn, the Black Donnellys
               will be abroad tonight.

FALSE MRS. DONNELLY: And that's one thing, son John, that you've done lately to strike terror into our enemies' hearts as should be struck and struck again and again and again till they leave us alone! Till alone us they leave!

FALSE JOHN: So they say we derailed the train, hunh? What else are they saying we done, eh mither? Eh, fither?

FALSE MR. AND MRS. DONNELLY (*Alternately*): Burning two barns, cutting the tongues out of 20 horses and putting 400 iron pins in Gallagher's wheat sheaves so's the threshing machine would catch fire.

FALSE JOHN (*With a fistful of weapons*): Mike, get up! We'll show those blank blank so and so's they can't pin anything on us.

FALSE MR. DONNELLY: John, what are you going to do, avourneen?

FALSE MRS. DONNELLY: Sure there's been enough misery and tribulation now, do you want to bring my gray hairs with sorrow to the grave? (*Sudden manic change in her character.*) But there's one thing, son, I never hear them saying you done.

FALSE JOHN: What's that, Mither?

FALSE MRS. DONNELLY: Killing a man.

FALSE JOHN: Couldn't do that, mither.

FALSE MRS. DONNELLY: Then you're no son of mine. Until you've killed your man the way your darling father did, you're no son of mine.

CHORUS: By thefts they showed their father's blood
       By fights and drunken sprees
       Till the countryside, living in dread,
       Called them the Black Donnellys.

MRS. DONNELLY (*Standing forward*): Am I like that?

MR. DONNELLY: What everyone forgets is that **our** barns were burnt down in 1870. We suffered too.

MRS. DONNELLY: Everyone forgets—because—I once said that there were worse than my sons in the township of Biddulph but theirs is the larger gang and so the Donnellys go to the wall.

MR. DONNELLY: We're trapped—we should leave, we should have.

MRS. DONNELLY: I'm going to leave, Mr. Donnelly.

MR. DONNELLY (*Pause*): I'm going to stay and sue them for false arrest!

MRS. DONNELLY: And rouse them to final fury? No—I'm going to run away from Biddulph. (*Exit.*)

MR. DONNELLY: It's no use. Come back, Mrs. Donnelly. (*Exeunt.*)

EPHRAIM: Theresa? Where have you gone?

She looks out at him from behind one of the placards, laughs and disappears. The placards begin to revolve, the puppets as well, now the formal DONNELLYS, now the grotesque ones. Reprise the last 12 lines at the beginning of the St. Marys sequence, then fade and in the twilight EPHRAIM'S sleigh is nearing Southwold township (signpost—one way Southwold, another St. Thomas).

EPHRAIM: For the rest of the day I tried to forget the Donnellys and remember that originally I had intended on this journey south to visit certain of my relatives in Southwold. But, again, curious things began to happen. When my horses reached the crossroads where a left turn meant St. Thomas and a right turn the village of Southwold—I could not turn the sleigh the right way.

A VOICE: Flummerfelt, I want you to let me off in St. Thomas at 5 Fifth Avenue.

EPHRAIM: Fifth Avenue. We're not going as far as New York surely.

A VOICE: No, no, you blockhead! Fifth Avenue, St. Thomas!

MRS. DONNELLY stands up from hiding under a sleigh blanket.

EPHRAIM: It was Mrs. Donnelly, and for the very first time—I was afraid of her. (*Sleigh stops.*)

MRS. DONNELLY: Now, give me your jack knife —

EPHRAIM: Why do you want my jack knife, Mrs. Donnelly?

MRS. DONNELLY: To cut the bells off your sleigh—then he won't be able to hear where we're going—in the dark.

EPHRAIM: Who's he?

MRS. DONNELLY: Constable Jim Carroll.

CARROLL (*In sleigh with St. Thomas POLICE CHIEF*): Arrest that woman. She was told not to leave the township. Let me give these horses a larrup—

We hear the sleigh bells of EPHRAIM'S sleigh, then they stop.

POLICE CHIEF: We're at the crossroads, Jim. It's getting dark for seeing—I've been following them by the sound of their bells. (*Silence.*)

CARROLL: Either they're resting, or—maybe they'll light a lantern.

EPHRAIM: Mrs. Donnelly, it's against the law to drive a sleigh without bells. You might run right over another sleigh or cutter and they'd have no warning. So, if you won't let me have my bells, at least let me light a lantern. The law says too that we should have a red lantern at the back of the sleigh.

MRS. DONNELLY: You young simpleton—so Constable Carroll can follow us with his eyes instead of his weasel ears? Law, what good has law done us?

POLICE CHIEF: Why's she going to St. Thomas, Constable Carroll? Just anywhere to get away?

CARROLL: Oh some sob story about seeing her daughter who lives there and her grandchildren. Mike's widow's in the same house … on Fifth Avenue, St. Thomas.

POLICE CHIEF: Mike? Oh, you mean the one who got murdered in Waterford lately. Why not let her visit her grandchildren? Maybe she intends returning?

CARROLL: Not that hardened harridan witch. No, she shall not see her daughter or her grandchildren ever again before she dies! (*There is a chase but Mrs DONNELLY'S trick works and CARROLL loses the trail for a while. A lighted window in a St. Thomas street comes closer, but frosted over with snow and rime. Train whistles.)*

MRS. DONNELLY (*Looking in the window towards audience*): Oh, young Mr. Flummerfelt—help me rub the frost off this window of my daughter Jenny's house—so I can hear her dear voice again and see her face and my grandchildren.

EPHRAIM: Mrs. Donnelly, why don't we knock on the door and …

MRS. DONNELLY: No, it's too late for that. Blow on the window and rub it off with your sleeve. Have you no brains?

Sleigh bells getting louder as EPHRAIM does this, and …

POLICE CHIEF: Mrs. Donnelly. You are to come along with me to the police station, and from there Constable Carroll will take you back to Biddulph Township.

MRS. DONNELLY: Read the warrant first, if you please. Where is the warrant? I know my law. Before you handcuff me and put me in your sleigh and drag me back.

EPHRAIM (*Over the last part of this scene as MRS. DONNELLY is carried off*): I could not stop him—he would not let her see her daughter, and—I did not see the Donnellys again until the following Sunday when I was going home north to Perth County through the Irish Settlement again.

SCENE 6
HURON HOTEL, GRANTON

CLERK: In the case of Ryder versus James and Julia Donnelly met at Granton at the Huron Hotel Tuesday 27th January 1880 and was opened in due form.

RYDER: My name is Patrick Ryder. My reasons for suspecting the Donnellys of burning my barns was—that I heard a neighbour, Mrs. John Carroll told my daughter Mary that my son would not be long riding in his new buggy—and this buggy was burned in the barn, in the driving shed. Further, she said that Mrs. Donnelly made this threat. Yes, this threat alarmed me.

LAWYER McDIARMID: Have you any other reason, Mr. Ryder?

RYDER: No.

CASEY: Mrs. John Carroll.

MRS. JOHN CARROLL: Mrs. Donnelly visits with me sometimes. Mr. Ryder, Mrs. Donnelly did not say that your son would not have his buggy long, I am positive of this. What she did say was that…

MRS. DONNELLY: I'll put a blush in his face and make him lie back in his grand buggy because that particular Ryder boy had been part of a mob trampling through our yard in search of the famous cow that was lost.

MRS. JOHN CARROLL: No, I have not heard Mrs. Donnelly say anything against the Ryders since.

MR. DONNELLY: You are treating us like mad dogs. We have been dragged all across the township to make us laughing stocks, an old man and an old woman over 60 years old. We are being advertised as barn burners.

MRS. DONNELLY (*Turning back*): Mr. Casey. Magistrate Casey, your Honour.

CASEY: Why, Mrs. Donnelly, are you showing me this knife?

MRS. DONNELLY: Because I once was the woman who stopped you from tormenting a man with this knife and I am now the woman who tells you that my husband and myself are being tried, accused and judged by thieves and murderers. (*She throws the knife at his feet; he picks it up. Exeunt all but CARROLL, RYDER.*)

CASEY (*Starts to whet the knife on a stone*): Carroll, I'm not facing that woman again in daylight. I'll show her who's master of this neighbourhood—get me a calendar. Ryder, can we use your old house to meet in?

CARROLL: We'll need some whisky. Better make up a list of our men.

CASEY: Everybody got a pen and some ink. Here's some paper.

CARROLL: Sunday's out. There are only two possible days—this and this.

RYDER: Why?

CARROLL: Unless you want to wait until after the hearing which is going to fall through and then they're at our throats for malicious arrest.

RYDER: Tell us what to write. No, Ash Wednesday would be bad luck, you're ...

CARROLL (*Directly to us*): Tie up your dogs tonight. Keep them inside. If you hear any noise outside, pay no heed. We'll need 50 copies of that.

RYDER: When do we hand them out ? *They tear paper.*

CARROLL: Not until after we hear what this priest has to say at mass on Sunday.

CHORUS: Oh, three men went to Deroughata
      To sell three loads of rye.
      They shouted up and they shouted down
      The barley grain should die.
      (Refrain)
      Tiree igery ary ann, Tiree igery ee,
      Tiree igery ary ann, The barley grain for me.

SCENE 7
MASS AT ST. PATRICK'S, FEBRUARY 1880

Bell rustily ringing. Narrator (EPHRAIM) looks on, helps arrange all the carts (thaw) needed and general big effects. But don't wait for this to be finished. Begin the scene and let assistants work on as best they may in getting ready. Use kids' wagons and sleighs. Inside the church, a CHOIR sings loudly the Dies Irae. As the church opens, it reveals a FATHER CONNOLLY in a wolfskin coat plus a large congregation, all of whom are standing.

CHOIR: Dies Irae, dies illa
      Solvet saeclum in favilla,
      Teste David cum Sibylla.

Organ, then ...

FATHER CONNOLLY: And no one is to give the Donnellys water for their horses. And no one is to forget that last September, their buggy was standing outside their log shanty when a whirlwind came thundering up to its divine destruction.

CHORUS: Amen.

FATHER CONNOLLY: Then at the harvest-time, I will order the harvesters: Collect the weeds first, and bundle them up to burn. But gather the wheat into my barn. ... Bundle them up to burn. And I say to you that whoever has burnt down the barns of Patrick Ryder, their house—a ball of fire from Heaven shall fall on that house before this month is out. Kneel, all those who propose to obey this driving out.

Thunderously, nearly everyone kneels, but not all—three or four families—all of the KEEFES, some of the RYDERS, anybody not from Tipperary—do not kneel. MR. and MRS. DONNELLY proceed to the church steps and wait to see who will give them a ride home.

PRIEST: Ita, missa est ...

Scores walk by the DONNELLYS. We hear the scrapes of scores of carts and sleighs.

MR. DARCY: Good morning, Mr. and Mrs. Donnelly.

MR. DONNELLY: Mr. Darcy ...

MR. DARCY: Well, I'm surely sorry Mr. and Mrs. Donnelly, but my wife and I, in view of what Father Connolly has just said, dare not offer you the ride home we gave you from home.

MRS. DONNELLY: How are we then to get home, Mr. Darcy?

MR. DARCY (*Pause*): Shanks mare? I do not know. Perhaps you should not have come.

MRS. DARCY: One thing I never have understood, Mr. and Mrs. Donnelly. You still have five sons and one daughter. Your crippled son, William? He has a fine cart. Why does he not bring you to mass and home ?

MRS. DONNELLY: My sons refuse to attend mass where they are preached at from the altar time after time. They get up early and drive down to Father Flannery in St. Thomas for mass and confession. Actually we do not need such a long ride as home. We are invited to the Armitages for dinner. But a mile away.

MRS. DARCY: That is out of our way. Good day.

MRS. DONNELLY: And good day to both of you, Mr. and Mrs. Darcy. We shall see you next Sunday.

Swarms of carts, wagons, even a sleigh go by steps of church. FATHER CONNOLLY in wolfskin coat talks to parishioners. Crowd thins a bit.

SCHOOLMASTER: Father Connolly (*He is recently married to MARIA KEEFE whose wedding dance the DONNELLY boys were attending January 14 at start of play*).

PRIEST (*Growling*): Good morning, schoolmaster Panton.

PANTON: Father Connolly, Maria and myself were just saying how ridiculous these incendiary charges are against Mr. and Mrs. Donnelly. How could people their age be expected to run across fields of snow?

PRIEST: Oh, is that what you think, eh?

PANTON: Four feet deep. How absurd?

PRIEST: Oh yes, how absurd.

MARIA: Father Connolly, they are only accused because James Carroll could not bring a case at all against the boys.

PRIEST: Because you played the tawdry, cheap little bride dancing all night so the barn had to be burnt down by the old people. Look at them. They're no weaklings.

PANTON: (*Pause.*) Good morning, Father Connolly.

PRIEST: Who do you think you are?

PANTON: One of your parishioners, sir.

PRIEST: And a mere schoolmaster. Stick to your rod and your abacus and your slate. Parish policy is my preserve. And, Mrs. Panton, don't try the strong minded woman bit with me. You see where that has got your tall friend over there. Alone on the steps of my church. Alone! No one shall give them aid.

MARIA: May we go now, Father Connolly?

PRIEST: What care I. Go. *He turns just in time to see MARIA'S FATHER, JAMES KEEFE, address the congregation from his wagon. The PANTONS move to comfort the DONNELLYS.*

JAMES KEEFE: I, James Keefe, wish to tell the people (*Pause*) to tell you that as long as I have horses and wagons to my name (*Pause*) I shall always have room in my cart for James and Judith Donnelly to ride wherever they wish to go for as long—as long as ever!

FATHER CONNOLLY shakes his fist at him and backs up the steps into his church. The KEEFES, PANTONS, and DONNELLYS drive away. Snow. Darkness. A lantern.

SCENE 8
FAREWELL

Suddenly, we are back at the DONNELLY house first seen at the start of the play. This time in the house EPHRAIM has just risen, dressed and eaten breakfast with the DONNELLYS.

EPHRAIM: Yes, I'm sorry to leave you so early in the morning, Mr. and Mrs. Donnelly, but—oh John's hitched up my team—it'll be nightfall before I land home in Logan.

THE DONNELLYS, THE TWO GIRLS (*Faintly*): Goodbye, Mr. Flummerfelt.

EPHRAIM: Um Gott Willen, I shall see you next summer and help you harvest your wheat.

Ghostly laughter. JOHN (Lantern) hands over sleigh to narrator, fades away. Suddenly, MRS. DONNELLY dressed and bonnettted for travel, runs toward FLUMMERFELT's sleigh —

MRS. DONNELLY: Ephraim Flummerfelt! Please. Could you take me to the railway station at St. Marys?

EPHRAIM: Where is it you wish to go Mrs. Donnelly?

MRS. DONNELLY: Out of Biddulph. For the first time in my life, I'm afraid. Jim, don't try to stop me. They won't recognize his sleigh at the toll gates and I'll take the train to London, then transfer to the L & PS for St. Thomas.

MR. DONNELLY: Go, Judith. Give my love to our daughter Jenny and our grandchildren. And Mike's widow and hers. This will blow over when we sue them for making us suffer so. Safe home. Thank you and farewell Mr. Flummerfelt.

They wave goodbye.

We get one last mesmerizing shot of EPHRAIM coming towards us thro' snow white out with MRS. DONNELLY then lantern and lamp spark, blink, go out.

Epilogue

Suddenly, loud bird song, summer light, old woman in ditch picking strawberries, sleigh fades. Instead a wagon and horses are feeding under the shade of trees not there in 1880. But sleigh bells take a while to fade. We see that there is also an old man sitting watching the old woman. He is shorter than she is. After a while, we recognize the ghosts of MR. and MRS. DONNELLY. But we don't see their faces. Real live men now appear, and they walk without the "float" quality of the ghosts who often fade away as their viewers' minds gutter like candles. The white cloth (snow) on the downstage centre slides away to reveal the puppet EPHRAIM asleep on a plot of green grass. He lies inside a square formed of four stones. The two men are UNDERTAKER MUDIE who buried the DONNELLYS and McDIARMID, their lawyer.

McDIARMID: Good morning, young fellow, whoever you are.

EPHRAIM: I was just helping Mrs. Donnelly into the sleigh when—it was a bright morning with white clouds and blue sky and a fresh breeze—I could see an old woman picking strawberries in the ditch—strangely familiar. (*Pause. Puppet stands.*) And tying their horses to a fencepost—Mr. McDiarmid, the Donnellys' lawyer whom I had met at Lucan and Granton accompanied by a very sombrely clad gentleman just a shade too smooth in his manners.

EPHRAIM PUPPET: Good morning, Mr. McDiarmid. Mrs. Donnelly and myself are going to the railway station at St. Marys. Mrs. Donnelly, we'll be late for the London train. Please get into the ... *He is puzzled by the wagon.*

McDIARMID: You're not from these parts, lad. Where did you stay last night if I might ask?

EPHRAIM: With Mr. and Mrs. Donnelly. They very kindly took me in when it snowed so hard on January 14th. Oh, I was lost in the snowstorm coming south from Perth County. We met at their trial for incendiarism, Mr. McDiarmid.

McDIARMID: I have never met you before in my life!

EPHRAIM: Yes, you have. You asked me to witness on Mr. Donnelly's behalf before I made an errand to Southwold and once when I came back from there—why, yesterday.

McDIARMID: Nonsense! Where did you sleep last night?

EPHRAIM: Why, at the Donnellys' house over there. Where else? (*Music. House has gone. Screams as he turns and sees nothing but four stones on the green grass that mark where DONNELLY'S house used to be seven years ago!*) Where have they gone? Mrs. Donnelly! Come back, please. Where are you?

MUDIE: Young man, get hold of yourself. You may be driven mad by what I have to tell you so powerful and dangerous has been the illusion or spell someone has cast upon you. (*Music*) Young man, seven years ago, I received a box of burnt bones and tortured flesh already picked over by souvenir hunters.

EPHRAIM: Who are you, sir? I'm ... I'm Ephraim Flummerfelt, mein gott willen, from Perth County. My sleigh's turned into a wagon!

MUDIE: I am Undertaker Mudie of Lucan.

EPHRAIM: Whose bones?

MUDIE: Battered and smashed by a mob of 40 vigilantes who broke into their house on the night of February 4, 1880, murdered Tom, Bridget, their mother, their father. Burned the house over their heads. Ran to Whalen's Corners, called out Will Donnelly, got John Donnelly instead and shot him. *Lay puppet away.*

Human actor now. *Big death portrait of JOHN DONNELLY in coffin projected above.*

EPHRAIM (*Cries out, runs to the four stones. picks them up, kisses them, rolls about the site of his dream visit in howls of grief*): Then I did not help her escape. My Donnellys. My wonderful, lovely Donnellys. How could they have made so many hate you when—you weren't like that! I know. I met you. I want to die with them! *Pulls out knife. The two older men lift him up and comfort him.*

McDIARMID: There, Mr. Flummerfelt. It was only a dream. But many in these parts have seen them walking, in broad daylight, at twilight. They died unshriven.

EPHRAIM: But, Mr. McDiarmid, it was not a dream. They invited me to stay the night and they fed me.

MUDIE: Generally speaking, Ephraim Flummerfelt, it's not wise to accept food from the shades of the departed. Occasionally, in a professional way, I am afflicted with a supernatural visitant at my undertaking parlour. I never accept food or gifts or conversational sallies.

EPHRAIM: Why, there's the impression of my body in the grass between the four stones. That's (*Pause*) where I fell asleep.

McDIARMID: Yes, Mr. Flummerfelt. Aye yes, whoever slept between those four stones might dream of the Donnellys.

MUDIE: Neighbours here, customers, (*Pause*) tell me that at night suddenly the house appears all lit up, but run across the road to have a closer look and—vanishes in a puff of smoke. (*Takes out scissors, gives them to EPHRAIM.*)

EPHRAIM: Where was I really then? Why are you giving me these scissors ?

McDIARMID: Your hair and your nails have grown long wherever you have been, sir, down among the restless dead. Let Mr. Mudie tonsure you. He's good at it.

EPHRAIM: I let him, though the thought occurred to me that I had died and was being prepared for burial.

McDIARMID: There are certain things we must now tell you. (*Pause*) Mudie?

MUDIE: Information reached me through the relatives of a recent customer that someone had put their wagon in the Donnelly yard and had fallen asleep two nights back inside the four stones.

McDIARMID: When Mr. Mudie passed this on to me, I telegraphed Constable William Donnelly in Glencoe, and asked for procedural advice.

MUDIE: He told us that any trespasser on his parents' farm should be told to leave, but when we came yesterday you looked so innocent and to be enjoying yourself so much that we threw an old blanket over you, told the neighbours to feed and water your horses, and—decided to wake you up today.

EPHRAIM: Which is?

McDIARMID: You tell me.

EPHRAIM: February the 3rd, 1880. *The older men laugh.*

McDIARMID: June 21st, 1887.

EPHRAIM: But it was so real!

MUDIE: If it was real, then perhaps you have some memento of your visit.

EPHRAIM: John Donnelly gave me some sleigh bells. One, a tiny one, I kept back in my pocket. (*He produces it, it rings, but then it fades away.*)

McDIARMID: Ah, fairy bells melt like dewdrops in the sun.

EPHRAIM: Wait! Mrs. Donnelly, in gratitude for my financial help with the bail, gave me a handkerchief edged in black, sewn in remembrance of her son Michael's death. (*He produces the handkerchief! The DONNELLY ghosts reappear.*) Look. There they are now. Picking wild strawberries. Look! They beckon me to accept some berries.

McDIARMID: Do not go over. Ghosts kill friends too, you know. Anything to have some company in Limbo. They're lonely, are the dead.

MUDIE: We can't see the ghosts, by the way, Mr. Flummerfelt. Or can you, Mr. McDiarmid?

McDIARMID: No, no. Now this handkerchief is a marvel. It has Judith Donnelly's name sewn upon it and should not exist because all the household linen was destroyed in the fire. *Slowly, he slides it into his pocket.*

EPHRAIM: I wanted so much to taste the strawberries.

The ghosts show their faces which are horrifying skulls. Laughing shrilly, they throw the berries at EPHRAIM and vanish. He screams at their skull faces. Pause. MUDIE and McDIARMID walk EPHRAIM over to his wagon. Help him up.

EPHRAIM: I drove out of the yard in my wagon. I knew my life would never be the same again. They warned me that at the river, the ghosts might cause me trouble again.

He comes to a bridge at twilight. Owl. Moon. From the water, four black gloved hands reach up and grasp the ankles of the horses who panic.

EPHRAIM: Whoa, Wilhelmina! Quiet, Golden!

A young girl (THERESA) steps up from under the bridge.

THERESA: Cross yourself, Ephraim Flummerfelt. It was myself sewed that handkerchief. Cross yourself.

EPHRAIM: No, Theresa. I'm not in the habit of ...

THERESA: Like this. *She crosses herself. Vanishes as he does cross himself. Music as he drives on out of sight.*

EPHRAIM: Crossing the river, crossing the river broke the spell I had been under.

The end.

Alan Filewod

THE TOYSHOP OF MYTH: JAMES REANEY AND *SLEIGH WITHOUT BELLS*

Few evenings in the theatre are engraved as brightly in my memory as the night in 1973 when James Reaney's *Sticks and Stones* opened in Toronto at the Tarragon Theatre. This was the first instalment in what would later be known as the Donnelly Trilogy, an epic, playful and mythic retelling of the history of the Black Donnellys, a history, largely passed into folklore, of the bloody feud in a community of Irish immigrants in southwestern Ontario in the late 19th century.

When *Sticks and Stones* opened to astonished audiences twenty years ago, it seemed as if Canadian theatre had made a quantum leap. I remember sitting in awe as the ensemble of actors returned us to the story-telling sources of theatre, combining lyric poetry, ribald physicality and stern melodrama to reveal that the local details of regional culture—the details of our own back-yards—carried echoes of deeper myths. During the interval I did something I had never done before, had never thought of doing before: along with many others in the audience, I walked onto the playing space to touch the great assembly of *objets trouvés* that comprised the set. These simple objects were the materials from which the play was made: on the stage sat an assortment of ladders, stones, barrels and wagon-wheels; the walls were covered with pro-clamations, old newspapers and archival photos, and the set was littered with (to quote from the stage manager's prop list):

> breaking fiddle, 2 thorn branchs, handspike, surveyor's peg, bamboo cane, slingshot, 1 sawing block, 7 medium stones, 1 house window, cats cradle string, turnip sword, 5 water cloths, Mr D[onnelly] silver glasses, rope handcuffs, 1 petition, 2 Union Jacks, census book, deed, mouth horseshoe, pregnancy pillow, &c.[1]

A recurring image in Reaney's poetry and drama is that of the kalaidoscope; in *Sticks and Stones* he turned his kalaidoscopic eye to our colonial history, and revealed it as a place of wonder; in his theatre we become children in a toyshop.

Sticks and Stones was followed in quick order by the other two parts of the trilogy: *The St Nicholas Hotel* in 1974, and *Handcuffs* in 1975. All three plays were created out of workshops with NDWT [Ne'er-Do-Well Thespians] Theatre under the direction of Keith Turnbull. The workshops were public and often involved children; Reaney and Turnbull would invite participants to play with

---

puppets, household objects and lists—lists of names, of places, of dates—and Reaney would weave these patterns together with his poetry. He is at once the most poetic and the least literary of Canadian playwrights.

Three recurring elements can be found in Reaney's dramaturgy, and they explain why *Sleigh Without Bells* (published for the first time in this volume) is both a logical extension of *Sticks and Stones*, and a curious anomaly in contemporary Canadian playwriting. The first of these is Reaney's deep attachment to the idea of myth, which he explored as a scholar when studying under Northrop Frye, and which he mined as a poet and a dramatist. The teachings of Frye and Jung form a substratum in all of Reaney's writings, including his idea that

> the basic plot of all dramas revolves around a dragon and a witch meeting up with a knight and a helpful dwarf who save a beautiful half of the knight's full self called, in William Blake, his emanation or ... girl friend. To this add gracioso, agroikos, pantaloon, old, old women, really sweet ingénues (for the subplot); make the dragon into King Lear as hero, and the young mesomorphic knight into an Edmund (the eiron character is reversible) and you have the plot of tragedy, turn it again and you have romantic comedy.[2]

In the Donnellys trilogy, Reaney transforms a bitter rural feud between warring factions of Irish settlers into a cosmic battle of archetypes. The best description of his mythic retelling can be found in his own preface to *Sticks and Stones* which was itself lifted from the programme notes of the original production:

> The play is based on the story of an actual family who came out from Ireland in 1844 to Biddulph Township 18 miles from London, Ontario, and were nearly annihilated by a secret society formed among their neighbours 36 years later. In the text before you the reader will meet Mr and Mrs Donnelly, their son William and their only daughter Jennie. The other six sons appear but they appear most clearly in the form of their shirts on Mrs Donnelly's washing line. Watch for friends of the Donnellys—Andrew Keefe, the taverner, and Jim Feeney, the traitor. Their neighbours form a Catholic road of farmers' names and a Protestant road. Then there are enemies: George Stub, a Protestant merchant in the nearby village; and Tom Cassleigh, a neighbour who was tried several times for killing an Englishman named Brimmacombe. Both these gentlemen are also local magistrates! Two more enemies are close neighbours—called here Mr and Mrs Fat; also Pat Farl whom Mr Donnelly killed at a logging bee. There is also a Medicine Showman who puts on a rival play to mime how fiendish the Donnellys were; there are constables, census takers, gaolers, Negro settlers, surveyors, the pyromaniac eight Gallagher boys, Mrs Farl, a bishop and many others.[3]

This description seems to promise a boisterous melodrama, and to a large extent that promise is fulfilled: *Sticks and Stones* is crowded with character and incident. In that regards it bears comparison to the Royal Shakespeare Company's later *Nicholas Nickleby*, which used similar ensemble storytelling techniques. But *Sticks and Stones* is also a poetic drama, in which formal structures of recitation and lyric emotion provide the mythic counterweight to the prosaic ribaldry of melodramatic performance. Consider, for example, Jennie's speech in the final scene towards the end of the play, when she answers her brother's question, "Why was I a Donnelly?"

JENNIE

[*Distribute this speech among the women; some men join in later*]

Because from the courts of Heaven when you're there you will see that however the ladders and sticks and stones caught you and bruised you and smashed you, and the bakers and brewers forced you to work for them for nothing, from the eye of God in which you will someday walk you will see [*use ladders held up and moved back and forth by the cast*] that once, long before you were born [*sometimes together, sometimes solo*] you chose to be a Donnelly and laughed at what it would mean [...] So I am proud to be a Donnelly against all the contempt in the world. I am proud that my mother confirmed my brother in the forest with a fiddle [...]

Because you were tall; you were different / and you weren't afraid, that is why they burnt you first with their tongues / and then with their kerosene.[4]

Almost all of Reaney's poetry and drama resonates with similar passion expressed through enhanced but still idiomatic language. The manichean structures of melodrama restate the deeper conflicts between good and evil, order and chaos, made known through poetry. As poet and dramatist, Reaney's particular genius lies in his ability to locate these conflicts in simple, familiar objects and places. His key in this is his talent for recapturing the perceptions of childhood, in which wonder and delight are offset by exaggerated fears and nightmares—including the ghosts that figure so largely in his Donnelly plays, especially in *Sleigh Without Bells*. It is no accident that much of *Sticks and Stones* is constructed through children's games and songs; the actors quite literally play with the various ladders, barrels and objects that comprise the stage setting.

The idea of the theatre as a toyshop is the second recurring element in Reaney's writing. At its simplest, the toyshop is the transformation of commonality into objects of wonder, just as a kaleidoscope fragments and reconstitutes the images it receives. Reaney has spoken of his "catalogue philosophy," which delights in lists:

the catalogue is an exuberant, elastic structure, a segmented boa constrictor with which you can swallow your neighbourhood, your town, your province—tomorrow the universe![5]

In a famous example from his play *Colours in the Dark*, actors form a family tree pyramid:

It takes
Two parents
Four grandparents
Eight Great grandparents
Sixteen Great great grandparents
Thirty-two Great great great grandparents
Sixty-four Great great great great grandparents
One hundred and twenty-eight Great great great great great
grandparents
Two hundred and fifty-six Great great great great great great
grandparents
Five hundred and twelve Great great great great great great
great grandparents
One thousand and twenty-four Great great great great great great
great great grandparents[6]

In his staging notes, Reaney acknowledges that "It would take over a thousand people to do this scene." The process of finding ways to theatricalize such information is the essence of his stagecraft; with a thousand actors, the scene would be pedantic and likely boring; with thirty-two it becomes an act of metonymic fancy. In *Sticks and Stones*, catalogues of names form a lacework of oral geography through the action. The names are pieces in a verbal game constructed of chants and recitation:

[*Use a long ladder as the core of this: whistle "Lillibulero" under—this tune will meet the banjo tune behind the Negro settlers' protest—the chorus forms a double line that faces us with one black in its midst.*

Who settled the third & fourth concessions?
Protestants Johnsons

STICKS HALF CHORUS	STONES HALF CHORUS
Big Jim, Little Jim, Jerry Jim	Johnson
Big John's John's George	Johnson
Big Tom's John's George	Johnson
and	

	Attery	Stubb
	Armwright	Latchett
	Courcey	Blackwell protestants
and pioneers! The Guernseys		& the Cobbetts
came with them it appears		And then
BLACK *banjo* What about the Mescoes		& the Washingtons
	Taylors	Runcimans
	Delkeys	& the Bells[7]

Along with catalogues, the second revealing item to be found in Reaney's toyshop is the ubiquitous figure of the puppet. For Reaney, a puppet is any semiotic device that can be manipulated in front of an audience, whether it be the hand-puppets he introduced in *Sticks and Stones* to represent the Governor General and his Lady, or the seven shirts on a line that speak for the seven Donnelly boys. In *Sleigh Without Bells*, one of several recent works written for puppets, the most memorable image may be the puppet that represents Mr Donnelly: a lantern with a hand attached to it. In every case, the puppet is an object handled visibly by an actor. Delight in puppetry is a typifying feature of Reaney's drama, not just because the puppet is a common childhood toy but also because puppetry constructs a relationship between puppet and manipulator that creates new opportunities for gestural story-telling. In that sense, the puppet liberates the actor, just as a mask can liberate a clown.

Puppets also bring to mind the puppet theatres of Reaney's childhood, which surface in his plays in the form of lurid medicine shows. The first act of *Sticks and Stones* is interrupted by the entrance of just such a show, which plays two exaggerated scenes that recapitulate the rural legend of the demonized "Black Donnellys". The scene functions to situate Reaney's version of the story against popular memory, but at the same time it is a tribute to the rough theatricality of the playwright's own childhood.

The third recurring element in Reaney's work is his deep attachment to his geographical home in south-western Ontario (which he has in his poetry renamed "Souwesto.") Reaney was born near the Donnelly's homestead, and has since lived and worked (as a Professor of English at the University of Western Ontario) close to his birthplace. In his attachment to his place and its history, we can see a replaying of a common postcolonial paradox, in which attachment to place is complicated by a nostalgia for cultural authenticity the place cannot fulfil. The postcolonial subject lives in a state of disruption, in which a sense of belonging to the land is mediated by a feeling of imposition. In his 1962 poem, "To the Avon River above Stratford, Canada," Reaney expressed this paradoxical love for a place that is given meaning only in terms alien (indeed invasive) to it:

What did the Indians call you?
For you do not flow
With English accents.
I hardly know
What I should call you
Because before
I drank coffee or tea
I drank you
With my cupped hands
And you did not taste English to me [...][8]

This desire to understand *place*, to reconcile the displaced European traditions with the North American land, is a passionate motif in Reaney's work. The passion is genuine but Reaney's equal passion for deep myth leads him away from sentimental romanticism or cheap patriotism. Reaney's attachment to place is not an ideological abstraction but rather a sharing of community and family experience—a life-long attempt, perhaps, to uncover the true name of the place that formed him.

These three imperatives—of myth, play and place—find remarkable expression in *Sleigh Without Bells*. Here we have a ghost story written for puppets by a playwright considered by many to be the finest in Canada; indeed, my suspicion is that he is one of the handful of great playwrights writing in English today. And yet, like much of Reaney's recent work, *Sleigh Without Bells* is shrouded in obscurity and in all likelihood destined to be read as a curiosity. The play deserves a better fate than that, but its marginalization may be an inevitable result of Reaney's problematic relationship with the Canadian theatre community.

Sleigh Without Bells is a play of intertexts and gestures, a theatrical footnote to the Donnellys trilogy which expands motifs found in the earlier plays and which can be read as a reflective commentary on them. The story roughly parallels the events of *Handcuffs*, which narrates the final months of arrests, harassment and conspiracy which culminated in the infamous murder of the Donnelly family in 1880. Several sequences, notably the trial of Judith Donnelly and the subsequent plotting of the conspirators in scene seven, are compressed quotations from *Handcuffs*, just as the False Donnelly puppet play in scene five is taken directly from the Medicine Show in *Sticks and Stones*. But the framing ghost story of the rustic Ephraim Flummerfelt, who meets the ghosts of the Donnellys seven years after their death, is entirely new. The tone of the play is elegiac; in its poetic recreation of the moods of the Canadian winter, it suggests a mysterious natural order which directs human action. As young Ephraim wanders through the storm that begins the play (signified by shadows, waving semi-transparent curtain and muted sound effects), we hear the voices of the world that surrounds him:

HAWK:	I was the hawk that watched him make his first mistake from my tree. He chose the road I wanted him to take, not the safe one his mother and father, good Protestant souls, sagely advised.
DEER:	We were the deer whose antlers he glimpsed in the swamp bottom. We could smell him and his sweaty horses.
RIVER:	I was the river that last week knocked out the bridge he should have used so that he would lose his way and find the place he was most afraid of.[9]

Ephraim is lost in a mythic world, a world where young heroes encounter dragons and dwarves, or in this case, murdered souls. The structure of *Sleigh Without Bells* is taken from fairy stories, themselves repositories of literary archetypes: finding himself in a haunted place, Ephraim falls asleep and enters the dream world where the Donnellys relive their trials; when he awakes it is summer again and he continues his journey, gifted with special knowledge.

Two questions need to be posed against this play: Why did Reaney reconfigure the Donnellys as a ghost story? And why did he write this as a play for puppets? The first is the more easily answered. *Sleigh Without Bells* removes the play of the Donnellys even further from its archival sources, and in this expresses Reaney's own experience with the material. As he has written, the original Donnelly's project began with historical and archival research, a process that was built into the trilogy by the inclusion of documentary evidence. In his forword to *Sticks and Stones*, Reaney wrote that,

> When you immerse yourself in this play, you may find that your experience matches my own when I immersed myself some eight years ago in documents which had lain for years and years in the attics of two local courthouses: after a while I couldn't stop thinking about them.[10]

In the twenty years since he created *Sticks and Stones*, Reaney has clearly continued to think about those documents, but his thinking has gone more deeply into their underlying structures and myths—from history to story to archetype. The quotations from *Sticks and Stones* and *Handcuffs* perform the same authentifying function in *Sleigh Without Bells* that documentary evidence did in the original plays by providing a foundation of public knowledge. The fairy story frame enables Reaney to tell his own story, the story of the innocent who finds himself immersed in the Donnellys and caught up in their fate, but who in the end awakens and leaves them in the past. In that sense, *Sleigh Without Bells* is a dramatic autobiography of one man's obsession with the Donnellys.

Reaney's decision to write this introspection as a play for puppets is a more complex problem, because it raises the question of his ambiguous reception in the professional theatre community in Canada. *Sleigh Without Bells* is written to be performed by an eclectic assortment of hand-puppets, cut-out dolls and manipulated objects, and in this regard it extends the occasional puppetry found in the trilogy. Unquestionably it attests to Reaney's abiding love for pure theatricality. But at the same time, his return to puppets is a gesture of defiance to a professional theatre that has rejected him. The Donnellys trilogy was the high tide of Reaney's career in the professional theatre; since then most of his work has been with community and university theatres, and more recently, in opera. In part this is because Reaney's plays usually require larger casts and longer rehearsal periods than most theatres can afford, but in equal measure it is because Reaney has refused to compromise his vision to meet the demands of the theatres; his most recent Toronto production, *Gyroscope* (a realistic chamber comedy), was received as a disappointing retreat from his characteristic dramaturgy. But if critics wanted another *Sticks and Stones*, the theatres themselves weren't interested. In the 1970s the trilogy was widely acclaimed as a masterpiece of Canadian playwriting, but it has rarely been performed outside of universities and high schools since. And whereas in England the Royal Shakespeare Company was willing to devote time and energy towards an epic like *Nicholas Nickleby*, it is a sad comment on Canadian theatre that the Stratford Shakespearean Festival, Canada's answer to the RSC, has not performed any Reaney play at all since its 1967 production of *Colours in the Dark*. That fact is bitterly ironic when one considers that the Stratford Festival is situated in Reaney's "Souwesto," less than fifty miles from his home, and is built on the banks of the same river—the Avon—that Reaney pondered in his 1962 poem. In what other country could the greatest living dramatist live so close to the largest theatre and be so totally isolated from it? In a word, the Canadian theatre community has treated Reaney shabbily.

Reaney's return to puppets has enabled him to continue his creative work on his own terms, although he has often spoken in public of the anger he holds towards the professional theatre. On several occasions Reaney has announced his dream of touring a puppet production of the Donnelly trilogy across Canada, and although few have taken him seriously, *Sleigh Without Bells* is welcome evidence that he was not merely speaking whimsically.

Bibliography

Jean McKay, "Interview with James Reaney," in: Stan Dragland (Ed.), *Approaches to the Work of James Reaney* (Toronto: 1983).

Gerald D. Parker, *How to Play: The Theatre of James Reaney* (Toronto: 1991).

James Reaney, *The Donnellys* (Erin, ON:. 1975).

James Reaney, *14 Barrels From Sea To Sea* (Erin, ON.: 1977).

James Reaney, *Performance Poems* (Goderich, ON.: 1990).

James Reaney, *Poems* (Toronto: 1972).

James Reaney, *Sleigh Without Bells* published in this volume.

James Reaney, *Sticks and Stones* (Erin, Ont.: 1975).

Notes

[1] Reaney 1977, 7.

[2] Reaney 1990, 83.

[3] Reaney, *Sticks and Stones*, 1975, 7.

[4] Reaney, *Sticks and Stones*, 1975, 154.

[5] Reaney 1990, 82-83.

[6] Reaney 1972, 277.

[7] Reaney, *Sticks and Stones*, 1975, 50.

[8] Reaney 1972, 211.

[9] Reaney, *Sleigh Without Bells, 266.*

[10] Reaney, *Sticks and Stones*, 1975, 7.

Banuta Rubess

STONE AGE
(Part Two of HEAD IN A BAG)

STONE AGE is a companion piece to *HEAD IN A BAG*, even though it is not, properly speaking, the second act. The action happens in the present, even the future. It is about ice cracking, about fissures. Large boulders toppling down a mountain. Where in Part One, everything is interwoven, here pieces are discrete. Chunks toppling down, one by one. Organizing principles are the corpses found underneath the ice and the snow, how the stones are put to use, and a primitive, public violence as punishment and proof that tormentors have (supposedly) been eliminated.

All characters except the CRONE have an unrealistic pallor, they are in GREY FACE—the color of stones, dried mud, of death.

The stage is dominated by a long wall with several doors and filing cabinets.

STONE AGE requires immediacy: work with an ensemble to be in touch with the current political and moral debate. It is always unfinished, even on closing night.

Scenes and Characters

In all scenes, CRONE, an ancient woman

SCENE 1: 1989-90.

NICOLAE and ELENA CEAUCESCU, the dead Romanian dictators.
NICOLAE 2 and ELENA 2, the dictators in better times
A TOURIST

SCENE 2: SUMMER 1991.

MINISTER OF EXTERNAL AFFAIRS, anxious and ill-informed
AIDES A, B, C

SCENE 3: A TRAIN IN PARIS, 1992.

A VEILED MIDDLE EASTERN WOMAN
DAGMAR AND DETLEF, prosperous people
AN AMERICAN TOURIST
A SHABBY MAN, from East Berlin

SCENE 4: A SMALL PRIVATE PLANE OF A LARGE AMERICAN COMPANY.

PILOT CORPSE
PUBLIC RELATIONS (PR) PERSON for Benefax Corporation
STEWARDESS, a North American
THE PRIME MINISTER OF A NEWLY INDEPENDENT COUNTRY

SCENE 5: CRONE DRAWS CONCLUSIONS

DAGMAR
SHABBY MAN

SCENE 6: ADVANCED CAPITALISM VS. PRIMITIVE CAPITALISM

BOBBY, the Canadian businessman
TWO THUGS, ANNA and MARIKA, shabby but fashionably dressed, long suffering East European women

SCENE 7: THE FACILITIES.

WOMAN IN PINK (with child), an East German
TOILET CUSTODIAN, a sour old man, a West German

SCENE 8: A WAR

MINISTER OF EXTERNAL AFFAIRS
AIDES A, B, C

SCENE 9: A LETTER FROM THE PLAYWRIGHT.

TOURIST

SCENE 10: THE WALL, CANADA.

ELLEN, as in HEAD IN A BAG: PART ONE, only transposed to the future—the idealist
SAPPHIRE, as in HEAD IN A BAG: PART ONE, only transposed to the future—the pragmatist
MOUNTIE CORPSE
HOODED EXECUTIONER

SCENE 11: FINALE.

ENSEMBLE

SCENE 1
1989-90

The world is covered in snow, or is it bone dry dust? Nothing moves. Everything that happens is on the principle of vivid colour against white or grey.
CRONE is caught in the light, a survivor.

CRONE: The first time it gets cold you just build a big fire. You think it will go away. Then you find a frozen monkey at your door. Then you notice you haven't

---

heard a pterodactyl for a long time. Then you start counting your goosebumps and you know it's the Ice Age.

People didn't know what to do. A lot of them tried to run away from the cold. A lot of them died. Some people painted in dangerous places. In hidden caves. You had to be mighty courageous to do a thing like that. You had to manoeuvre torrentious waterfalls, crawl through underground tunnels. It was crazy. I mean, even when you got there ... lions and bears. The painting. It's not for you to see. It's for the great power. It's for the ice. It was a sacrifice. Elsewhere, some people were bludgeoned and eaten. This too was a sacrifice.

There's one picture in particular. There's a bison, a hunter and a rhinoceros. The hunter was lying on his back. He'd been gored. Gored. He was bleeding, he was going to die. In the other neck of the woods, the bison stared at the hunter's spear in his stomach. "What kind of animal is this biped? Who thought of this mutation?" the bison wondered in his agony. Or did he?

And then there's the rhinoceros. Big strong rhinoceros standing off in the corner doing nothing. Couldn't he trample on the bison, flip the hunter over and break his neck? Lick their wounds and tears? Do something? Standing still.

This was the painting. The bison, the hunter, the rhinoceros. This was the sacrifice. They vanished in the snow.

CRONE crosses the stage excruciatingly slowly. She discovers a CORPSE lying on the ground, steals matches from it. Its bloodsoaked shirt says 1 9 8 9. She scavenges throughout the play.

CRONE: And when the ice cracked, all you could see was corpses floating up. Two woolly mammoths, frozen and preserved. A baby crocodile, thawing quickly. An ice cube full of mice. Yeah, the sun. The occasional chinook. I had to look for fire. Where's the fire?

The match illuminates NICOLAE and ELENA CEAUCESCU. They lie on the ground, their heads leaning against each other, wearing winter coats, looking up at the sky. They are dead. Gunshots in their chests and head. They are covered in light snow.

Two more corpses are slumped against the wall, looking dazed. They are NICOLAE 2 and ELENA 2.

ELENA: Kiss me.

NICOLAE: I can't.

Loud music suddenly plays, stately and sombre anthems, all cast singing along loudly and lustily, out of synch. The music ends abruptly.

ELENA: Nicolae, darling, are you uncomfortable? Darling, are you uncomfortable?

NICOLAE: No, why? I like lying on the stone cold ground in the middle of winter.

ELENA: But it's the ground of Rumania. The ground of our homeland. Our ground.

NICOLAE: Scum. Terrorists. CIA.

ELENA: We never take time to relax like this. To just look at the sky. Look at the sky. To think about life, our lives, our children's lives.

NICOLAE: Well, now we're looking.

ELENA: Why don't you kiss me, you should kiss me.

NICOLAE: I can't, you know I can't.

CRONE searches the other corpses.

NICOLAE: Everything's falling apart. People don't care anymore. They say one thing and they mean another. You promise them their own private home with running water and they're babbling away to foreign correspondents behind your back .

ELENA: Hearts of stone.

NICOLAE: Hearts, who's talking about hearts?

ELENA (*Puckers up stiffly*): Please. Kiss me.

NICOLAE: You're being impossible! You know I can't.

The loud music resumes, the cast sings along again, then stops abruptly again, as if two people are disagreeing whether a radio station should be played or not.

A TOURIST strides briskly across the ledge of the wall. CRONE is still inching along.

ELENA: I'm so disappointed. Bogdan said he would come by with the porcelain, he never came. Admiral Flotescu said he would do it instead and he didn't. He couldn't blackmail a syphilitic priest, let alone—

NICOLAE: Flotescu, ha!

ELENA: Hearts of stone. Rumanian stone.

NICOLAE: We shoulda had a lawyer.

Loud music and singing resumes. NICOLAE 2 and ELENA 2 scramble to their feet. They are hysterical with fear. They back up against the wall as if facing a firing squad.

NICOLAE 2: A lawyer, a lawyer, you CIA terrorists.

ELENA 2: Nicolae, they're going to shoot.

CRONE raises her walker in the air. The stage is suddenly very very bright, the couple No. 2 fall against the wall as if shot. The music stops.

ELENA: You shoulda bribed the driver. You shoulda bribed the pilot and the driver.

NICOLAE: They weren't going to take it.

ELENA: You shoulda promised them something better.

NICOLAE: I promised them.

ELENA: Something better.

NICOLAE: What what what better to promise I promised! Ten thousand Swiss francs isn't that enough?

ELENA: Ten thousand Swiss francs, what does ten thousand Swiss francs mean to a Neanderthal?

NICOLAE: Maybe he wanted dollars.

ELENA: They are not like us, you know. They are the dull, plodding sons and daughters of the soil, they need something they know what it looks like and how it's gonna feel running down their leg. You shoulda promised them something better, all the butter they can eat, exit visas for their second cousins, a year's supply of sausages, something to stop them thinking for one split second of the one thing they are thinking about all the time which is how to stab us in the back, stab us in the back, stab us, stab us, stab us in the back.

NICOLAE: Well, now we're stabbed.

Pause.

NICOLAE: We shoulda had a lawyer.

A brief burst of loud music and singing. NICOLAE 2 and ELENA 2 get back to their feet, with champagne glasses in hand, very jovial, as if on TV.

NICOLAE 2: If you ask me whether I would do it all again, I would say I wouldn't change a thing, thank you very much. Thank you very much, except I would get a pilot's license.

ELENA 2: Nicolae was knighted by the Queen of England. Jimmy Carter treated us like kings. And Yasser Arafat is like a second cousin.

NICOLAE 2: If I've learned anything, it's take care of the family. Every ancient civilization knows this. The Aztecs know this. The Mafia knows this.

ELENA 2: Baboons know this.

NICOLAE 2: You stick to your family because blood is thicker than water.

ELENA 2: And you can't squeeze blood from a stone.

NICOLAE 2: That's right, sweetheart. You can't squeeze blood from a stone. Now this sounds complicated but it isn't. People who are not your family - you have to think of them as stones. Now you gotta respect them because they're hard, they're tough, and they're not going away. But in the long run, they're just stones. And you can't squeeze blood from them.

ELENA 2: But you can try.

They pop the cork and they drink the champagne. Tight spot on the couple on the ground. NICOLAE raises his head with tremendous difficulty. Tremors shake his entire body.

NICOLAE: We'll be back.

ELENA 2 waves royally.

ELENA 2: We'll be back!

LOUD MUSIC. ELENA 2 and NICOLAE 2 throw themselves against the wall, they fall through it. The wall becomes a mass of colour. It develops a crack. NICOLAE and ELENA struggle to their feet, singing rigidly. CRONE searches them both, ELENA stumbles offstage. She finds a match in NICOLAE'S pocket. She lights it, and pushes NICOLAE over her walker. She leaves the stage.

After a long pause, NICOLAE begins to move with the walker, like a grotesque spider. Music returns: Beethoven's FREUDE SCHOENER GOETTERFUNKEN.

SEGUE # 1: The stage is empty. LOUD MUSIC. The doors tremble. A MAN LIKE GORBACHEV appears through one door, in his pyjamas, carrying a candle. The back of his pyjamas says 1 9 9 1. He sits down and falls asleep, wakes up suddenly. He trips over a CORPSE. A door opens and slams. He turns as if caught. A dog barks. He tries to rip open another door, it's locked. All the doors are locked. They shake, and many dogs bark. Then the stage is silent. He pulls out a pink pencil and taps on a door. Then suddenly—

SCENE 2
SUMMER 1991

The MINISTER OF EXTERNAL AFFAIRS walks a zigzag through the space. People frantically open files and pass her telephones.

AIDE A: It's a coup. It's a coup. It's Russia.

AIDE B: Hairspray, minister.

MINISTER: It's too early for a coup.

AIDE C: It's not early over there, minister. There's an eight hour difference between Ottawa and Moscow.

MINISTER (*Withering*): I know that, Sneezy. Is this going to involve refugees? We've got enough of them already.

AIDE A: Just the usual statement from External Affairs.

AIDE B: I like the scarf, the scarf is good.

AIDE A: It's a group of hardliners. They claim Gorbachev is sick, he might be dead. Yeltsin is still alive, and people are gathering in the square.

AIDE C: Lots of tanks. Lots of soldiers.

AIDE A: Could get bloody. We've been working all night. Here's the file.

MINISTER: Oh please. (*waves A off*) Just teach me how to pronounce their names.

AIDE C: It's more complex than that.

MINISTER: I doubt it. Power is simple. It shifts. Hit me with the names, Danny.

AIDE A: It's a coup, goddamit.

MINISTER: They're used to coups. What am I supposed to do, send in the Canadian Army? Now get me their names and a blueberry muffin!

AIDE B has a muffin at the ready, the team exits.

SEGUE #2: CRONE, walking with a cane, opens the door to the TAPPING GOR-BACHEV. He exits, looks around him, immediately wants to return to the room, she slams the door on him. A forlorn tapping sound resumes. She opens the door, and the ENSEMBLE bursts in and ransacks the files—the Stasi offices of East Germany. The only text for this scene are a choice of words "Me" "You" and "Hey." The actions are improvised. Someone finds files full of information about themselves, someone else finds their spouse has informed on them, someone laughs hysterically, someone weeps bitterly. The year 1992 is found on a file folder. Loud playing of doomed anthems.

SCENE 3
A TRAIN IN PARIS, 1992

A VEILED MIDDLE EASTERN WOMAN and a prosperous couple, DETLEF and DAGMAR on a train. DAGMAR offers food to DETLEF (the muffin bag), he refuses, wincing.

Elsewhere on the train, an American TOURIST reading a big YELLOW NEWSPAPER, and listening to her Walkman, sits in a different part of the train. Now and then she sings along with her tape.

The CRONE sits in the middle of the train, occasionally singing snatches of anthems.

A SHABBY MAN appears in the doorway. He doffs his hat.

SHABBY MAN: Excuse me ladies and gentleman attention all German speakers on the train Paris-Berlin, I wish you a pleasant journey and ask for a moment's attention. I come from East Berlin and I have had my wallet stolen and now I can't get home. I wonder if by any chance you could help me financially for a ticket, even a few franc would do.

DETLEF and DAGMAR studiously ignore the SHABBY MAN. The VEILED WOMAN gives him money. He thanks her profusely and exits. DETLEF and DAGMAR shake their heads in disapproval.

DAGMAR: You shouldn't have done that you know. Excuse me—(*Over emphatically*) no should do that, no do. (*Enunciating*) NO. He's not going back to Berlin, he's going to stay here and pick pockets in Paris. Wander into restaurants and eat off plates the diners haven't finished. Get lost on the metro and make everybody late with his aimless dawdling. The trains are full of this Eurotrash.

DETLEF: When the wall came down,—brothers and sisters! (*Mimes kissing, embracing, then gestures with disgust*) Now: riots and refugees! Neo-Nazis and taxes, taxes!

DAGMAR: No do, no do.

VEILED WOMAN nods painfully.

DAGMAR (*Sotto voce to husband*): How she can stand to wear that thing.

DETLEF (*Sighing, shaking head*): Tribes.

The SHABBY MAN appears in the doorway of the TOURIST'S compartment. He doffs his hat.

SHABBY MAN: Excuse me ladies and gentleman attention all German speakers on the train Paris-Berlin, I wish you a pleasant journey and ask for a moment's attention. I come from East Berlin and I have had my wallet stolen and now I can't get home. I wonder if by any chance you could help me financially for a ticket, even a few franc would do.

THE TOURIST doesn't hear him.

SHABBY MAN: Excuse me, you are American?

He taps her roughly on the shoulder, she turns around and smiles.

SHABBY MAN: American?

He stretches out his hand to beg, she turns away. He insults her, at first with a smile, then more and more bitterly.

SHABBY MAN: American parasite. Multinational bloodsuck. Michael Jackson pig. No oil in Yugoslavia, yes? Kuwait, okay. Dan Quayle for you. Thank you, American.

The SHABBY MAN exits. He approaches the CRONE. He takes off his hat.

SHABBY MAN: Excuse me madame you speak German? I wish you a pleasant journey and ask for a moment's attention. I come from East Berlin and—

CRONE: This is terribly embarrassing. I have had my wallet stolen and now I can't get home. I wonder if by any chance you could help me out financially to collect money for a ticket, even a few franc would do.

THE SHABBY MAN pretends he doesn't understand what the Crone is saying.

SHABBY MAN: Non comprende. Ni ponimaio. Je ne comprends. ['I don't understand' in Italian, Russian, French]

The CRONE begs from everybody, they all leave. DAGMAR falls dead on the floor. The VEILED WOMAN gives the CRONE an orange and exits. The CRONE is about to eat the orange when she notices the SHABBY MAN hovering in the doorway. The CRONE leaves the orange on a chair for him, and exits. The SHABBY MAN staggers to the chair, picks up the orange, sits down, holds the orange to his heart and slumps back, dead.

American music plays.

SCENE 4
A SMALL PRIVATE PLANE OF A
LARGE AMERICAN COMPANY

A CORPSE-PILOT lies on top of the wall. The PUBLIC RELATIONS (PR) PERSON and the STEWARDESS stand at the doorway of the plane. PR PERSON brings a large basket filled with fruit, especially bananas. The basket is wrapped in cellophane.

PR: His English is excellent. It's admirable. Compared to some of the other prime ministers we've had on this plane, let me tell you, it's FLUENT. Fluent English. Hallelujah. (*Looking for a place for the fruit basket*) Put it here. Here? Here. Okay. Prime Minister over here, fruit over here. He's only been prime minister for a year, so you want to keep that in mind.

STEWARDESS: He was the playwright.

PR: No that's Czechoslovakia.

STEWARDESS: Oh. The music teacher.

PR: No that's Lithuania.

STEWARDESS: Oh. The movie star?

PR: I'll tell you all you need to know honey: he ain't no lawyer.

THE PRIME MINISTER OF A NEWLY INDEPENDENT COUNTRY (PM) steps onto the plane. He is a tired man. He has cut himself shaving, it's covered with a bandaid that seems too large. THE STEWARDESS is excited and awkward.

STEWARDESS: Welcome aboard, your honor. Sir. Please. Here.

PM: Thank you.

She shows him his seat. PR person pulls her aside, leaving PM alone with THE FRUIT. (See directions below regarding PRIME MINISTER and FRUIT)

PR: The Benefax brass wants all these new countries to get a real taste of our knowhow. Of service. Real service. I'm not talking about blow jobs. The little Polish girls giving blow jobs up and down the Autobahn these days for foreign currency, that is absolutely not what I am talking about.

STEWARDESS: I didn't think you were.

PR: I'm talking about basic American customer service. Hello. Good morning. Can I help you?

STEWARDESS: Sure.

PR: I wouldn't go into all this song and dance but you are going to be the only people on this plane, so ...

STEWARDESS: It's a small plane.

PR: A few more things to watch out for. These guys have been flying Aeroflot all their lives, so they don't know from seat belts. Fasten his for him. But when you do, try not to touch. They don't like being touched. Okay. Fine. And their dental service is terrible. So his breath stinks. He can't help it. You'll live. Okay. Have a nice flight. Any questions no. Ciao, baby.

The PM is alone with the fruit. The fruit tortures him. He's not sure whether he can eat it or not. It makes him very uncomfortable. Finally he goes over to the fruit basket, tears it open, pulls out the bananas, stuffs fruit into his pockets, eats as much as he can very quickly, puffs up the other stuff in the basket, hides the banana peel, wraps it all up in cellophane again, sits down abruptly when he hears the stewardess approach. He feigns asleep.

The STEWARDESS returns to the plane. She reaches over to do PM's seat belt. He reacts violently.

STEWARDESS: Sorry, seat belt, sorry, belt, here, lap, shut, danger, safety, simple.

PM (*Light accent*): Do you speak English?

STEWARDESS: (*Laughs too shrilly*) (*Scolds him*) Sure, yes, in fact, on behalf of myself, Captain Faznani and the crew, we'd like to welcome you aboard the American Way, a D-855 propeller plane, courtesy of Benefax International. During the flight, I'm at your service. That means drinks, blankets, whatever you need. Oh and this Celebration of Summer Fruit Cornucopia is for you. It's just another touch from Benefax to show you We Care.

A deep silence.

STEWARDESS: Really, have some fruit.

PM: Thank you. I'm not hungry.

STEWARDESS: They said you'd be starving.

PM: Thank you.

STEWARDESS: They said you'd gorf all these bananas in a minute.

PM: Thank you.

STEWARDESS: They said you probably hadn't seen bananas in years.

PM: It's a civilized country. What else did they say?

STEWARDESS: They said you've never had a credit card, your TVs have two channels, no Evian, no Elvis, no Tampax, no fax, can't drink the water, don't speak da English, your children are diseased, your abortions are brutal, your industry is rusty, your grammar is antiquated. They said you're anti-Semitic, homophobic, racist, sexist, computer illiterate alcoholics. That's what they said.

PM (*Leans forward and speaks right into her face*): Well, they lied. And we have excellent choirs.

The PRIME MINISTER'S breath could kill a cat.

STEWARD: Well! Then. Let's fasten our seat belts.

She fastens hers, he has no intention of doing so, she refuses to notice.

PRIME MINISTER sings to himself. They both slump forward, dead.

SCENE 5
CRONE DRAWS CONCLUSIONS

Primitive music. The CRONE throws the PILOT CORPSE off the wall. During CRONE'S text, DAGMAR and the SHABBY MAN slowly get up to their feet, swaying, staring dully at each other, the image of the prehistoric drawing in the cave. Dead adversaries.

CRONE: I saw a picture once in a cave. A hunter, a bison, and a rhinoceros. This one had hurt that one. That one had hurt this one. Both of them were dying. The rhino just stood there. What else could he do? It was very cold. The snow was falling all over. And I had to look for … fire.

CRONE lights a few candles.

SEGUE #3:

The CORPSE of STALIN marches onto stage and towers angrily over the audience.

STALIN: (*British accent*) What the HELL goes on here?!!!

STALIN slumps dead against the wall.

SCENE 6
ADVANCED CAPITALISM VS. PRIMITIVE CAPITALISM

A new office in some East European or Russian city. A dusty picture of Gorbachev still adorns the wall. BOBBY, a Canadian businessman, enters with two female THUGS, ANNA and MARIKA. MARIKA carries a big box containing a fax machine. The women don't look like thugs, but deep in their hearts, they are. They seem to be very friendly. MARIKA speaks hardly any English. ANNA has an accent, but can be understood. When the thugs speak with no accent, they are speaking in their own language and to each other.

BOBBY: Coming in from the airport, I thought WOW I'm really here. THIS used to be the SOVIET UNION. The Evil Empire. And I'M HERE. All the way from Canada, me. Here. And we're going to lick this sucker together. You, what's your name again?—

MARIKA (*Very softly*): Marika.

BOBBY (*Doesn't understand her, doesn't ask her to repeat it.*): —and you—

ANNA (*Loudly*): ANNA.

BOBBY: Anna, I can pronounce that, and you and me and my fax here. We're gonna do it. We're gonna do bizness. And we're gonna do it starting NOW. (*Looks at his watch.*)

MARIKA (*Accent*): Is Timex?

BOBBY: Pardon?

MARIKA (*Accent*): Timex, you wear Timex? (*No accent*) You can get one thousand roubles on the black market for a Timex.

BOBBY: Hey, hey, no talking in foreign languages around here, Bobby doesn't understand.

ANNA (*Warning*): Marika. (*To BOBBY, accent.*) I think she is a little in love with you, sir.

BOBBY: None of that, we don't do that in my country. It's a Swatch. Now where can we hook up the fax? The fax. Hook it up. Wait a minute. Where's the phone around here?

ANNA (*Accent*): You have to register for phone.

MARIKA (*Accent*): I wait five years for phone.

BOBBY: Yeah, but that's all changed now. Are you trying to tell me I can't hook up this fax? But then how—if there's no—I can't possibly—!!!

The THUGS shrug. BOBBY fumes and paces. He wrestles with his rage as the THUGS talk about him.

MARIKA (*No accent*): Look at his suit. And his shoes. They're made of butter, his shoes.

ANNA (*No accent:*) He has fifteen ballpoint pens.

MARIKA (*No accent*): 100 rubles.

ANNA (*No accent*): And a calculator.

MARIKA (*No accent*): 1,000 rubles.

ANNA (*No accent*): And a videocamera.

MARIKA (*No accent*): A camera! That's worth half a house.

BOBBY: These conditions are primitive. If you people don't improve your telecommunications you're just going to be stuck in the Stone Age forever. And you've got to learn English, Maria, I don't want to nag, but learn English!

ANNA: Marika.

BOBBY: Whatever. By the way there's no water in my apartment.

ANNA: Ohhhhh. (*Accent*) What floor you live?

BOBBY: What does that matter?

ANNA (*Accent*): Well anybody living more than third floor, water is problem.

BOBBY: You're telling me in this entire city people living in apartments don't have water?

ANNA (*Accent*): After midnight is water. Weekend, warm water.

BOBBY: Somebody please invent the wheel around here!

MARIKA (*No accent*): Did he bring soap?

BOBBY glares at her.

BOBBY: Marina!

MARIKA (*Accent*): You have soap? Very difficult, soap.

ANNA (*Accent*): You can buy for dollars no problem.

BOBBY: I have SOAP, it's WATER I would like. How can I possibly work—just look at this office—it's a dump. Anna, make sure this place gets painted. Or is paint a problem? Paint is a problem. (*Note to himself*) Phone head office. When I get a phone. (*Pointing at portrait*) Gorbachev has definitely got to go.

ANNA: Marika! (*Gestures that Marika do the work.*)

Marika pulls up a chair to take Gorbachev down.

MARIKA (*No accent*): That's life for you. Gorbachev wins the Nobel Prize and the American turfs him out. (*An unnerving bray of laughter*) Anyway, Gorbachev's a stinking Communist so I don't care. (*Another big laugh*)

ANNA (*Accent, to Bobby*): She says great idea.

BOBBY: Good. Got some of my own souvenirs here. You girls can tell me where to put them. Then we'll call it a day. We'll all go home, and NOT have a shower. (*Opens briefcase*) Number One: (*Pulls out a big brightly coloured rock*) From the Berlin Wall. Wife got it in New York for twenty bucks. Guy was asking for fifty, but he'd had a bad day.

ANNA (*Accent*): Berlin Wall, Marika.

MARIKA (*Accent*): Very nice, Mister.

BOBBY: Bobby. (*Pulls out a big red granite rock*) The Lenin statue in Smolensk. Barry from head office gave it to me. Says it cost him five bucks and two packs of condoms.

ANNA: (*Accent*) Awesome, Bobby.

BOBBY: Yup. (*pulls out an even redder rock*) Number three. From the Great Wall of China. Smuggled it out myself. Not supposed to do it, but …

He puts the three rocks in front of himself and smiles fatuously at the THUGS.

BOBBY: Where's the crapper?

ANNA (*Accent*): Pardon?

BOBBY: You know, the facilities. Toilet. WC.

ANNA: Oh. The lavatory is on the left. But—

BOBBY: I know! (*Pulls roll of toilet paper out of briefcase*)

BOBBY exits. MARIKA immediately goes to his briefcase and pulls out a pack of cigarettes. From now on, the THUGS speak with no accent.

MARIKA: Did you get the gas?

ANNA: Fifteen litres. All I could get. Cost me a (*Touches her lips, indicating a blow job*).

MARIKA (*Shrugs*): If that's what it costsÁ (*Cradles the biggest rock*) You know the house Yvette and her new boyfriend Gustav bought with the money from their American relatives?

ANNA: Yeah?

MARIKA: Someone stole it. The whole house. They just took it all apart. Every little nail. It's gone. It's true. I saw it on TV. Gustav looked hysterical.

MARIKA goes over to the door, as ANNA picks up the second biggest rock.

ANNA: She's going out with Gustav? The bartender?

MARIKA: Yeah.

ANNA: I was married to him once.

MARIKA: Really? Is he nice?

ANNA grimaces "No." MARIKA gets ready to bean BOBBY.

MARIKA: You can take the Timex.

ANNA positions herself by the door with a rock.

ANNA: It's a Swatch.

The door opens, in comes the CRONE. She takes the rocks from them. ANNA and MARIKA slink out the door. THE STALIN CORPSE gets up and becomes the TOILET CUSTODIAN. Someone is knocking on a door. CRONE opens it, and lets in the WOMAN IN PINK.

SCENE 7
THE FACILITIES

A young WOMAN IN PINK from East Germany and her child. The WOMAN is dressed very warmly, in a pink ski jacket. She faces the TOILET CUSTODIAN, a sour old man.

WOMAN: There's someone here who needs to use the facilities.

CUSTODIAN: Thirty pfennigs. Soap and towel extra.

WOMAN: I don't have thirty pfennigs.

CUSTODIAN: Then you can't use the facilities.

WOMAN: It's not for me, it's for my son. He's only two and he'll be very quick, I promise.

CUSTODIAN: If you don't have the money, you can't use the facilities. You speak German, you can read the sign. Thirty pfennigs.

WOMAN: Well, here. (*Rummaging in her purse*) I have thirty pfennigs, but they're old East German pfennigs, I thought you wouldn't take those.

CUSTODIAN: Oh, you're from East Germany are you?

WOMAN: The former East Germany, yes.

CUSTODIAN: Our brothers and sisters.

WOMAN: Yes, when the wall came down, he was just a baby. It was like a dream. To know he would grow up in a free world. But I think he really has to go now.

CUSTODIAN: Your money is worthless. You need thirty contemporary German pfennigs. There are free toilets in the square.

WOMAN: The square is ten minutes away.

CUSTODIAN: It's good for you. It builds the character.

WOMAN: He has no problems with his character. He needs the pottie. Now.

BOBBY' enters from a door and dies quietly in a corner of the stage.

WOMAN: Look, that booth is free.

She makes a move, CUSTODIAN blocks her.

CUSTODIAN: We're supposed to roll out the red carpet for you, are we? Just because you've suffered all those years? Voted like a pack of sheep, enjoyed full employment doing nothing, sent millions to the salt mines, your own friends and family, destroyed the reputation of several great German philosophers, especially Karl Marx, who never deserved this, because you people built your own walls, your own iron curtains, took out your own party memberships, chanted your own ridiculous slogans, had your own state take care of you from cradle to grave, and now we're supposed to let you in here so you can shit wherever you want whenever you want without paying one single solitary pfennig? You're just squeezing us like golden mashed potatoes through your fatty greedy lazy Eastern fingers.

WOMAN: This is a two year old child. We are having an emergency.

CUSTODIAN: An emergency. But when people get shot climbing over the wall it's not an emergency. When your nuclear Chernobyls poison the atmosphere all the way to Labrador it's not an emergency. When your little boy has to sing songs for Lenin it's not an emergency.

WOMAN: I've had enough of this.

They fight. She wins (i.e. gets into the booth, through the door).

CUSTODIAN angrily kicks the door.

CUSTODIAN: I HAVE WORKED AND STRUGGLED ALL MY LIFE IT WASN'T EASY! Can I go over to your country and say please I am going to use your RATINFESTED BLOOD AND SHIT SMEARED CESSPOOL OF A LAVATORY and not pay a single PFENNIG! If your lavatories are free then we are all paying for it now aren't we! (*He kicks the door violently.*) Listen to me. I can hear you. I can smell you. I'm imagining you. I know exactly what you're doing.

CRONE finds a letter in BOBBY'S suitcase.

CRONE: I have a letter here from the playwright!

THE MINISTER OF EXTERNAL AFFAIRS enters suddenly with her entourage, snap change to SCENE 8.

SCENE 8
A WAR

AIDE A: It's war. It's war. It's Bosnia.

AIDE B: Powder, minister.

MINISTER: Is it the Serbs or the Croatians?

AIDE C: It's very complicated, minister.

MINISTER (*Withering*): I know that, Sneezy. Is this going to involve refugees? We've got enough of them already.

AIDE A: Just the usual statement from External Affairs.

AIDE B: I like the pin, the pin is good.

AIDE A: Our peacekeepers are finding an impossible situation.

AIDE C: They're not exactly getting a hero's welcome.

MINISTER: Can we pull out?

AIDE C: It's pretty desperate. Here's the file.

MINISTER: Oh please. (*Waves A off*)

AIDE A: It's a war, goddamit.

MINISTER: They're used to wars.

MINISTER exit, the others remain dead on the floor.

SCENE 9
A LETTER FROM THE PLAYWRIGHT

CRONE: There's a letter here from the playwright.

A CORPSE brings a CANDLE and helps light the long, long letter as CRONE reads it by candlelight.

CRONE: TO WHOM IT MAY CONCERN: In my father's house, there was a drawer. In fact, it wasn't just my father's house, my mother also lived there. In fact, so did I and my siblings. In fact it wasn't even a house, it was an apartment, and the landlord downstairs was really scary, you could hear him beating his sons at night, they banged around the rooms like frightened colts. Anyway, there was this drawer. When I was thirteen my father opened it. He had pictures of mass graves. He said he had searched for his father's body in one of them. When he was thirteen. Yeah, okay, so. My father wasn't dead. My father had an accent and a company car. He had before and after photographs of a schoolteacher who had been tortured because he collected foreign stamps. Oh, yeah, sure, I really believe that. My father said he had a picture of a boy scout leader whose eyes were poked out, but he didn't make me look at it. My father showed me lots of other pictures but I don't remember them because I really did not did not did not want to look. Because these dead people were killed by Communists. Hitler, okay, get killed by Hitler, but Stalin—I mean I hate the right-wing. I hate these people who criticize the Communists and then say something anti-Semitic in their very next breath. He was shoving these photos at me.

The TOURIST glides into the darkness, camera at the ready.

CRONE: But I was otherwise engaged. I had to go and demonstrate for the suffering people of North Vietnam. I had to demonstrate on behalf of the 93% of the world population who had gotten the distinctly short end of the stick. And that didn't include those guys in the mass graves. Don't give me any of this Latvian folk dancing. This Ukrainian nostalgia. These Rumanian handkerchiefs. My father shut the drawer. I gave it a wide berth from then on. Yours in the struggle, Banuta.

P.S. There was another drawer, the record drawer. I had to avoid it because of Wanda Landowska. The harpsichordist. She was dead. Her black and white record cover made her look very dead. Her dead profile. Her dead hair in a dead bun. She looked pretty mad about it. It was hard to use our record collection. I couldn't touch that record cover. Because the dead are so bitter.

The TOURIST snaps a photo.

SEGUE # 4:

CRONE begins to weep. The ENSEMBLE on stage stirs and tries to comfort her. The CRONE falls silent and the ENSEMBLE sways in the wind. WANDA LANDOWSKA music plays crazily as the CRONE improvises an aria combined of silence, weeping, anthems, war sounds, and rabid dogs. The ENSEMBLE has agreed responses to each sound. The tapestry of history. The CRONE chases everyone off the stage, and crawls away to weep. The year 1999 appears.

SCENE 10
THE WALL, CANADA

ELLEN makes herself comfortable under a sunlamp. She is in Canada,
in an alternate reality in 1999. SAPPHIRE enters, carrying shopping bags.

SAPPHIRE: Ellen! What are you doing here? I thought you'd be gone by now.

ELLEN: They won't get away with it.

SAPPHIRE: They are.

ELLEN: People won't stand for it.

SAPPHIRE: They don't have a choice.

ELLEN: They've got lots of choice. They can go out into the streets.

SAPPHIRE: Uh huh. For a day or two. You better get going. Take all my vitamins and chocolates with you. (*Gives her a bag.*)

ELLEN: If you insist. (*Starts to move towards getting dressed*) They can't just build a wall and divide the city. We'll demonstrate. We'll throw rocks.

SAPPHIRE: You'll get used to it. You won't notice it. They'll decorate it. It'll be a tourist attraction. Maybe they'll get your Buster to design.

ELLEN (*Sits down again*): He's not my Buster. We're an independent couple.

SAPPHIRE: Ohhhh. I guess you finally had that talk.

ELLEN: He didn't show.

SAPPHIRE (*Truly shocked*): Again!!?

ELLEN: Yeah. It's awful. I should call it quits. But—

SAPPHIRE: What?

ELLEN: He's got so much hair on his chest.

SAPPHIRE: It's the only interesting thing about him.

ELLEN (*A second interesting thing*): He's been to the Galapagos Islands. I should break up with him.

SAPPHIRE (*Laughs*): See you already forgot.

ELLEN: What?

SAPPHIRE: The wall. You wanted to throw rocks and now you're talking about Buster's chest.

ELLEN (*Horrified*): You're right! That's so disgusting.

SAPPHIRE: Okay now scram …

ELLEN: I hate to do this Sapphire. But all my friends live on that side of town.

SAPPHIRE: So I'll get new friends.

ELLEN: You don't want new friends.

SAPPHIRE: You better cross the lines before they're bricked and mortared. Go register at the central committee and the only friend you lose is me. Go. THEY have the beach. (*Gives her a blanket*) Take this, I don't need it.

ELLEN: Oh boy, who's to know what to do, I don't know.

SAPPHIRE: How Canadian of you.

ELLEN: What kind of Canadian? That's the thing these days.

SAPPHIRE: You don't have a choice anymore. You're an Eastern Canadian.

ELLEN: I do still have a choice. It's just a wall. And the trains still run in that direction.

SAPPHIRE: So get going and stay there. Stay there forever.

ELLEN: It won't be forever, it's never forever.

SAPPHIRE: Forty-five years before they pull this sucker down.

ELLEN: Five years.

SAPPHIRE: You said they wouldn't do it. You said they couldn't get away with it.

ELLEN: They won't, they can't, but they might and if they do it'll be five years.

SAPPHIRE: Forty-five. Anyway. (*Gives her a frilly dress*) Take this, I never liked it. There's nothing we can do.

ELLEN: Yes, there is. I'm going to call my MP.

A MOUNTIE CORPSE slides into the corner of the stage.

SAPPHIRE: Do you still have an MP? (*Implying the MP is arrested, deported, dead*)

ELLEN: Sure I do.

SAPPHIRE finds a severed head, a large wrapped object in a gray bag, in a drawer. The shock gives her a violent attack of hiccups.

ELLEN: I saw her on her bicycle just yesterday.

SAPPHIRE (*Gasping*): Ellen—! (*hiccup*) It's a severed head, Ellen!

ELLEN: What?!! Blimey! Okay, don't get excited. I bet this is just Buster's idea of a practical joke. Big ha ha. (*Looking closer at the head*) Wait a minute. It can't be. It's the prime minister.

SAPPHIRE (*Hiccups throughout*): You don't know it's him. You've just seen him on TV.

ELLEN: It's him alright.

SAPPHIRE: I don't think his chin was that big. (*Fervently*) Let's run away to my cottage until all this blows over. We'll learn to build fires and we'll plant healthy food, we'll plant turnips, we'll play Trivial Pursuit.

ELLEN: For the next five years? You have got to get rid of those hiccups. My Auntie Mavis had the cure. You put a paper bag over your head, and bob's your uncle. (*She looks for a bag.*)

SAPPHIRE: Let's get out of here. You've got to get out of here.

A knock on the door. SAPPHIRE yelps.

ELLEN: Oh! I bet that's Buster.

SAPPHIRE: Ellen, I'm sorry ...you're my friend but I (*She hiccups dreadfully.*) they asked me some questions and ... I tried to get you out of here but ...

ELLEN pulls the door open. A HOODED EXECUTIONER stands there, she doesn't see him. SAPPHIRE stops hiccuping.

SAPPHIRE: I thought you wouldn't mind if I just told them a few things.

ELLEN: Buster? It's over, Buster.

The image freezes for a moment. A member of the ensemble runs in and steals the executioner's hood; he chases after it; all others participate in this game of chase and catch. Loud primitive music. CRONE begins to build a barricade between the audience and the wall. When the rest of the ensemble are gone, the music dips and CRONE speaks.

SCENE 11
FINALE

CRONE: It was a murderous time and a murderous year. The ice cracked so loudly your ears hurt. The air was burned soup, you couldn't see. Cabbages grew as big as boulders. Infants were born with skin on their legs like frogs. They took one look at the world and turned their back on it. Died as fast as they could. We waited. We counted our pennies. We ate our dog.

CRONE exits. The rest of the ENSEMBLE returns haphazardly, each with an object precious to themselves: a gun, alcohol, a child. They face the wall as if about to witness an explosion. The wall begins to glow red. The area backstage is also red. Now and then a member of the ensemble dares to go back out. The CRONE appears at the top of the wall, surrounded by candles.

CRONE: Those women in the fields. They never stop. No rock can block them. It's true, I saw them. There's the stone. A giant stone, bigger than anybody. Can't move it. You heat it up until it glows. Hot and red, can't touch it. You stand around the stone and sweat. Then you douse it with cold water. Then you run. The stone explodes.

Curtain.

Coral Ann Howells

'REVISIONING HISTORY'

Stone Age, despite the paleolithic connotations of its title, is a play about contemporary European history which ends with a vision of the future set in Canada. This freewheeling through time and space is only the first challenge posed by the play/text and its author-director, for Banuta Rubess with an Oxford D. Phil. in history has written a play which subverts the authority of history, presenting the facts of the disintegration of Europe since the end of the Cold War through a theatrical representation which highlights not those facts themselves but the artifice of representation, thereby calling into question both the grand narratives of history and nationalism and the existence of a reality behind the illusory world of the play. This combination of historical record and postmodern performance is the most distinctive feature of Rubess's dramatic mission:

> So, 'revisioning' history to me means disclosing information—don't forget my Latvian roots, which to me has meant an absence of information—and it means telling the story from a new perspective, often the perspective of women, or a woman.[1]

What looks like an explanation turns out to release several cats from the bag (*Stone Age* is a companion piece to *Head in a Bag,* written and directed by Rubess at Theatre Passe Muraille in 1992) for Rubess's perspective is that of a Latvian-Canadian woman, a 'transcultural' female subject. Canadian born of Latvian parents, whose first language is Latvian (she did not learn English till she went to kindergarten) and who has written and directed several plays in Latvian,[2] Rubess combines an extreme sensitivity to European politics with a Canadian scepticism of absolutes:

> In Canada we have a sharp awareness that there's something in between. That might seem like a boring or bland middle-ground, but it isn't neces- sarily. It's potentially a fertile ground where the black and white rub up against each other and discussion ensues.[3]

The emphasis on dialogue is a version of that 'positive contamination' or hybridisation of cultures which critics like Lola Tostevin and Janice Kulyk Keefer have identified as the transcultural contribution to the multicultural debate in Canada, and which arguably could provide a model for contemporary Europe with its violently competing local nationalisms and ethnic conflicts.[4] If politics is a matter of perspective, then the woman playwright's view of politics

---

and of history needs to be taken into account as she engages her audience/readers in this political satire which is also her revised version of history.

Speaking of perception and reception, there is yet another matter to be negotiated, for what we see on the printed page is a postmodern performance refracted as text. This is a scripted version which is always provisional (indeed there are slight variants in scene definition between the initial lists and the printed text) and always an incomplete representation of the play. The play itself as refractor of current events is endlessly changing in performance, so that as the Preface states, it is "always unfinished, even on closing night." (296)[5] This instability of the text owes as much to the dynamics of ensemble playing as to the shifts in current political and moral debate to which it is a response. In its present form this play occupies a textual space which incessantly pushes against the limits of written representation, for it is crowded with signals acknowledging a relationship to the dramatic genre with its "intrinsically theatrical language of light, colour, movement, gesture and space,", as Steven Connor characterises the postmodern performance.[6]

My own critical procedure is designed to show up the ways in which this is and is not text, for I propose to read *Stone Age* by setting it against T.S. Eliot's *The Waste Land*, my intention being to indicate historical and genre differences, such as modernist v. postmodernist, poem v. play, male v. female perspectives. Writing seventy years apart, both Rubess and Eliot offer narratives of historical crisis and interpretive analyses of European cultural disintegration, in one case dealing with the 1920s in the aftermath of the first World War, and in the other with the 1990s in the period following the Cold War. *Stone Age* opens with a waste land scenario where the stage is "covered in snow, or is it bone dry dust" (297) (Scene 1) in a suspended time-space which is delineated by the first speaker as the earliest phase of cultural history. However, the speaker herself is positioned against "a long wall with several doors and filing cabinets" (296), thus signalling continuities between prehistory and the present which challenge the linear narrative of history. On a first reading, the impression is one of fragmentation—a collage of scenes, multiple voices, incomplete stories—in a text whose formal disruption images the kaleidoscope of events and casualities in Eastern and Central Europe since 1989. As in *The Waste Land*, here again European civilisation is reduced to "a heap of broken images" and the crucial questions of survival recur: What fragments can be "shored against my ruins?" and what visions for the future might grow "out of this stony rubbish?"[7] There are obvious continuities of theme and form between the two texts, plus a similar parade of ghosts, hooded figures, corpses and bizarre resurrections, for arguably Rubess depends on modernist poetic models and expressionist drama, just as her narrative depends on the facts of recorded history. Yet the differences too are obvious, for instead of the vestiges of Christian and Classical mythology and the remains of high culture used by Eliot and James Joyce, Rubess evokes prehistory with its paleolithic cave paintings of hunters and animals hidden by the Ice Age but endlessly recalled in folk memory. Her revisions of history in the present, though fixated on traumatic events in the recent past, is projected forwards as well as backwards into visions of the future where the Berlin Wall assumes its place in a typology which links the Great Wall of China to a Wall in Canada, said to be in process of being built at the end of the play. The final image is that of a glowing red wall, "highlighting" the stage prop which has been visually dominant from the beginning, and indeed from before the beginning.[8] Like the "hypocrite lecteur" addressed by Baudelaire and addressed again by T.S. Eliot, Rubess's readers/audience are forced to recognise our complicity as the events of history are endlessly replayed. Yet likeness and difference are ambiguously balanced, for though the strategies of involvement are similar, the motivation is not, the difference being the explicitly political dimension in Rubess's play/text. This is a crucial difference in postmodern theatre according to Connor:

> Much postmodern aesthetic theory concerns itself precisely with the denial of the modernist separation of the sphere of art from other social activities and concerns, and attempts to restore the repressed political dimensions of aesthetic and cultural activity of all kinds.[9]

Whereas Eliot's poetic urge is primarily metaphysical and *The Waste Land* ends with a yearning for visions of transcendental order (cf. Joyce's 'Epiphanies' and D. H. Lawrence's 'Living Moments') Rubess shows no such faith in the power or even the possibility of absolute truth. Writing in what Anthony Giddens calls the "late modern post-traditional world," where the grand narratives have lost their meaning,[10] Rubess's emphasis is on the artifice of social, cultural and literary constructions, imaged in the Wall(s) itself.

Rubess's dramatic method highlights theatricality, stepping outside the conventions of realistic representation in order to render problematic the very historical facts on which her documentary narrative depends. Scene 1 is a brilliant demonstration of her 'double' technique, as the ageless Crone (Eliot's Tiresias figure here cast in the feminine) stumbles out of her monologue about prehistory on to the corpses of Nicolae and Ellena Ceaucescu. Factual information is provided for the audience by a bloodsoaked shirt marked 1989, a technique similar to one Rubess recalls having used in the 1982 production of a play by the female Latvian writer Aspazija, *The Silver Veil*.[11] Multiple perspectives on the 'December Events' as the Roumanians still refer to the shooting are figured onstage by two couples—the snow-covered corpses of the Ceaucescus over which the Crone stumbles, and two more Ceaucescu corpses 'slumped against the wall', who revive and converse then are shot again (incidentally learning nothing in the process) until they fall through the wall, only to get up again singing. Such grotesqueries challenge the audience to take a more critical view of the effects of shooting dictators; nothing is ended and instead everything remains to be done again and again. A related point—this time a satirical elision of difference and a construction of parallels—is illustrated in the paired scenes (Scenes 4 and 6) where 'The American Way' of global capitalism is replayed with variations in "Advanced Capitalism v. Primitive Capitalism" (305) as the naive Bobby, "All the way from Canada, Me. Here" (306) is two timed by Anna and Marika in a "new office in some East European or Russian city." (305) Indeed such structures of correspondence recur throughout, and culminate in the Canadian Wall at the end—with more corpses, a severed head (not a 'Head in a Bag' but the head of the Canadian Prime Minister whose image has just appeared 'live' on television). There is a refocussing of the dominant verbal-visual images of snow and fire, heat and cold, stones and violence in powerful theatrical finale performed in front of the glowing red wall. This figures an "insupportable situation of tension and explosive risk," a phrase used by Julia Kristeva in her essay "Women's Time" and encodes what I take to be an allusion by Rubess to a feminist revision of history as cyclical or mythical, which is closely akin to her own.[12]

The woman's 'time-less' perspective is given voice by the aged Crone, a figure who is there from beginning to end. It is she who remembers back to the hidden cave paintings with their images of sacrifice, just as she alone recalls other corpses in other eras, so blurring differences between present and past. Sometimes she is the sole survivor, but in other scenes (like 'The Filing Cabinet of History' and 'The Tapestry of History,' Segues 2 and 4) she is accompanied by the ensemble in multivoiced choric commentary. Though *Stone Age* could not be simply defined as a feminist text (the figures of Ellena Ceaucescu, the Canadian Minister of External Affairs, and Sapphire pose too many challenges to concepts of sisterhood) yet the woman's point of view with its emphasis on process and continuity offers an alternative version to the male symbolic order of recorded history. Significantly it is the old woman who alone seems to retain any affective response to human suffering. Faced with the Tapestry of History she weeps inconsolably, just as it is she who makes the only charitable gesture in the play. She leaves the orange on the Paris-Berlin train for the penniless East Berliner, rejected by his new wealthier fellow citizens as "Eurotrash" (Scene 3, 302). Even at the end as the Crone stands on the glowing wall warning of apocalypse, her story also recalls the endurance of peasant women in the fields: "They never stop. No rock can block them. It's true. I saw them" (Scene 11, 314) Through that anecdote and image she offers a muted prospect of survival, for the determinism of history is never absolute.

It is the Crone who reads aloud the Playwright's Letter in Scene 9 where Rubess addresses her audience in order to establish the position from which she represents history. Using another kind of documentary evidence, she speaks out of her personal history to construct her transcultural perspective, projecting a narrative identity based on memories of a childhood haunted by the ghosts of her parents' East European past and her own adolescent refusals to confront those traumatic memories: "I was otherwise engaged. I had to go and demonstrate for the suffering people of North Vietnam … Don't give me any of this Latvian folk dancing. This Ukrainian nostalgia." (311) The effect of this autobiographical intervention is to add a subjective dimension to the historical record being enacted and revised in the play, underlining the importance of remembering as well as the correspondence between two women's perspectives on a historical process where 'now' is continuous with the past.

This blurring of boundaries as voices merge and diverge across time foregrounds Rubess's method of revisioning history, where "Who is telling the story is the crucial question."[13] The reference to discursive process serves as a reminder that this belongs to the genre of postmodern narrative which Linda Hutcheon has called "Historiographic Metafiction"[14] though in this instance it might more accurately be described as "Historiographic Metadrama."[15] Perhaps it is not the "fictionality of history" (Hutcheon's term) but rather the provisional nature of historical representations which is foregrounded here, for theatrical artifice insistently draws attention to the form in which the message is communicated: "I knew that history and theatre were a matter of presentation, of story-telling."[16] As Hayden White has shown, the narrative forms that recorded history takes have as much to do with subjective interpretation and particular socio-cultural context as with the facts themselves.[17] It is therefore interesting to speculate that the disrupted parodic structure of Stone Age represents not only the collapse of grand narratives in the postmodernist era, but also Rubess's feminist comment on the fabrications of history. This would seem to be confirmed by her own remarks on gender and aesthetics:

> I think it's true that there is a feminist dramaturgical aesthetic, which spurns the structure based on conflict and resolution. The one where everything gets built up to one screaming point and then everything is suddenly released. Women often write in waves, repeated climaxes, collages. It's true that often male critics will then complain about a lack of build or something ... I think my work, collective or solitary, has almost only received raves by women—understanding, perceptive assessments.[18]

While Rubess refers to tensions in the reception of her work which may be based on a politics of gender, there are also, I believe, real tensions generated within the play itself, which revolve around the crucial question of authority. Where does it reside?—in the text, with the author, or with history? In this case none of the traditional answers will quite suffice. As we have seen, the playscript depends for its completion on performance, and possibly also on its predecessor Head in a Bag, to which it is neither supplement nor sequel though containing elements of both (e.g. it shares the same stage set and several of the same characters). The dimension of 'performance' also raises questions related to author and authority, for although Rubess wrote the play she designed it for ensemble work, so that there are scripted moments when "actions are improvised" (Seque 2) and "the rest of the Ensemble return haphazardly"(Finale, 314). It is precisely at these points of potential dissolution of the playwright's authority that the action mimes the dynamic interrelationship between disintegration and centring which constitutes the theme of the play. Dependent though it is on the records of documentary history Stone Age deconstructs those boundaries, setting up an elaborate interplay between the determinism of history and the inventiveness of the creative artist, presenting history not as fact but as theatrical representation which is always open to revision through performance.

At the EC Summit meeting called to celebrate the entry into force of the Maastricht Treaty on 1 November 1993, President Francois Mitterand offered his commentary on one possible future for Europe: "We are confronted by ethnic massacres which could turn into regional wars. There is a serious risk of a European conflict at the beginning of the next century."[19] Looking at the same situation, not from a male Eurocentric perspective but from her female transcultural one, Rubess figures her warning differently as she seeks to make the European narrative significant for a North American (Canadian) audience. The play offers "an alternate reality in 1999" (311), with a Canadian Wall (modelled on the Berlin Wall), which is about to explode. So the dramas of history are manifestly available to be transformed into scenarios for the future by artists and politicians in an endless process of recording and 'revisioning', which is signalled by those prehistoric cave paintings at the beginning of the play: "You had to be mighty courageous to do a thing like that" (Scene 1, 298). In Rubess's theatrical reinvention of history differences between fact and fiction, present, past and future, Europe and North America are eroded as the emphasis falls on representation, story-telling. So it seems fitting to end this commentary with the words of another postmodern writer in a different genre, Timothy Findley, whose description in his novel *Famous Last Words* of an ancient handprint in the Altamira Caves (another survival from the Stone Age) might itself be read as commentary on Rubess's project, gesturing towards the centring of history—or at least its retelling—through the subjective vision of the artist:

> All I can tell you of myself and of my time and of the world in which I lived is in this signature: this hand print: mine.[20]

Bibliography

Steven Connor, *Postmodernist Culture: An Introduction to Theories of the Contemporary* (Oxford: 1989).

T.S. Eliot, "The Waste Land" (1922) in: *Selected Poems* (London: 1967).

Timothy Findley, *Famous Last Words* (Toronto/Vancouver: 1981).

Anthony Giddens, *Modernity and Self-Identity: Self and Society in the Late Modern Age* (Cambridge: 1991).

Linda Hutcheon, *The Canadian Postmodern: A Study of Contemporary English-Canadian Fiction* (Toronto: 1988).

Janice Kulyk Keefer, "From Mosaic to Kaleidoscope," *Books in Canada*, September 1991, 13—16.

Richard Paul Knowles, "Replaying History: Canadian Historiography and Metadrama," *Dalhousie Review* 67, 2/3, 1987, 228—43.

Julia Kristeva, "Women's Time" (1981) in: Catherine Belsey and Jane Moore, Eds., *The Feminist Reader: Essays in Gender and the Politics of Literary Criticism*, London 1989.

Judith Rudakoff and Rita Much, Eds., *Fair Play: 12 Women Speak: Conversations with Canadian Playwrights* (Toronto: 1990).

Lola Lemire Tostevin, "Contamination: A Relation of Difference," *Tessera*, Spring 1989, 13—14.

Hayden White, *Tropics of Discourse: Essays in Cultural Criticism* (Baltimore: 1978).

Notes

1

"Interview with Banuta Rubess," in: Judith Rudakoff and Rita Much, *Fair Play: 12 Women Speak: Conversations with Canadian Playwrights* (Toronto: 1990), 49-73.

2

Plays in Latvian by Rubess include *Heroica* (1979), *The Last Latvians* (1983), *Tango Lugano* (1989).

3

Rubess interview, Rudakoff and Much, 1990, 71.

4

Lola Tostevin, "Contamination: A Relation of Differences," *Tessera* (Spring 1989), 13-14, and Janice Kulyk Keefer, "From Mosaic to Kaleidoscope," *Books in Canada* (Spring 1991), 13-16.

5

Banuta Rubess, *Stone Age*, Preface.

6

Steven Connor, *Postmodernist Culture: An Introduction to Theories of the Comtemporary* (Oxford: 1989), 135.

7

T.S. Eliot, *The Waste Land* (1922), in: *T.S. Eliot: Selected Poems* (London: 1967). Quotations are from Sections 1 and 5.

8

The Wall was also the main stage prop in *Head in a Bag* (1992).

9

Connor, 1989, 224.

10

Anthony Giddens, *Modernity and Self-Identity: Self and Society in the Late Modern Age* (Oxford: 1991).

11

Rubess interview, Rudakoff and Much, 1990, 57.

12

Julia Kristeva, "Women's Time" (1981) in: Catherine Belsey and Jane Moore, *The Feminist Reader: Essays in Gender and the Politics of Literary Criticism* (London: 1989), 155-74.

13

Rubess interview, Rudakoff and Much, 53.

14

Linda Hutcheon, *The Canadian Postmodern: A Study in Contemporary English-Canadian Fiction* (Toronto: 1988), 61-77.

15

Richard Paul Knowles, "Replaying History: Canadian Historiography and Metadrama," *Dalhousie Review*, 67, 2/3 (1987), 228-43, Knowles adapts Hutcheon's "Metafiction" to read the plays of Rick Salutin, James Reaney, and Sharon Pollock, arguing that they all use devices which self-consciously foreground theatricality in their reinventions of history.

16

Rubess interview, Rudakoff and Much, 53.

17

Hayden White, "The Fictions of Factual Representation," in: White, *Tropics of Discourse* (Baltimore: 1978), 121.

[18] Rubess interview, Rudakoff and Much, 68.

[19] *Guardian*, 30 October, 1993, 11.

[20] Timothy Findley, *Famous Last Words* (Toronto/Vancouver: 1981), 180.

Willy Russell

TERRACES
(A Thirty Minute Film For Television)

CAST

Billy

Joey

John

Eddie

Joyce

Debbie

Michelle

Carol

Danny

Susan

Michael

SCENE 1
PUB INT: DAY: DAY 1

The pub is crowded and noisy, the atmosphere, high with elation and the sense of celebration.

Behind the bar, the wall is decked out with football memorabilia—yellow scarves, framed pictures, badges, fading newspaper articles. All relating to a team identified in one of the pictures as being 'Northgate.'

Throughout the title sequence, the camera picks its way through the throng of drinkers. We catch snatches of dialogue as we pass various groups.

BILLY: An' I'm talking history, right. When the referee blew the final whistle today, it was a fanfare! With that whistle, he blew Northgate into the final and into the history books. An' I'll tell you somethin' else ...

(But we don't hear what it is as the camera has passed on and the dialogue from another group segues over BILLY'S dialogue.)

JOEY: I feel proud, I do, proud. Even if we don't make it in the final, I'll still never forget what was achieved on this day. I've supported Northgate ever since …

(*Again we do not hear the end of the speech as the camera has passed on to another group.*)

JOHN: The underdogs, that's what we were the underdogs, but we showed 'em today, we showed 'em alright.

(*As the camera moves on, we see the pub door open, EDDIE and his wife enter. EDDIE stands for a moment, his eyes bright and glistening. A hush begins to fall as those gathered in the pub note his arrival. When he feels that he has their attention he slowly lifts both fists before shouting.*)

EDDIE: YEeeeeeeeeeeee!

(*He leads the gathering into the chant.*)

EDDIE: 'Northgate' 'Northgate.'

(*As EDDIE and his wife make their way towards the bar.*)

Come on Joyce. 'Northgate' 'Northgate.'

JOYCE (*Good-naturedly - parodying him.*): 'Northgate' 'Northgate.'

(*We track with JOYCE as she moves to a table and sits with a group of other women.*)

JOYCE: I'll tell you something, I wish they'd get into the final every bloody week if it'd keep him as happy as this.

DEBBIE: I usually hate football, but something as special as this, it's a real tonic. You can feel it in the air can't y'.

MICHELLE: A bit of success! That's what this community's needed for a long time, a bit of success.

(*EDDIE, BILLY, JOEY and JOHN appearing at the table. EDDIE laying down a tray of drinks.*)

EDDIE: I'll drink to that. A win like we had today. It's important for everyone. Everyone.

Handing drinks around.

SCENE 2
DANNY'S HOUSE—LOUNGE INT: DAY: DAY 1

MICHAEL, DANNY'S son, is doing a crossword in the paper. DANNY is reading a novel.

SUSAN: Are we goin', Danny?

DANNY (*Absent*): Mm?

SUSAN: Are we goin' down there or not?

MICHAEL: Dad … what's a (*Reading*) a 'Historical gang' beginnin' with M … three letters?

DANNY (*Looking up. Puzzled*): A what? Here … let's have a look.

MICHAEL: A historical gang.

DANNY (*Getting up and looking at the paper*): Historical! Hysterical... you nutter!

MICHAEL: Oh yeh.

DANNY: Mob it is ... mob! (*Tuts*) Historical!

SUSAN: Are we goin'?

DANNY: D'y' fancy it?

MICHAEL: Dad ... what's a ten letter word that means 'one who always agrees'?

DANNY: Who's supposed to be doin' this crossword?

SUSAN: I thought y'd want to celebrate gettin' through to the final.

DANNY: That's not celebratin'. It's just drinkin' for the sake of it an' going over every last detail a thousand times.

SUSAN: You're a real killjoy, you are. Other fellers would be overjoyed if their team got through to the final.

DANNY: I am overjoyed. I just can't see much point in goin' over it again an' again. Eddie an' that lot, they're like bloody television commentators.

SUSAN: So we're not goin' out?

DANNY: I didn't say that. Do you want to go out, love?

SUSAN: Well, it is Saturday night.

DANNY: Yes, but do you want to go out?

SUSAN: Yes. Yes!

DANNY: Well get your coat on. If you want to go out, we'll go out.

SUSAN: Well why didn't you say that in the first place? Come on. I bet it's a riot down there tonight!

SCENE 3
PUB INT: DAY: DAY 1

EDDIE, JOHN and JOEY are stood at the bar.

JOHN: What I mean is that the street should show its support.

JOEY: There's not a family in this street that doesn't support the team.

JOHN: Yes, but what I'm talkin' about is demonstratin' that support.

EDDIE: John's right. It's a great achievement this is and must be treated as such. To some people it might just be a game of football, a team, but to me it's a game of life!

JOEY (*Laughing*): I like that, 'a game of life.'

JOHN: What we could do is, every house, every one of us put pictures of the team in all the windows?

EDDIE: No ...! That's what y'do at Election time. What we're talkin' about is somethin' serious!

Cut to the door to see DANNY and his wife enter. The women call out to SUSAN and make way for her to sit with them. DANNY comes across to EDDIE and co.

DANNY: Alright? Celebration pints all round, is it?

EDDIE: What a victory though, Danny, eh, eh?

DANNY (*Laughing to barmaid*): Four pints an' a vodka an' lime, Carol.

JOHN: The underdogs! The outsiders, the no hopers, but we bleedin' well showed them today.

EDDIE: And that's why I think we should make the most of this opportunity. Display the way we feel. Really show our support.

JOEY: We could get a bloody banner printed, with the name of the team and stretch it right across the street.

DANNY (*Just before taking SUSAN'S drink across to her*): Get out of here. The way you support a team is by going to see them play.

EDDIE: What we're talking about here Danny is whippin' up some y'know, some real interest. Some real enthusiasm.

DANNY: Y'don't need t'do that.

JOHN: Why not? It'd be good, Danny.

DANNY: It's the game that's important, John. Y'don't want to be gettin' into all these daft things like banners and pictures in windows an' slogans. It's a game, not something else, not something you go out and paint the streets for.

EDDIE (*Grasping him and it*): That's it! That's it! The whole bloody street, every inch of it in the team's colour!

JOHN: Yellow!

JOEY: The entire street painted yellow. Danny that's bloody brilliant.

DANNY (*Laughing*): Get lost! I didn't mean …

EDDIE: We're on. That's it! Right.

EDDIE banging on the bar for order. He gets it.

Is everyone listenin'?

DANNY: Eddie … listen …

EDDIE: Right. Now everyone here tonight knows that today our own team, this street's team, got through to the final.

There is a thundering cheer.

EDDIE: Well look, we've been talking and we think that this street should show its support for our team. Each and every family in this street can bind together and display a united front, a wave of solidarity in unanimous support for our boys.

JOHN (*Shouting*): Well, what are we goin' to do, Ed?

EDDIE: I'll tell you. I'll tell all of you. (*Effect pause*) It's dead easy. Everyone, all of us, we paint every house in the street in the colour of the team! The whole street tellin' the world of our support! Is everyone agreed?

Shouts of agreement.

EDDIE: Right. Billy ... where's Billy?

A head popping up from the crowd.

BILLY: Here, Eddie.

EDDIE: Billy ... ave y'got any yellow paint in the shop?

BILLY: I've got bloody gallons of it. It's been there for years.

EDDIE: Will y'open the shop tomorrow? So we can buy it?

BILLY: Buy it? Y'won't buy it. For somethin' like this y'can have it for free.

A spontaneous cheer for BILLY. The pub talk, excited, starts up again.

Close up on the group of women.

JOYCE: Don't tell me. Don't tell me that at long last I'm gettin' me house painted! Ohhh, I can't believe it.

SUSAN: Trust your Eddie. He's a laugh.

DEBBIE: I'll bet we get reporters around. An' the telly.

JOYCE: Oh God ... I'll have to get me hair done!

DEBBIE: This street could become famous.

MICHELLE: Do you really think the television people will come?

JOYCE: Well they wouldn't miss out on something like this, would they? Eh?

SCENE 4
THE STREET EXT: EVE: DAY 1

We see a line of terraced house, outlined against sky. Sounds of emptying pub. Cut to see the lit pub in long shot at the far end of the street. People spilling out. Two figures walking towards us. Shouts of 'Goodnight DANNY,' 'See y' DANNY,' 'Tarar Sue.'

DANNY and SUSAN walking along street arm in arm. Not drunk but glowing.

SUSAN: Joyce says the television cameras might turn up when it's done.

DANNY: Eh?

SUSAN: When the street's painted. (*She laughs.*) Ey ... they might even interview some of us. Don't y' fancy seein' me on telly, Danny?

DANNY: Don't be daft. The street won't get painted. Well, our house won't anyway!

SUSAN (*Stopping and swaying slightly*): And why not?

DANNY: Come on. It's just stupid.

SUSAN: Why? (*Not moving*)

DANNY: Come on ... it is.

SUSAN: Why aren't we havin' our house painted?

DANNY: Because I don't want it painted. Now come on.

SUSAN: Well you miserable swine.

DANNY (*Laughing*): Ogh … come on. (*Trying to get her to walk but she stands firm.*) Susan!

SUSAN: Everyone else is painting their house! Why aren't we?

DANNY: Everyone won't be paintin' their houses. If I'd thought they were serious in there I would have said something. They'll all have forgotten it by tomorrow. Now come on. It's freezin'.

(*She allows him to lead her up the street.*)

(End Day 1)

SCENE 5
DANNY'S HOUSE-LOUNGE INT: DAY: DAY 2

DANNY sitting in armchair reading paper. Curtains drawn behind him.

SUSAN entering in dressing gown. Carries cup of tea. Places it at the side of DANNY'S chair.

Pulls back the curtains.

Sees from her point of view the opposite side of the street, EDDIE is up a ladder and is painting his house.

SUSAN: Oh yes. 'They'll all have forgotten it by now.'

DANNY: Mmm?

SUSAN: Look.

DANNY: What?

SUSAN: Come and have a look.

DANNY gets up and sees EDDIE at work.

DANNY: The bloody lunatic!

SUSAN: Why is he?

DANNY: He's round the bend. Nobody else will do it. He'll be embarrassed out of his mind. The only yellow house in the street. The Lone Canary.

SUSAN: How will his be the only one? Everyone's doin' it.

DANNY: You mean everyone said they'd do it. What they said they'll do and what they will do are two different things.

MICHAEL comes rushing in. Excited, breathless.

MICHAEL: Dad … Dad … When are we paintin' our house? Dad, can I help y'? Everyone in the street's doin' it.

DANNY: Listen, Michael, Eddie Wilks is not everyone.

MICHAEL: I know. But John Cameron's dad's doin' his house down the other end of the street. An' Peter Wilksy's , an' Morgan's an' they said all the street's gonna be yellow.

SUSAN (*Smug*): Satisfied!

(*DANNY stretching out of window to see further down the street. From his POV we see a few ladders. SUSAN leaning out of window and shouting across to EDDIE.*)

SUSAN: Let's have a look, Eddie! Ahhh. It's lookin' lovely, Ed! Just what we need in this street, Eddie, a bit more community spirit.

EDDIE (*Shouting over*): Look at them, they're all gettin' stuck in now. Where's that feller of yours? Come on.

DANNY: Do you want the house painting yellow?

SUSAN: Well everyone else is doin' it.

DANNY: I didn't ask you that. Do you want the house painting yellow?

SUSAN: Danny! I want the house painting like the rest of the street and if the colour they've chosen is yellow then I'll have my house yellow!

DANNY: Would you have it painted yellow if nobody else was doing' the same?

MICHAEL: Ah come on, Dad!

SUSAN (*Becoming exasperated*): Of course I wouldn't. I don't even like yellow!

DANNY: Good. Because I'm not going to paint this house yellow.

SUSAN: And why not?

DANNY: Because I don't want to!

MICHAEL: Ah Dad! You're rotten.

SUSAN: You don't want to? What do you mean, you don't want to! It's not up to you. The street's decided …

DANNY: Yes! An' I've decided I don't want my house painting.

MICHAEL: Dad, why?

SUSAN (*Becoming heated*): I thought you supported the team.

DANNY: And will painting my house increase my support? When kids go spraying paint over bus shelters, scrawling the team's name on a wall, does that mean greater support? I support my team all right, but that's got nothing to do with painting a house.

Pause. SUSAN glaring at him

MICHAEL: Alright then. OK. I'll go an' help Wilksy paint his house!

Storms out.

DANNY: Michael!

SUSAN: Go on. You go, Michael love. You go an' help Mr Wilks.

SUSAN: Why do you begrudge your own child a bit of pleasure?

DANNY: It's got nothing to do with begrudging pleasure and you know it!

SUSAN (*As she storms out. To DANNY*): You make me sick!

DANNY (*Throwing down his fork onto plate*): Agh … this is ridiculous!

SUSAN (*Tidying up*): Yes … I know.

SCENE 6
THE STREET EXT: DAY: DAY 2

The street. Houses partially painted yellow.
MICHAEL in the street

SCENE 7
THE PUB INT: DAY: DAY 2

EDDIE, JOHN and JOEY drinking pints, stood at the bar, their working clothes showing evidence of yellow paint.

EDDIE: When Joyce telephoned them, the girl at ITV said as how she thought it'd make a very interesting feature.

JOHN: We're going on telly?

EDDIE: Well you think about it. It's a phenomenon this is. The TV companies won't pass up an opportunity like this.

JOEY: I'll have to get me suit pressed!

JOHN: D'you think we'll be interviewed?

EDDIE: Of course! Well, not everyone. But they'll want to interview the architect of the idea won't they?

JOEY: I thought it was Danny's idea.

EDDIE: Yeah. Danny thought of it. But what's an idea unless someone puts flesh and bones on it. Know what I mean?

JOHN: I wonder who'll they send to do the interviews.

JOEY: I hope it's someone from the sports side.

EDDIE: I reckon they'll send someone like Des.

JOEY: Desmond Lynam … in our street?

The barmaid, CAROL has been listening.

Cut to door as DANNY enters.

EDDIE (*Oov*): Aye, aye. I see some people still observe the Sabbath round here.

JOEY: Just got up have y' Danny?

CAROL pulls a pint for him.

JOHN: I hope you noticed the work that's been done while you've been sleepin'.

EDDIE: Better get y'finger out, Danny. Des Lynam's comin' y'know, Dan.

DANNY: What?

CAROL: I hope they send Jeremy Paxman. Ooh, he's lovely.

EDDIE and JOEY looking at her dismissively.

EDDIE: It could end up with them devotin' a whole programme to this y'know.

DANNY: Listen, Eddie, I think y'd better know. I've got no intention of paintin' my house.

EDDIE (*Pause, puzzled*): What d'y' mean?

DANNY: What I say. I'm not painting my house.

There is a silence in which they all look at him.

DANNY: Look, lads. It's quite simple—I don't want to paint my house! Now can we just leave it there? (*Pause*) Come on, let's talk about somethin' else.

EDDIE (*Stunned*): Somethin' else!

JOEY: What's wrong with y', Danny?

DANNY: Nothing's wrong with me, Joe. But I don't want to paint my house.

JOHN: And why not?

DANNY: No reason, John. I just don't want to.

EDDIE: But Danny, Danny, is it a question of what you want?

DANNY: It is my house. It's my decision.

JOHN: But you live in a community, Danny. You've got to think of others as well.

DANNY: I've thought of others, John, an' if my house remains unpainted it won't hurt one insect, animal or human being.

EDDIE: How do you know you won't be hurtin' anyone?

JOEY: Des Lynam won't like it.

EDDIE: Now come on, Danny. Let's stop arsin' around. (*He puts his hand in his pocket and produces a tenner*) Carol, round of scotch. Make them large ones sweetheart.

DANNY: Listen, Eddie … I'm not going to paint the house.

EDDIE (*Laughing*): You're a case, you are, Danny. Always were a bit of the awkward one. A bit different. 'Eh, John, I'll bet he was an awkward bugger when he was a kid, eh?

JOHN and EDDIE laughing

DANNY: Eddie, y' can laugh, buy me whisky, bring in a troupe of dancin' girls if you like, but I won't be paintin' my house.

Eddie (*The laughter fading*): People won't like it, y' know.

(*DANNY shrugs.*)

JOHN: Come on Danny. Why try to be the odd one out?

DANNY: I'm not trying to be anythin', John, (*Sighs*) I just don't want … to. Alright? So can we just forget about it now?

(*DANNY reaches out towards the glass of scotch on the bar. EDDIE reaches across and pushes it away. Cut to see EDDIE from DANNY'S POV. He is shaking his head.*)

EDDIE: No way, Danny!

DANNY: What?

EDDIE: If a feller doesn't want to join in with me, then that's alright. That's OK. But if he's not with me in all things, he's not with me in any.

DANNY: For Christ's sake, hasn't this gone far enough? Stop bein' so bleedin' daft!

EDDIE: It's not me that's bein' daft, Danny. (*Pause*) Now, are y'gonna drink with me?

DANNY (*Pause. He looks at the glass.*): I'll drink with you.

EDDIE (*Beginning to push the glass towards him*): Good boy, good boy.

DANNY: But I won't paint the house.

EDDIE (*His hand pulling back to the glass*): Well y'won't drink with me either! (*Pause in which they look at each other. EDDIE drains the glass in one.*)

DANNY: Alright, stick your drink!

(*DANNY turns away and heads for the pub door.*)

EDDIE (*Shouting after him*): It's up to you, Danny. It's up to you!

(*DANNY bangs the pub door behind him.*)

(End day 2)

SCENE 8
DANNY'S HOUSE—LOUNGE INT: DAY: DAY 3

SUSAN and MICHAEL sit at table eating breakfast. DANNY enters.

DANNY: Any tea made?

SUSAN: If you want tea you know where the pot is.

DANNY glaring at her.

DANNY: We're not still carryin' this on, are we?

Looking at MICHAEL

SUSAN: Us? We're not carrying anything on Danny.

DANNY: Ogh for Christ's sake!

DANNY snatching up kettle and beginning to fill it.

SCENE 9
DANNY'S HOUSE: FRONT DOOR EXT: DAY: DAY 3

Front door.
Close up of knocker.
Hand.
Rap on door.

SCENE 10
DANNY'S HOUSE—LOUNGE INT: DAY: DAY 3

MICHAEL and SUSAN.
SUSAN getting up.

SCENE 11
DANNY'S HOUSE—HALL INT: DAY: DAY 3

Door being opened.

EDDIE, JOEY, JOHN and others seen from her POV.

EDDIE: Alright Sue love, can we have a word with Danny?

SUSAN: Come on in Ed. He's in the kitchen.

They stream in.

SCENE 12
DANNY'S HOUSE—LOUNGE INT: DAY: DAY 3

DANNY looking up from making tea.

See them from his POV.

Not a mob. More a deputation. Most are stood just outside the kitchen.

Cut to see DANNY from their POV.

EDDIE: Listen Danny … we've been talkin'.

DANNY (*Continuing to make tea*): Have you?

JOHN: We've been a bit rash, Danny!

(*DANNY looking up*)

DANNY: Well I'm glad you've realised it, John.

EDDIE: Look, Dan. I mean, OK. You don't wanna be bothered paintin' the house. So what we have done, Danny is a few of the lads an' meself have agreed that we'll do it for y'.

SUSAN (*From the back of the group*): Ah … now that's what I call real friendship, Eddie.

SCENE 12A
DANNY'S HOUSE—HALL INT: DAY: DAY 3

DANNY (*Following them to the door*): Eddie.

EDDIE: What's that Dan?

DANNY: You lay one hand, one finger on an inch of this brickwork an' I'll have the coppers on you.

SUSAN: Danny!

EDDIE: Danny! We're offerin' to do you a favour.

JOEY: We'll even paint it back to the normal colour when the final's over.

DANNY: No thanks.

EDDIE (*Pause*): I wouldn't push it too far, Danny.

DANNY: I'm not pushing it at all.

JOHN: Listen mate. We came round here to make things OK between us. Now if you're gonna start bein' unreasonable ...

DANNY (*Closing door after them*): Bye.

EDDIE (*Wedging his foot in door.*): I'm warnin' you. You'd better fuckin' well grow up. Or you'll be sorry.

(*DANNY closes the door.*)

SUSAN: You're warped! Did you know that? Warped, that's what you are. They're your friends.

DANNY: No! Friends will let you be yourself!

(*He walks past her and into the kitchen*)

(End Day 3)

SCENE 13
STREET EXT: DAY: DAY 4

JOYCE and other women queuing at check out. SUSAN enters.

JOYCE: We're just sayin', Sue. The television people are coming, you know.

MICHELLE: When's that feller of yours goin' to get started?

SUSAN: Danny'll do it. Don't worry.

DEBBIE: Someone was saying that John Major's opening a school over in Grant's Parade on Friday.

JOYCE: He's gonna come here and see the street?

DEBBIE: Well they didn't exactly say ...

JOYCE: Oh my God. This is fantastic. Wait till I tell Eddie. (*Pause*) The Prime Minister comin' to our street! You'll have to get him moving Susan. We can't have you letting the whole side down.

SCENE 14
DANNY'S STREET EXT: DAY 4: DAY

DANNY is walking along on the way back from work. Even more houses are painted now. The street is taking on an overall yellow look.

Tight on DANNY as he walks along the street.

From DANNY'S POV JOEY getting out of his car. The two men looking at each other but making no acknowledgement as DANNY walks past.

JOEY nervously looks up and down the street: Danny. Danny.

DANNY (*Stopping*): What?

JOEY (*Running up to him*): Listen I don't think they're gonna be comin' till tomorrow, the television people.

DANNY: Yeh. Well?

JOEY: Danny. I'm trying to help you. I shouldn't even be seen talkin' to you, mate. What I'm sayin', Danny, is you've still got time. Y' could get it painted by tonight.

(*DANNY turns and walks away.*)

SCENE 15
DANNY'S HOUSE—LOUNGE INT: DAY: DAY 4

Close up of three gallon tins of yellow paint and a large brush.

Pulls back to reveal SUSAN sitting in armchair. DANNY standing in doorway.

DANNY: What's that?

SUSAN: Paint.

DANNY: I can see that. What's it for?

SUSAN: You're going to paint this house, Danny.

DANNY: Oh am I?

SUSAN: I'm not going to be humiliated any longer. It's all right for you. You don't get it. You're out at work all day. But I have to live here in this street. All day, people goin' on at me, makin' me feel small. Well I'm up to here with it, Danny and I'm not bein' humiliated again.

DANNY: You don't have to be humiliated. Stand by me and there'll be no humiliation.

SUSAN (*Bouncing out of the chair*): I'm not arguin' with y', Danny. I've had enough of bein' the reject. Now listen, I'm givin' you a warning', either you paint this house tonight ... or I'm gettin' out!

DANNY: Don't be so bloody stupid!

SUSAN: Stupid! You call me stupid?

DANNY: Yes, you're acting like a child.

(*We hear the pound of a door opening and a child crying. MICHAEL, tear stained and screaming, rushes in, DANNY tries to take him, but he runs to his mother.*)

SUSAN: Michael ... Michael ... what's wrong?

MICHAEL (*Between sobs*): They won't ...they won't ... play with me ... they all said ... Wilksy and all of them ... they said ... (*Breaking down*)

SUSAN: Said what, love? What did they say?

MICHAEL: Said our house ... is a ... a house for freaks! (*Breaks down*)

SUSAN (*Screaming at DANNY*): See! See what you and your stupid bloody ways have done!

She puts her arms around the child and leads him to the door.

Don't cry, love. Don't cry. You're right. It is a freak's house. Look, there's the freak ... y' father! He's the one who's turned it into a house for rejects. Well he'd better do somethin' about it quick or else he'll be the only one livin' here!

They exit and leave DANNY alone in the room.

Run sound of child crying.

DANNY looks at the paint, sighing, taking off his coat.

SCENE 16
DANNY'S HOUSE—HALL INT: DAY 4: DAY

DANNY in overalls. Paint brush and can of paint in one hand. Step ladders leaning against wall. DANNY moving to pick up step ladder.

Loud bang on the door.

As DANNY moves towards the front door, we see from his POV a note being pushed through the letter box.

DANNY picks up and opens the note,

We read with him.

DANNY: 'This is a warning! Paint the house or find somewhere else to live!'

Cut to DANNY's reaction, staring, breathing hard.

SCENE 17
DANNY'S STREET EXT: DAY: DAY 4

Door opening.

DANNY stepping out.

Places three cans of paint on to the pavement.

All yellow. See houses from his POV. Curtains moving.

DANNY (*Shouting at houses*): Are you all watching? All listening? Are y'? (*Laughs*) Come on … come out and have a look. (*Pause*) Where are y'? Come on … come on out! (*Pause*) See … look … the paint's here. Come on, you can come out.

(*Slowly front doors begin to open.*)

Come on … all of y' … COME ON.

Pan street and faces slowly from DANNY'S POV.

(*Neighbours begin to emerge.*)

See … look … there's the paint. It's yellow, see. Right? (*Pause*) Now someone wants me to paint my house eh?

EDDIE (*Shouting across*): I'm glad you've seen some sense, Danny.

DANNY: Sense? Oh yes, I've seen sense. (*He stands and surveys the onlookers.*) I've seen sense all right. You all want to paint the house, do y'?

EDDIE: Good lad, Danny.

JOHN: Good man … good man.

DANNY: Watch … just watch.

(*He slowly bends and prises open one of the cans. He lifts it.*)

EDDIE (*To a neighbour*): I knew he'd see sense in the end.

(He turns back to look at DANNY.)

DANNY is pouring the paint down the grid.

DANNY: Well that's my answer. That's what I say to you. And just in case you didn't hear me.

(He quickly prises open another can and hurls the paint across the road.)

(Screaming at them all.)

Can you hear me now? Can'y?

(He grabs the third and final can.)

(Behind DANNY, SUSAN and MICHEAL emerge from the house.)

DANNY: Go on ... Yes ... you go. Go and join your friends.

He watches as they cross the street and are comforted and taken in by JOYCE.

EDDIE *(Shouting across)*: I always thought there was somethin' about you, mate an' now I know what it is: You need treatment you do. Do you know that? You're soft in the head son.

DANNY rushes forward and grabs the paint brush. He swings and scoops up paint with it, hurling it along the street. It is a gesture of total and frustrated anger. There are screams as people try to get out of the way of the flying paint.

DANNY, his anger momentarily spent, stands glaring, breathing, go in very close.

SCENE 18
THE PUB INT: DAY: DAY 4

EDDIE and his cronies and others are drinking at the bar. Barmaid behind bar.

JOHN: He's not normal. He's a sick man. Sick in the mind.

JOEY: What the hell are we supposed to do? Half the cameras of the world are gonna be beamin' in on us tomorrow.

CAROL: Not now. No, they won't come here.

EDDIE: Why not?

CAROL: They'll go to Winfield Street. They've copied us, haven't they?

EDDIE: What?

CAROL: All the Winfield Street end have started painting their houses.

EDDIE: I don't believe it.

JOHN: She's right. I came home that way tonight. They're all painting away.

EDDIE: But the cameras won't go to Winfield Street. They weren't the originals we were.

JOHN: Yeah, we were Eddie. But Winfield Street is gonna be completely yellow. Not just almost yellow, yellow with a dark blob in the middle.

CAROL: That's why they'll get all the attention in Winfield Street.

EDDIE: Oh no.

JOEY: They will, Eddie. See, it's the visuals Eddie. And the continuity for the cameras. I mean you imagine a shot of a street where every house is painted apart from one. What is it that stands out? Not the fact that the street has been painted yellow. No. That just becomes the backdrop and the big feature becomes the one house that's not been painted!

EDDIE: This country is ruled by majorities. Not by the dick heads, the oddballs and the awkward arses. I'm up to here with Danny Harris. It's him and his sort who give this country a bad name, who'd drag it down into the sewer if they were given half a chance. We've got a marvellous opportunity here; an opportunity, to show the world the hard work and pride of this community. And to allow one headcase to deny us that opportunity would be a crime, a crime against the whole community. And I, for one, am not about to let that happen, I'm not John.

(End Day 4)

SCENE 19
DANNY'S STREET/HOUSE EXT: DAY: DAY 5

We see JOEY and JOHN walking along the street, glancing nervously from side to side, as they arrive at DANNY's house, we see that they are carrying paint and brushes.

They hurriedly open the cans and begin painting the walls, JOEY checking all the time that no one is coming.

JOHN: What you so nervous for? It's alright, he'll be at work.

JOEY: He's a bloody madman though. He's dangerous. I don't wanna be caught doing this.

JOHN: I've told you, he'll be at work.

(*But the two suddenly reel back spluttering as a bucket of water is flung at them: pull back and reveal from their POV, DANNY at an open upstairs window.*)

JOHN: Bastard, you bastard.

JOEY: Lunatic, bleedin' lunatic.

(*Hold DANNY watching from the window as they move off.*)

(End Day 5)

SCENE 20
DANNY'S HOUSE—LOUNGE INT: DAY: DAY 6

As we cut we hear the ringing of a telephone. We see DANNY picking up the receiver.

DANNY: Hello … Yeh, I'm Mister Harris …

(*DANNY's face. Shock.*)

What? What! Which hospital?

SCENE 21
DANNY'S STREET EXT: DAY: DAY 6

The door opens and DANNY comes running out, pulling on a jacket as he does so. DANNY begins running along the street.

From DANNY'S POV, JOEY getting out of his car.

DANNY running up to him.

DANNY: Joey, I've got to get to the hospital. It's our Michael. Would you give me a lift?

JOEY: Well, erm ... I've ...

(Uncomfortable, he glances beyond DANNY and sees EDDIE looking out of his window.)

Danny, you know I would but ...

(DANNY looks at him for a brief moment before turning and running down the street.)

SCENE 22
DANNY'S HOUSE EXT: DAY: DAY 6

There are ladders against the wall. EDDIE, JOEY and JOHN are painting the house. At the foot of the ladders, MICHAEL is helping them.

SCENE 23
DANNY'S STREET/HOUSE EXT: DAY: DAY 6

DANNY walks into shot. He stands and watches for a moment. From his POV the men painting his house.

His eyes closing as he sees MICHAEL amongst them, laughing and happily splashing paint on the brickwork.

DANNY, a low wounded scream welling up from within him as he begins to run towards the group.

Cut to EDDIE, JOEY and JOHN as they hear the scream and see the figure running towards them.

They begin to scramble down the ladders. JOEY is not quite fast enough.

DANNY kicks the ladder away and JOEY falls the last few feet to the ground.

He scuttles away to join the rest of his group.

Stand off. DANNY facing the group. Breathing hard and heavy.

The group, afraid of the wildness they see.

JOEY: My leg, my leg ... he's broke my bloody leg.

EDDIE: It didn't have to come to this you know. We'll win in the end. We will son. It's only fair Danny. We're the majority.

But *DANNY is not listening. He is staring at his son who cannot look him in the eye. We see tears in DANNY'S eyes.*

(End Day 6)

SCENE 24
DANNY'S HOUSE—HALL INT: EVE: DAY 7

The doorbell rings. DANNY cautiously approaches the door and looks through the fish eye. From his POV SUSAN standing outside. DANNY pulls back the bolts and opens the door slightly.

SUSAN (*Nervous, reluctant almost*): Hia ... Danny.

(*DANNY nods at her.*)

SUSAN: Well are you gonna keep me standing here?

DANNY: Who've you got with you?

SUSAN: For God's sake Danny!

DANNY peeping out and checking that all is clear. He opens the door just wide enough for her to enter. She does so.

SUSAN stands and watches as DANNY rebolts the front door.

SUSAN: It's like Fort bloody Knox.

(*Silence between them.*)

SUSAN: Well, aren't you going to offer me a cup of tea?

(*He looks at her blank.*)

SUSAN: Shall I make it?

SCENE 25
DANNY'S HOUSE—KITCHEN INT: DAY: DAY 7

She goes through to the kitchen. DANNY follows her. He watches as she fills the kettle.

DANNY: So?

SUSAN: So what.

DANNY: So why are you here?

SUSAN: Couldn't you have considered me an' Michael in all this Danny?

DANNY: Couldn't you have thought of me? (*Pause*) We're a family. (*Pause*) We didn't have to do what a street chose to do.

SUSAN: Where's the cups? I'll bet you haven't washed a dish, have y'? All the cups in the front room ... Go an' get a couple and I'll wash them.

(*DANNY goes through to the front room.*)

(*We remain with SUSAN in the kitchen and hear DANNY'S dialogue OOV.*)

DANNY (*OOV*): So why the visit Susan? Have they sent you to try and change my mind?

SUSAN (*Nervously glancing at the back door. From her POV, the bolts. She quietly pulls back one of the bolts.*): I told Eddie, when Danny gets an idea in his mind, he can be real obstinate.

(*She is about to pull back the second bolt when DANNY appears in the kitchen doorway. She wheels away from the door and beams a nervous smile at him.*)

(*Pause*)

You're just like a little boy over all this.

DANNY: I've missed you. And Michael.

SUSAN: Danny! Come here.

(*DANNY does so. SUSAN embraces him and leans back against the door.*)

DANNY (*Almost crying*): I just want you both to come back.

Close shot of SUSAN'S hand behind her back. She is gingerly releasing the second bolt.

SUSAN (*Also almost crying*): And we want to come back. We do Danny. Couldn't you just paint the house.

(*DANNY pulling back slightly*)

It's stupid Danny. Please Danny. Please. Before it's too late.

DANNY: What do y' mean, 'before it's too late'?

They stare at each other. SUSAN pulls the bolt the final inch. She looks away as EDDIE, JOEY, BILLY, JOHN and others enter.

DANNY staring in despair at SUSAN.

SUSAN: I'll come back, Danny … when it's painted. We'll be alright then, Danny.

(*She goes out of the back door.*)

EDDIE: We're sorry it had to come to this, Danny. But I hope we can make you see sense. (*Pause*) I want y' t' know son that when this is over, we can all go back to normal. There'll be a drink waitin' for y'in the pub.

SCENE 26
DANNY'S HOUSE/STREET EXT: DAY: DAY 7

Magic hour. EDDIE, JOEY, JOHN and others painting the exterior.

SCENE 27
DANNY'S HOUSE- LOUNGE INT: EVE: DAY 7

DANNY is sat on a chair, watched over by three men.

SCENE 28
DANNY'S HOUSE AND STREET EXT: EVE: DAY 7

Magic hour. The painting now completed. EDDIE and the others, including the men who were watching over DANNY looking at their work. They all move to the opposite side of the street. From their POV we see the entire length of the street, now a uniform yellow.

The front door opens. DANNY appears carrying a suitcase or hold-all. He momentarily looks at the group of men before turning and beginning to walk away. As he passes one of the doors it opens and MICHAEL, WILKSY and CAMERON spill out onto pavement and begin kicking a ball. We hold this group in the foreground as beyond them in the background DANNY continues walking away.

WILKSY suddenly stopping and noticing. Open mouthed, MICHAEL and CAMERON follow his gaze. The three of them, awed.

MICHAEL: Aaagh. It's all done. It's all the same.

(Calling)

Mum ... mum ... look, look.

(SUSAN and JOYCE emerge from EDDIE's house and this is the cue for us to begin to slowly track.)

(Up and away.)

As doors to the houses and to the pub open and the people in the street, as if drawn by some spiritually magnetic force spill out onto the road. Each and every one of them, staring, hushed and silent, awed and smiling at the result of their communal handiwork. And always, beyond them is the figure of DANNY walking away.

He pauses for a moment at the corner, turns, looks for a brief moment and then is gone.

The end.

Anne Frances Bulmer, Rurik von Antropoff
WIDENING THE HORIZONS

Willy Russell, internationally successful on stage and screen with plays like *Educating Rita* and *Shirley Valentine*, could be said to be a man with a message. First and foremost, however, he is an entertainer. From personal experience as a working class teenager in a fairly tough school environment[1] on the outskirts of Liverpool, England, he learnt that if you want to get a message across it is better to use humour than a hammer, and it is a mark of his skill as a humorous playwright that his work enjoys such popular appeal. Willy Russell is an educating entertainer, or an entertaining educator, and it is this combination that makes much of his work appealing not only to theatre and cinema audiences but also to young people in schools and colleges. Indeed, several of his plays have found their way into school curricula and university literature courses in Germany, thanks to the work of Albert-Reiner Glaap, in whose honour this present volume is published, and whose editions of Russell's plays[2] offer valuable guidelines for analysis as well as interesting interviews with the author himself. Russell's concerns are with the individual in relation to society. Whether he is dealing with women's liberation, or breaking down class barriers, or the narrowness of traditional education, behind the laughter (and sometimes the tears) there is a passionate concern with liberating the individual from the confines of conformity.

In the text *Terraces*[3] which Willy Russell has kindly contributed to this volume, and which was broadcast on September 6th, 1993 as part of the BBC Schools Scene drama series, we find various features which are characteristic of his work. The central theme in *Terraces* is the conflict between the desire for individuality and the group pressure to conform. It is a conflict which all children experience, particularly as teenagers, and particularly in Western society today. Russell, however, cleverly uses adults as his models, and makes the situation just slightly larger than life. The light-hearted, almost ludicrous, idea of an urban street in a close-knit working-class community in Northern England agreeing (almost unanimously) to paint itself yellow to support its local football team starts the play off in a mood of fun and enthusiasm. By the end of the play, however, there is a real sense of tragedy as Danny, the one who has steadfastly refused to conform with the majority, is betrayed by his wife, has his house forcibly painted, and can no longer count himself as one of the community. The final shot shows "Each and every one of them, staring, hushed and silent, awed and smiling at the result of their communal handiwork. And always, beyond them is the figure of DANNY walking away."[4] The audience is left sobered by the results of what had started out as a "bit of fun." It has seen how quickly positions become entrenched, and how little dialogue has taken place. The audience is left to speculate as to when and whether this bitter confrontation could have been halted, and whether a solution could have been found.

The questions raised in this short play about conformity, majority decisions, and ultimately the role of minorities within a democracy, are questions worth asking. Although she does not like the colour yellow, Danny's wife Susan bows to the will of the street and criticizes her husband's decision to assert his individuality. "It's not up to you. The street's decided ..."[5] Danny, on the other hand, cannot bring himself to do something he sees no sense in, even if it would make everyone else happy. Is Eddy, the one-time pal, now leader of the "yellow-shirts" right in resorting to threats and acts of violence in the interests of the community? In what situations does a group become a "mob" (the word being one of the crossword clues Danny's son is struggling with—the other, by the way, is "conformist")? When is individualism a threat to society, and when may an individual be restricted by the confines of a stifling community? By discussing the pressures on the adults in the street, and the motives for their behaviour, young audiences will become more aware of the problems which will confront them as they grow older, and understand how the needs of the individual must be balanced against the demands of the majority, whether it be in school, on the football terraces, in the work place, in the home, or even society at large.

The theme of the individual trapped in a limiting environment and pressurized to conform, but who, with a little effort can break out of that environment and learn to stretch his wings, was developed by Willy Russell in two of his most successful full-length plays—*Educating Rita* and *Shirley Valentine*. In *Educating Rita* Willy Russell shows how a lack of education reduces the options open to people. Education does not just mean formal education, but becoming open to new ways of looking at things. *Educating Rita* is the story of one particular working-class girl's attempt to achieve more choice in her life and therefore more control over her own life.[6] And the play is almost totally autobiographical. Like Rita, Willy Russell found the road to educational enlightenment rocky in the extreme. Like Rita, he came from a working-class background, failed to find much motivation at school (he was much more interested in watching the then unknown Beatles in the Cavern in Liverpool), left early and ended up as a ladies hairdresser. After five years of feeling the confines of this existence he decided, like Rita, to broaden his horizons. Rita goes to the Open University and struggles to understand what the educational establishment expects of her. Willy Russell, at the age of twenty-one, decided to go back to school, and then armed with the entrance requirements to college, and a lucrative, but physically demanding, part time job, he was ready to go to college and train, significantly, to be a teacher.

For those who have enjoyed a smoother path through the educational establishments it is worth reflecting how daunting the journey can seem. In his introduction to *Educating Rita*, entitled "Educating The Author," he describes the moment at school, when immersed in a novel in the only lesson he really enjoyed, an hour of "silent reading," he realized what he really wanted to be in life:

> I wanted to be a writer! It was a wonderful and terrible thought—wonderful because I sensed, I knew, it was the only thing for me. Terrible because how could I, a kid from the 'D' stream, a piece of factory fodder, ever change the course that my life was already set upon? How the hell could I ever be the sort of person who could become a writer? It was a shocking and ludicrous thought, one that I hid deep in myself for years, but one that would not go away.[7]

In a society which is still more class conscious than most in the Western world, where until fairly recently a strong accent and the wrong background strongly militated against the prospects of a decent job or social acceptance, summoning up the courage to climb over the class barriers was (and can still be) no easy task. Despite (or because of?) a comprehensive state school system aimed at increasing equality, the public (private) school system still operates an "old-school-tie" network which opens doors resistant to the pressure of others. As Rita points out, echoing the group dynamics in *Terraces*, there are pressures (amongst all classes) to conform. "They hate it when one of them tries to break away."[8] Rita herself is from a working-class background in the North of England, and it is her speech as much as her clothes and her attitudes which define her at the start of the play. But the problems of breaking out of the mould into which society or one's peer group have cast one are the same everywhere. In this connection a director in Atlanta, Georgia, asked Russell's permission to perform the play with a black Rita, and another American director saw the part in terms of a Jewish Rita. What is encouraging is that whether Rita is working class, or/and Black, or/and Jewish, her attempt to break through the confines imposed either by the pessimistic expectations of the peer group or those that the larger society seems to impose leads not only to the enrichment of Rita's life but also her tutor, Frank's.

In *Shirley Valentine* the confines are much more tangible. In this entertaining one-woman show, Shirley, the married martyr from a working-class background, is trapped by the role expectations of her boorish husband, her own children, and most of her neighbours. She has reached the material heights of her aspirations, but as she sits imprisoned in her respectable suburban semi-detached house with the fitted kitchen she is forced to talk to the wall for companionship. When she is offered the opportunity of two weeks of freedom by her feminist friend, Jane, in the form of a plane ticket for a fortnight in Greece, she feels she cannot possibly accept. She is forty-two and frightened.

This is, however, no heavy drama about a woman physically abused by a violent husband, or mentally tortured by a vicious spouse. Shirley is simply walled in by narrow horizons and limited expectations. They were confirmed in school with a less-than-encouraging headmistress, and reinforced by those of her husband, herself, and most of her peer group. As Willy Russell says in his introduction to Shirley Valentine:[9] "Working-class tribalism demands that working-class men live and behave in a strictly prescribed manner"… with rituals of beer drinking, fighting, football and the denying of any sensitivity. The men impose the same rituals on their women. They have been going on holiday to the same place for fifteen years because husband Joe gets culture shock if he goes anywhere new. After all "Greece is what y' cook (his) egg an' chips in."[10] Shirley is expected to have a meal on the table the moment her husband comes home and fears the consequences if she does not. She has toyed with the idea of leaving her husband, but her real fear—like that of so many people—is of mental and emotional agoraphobia. "I'm frightened of life beyond the wall,"[11] she says, and means, of course, that she is afraid of the unknown.

When Shirley finally summons up the courage to leap over the wall and fly to Greece, she begins to rediscover her own potential. As she sits by the sea in Mykonos she reflects on her life to date. "What I'd kept thinkin' about was how I'd lived such a little life. An' one way or another even that would be over pretty soon. … I'd allowed myself to live this little life when inside me there was so much."[12] Shirley Valentine "got lost in all this unused life."[13] She decides on positive action. She allows herself a liberating voyage of discovery with "Christopher Columbus"--Costas on his brother's boat. She decides not to go back to England to her role as "St Joan Of The Fitted Units" but to stay in Greece and support herself by working in the cafe. This is not, however, hardened feminism. When Shirley discovers who she is and decides she likes herself, she is not revengeful, or dismissive of Joe. She realizes that he, too, is trapped in his own narrow world, and he, too, needs liberating. The play ends generously with Shirley expecting a visit from Joe. "He needs to feel the sun on his skin an' to be in water that's as deep as forever, an' to have his wet head kissed. He needs to stare out to sea. And to understand. (Pause.)"[14]

The colloquial register, mixture of slang, mispronunciations which allow for humorous word play, and references to popular English culture and working-class clichés, all serve to show Shirley's roots. But although Shirley may not have had the advantages of a middle-class up-bringing, she has, by nature, an irrepressible wit and energy. She learns that not all that the middle classes revere stands up to close scrutiny. She discovers that Freud was not always right about sex and the female body. She discovers—in a country where accent is a strong class marker—that the right accent doesn't automatically make you one of the establishment. Elocution lessons can hide a multitude of sins: The elegant and wealthy Marjorie, Shirley's old school friend with the correct vowel sounds, turns out to be a high class whore. In *Shirley Valentine* Russell is preaching directly to his audience. He is saying that no-one should expect too little, either of himself—or others. As Michael Coveney in a review in the Financial Times said: "Russell's unerring ear for authentic working class speech and humour, allied to an optimistic belief in the ability of people to transform their own lives, given half a chance, explains why he enjoys the huge popular appeal denied to Royal Court dramatists."[15]

The conscious attempt to appeal to an audience on the entertainment level, as the first stage in getting a message across, is clearly evident in the popular musical play *Blood Brothers*, now in its eleventh year on the London Stage. The idea was first conceived as a play written for the Merseyside Young People's Theatre Company and premiered in a comprehensive school, and only later reworked as a musical. Using a story-telling structure based on old ballads Russell shows how influential social class can be on the upbringing and character of young people. The story deals with the fate of two twin brothers who were separated at birth. One of the twins grows up with his natural mother in a working-class environment, becomes an unskilled labourer, and later unemployed. The other, because his natural mother cannot keep him, is adopted and brought up by a caring middle-class couple desperate for a child of their own, and sent first to grammar school, and then to Oxford University. This twin succeeds his father as boss of the factory and finally becomes a local councillor. The two brothers meet at various stages in their lives, oblivious of their true relationship. As children they even innocently mingled their blood and swore to be "blood brothers". In keeping with the ballad tradition, however, the tragic and violent end is foreshadowed throughout the play with the superstition that twins once parted are doomed to die if either one discovers he has a blood brother (Act I, Scene 8).

As the boys grow older the class barriers become more difficult to overcome, and the less-advantaged Mickey finds to his distaste that he is dependent on favours from the more advantaged Eddie. In a sense all the characters are "trapped," either by their environment, or their fears. Finally, because Mickey feels he has no control over events in his own life, he loses his self-control, too. In a fit of frustration he threatens to kill Eddie, but he cannot even control that situation. In a melodramatic moment the twins discover the truth about their relationship and the fatal superstition comes about.

Although the play ends with the deaths of the two twins in a situation of misunderstanding, jealousy and hatred, it is by no means all a dark and dismal story. The issues that Willy Russell wants to highlight—the unemployment, the poverty, the apparent injustice in the distribution of opportunity, are all packed round with wit and humour. And even if the audience does not totally accept the all-"nurture" rather than "nature" interpretation of the twins' development, the basic social problems cannot be ignored. For young people a rock-ballad musical with a strong story-line is a more than acceptable introduction to the whole subject of drama, and even reading the play as a text in the classroom is likely to provoke strong feelings of identification with the struggling Mickies, and perhaps even the more fortunate Eddies of today, and consequently focus attention on the underlying social and political debate.

In all Willy Russell's plays, including those not dealt with here, there is a refreshing directness and frankness of approach which helps to make the plays accessible to a very wide audience. A major part of this appeal lies in his use of

---

language. Russell himself thinks of drama as ultimately a working-class form, based as it is on the spoken word. He emphasizes the fact that working-class culture is still orally based.[16] Although his characters enjoy a certain universality—at least in Western culture—in terms of their frustrations and aspirations, they have firm roots, both from the point of locality—usually suburban Liverpool, —and class—mostly 'respectable working-class.' The characters he creates are defined by the language they use—usually a colloquial register, full of local (Liverpool = "Scouse") dialect forms, common non-standard English, and accepted slang. The language, however, is never so exaggerated as to be incomprehensible, and it is often extremely funny. Accents, of course, can often be clues to personal histories, as they adapt to changing environments but seldom completely lose all their original markers. A strong regional accent helps to give the character a very local identity which can be both a comfort to the individual in the sense of belonging, and a limitation in the wider world of greater mobility and flexibility. As already mentioned, only recently in England have regional/social accents ceased to be such a negative factor in achieving high status professionally and socially. It is Russell's ear for convincing dialogue which gives each character such individuality and naturalness, and allows them, even without the benefits of higher education, to be lively, witty and amusing. In the case of *Educating Rita* language is used as a dramatic device, and Rita's development is reflected in her changing language. At a crucial stage in her education she underlines the point by saying: "I can talk now."[17] In Rita's case the use of language is bound up with her emancipation, with the whole issue of gaining control over her own life. In *Blood Brothers* Mickey almost fails to get Linda to go out with him because he lacks the language, and he has to be prompted by the fluent and better educated Eddie, who even as a child had access at home to things like dictionaries. In *Terraces*, with which this article started, and which was written for the more filmic medium of television, one of the features in the development of the comi-tragedy is the striking lack of real communication, of talking the issues through. Language is an important acquisition in the quest for personal liberation.

Apart from being a highly entertaining and humorous guide to England in the seventies and eighties, Russell's plays deal with the kind of personal, social and educational issues that are part of contemporary political debate. Although he is not so concerned with deep philosophical issues, or pain and passion, he is concerned to show the limitations of allowing oneself to be trapped in a working-class environment where many go "drinking for the sake of it,"[18] or regard Mecca as a fitted kitchen. His emphasis is always on the individual and the need for that courageous step to be taken towards a richer life. It is the personal voyage which interests him most. For this reason many of his plays,—those he himself has written particularly for younger people, as well as those mentioned here aimed at a wider audience—are particularly suitable for school performance and study. This does not, of course, rule out starting the process of theatre appreciation at any age. As many of the barriers to greater opportunity are within us rather than without it is never too late to set out afresh and discover new territory. Willy Russell himself has never forgotten the importance of learning, particularly post school. As he said in an interview in The Observer in Sept. 1993: "I'm much more a believer in continuing education." His latest project proves the point. He is still interested in processes. He is now trying to write a novel about five people who find their way to writing school.[19] This obviously combines his two enduring passions, writing and education— and in the process he will undoubtedly focus on widening not only the horizons of his characters but of all those who enjoy his work, as well.

Notes

[1]
Cf. Willy Russell, "Educating The Author," in: *Educating Rita, Stags and Hens,* and *Blood Brothers* (London: Methuen, 1986), 161-165.

[2]
Educating Rita (Ed. A. -R. Glaap) (Frankfurt: Diesterweg, 1984) (With Comments and Study Aids). - *The Boy with the Transistor Radio,* in: *Facing Life.* Short Plays for young People (Ed. A. -R. Glaap/ I. Hartmann-Scheer) (Düsseldorf: Cornelsen-Schwann (Courses in Literature), 1988). - *Blood Brothers* (Ed. A. -R. Glaap) (Frankfurt: Diesterweg, 1990) (With Comments and Study Aids). *Shirley Valentine* (Ed. A. -R. Glaap) (Frankfurt: Cornelsen Verlag Hirschgraben (TAGS), 1992) (+ Teacher's Book). - *Politics and Terror,* in: *Spotlights on Literature* (Ed. A. -R. Glaap, G. Haefner, F. Schmidt, T. L. Wullen) (Ismaning: Max Hueber Verlag, 1993).

[3]
First published in an earlier version in: *Second Playbill I,* ed. by Alan Durband. (London: Hutchinson, 1973); new edition of this collection as *Terraces,* 1979.

[4]
Terraces as published in this volume, 342

[5]
Terraces, 329

[6]
Cf. *Educating Rita,* Comments and Study Aids by A. -R. Glaap, 24.

[7]
Educating Rita, Stags and Hens, and *Blood Brothers* (London: Methuen, 1986), 162.

[8]
Educating Rita (Ed. A. -R. Glaap), 37.

[9]
Shirley Valentine (Ed. A. -R. Glaap), 7.

[10]
Shirley Valentine (Ed. A. -R. Glaap), 24.

[11]
Shirley Valentine (Ed. A. -R. Glaap), 24.

[12]
Shirley Valentine (Ed. A. -R. Glaap), 40.

[13]
Shirley Valentine (Ed. A. -R. Glaap), 41.

[14]
Shirley Valentine (Ed. A. -R. Glaap), 45f.

[15]
Financial Times, 29 June 1989. - The Royal Court in London specializes in new and experimental drama.

[16]
Educating Rita, Comments and Study Aids by A. -R. Glaap, 29.

[17]
Educating Rita (Ed. A. -R. Glaap), 64.

[18]
Terraces, 325.

[19]
The Observer, 5 September 1993.

LIST OF CONTRIBUTORS

Althof, Rolf; Anglistisches Institut V, University of Düsseldorf, Universitätsstr. 1, Geb. 23.31, 40225 Düsseldorf, Germany.

Andre, Marion; 59 Clifton Road, Toronto, Ont., Canada M4T 2E8.

von Antropoff, Rurik; Anglistisches Institut V, University of Düsseldorf, Universitätsstr. 1, Geb. 23.31, 40225 Düsseldorf, Germany.

Ayckbourn, Alan; c/o Margaret Ramsay Ltd., 14a Goodwin's Court, St. Martin's Lane, London. WC2N 4LL, Great Britain.

Bader, Rudolf; Römerstr. 35, 3047 Bremgarten near Bern, Switzerland.

Beissel, Henry; P.O.Box 339, Alexandria, Ont., Canada K0C 1A0.

Boireau, Nicole; University of Metz, Faculte des Lettres et Sciences Humaines, Ile du Saulcy, 57045 Metz Cedex 1, France.

Bulmer, Anne Frances; Anglistisches Institut V, University of Düsseldorf, Universitätsstr. 1, Geb. 23.31, 40225 Düsseldorf, Germany.

Cook, Michael; 43 Shrewsbury Street, Stratford, Ont., Canada N5A 2V4.

Filewod, Alan; University of Guelph, College of Arts, Dept. of Drama, Guelph, Ont., Canada N1G 2W1.

French, David; 254 Brunswick Avenue, Toronto, Ont., Canada M5S 2M7.

Griffiths, Linda; 224 Markham Street, Toronto, Ont., Canada M6J 2G6.

Groß, Konrad; University of Kiel, Englisches Seminar, Olshausenst. 40-60, 24118 Kiel, Germany.

Gunnars, Kristjana; University of Alberta, Dept. of English, Faculty of Arts, 3-5 Humanities Centre, Edmonton, Alberta, Canada, T6G 2E5.

Hall, Roger; 298 York Place, Dunedin, New Zealand.

Harwood, Ronald; c/o Judy Daish Assocs., 83 Eastbourne Mews, London W2 6LQ, Great Britain.

Hermes, Liesel; University of Koblenz / Landau, Seminar Anglistik, Rheinau 1, 56075 Koblenz, Germany.

Howells, Coral Ann; University of Reading, Faculty of Letters and Social Sciences, Dept. of English Language and Literature, Whiteknights, P.O.Box 218, Reading RG6 2AA, Great Britain.

Klooss, Wolfgang; Fachbereich II - Anglistik, University of Trier, Postfach 3825, 54286 Trier, Germany.

Probert-Gromüller, Janice; Anglistisches Institut V, University of Düsseldorf, Universitätsstr. 1, Geb. 23.31, 40225 Düsseldorf, Germany.

Rau, Albert; Auf der Pehle 44, 50321 Brühl, Germany.

Reaney, James; c/o Sybil Hutchinson, Apt. 409, Ramsden Place, 50 Hillsboro Ave., Toronto, Ont. Canada.

Rubess, Banuta; 13 Fennings Street, Toronto, Ont., Canada M6J 3B9.

Rubin, Don; Department of Theatre, York University, 4700 Keele Street, North York, Ont., Canada M3J 1P3.

Russell, Willy; c/o Margaret Ramsay Ltd., 14a Goodwin's Court, St. Martin's Lane, London. WC2N 4LL, Great Britain.

ACKNOWLEDGEMENTS

Marion Andre, CAPTIVE OF YESTERYEAR, © 1990 by the author. Published by permission. All rights reserved. Inquiries concerning rights should be addressed to the author, 59 Clifton Road, Toronto, Ont., Canada M4T 2E8.

Alan Ayckbourn, SERVICE NOT INCLUDED, © 1974 by the author. Published by permission. All rights reserved. Inquiries concerning rights should be addressed to the author, c/o Margaret Ramsay Ltd., 14a Goodwin's Court, St. Martin's Lane, London. WC2N 4LL, Great Britain.

Henry Beissel, WHERE SHALL THE BIRDS FLY?, © 1992 by the author. Reprinted by permission. All rights reserved. Inquiries concerning rights should be addressed to the author, P.O.Box 339, Alexandria, Ont., Canada K0C 1A0.

Michael Cook, THE GREAT HARVEST EXCURSION, © 1987 by the author. Published by permission. This play was commissioned by the Stratford Festival in 1986. All rights reserved. Inquiries concerning rights should be addressed to the author, 43 Shrewsbury Street, Stratford, Ont., Canada N5A 2V4.

David French, MEMOIR, © 1993 [work in progress] by the author. Published by permission. All rights reserved. Inquiries concerning rights should be addressed to the author, 254 Brunswick Avenue, Toronto, Ont., Canada M5S 2M7.

Linda Griffiths, THE RED SPRAY CAN, © 1993 [from: SPIRAL WOMAN AND THE DIRTY THEATRE] by the author. Published by permission. All rights reserved. Inquiries concerning rights should be addressed to the author, 224 Markham Street, Toronto, Ont., Canada M6J 2G6.

Kristjana Gunnars, FORGED LETTERS, © 1992 by the author. Published by permission. All rights reserved. Inquiries concerning rights should be addressed to the author, c/o University of Alberta, Dept. of English, Faculty of Arts, 3-5 Humanities Centre, Edmonton, Alberta, Canada, T6G 2E5.

Roger Hall, THE DREAM FACTORY, © 1992 by the author. Published by permission. All rights reserved. Inquiries concerning rights should be addressed to the author, 298 York Place, Dunedin, New Zealand.

Ronald Harwood, STARRING LAURENCE OLIVIER, © 1978 by the author. Reprinted by permission. All rights reserved. Inquiries concerning rights should be addressed to the author, c/o Judy Daish Assocs., 83 Eastbourne Mews, London W2 6LQ, Great Britain.

James Reaney, SLEIGH WITHOUT BELLS: A GHOST STORY ABOUT THE DONNELLYS, © 1993 by the author. Published by permission. All rights reserved. Inquiries concerning rights should be addressed to the author, c/o Sybil Hutchinson, Apt. 409, Ramsden Place, 50 Hillsboro Ave., Toronto, Ont. Canada.

Banuta Rubess, STONE AGE, © 1993 by the author. Published by permission. All rights reserved. Inquiries concerning rights should be addressed to the author, 13 Fennings Street, Toronto, Ont., Canada M6J 3B9.

Willy Russell TERRACES, © 1992 by the author. Published by permission. All rights reserved. Inquiries concerning rights should be addressed to the author, c/o Margaret Ramsay Ltd., 14a Goodwin's Court, St. Martin's Lane, London. WC2N 4LL, Great Britain.

TABULA GRATULATORIA

Ahrens, Rüdiger
Würzburg

Altendorf, Ulrike
Düsseldorf

Althof, Sigrid
Neuss

Antropoff, Christoph von
Düsseldorf

Bach, Ulrich
Kürnach

Bastein, Friedel H.
Hamburg

Berger, Dieter A.
Regensburg

Bliesener, Ulrich
Hannover

Bruijns-Pötschke, Marita
Monheim

Busse, Wilhelm G.
Düsseldorf

Carlsen, Jørn
Aarhus

Cencig, Elisabeth
Vülkermarkt

Christ, Herbert & Ingeborg
Düsseldorf

Clever-Vossen, Almuth
Düsseldorf

Cornelsen Verlag
Berlin

Dietrich, Heinz
Schwalmtal

Diller, Hans-Jürgen
Bochum

Donnerstag, Jürgen
Dortmund

Dresen, Margarete
Mönchengladbach

Düsterhaus, Gerhard
Bonn

Eromenger, Manfred
Braunschweig

Fechner, Emil
MG-Beckrath

Fink, Harold
Montreal

Fricke, Dietmar
Köln

Friedl, Herwig
Düsseldorf

Gaboriau, Linda
Montreal

Gibson-Bray, Sarah
Perth

Golisch, Petra
Düsseldorf

Grabes, Herbert
Giessen

Grub, Adolf
Jdar-Oberstein

Günter, Bernd
Mettmann

Hagge, Helmut P.
Hamburg

Hartmann, Malte
Köln

Hartmann-Scheer, Ingrid
Kaarst

Hauschild, Margret
Stuttgart

Hennrich, Antje & Lutz
Düsseldorf

Herbst, Dietrich
Frankfurt am Main

Hinz, Klaus
Düeren

Hohmann, Delf Maria
St. John's

Holtei, Christa & Rainer
Ratingen

Hortmann, Wilhelm
Duisburg

Hunt, Alan & Meredith
Düsseldorf

Hütten, Berthold
Goch-Gaesdonck

Kastovsky, Dieter
Vienna

Klebes, Ferdinand
Meerbusch

Klopstock, Wolfgang
Langenfeld

Korte, Barbara
Chemnitz

Kuester, Martin
Augsburg

Kuhlmann, Meike
Düsseldorf

Langner, Manfred
Aachen

Lauerbach, Gerda
Frankfurt am Main

Legenhausen, Lienhard
Münster

Lippke, Wolfgang J.
Siegen

Lorenz, Isabell
Düsseldorf

Mann, Renate
Köln

Mathis, Ursula
Innsbruck

Mengel, Ewald
Bamberg

Nies, Fritz
Düsseldorf

Optekamp, Yvonne
Iserlohn

Ormelius, Sven-Erik
Lund

Pache, Walter
Augsburg

Page, Malcolm
Burnaby

Pasch, Peter
Tuebingen

Perkyns, Richard
Halifax

Pickhardt, Wolf-Werner
Meerbusch

Plant, Richard
Whitevale

Porteous-Schwier, G.
Moers

Raider, Donald & Ute
Düsseldorf

Ross, Ingrid
Kempen

Sachse, Klaus A.
Düsseldorf

Saddlemyer, Ann
Toronto

Schrey, Helmut
Duisburg

Schuhmann, Kuno
Berlin

Sliwinski, Ilse
Düsseldorf

Stanzel, Franz Karl
Graz

Stilz, Gerhard
Tüebingen

Sturm, Berthold
Verden-Dauelsen

Thomas, Carin
Ratingen

Thomsen, Christian W.
Siegen

Trutnau, Wendy & Peter
Winsen/Luhe

Universitäts-und Landesbibliothek
Düsseldorf

Verderber, Heide-Rose
Köln

Wagner, Karl H.
Köln

Weizsäcker, Volkhart
Stuttgart

Weller, Franz-Rudolf
Brauweiler

Wilke, Gundula
Osnabrueck

Wodsak, Mona
Düsseldorf

Wüst, Rolf
Neuwied

Yvard, Pierre
Nantes

Zens, Christa
Düsseldorf

Zirker, Herbert
Kenn